Psychology Moving East

About the Book and Editors

Psychologists from nineteen countries in Asia and Oceania report on the expansion of western psychology in the region at both the academic and the professional levels. With its own network of associations, conferences, and journals, the community of psychologists in the East has braved new frontiers for the discipline, yet its achievements are little known to the rest of the world. The contributors adopt a socio-historical orientation for their discussion of how the essentially western discipline of psychology has been accepted and modified in cultures quite different from each other and vastly different from those of the West. One major point of controversy is whether western applications are appropriate in Asian settings or if scholars and practitioners should develop distinctive indigenous varieties according to the idiosyncrasies of the local cultures.

Geoffrey H. Blowers is senior lecturer in the Department of Psychology at the University of Hong Kong.
Alison M. Turtle is senior lecturer in the Department of Psychology at the University of Sydney.

Psychology Moving East

The Status of Western Psychology in Asia and Oceania

edited by Geoffrey H. Blowers
and Alison M. Turtle

Westview Press / Boulder and London

Sydney University Press

A Westview Special Study

This Westview softcover edition is printed on acid-free paper and bound in
softcovers that carry the highest rating of the National Association of
State Textbook Administrators, in consultation with the Association of
American Publishers and the Book Manufacturers' Institute.

Published in 1987 in the United States of America by Westview Press, Inc.;
Frederick A. Praeger, Publisher; 5500 Central Avenue, Boulder, Colorado
80301

Published in 1987 in Australia by Sydney University Press, The University
of Sydney, New South Wales, Australia 2006

Library of Congress Cataloging-in-Publication Data
Psychology moving East.
    (A Westview Special Study)
    1. Psychology--Philosophy. 2. Psychology--Asia.
3. Psychology--Oceania. I. Blowers, G. H. (Geoffrey H.)
II. Turtle, Alison M. III. Series.
BF38.P83 1987   150'.95   86-23388
ISBN 0-8133-7331-X

National Library of Australia Cataloguing-in-Publication Data
Psychology moving east: the status of western psychology in Asia and
Oceania.
    1. Ethnopsychology. 2. Cross-cultural studies--Asia.
3. Cross-cultural studies--Oceania. 4. Psychology.
I. Blowers, G. H. (Geoffrey H.). II. Turtle, Alison M.
155.8
ISBN 0 424 00127 6.

Composition for this book was provided by the editors.
This book was produced without formal editing by the publisher.

Printed and bound in the United States of America

 The paper used in this publication meets the requirements
of the American National Standard for Permanence of Paper
for Printed Library Materials Z39.48-1984.

6   5   4   3   2   1

To Erik Kvan and W. M. O'Neil,
our mentors and activists in promoting the study
of the theoretical bases of psychology
in Asia and Oceania

Contents

PART 1
SOUTH ASIA

PART 2
MAINLAND SOUTHEAST ASIA

PART 3
EAST ASIA

PART 4
INSULAR SOUTHEAST ASIA

PART 5
OCEANIA

Preface

The present volume grew out of a symposium entitled 'Historical Development of Psychology in Asia' which Geoffrey Blowers organised at the invitation of Dr. Yang Kuo-shu of National Taiwan University's Psychology department for the joint Second Asian Regional Conference of the International Association for Cross-Cultural Psychology and First Asian Conference of the International Council of Psychologists, held in Taipei in August of 1981. At that conference only six countries were represented: China Mainland, Taiwan, Hong Kong, Australia, Malaysia, and Japan. Potential authors of papers in a few other countries were unable to make the event. At the time, pressure of the conference deadline and ignorance of both the geography of the region and the extent to which psychology had perpetrated it, led to only about nine countries in Asia being contacted. The original idea was to see the extent to which western, that is, Euro-American psychological ideas had been absorbed in academic psychology circles in Asia, the extent to which they were being met with resistance, distortion and amendment and whether there could be distilled from the varied accounts something akin to an "Asian psychology".

The symposium proved to be very popular and the papers turned out to reveal some interesting and important themes. As a result of informal discussions with participants, most notably Alison Turtle who has for some years been specialising in the history of psychology, it became clear to us that an extended work encompassing all countries in the region would prove beneficial to both the slowly expanding literature of Asian cross-cultural psychology, and the history of psychology in a social

context. We also felt that with the growing interest
shown in the region, evidenced by the increasing fre-
quency of visits from overseas psychologists particularly
from North America, a volume of background material on
psychology in each country would be a useful starting
point for any future cross-cultural research in Asia. The
impetus for the work presented here therefore was in part
derived from the dissatisfaction shared with other
psychologists for cross-cultural research undertaken in
cultures with which the psychologist had little familiar-
ity. The essential difficulties of conducting such
research stem from two sources. In the first place there
has been a dearth of suitable theory which has impeded
the formulation of suitable research questions, and in
the second, an unsuccessful marriage of derived extra-
(etic) and intra- (emic) cultural concepts, the trials
and tribulations of which have become known as the
'emic-etic' debate. This has been documented in several
places, most notably in <u>Basic problems in cross-cultural
psychology</u> (Poortinga, 1977).[1] Hopefully this volume is a
corrective to some of the problems discussed in the pages
of that earlier work in that it offers a first-hand
account of how Asian psychologists have been able to
respond to the imposition of 'etic' concepts upon 'emic'
ones.

What this volume therefore comprises is a collection
of papers from all those countries in the areas of Asia
and Oceania where psychology has attained some sort of
official foothold, denoted either by the subject's being
taught as an identifiable unit at university level, or by
the existence of a professional psychological organization.

Two countries are represented here which do not
fully match up to this criterion: Fiji, which has been
included as an example of an early stage of evolution of
a discipline in institutional terms, and Singapore, where
psychology has a long history of being taught as a
segment of other disciplines, and which has witnessed the
formation of two organizations devoted to the study of
psychology, although neither has required a professional
qualification in psychology for membership. The authors
are employed as psychologists in all but two of the
countries they respectively describe, and in the case of
those two countries (Malaysia, and Mainland China) their
experience has been both first-hand and recent. Their
perspectives are therefore local and immediate. The
majority are natives of the countries about which they

write, though there was no deliberate policy formulated in this regard. They were encouraged to take a socio-historical stance, and to address questions such as the relationship between the indigenous culture and the concepts and ambitions of modern psychologists, and factors affecting interaction between local and foreign manifestations of the discipline, such as finance, political status and language. A standardized set of some thirty questions was sent to each of them. These were questions concerned with the teaching, admission and failure rates, language of instruction, the amount of contact with international psychology, the way research was funded and with what were thought to be the basic conceptual issues of the subject. With the questionnaire was sent the proviso that it was to serve as a set of guidelines and not as a definitive directive.

No consistent recruitment procedure for contributors was followed, as none seemed feasible. We used our personal networks of contacts as well as the Inter-national Directory of Psychologists (3rd edn., 1980). A scanning of the contents pages of the Proceedings of the International Association for Cross-Cultural Psychology in 1981 and 1983 proved to be fruitful; likewise with the contents pages of the journal Psychologia to which mainly Asian psychologists contribute. In a few instances we wrote to the secretaries of the national psychological associations asking for contact persons with an interest or specialisation in the history of psychology. The final author population covers a range of age, seniority levels, areas of interest and expertise within psycho-logy; nearly all have at least one degree in psychology, and most though not all are academics. Some are among the first generation of psychologists trained in their own countries, though where the discipline has reached maturity they are the result of two or more generations of home production; still others have studied abroad. In general terms, their attitudes towards the future of psychology in their countries are, predictably in view of their involvement with its present state, most usually optimistic. But their advocacies of the future direction that psychology should take are very diverse.

All contributors were asked to write their papers in English, a policy which has meant that the amount of input by the editors has varied greatly, depending on whether or not English was the writer's first language and on his or her level of fluency in it. A serious endeavour was made to avoid editorial misinterpretations by referring back to the authors both particular points for clarification when in doubt, and full edited manuscripts (if necessary more than once) for their consideration and final approval.

In order to achieve some consistency in matters of spelling, we decided to anglicize throughout, even for those countries where American influence was thought to be strong. In matters of usage of Chinese proper names however, we felt that imposing a policy of uniformity would involve an unacceptable level of misrepresentation. In 1975 the government of Mainland China introduced a system of _pinyin_ romanization which replaced the established English rendition of many Chinese words, especially proper names, by a form of spelling closer to the phonetic expression. This system has been used throughout the paper on psychology in that country, with the old-style (Wade-Giles) system of spelling given in brackets for references to works published before its introduction. Taiwan, Hong Kong, and other countries where Chinese is extensively spoken, such as Singapore, have not adopted the same system of _pinyin_ romanization, and Wade-Giles spelling is therefore used in their papers. Similarly, the Chinese convention of positioning an individual's given names after the family name rather than before it, as in the West, is employed in the paper on Mainland China but not in these other countries, where the convention has been variously modified when writing in English or speaking to a western audience.

For two countries, Macau and Burma, the information gathered on psychological developments is presented in note form as appendixes rather than as full papers. In the case of Macau this was because psychology has only very recently been introduced into the newly opened university there and is offered as only a service subject in other social science curricula. While, on the other hand, psychology in Burma has been established for many years, the availability of information in English is restricted to one publication printed in 1962 and some additional notes offered by a contributor who has been unable to report more fully on developments there. In each case we felt that there was insufficient information to justify full paper status but the respective contributors to some of the information gathered are acknowledged at the end of each appendix.

In its subtitles for the region the Table of Contents follows current United Nations usage, which has recently incorporated the Orwellian term "Oceania."

1. See in particular the papers by A. R. Davison, G. Jahoda, R. Malpass and L. Sechrest in Y. Poortinga (ed.) <u>Basic problems in cross-cultural psychology</u>, Amsterdam and Lisse, Swets and Zeitlinger, 1977, p.49-82.

Geoffrey H. Blowers
Alison M. Turtle

Acknowledgments

Thanks are owing to the Dr. Yang Kuo-shu of National Taiwan University for the opportunity given to Geoffrey Blowers to organise a symposium on the history of psychology in Asia. This took place at National Taiwan University during the joint Second Asian Regional Conference of the International Association of Cross-Cultural Psychology and First Asian Conference of the International Council of Psychologists, held in Taipei from August 10-12, 1981. We gratefully acknowledge both organisations for their sponsorship of the event.

The Conference Grants Committee of the University of Hong Kong provided a travel grant in 1982 to Geoffrey Blowers enabling him to visit the University of Sydney in August of that year when the project was at the initial stage. The University of Sydney provided funding to Alison Turtle for the early stages of the project from its Special Research Grants in 1982 and 1983. Much of the editing work was done whilst Alison Turtle was on a Special Study Programme from the University of Sydney from February to June 1984, during which the Psychology Department of the University of Hong Kong provided her with office accommodation. The latter department also provided considerable backup clerical services for the project, and thanks are owing to its secretarial staff, especially to Jane Lee.

Many people have provided comments and advice on the individual papers, and their contributions are acknowledged in context by the respective authors. The editors also wish to thank them for their assistance. In addition, a number of others have offered encouragement and assistance with the project overall, and the editors wish to express their appreciation - in particular to

Michael Bond (the Chinese University of Hong Kong), Josef Brozek (formerly of Lehigh University, U.S.A.), Ronald Hill (University of Hong Kong), and Ronald Taft (formerly of Monash University, Australia).

G.H.B.
A.M.T.

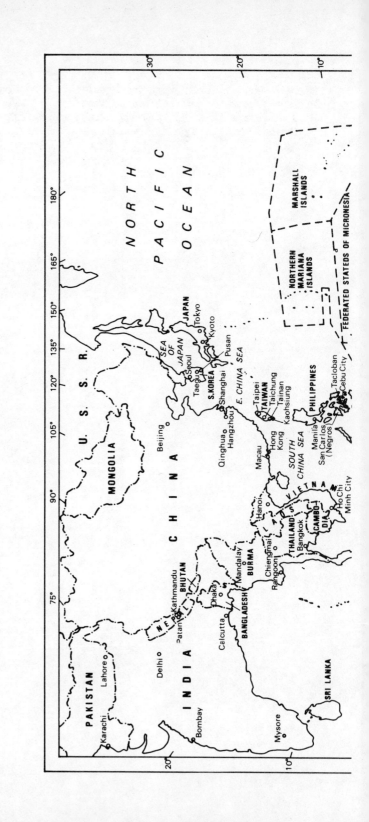

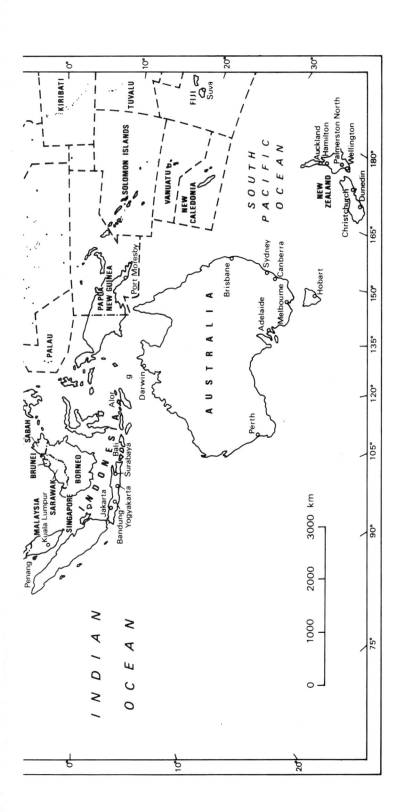

Introduction: A Silk Road
for Psychology

Alison M. Turtle

Modern psychology is moving east with impressive rapidity. To superimpose itself upon already highly developed views of the nature of the human mind, beliefs in the power to predict future fortunes in this life and in the possibility of continuation of existence in another, is no mean feat for a discipline with strong (if not total) adherence in its own attempts at theory formulation to the fundamental principles of materialism, empiricism and determinism. To offer practical solutions to problems of social planning, to advise on maximal utilization of capacities of individuals, to claim the ability to counsel, to comfort and to cure those in trouble and distress, in the face of firmly established beliefs about the proper forms of social organization and the relation of the individual thereto, and of highly valued practices of guidance, consolation and spiritual healing, gives evidence either of remarkable self-confidence and/or powers of salesmanship in modern psychologists, or of extraordinary social disruption in the East, or of both.

Spawned by British mental philosophy and evolutionary biology in interaction with German physiology and philosophy, and conceived against the rising swell of nineteenth century positivism, modern psychology arrived in Asia, specifically Japan, almost as early as it did in the United States, the subject being introduced into a Japanese university around 1890. It made an appearance in China before 1920, and in some of the colonized countries, such as India and Viet Nam, before World War II, somewhat later than in the Australian and New Zealand colonies, where the intellectual life and educational institutions of the new population were little influenced by the original inhabitants. But despite having had a long history in the area overall, signs of widespread and large-scale growth are only recent. Very recent examples here are: the formation of the first psychology department in Malaysia in 1979 and the inauguration of a new Singapore Psychological Society in the same year, the establishment of the Nepalese Psychological Association in 1982, and of the Department of Psychology and Philosophy at the University of Papua New Guinea in 1983. The number of academic psychologists in South Korea has trebled since 1976, while that of students majoring in the subject there has multiplied by six. In Mainland China, the Chinese Psychological Society resumed post-Cultural Revolutionary existence in 1977, and in 1983 a new society, the Chinese Society for Social Psychology, a subject hitherto inadmissible in that country, was founded. The techniques and ideology of modern psychology are thus being overlaid, in some cases in considerable haste, upon an ideological background composed variously of Hinduism, Islam, Buddhism, Taoism, Confucianism, Shintoism and Marxism-Leninism, themselves occurring in a range of combinations and combination styles.

With a few exceptions, the region has kept largely to itself until the last few years, though there has been a steady procession of individuals in various capacities sallying forth to the United States, the United Kingdom, Europe and the USSR. The usual posture adopted has been very much that of disciple rather than of apostle. Recently a more egalitarian stance is being assumed, with Asian and South Pacific countries offering themselves as venues for international conferences. The first such to be held was the XXth Congress of the International Union of Psychological Science at Tokyo in 1972, followed immediately by the first ever meeting of the International Association for Cross-Cultural Psychology, in Hong Kong. Subsequent Asian regional meetings of the latter group have been held at Hong Kong in 1979, Taipei in 1981, and Bangi (Malaysia) in 1983. A series of Asian Workshops on Child and Adolescent Development has also commenced, the first in Jakarta, the second in Bangkok (1982), and the third in Kuala Lumpur (May 1984). The IUPS plans to hold its XXIVth Congress in Sydney in 1988. Only Japan was a foundation member of the IUPS in 1951, but by 1980 seven other countries from the region had joined as well.

This collection of papers is intended to serve a dual purpose. Firstly, it should indicate to those unaware of the present situation of psychology in Asia and the Oceanic region of the Pacific, the state of affairs prevailing in the nineteen different countries herewith represented, as well as the major developmental stages and influences. One indication of the need for this is the fact that the latest edition of the International Directory of Psychologists (Jacobson and Reinert, 1980) does not include China Mainland, Indonesia, Bangladesh or Viet Nam, despite the fact that all these countries have well established psychology departments, and all but the latter have professional associations of psychologists. Another is the omission from Wolman's (1979) International Directory of Psychology: People, Places and Policies of any reference to Taiwan, Thailand, Malaysia, Bangladesh, Viet Nam or Papua New Guinea, although again all but the last two have both well established psychology departments and professional organizations, and those two each have one of these.

Secondly, it should prompt psychologists, historians of science and sociologists of knowledge internationally to raise a number of questions pertinent to the history and philosophy of the discipline. Such questions would include the following: What are the patterns of interaction between colony and imperialist power in the areas of scientific and technological development, in terms of the derivation of ideas, exploitation one-way or mutual, emulation or rejection? To what extent do the local religions and world views of the countries under consideration contain ideas comparable to or in conflict with the concepts of modern psychology, and to what extent are such comparisons in fact made by these new practitioners of psychology? How do local customs, such as patronage of faith healers and fortune tellers, in fact blend with the technology of modern applied psychology? Where modern psychology has had a long history, as in Japan, China, Australia and New Zealand, has it in fact followed similar or different paths to those in the regions where it first began its course? If different, why? At least in countries where it has had only a short history, does there seem to be a regular developmental sequence? Is psychology nowadays an inevitable part of the process of industrialization and urbanization? Can it be handled just as a technology, or must it be interpreted as invoking a world view? If so, what is this world view? To what extent can it be blended with or assimilated into a variety of different cultures and ideologies and still retain a recognizable common form?

Some of the foregoing issues have of course been raised in other contexts; many have not. Though recognizing that the present venture is, in terms of providing a data base for the history of modern psychology in these particular regions, very much of pilot status, its participant bias resulting in inevitably limited perspectives, the editors certainly make no claim that any further explorations will result in answers to unanswerable questions in the philosophy of psychology. Though the material arrays itself tantalizingly around the perennial problem of the ultimate objective truth status of psychology, it will not solve it. Rather, the interpretation of much of the material presented by the authors of these papers will very largely depend on the reader's own fundamental stance, realist or instrumentalist, towards psychology.

Notwithstanding that from its inception modern psychology has had a history of transplantation, there is no theoretical framework readily available for analysis of this situation. This offshoot of European and British systems of thought has thrived to such an extent in the favourable climate of the United States that questions of what was involved in that particular cultural shift have until recently largely been overlooked. Over the last two decades a wide spectrum of historians of science have indicated increasing concern with the interdependence of cultural tradition and social context (see for instance Buck, 1980 on American science in modern China), and more recently the specialist historians of psychology have been voicing the same theme (such as Coan, 1973, and Buss, 1979). But very few detailed analyses of such cultural interactions have been forthcoming for the psychological field, and such as have are almost totally exclusive to the European/British/North American exchange (see for example papers by Green and Rieber, and Blumenthal, in Rieber and Salzinger (eds.) 1980). Only a handful of publications has appeared to date on psychology in developing and Third World countries (such as by Jahoda 1973; Sinha 1973; Bloom 1982; and Blackler 1983). One available subset of analytic frameworks within the historiography of science covers the role of science in imperial impacts (outlined in MacLeod, 1982), but this framework has only limited relevance to the history of mental and behavioural science in Asia, where the burgeoning of the field post-dates the heyday of colonialism and direct imperialist domination.

ESTABLISHING THE ROUTE

Answers to the questions listed above are not quite as numerous as the countries represented in the volume. But they _are_ very numerous, a fact which may not unreasonably give rise to doubts as to the value of grouping them into a region. A more usual grouping is in terms of level of economic development, such as an Asian segment of the Third World (for example Atal 1974). Justification for the present grouping is of course first and foremost in geographical terms. The first obvious question to arise within such a framework is why the cutoff point has been set at Pakistan. But moving west from Pakistan into the Middle East, there appears to be a substantial physical area with a vacuum as far as modern psychological activity is concerned; even prior to the Russian incursion into Afghanistan there was no psychology department in Kabul University and no professional psychological organization in the country (Rahimi 1974), and the recent upheaval in Iran seems to have completely terminated activities of psychologists there (Agahi and Spencer, 1982).

Next, it will be asked why the region has been extended to include places as far east as New Zealand and Fiji, countries culturally very different from those of Asia. The answer here contains reasons which are pragmatic within a scholarly context. Papua New Guinea and Fiji represent very early stages in the evolution of the discipline, examples of which were not so easily located in Asia. Australia and New Zealand represent the distinctive situation of an extension of imperial science into a cultural vacuum, as the Australian aborigines and New Zealand Maoris were sufficiently few in number to exert any influence on such matters; these countries thus provide a good ground for comparison with the superimposition elsewhere of psychology onto sets of previously established practices and beliefs.

Furthermore, as perusal of the papers will indicate, the relative proximity of the Asian/Oceanic countries to each other is producing colleagual ties between psychologists in the locality. These relationships of course vary not only in strength but in character; they include dependence both economic and academic, and the conference interactions usual amongst neighbours. But the resemblances between many subgroups in the region, such as in cultures, subcultures or stage of urbanization, are also beginning to produce participation in joint research

projects on matters of mutual interest, and more focussed
conference discussions. Resounding with great audibility
from almost all of the papers is an admission of the
derivative character of psychology in its contemporary
condition within the respective countries, including in
the case of those where the discipline has had time to
become firmly established, an account of continuing if
not altogether unquestioning adherence to western models
(though not all from the same source). As has already
been remarked, the progenitor countries nevertheless
remain in quite considerable ignorance of the growth of
this particular group of offspring.

To attempt to draw general conclusions from our
range of regional "perspectives" is a formidable task,
and one that must be qualified in advance by an awareness
that each writer will have his or her individual bias, as
well as, presumably, giving some sort of national
colouration to their stories. It is conceivable that
certain information available to contributors themselves
is restricted for publication purposes, for instance
regarding the employment of psychologists in military
activities such as espionage or propaganda. Data which
permit of interpretation for the most part unequivocal
are presented in the following Table, which lists the
dates of formal establishment of the first departments
devoted exclusively to psychology in each of the countries under consideration, as well as of their extant
professional societies (if any). Where anomalies of any
sort have occurred for any reason, such as disruption to
the existence of a professional body or its achievement
of a fully independent status, the date of resuscitation,
reconstitution or whatever follows in brackets.

Establishment of first departments of psychology
and professional organizations of psychologists
in the Asian/Oceanic region

JAPAN   1903:   Imperial University of Tokyo
               1926:   Japanese Psychological Association

INDIA   1916:   Calcutta University
               1925:   Indian Psychological Association

CHINA - PRC   1920:   Southeastern University
               1921:   Chinese Psychological Society
                      (resumed functions 1977 after more
                      than ten years' enforced inactivity)

AUSTRALIA   1920:   University of Sydney
               1945:   Australian Branch of British Psycho-
                      logical Society (from 1965 the
                      Australian Psychological Society)

KOREA   1946:   Seoul National University
               1946:   Korean Psychological Association

TAIWAN   1949:   National Taiwan University
               1931:   Chinese Association for Pychological
                      Testing (founded on the Mainland, and
                      revived in Taiwan 1951)
               1953:   Chinese Psychological Association

THE   1954:   University of San Carlos
PHILIPPINES   1962:   Psychological Association of the
                      Philippines

THAILAND   1955:   International Institute for Child
                      Study, Srinakharinwirot University.
                      (Founded as a research centre, this
                      body from its inception conducted
                      courses at Master's level in con-
                      junction with the University's
                      Graduate College. In 1966 psychology
                      departments at Thammasart and
                      Chiengmai Universities began to offer
                      Bachelor's degrees.)
               1961:   Psychological Association of Thailand

Establishment of first departments of psychology and professional organizations of psychologists in the Asian/Oceanic region

continued

BURMA	1955:	University of Rangoon
VIET NAM	c.1955:	Hanoi Teacher Training College
PAKISTAN	c.1956:	Universities of Karachi and Sind
	1968:	Pakistan Psychological Association
BANGLADESH	1956:	Rajshahi University
	1972:	Bangladesh Psychological Association
INDONESIA	1961:	University of Indonesia
	1959:	Association of Indonesian Psychologists
HONG KONG	1967:	University of Hong Kong
	1968:	Hong Kong Psychological Society
MALAYSIA	1979:	Universiti Kebangsaan Malaysia
NEPAL	1980:	Tribhuvan University (Trichandra Campus)
	1982:	Nepalese Psychological Association
PAPUA NEW GUINEA	1983:	University of Papua New Guinea (Department of Psychology and Philosophy)
	1972:	Papua New Guinea Branch of the Australian Psychological Society (since 1975 Papua New Guinea Psychological Association. This body has not met since 1980)
SINGAPORE	1979:	Singapore Psychological Society (with non-restrictive membership)

After silk became a favourite with the Roman patricians in the second century B.C., the Silk Road followed a relatively straightforward route through China and Central Asia to Europe, plied for many subsequent centuries. The psychologists' path has not proceeded thus simply in geographic terms. Transmission of their concepts and technology has been achieved in a sequence influenced both by simple imperialist domination (as in India, Australia and New Zealand), and self-imposed emulation of foreign models. The latter has occurred as systems of government and social organization have changed, to take on the semblance either of capitalist democracy (as in Taiwan or South Korea) or Soviet socialism (as in Viet Nam and initially in Mainland China), or as speeded-up economic development has produced pressures from a rapidly industrializing society (as in Thailand and Malaysia). Where political independence is recent and industry undeveloped (as in Fiji and Papua New Guinea), psychologists have barely found a foothold.

Furthermore, the routes via which psychology has arrived at local destinations of academic recognition and professional organization have been numerous. In many of the British colonies (Australia, New Zealand, Hong Kong and on the South Asian subcontinent), it has followed the track well beaten out in the mother country, and proceeded via the gateway of departments of philosophy. In the former Australian protectorate of Papua New Guinea, it still functions as a joint department with philosophy. The British colonial system did not however always operate to produce this effect; generally in countries where a university system has been more recently introduced, different bonds were forged with psychology. In Malaysia the initial links, still partly extant, were with education and medicine; in Singapore and Fiji, neither of which has as yet established a separate department of psychology, the tie is in both cases with education, and in the case of the former, with social work, sociology and business administration, and medicine as well. In fact F. Y. Long argues very strongly in his paper on psychology in Singapore that the absence of a psychology department in that country is due to just this very tie with medicine in the "Lunatic Asylum," formed early in the century. In Indonesia, the discipline appears to have been significant first in a military (personnel selection) and then an educational context; not altogether dissimilarly, it was imported to Thailand

as an independent technology in the fifties, to assist
with handling problems of child development.

In purely organizational terms, there is a trend
clearly discernible across the board for psychologists of
academic and non-academic persuasions to join together in
professional associations to further the interests of
their discipline in political and intellectual
directions. In numerous cases in Asia (for example in
Hong Kong, Taiwan and Malaysia) such general associations
have been preceded by bodies devoted specifically to the
cause of mental health.

PROCESSING THE MERCHANDISE

What is being transported to the Asian/Oceanic
countries has been most often western but sometimes
Soviet psychology, in each case in a form very largely
unadulterated. The pattern virtually universal across
colonized and non-colonized countries is for foreign
academics to move in and train a first generation of
students, who then take higher degrees overseas and
return to replace their teachers. Depending on the wealth
of the country, this process may be extended over several
generations (as in Australia), or restricted to one (as
in Bangladesh). Availability of funding by international
agencies for these purposes also causes the pattern to
vary somewhat.

The particular problems both caused and experienced
by expatriate staff are well dealt with by Barry
Richardson in his paper on psychology in Papua New
Guinea. Transience and ensuing lack of commitment in
expatriates, preferential treatment of this group in
matters of housing, salary and terms of leave, and
ensuing lowering of morale of local staff, are of course
unique neither to psychology nor to Papua New Guinea.
They may be observed as well for instance in Hong Kong,
where, in spite of the signing in Beijing in september
1984 of the joint agreement over the colony's future, a
continuing uncertainty is being experienced by both
expatriate and local academics and other professionals as
the year of "Youknowhen" (1997) approaches.

A problem not to be overcome by the exodus or
deportation of the expatriates is that of language.
Textbooks are rarely available in the local languages of
the region, either in original or translated form.
Interestingly, Viet Nam faced up to this situation as

early as the mid-fifties, Taiwan about the same time, while some other countries, such as Bangladesh and South Korea, report themselves to be actively working on it right now. More elaborate steps towards resolution of the language problem have however been taken in some other countries. For instance, when in Burma in 1964 Burmese became the medium of instruction, textbooks began to be translated into Burmese, but this trend stopped at the undergraduate level. Despite this country's high level of isolation from personal contacts with the West, students of psychology there must now take English as a supporting subject for four years, and graduate students are both taught and examined in English. In an attempted resolution of its bilingual situation, in Hong Kong two universities now flourish, one teaching in English and one in Chinese. Others have not yet faced the issue, including even Malaysia, where the promotion of Malay as the national language is a prime policy objective of the government. Perhaps psychologists there are just too hard-pressed to take the time for textbook production. Some countries of course cope with polylingual cultures better than others; for example Singapore and Fiji display much more widespread fluency in English than is found in either Malaysia or Hong Kong, though all four have been colonies or protectorates of Britain.

Extremely heavy teaching loads in psychology are frequent across many of the Asian/Oceanic countries, especially where the subject is increasing in popularity with students, as detailed in several papers such as those on South Korea, Thailand and Papua New Guinea. The rise in popularity is not universal; it is not for instance to be seen in Nepal. A widespread trend is for psychology to be particularly favoured by women students, a possible explanation here being their lower career aspirations, as nowhere is it claimed that psychology is one of the top professions in terms of status. Other notable features of the students described in many of the chapters are their passivity, and their refusal to question authority (Nepal, South Korea, Burma and Papua New Guinea among others), a state of affairs which may well assist in the acceptance by them of western models of human nature. But it may also create a problem for the production of critical thinkers.

The question of parity of standards with the West, even with those of the colonizing or parent country where applicable, is a delicate but not unrecognized one. A number of countries continue to utilize a system of

external examiners from overseas for undergraduate
students, and some (such as Australia) just for doctoral
students, while at the University of the South Pacific in
Fiji outside examiners are called in annually to assess
the performance of the staff. Universities established on
the British model in British territories tended in the
early days to invite psychologists of quite outstanding
repute to act as external examiners; this, and transfer
of staff between the colonial and parent countries, has
had the deliberate effect of sustaining standards high in
western terms in countries such as Australia, New Zealand
and Hong Kong. Heavy teaching demands in poorer countries
militate against productivity in research, even where the
government is applying pressure for such to occur, as in
Bangladesh. A less obvious deleterious influence on the
quality of research is well outlined in the paper in
Thailand, where recent widespread enthusiasm for the
behavioural and social sciences is leading to a blind
faith in research output and a consequent over-investment
in underqualified people. A somewhat similar process
appears to be taking place in Papua New Guinea and in
Indonesia.

Of course not all the countries in the region are
developing contemporary psychology along identical lines.
Inevitably there is a selection amongst the goods
available, to fit local needs and tastes. A majority of
the authors refer to a strong local emphasis on applied
psychology; naturally such research focusses on issues
relevant if not peculiar to the particular country.
Methodologically as well, applied psychology is
selective, depending not only on financial but on broader
social circumstances too. For instance, the attitude and
opinion surveys so popular in the West seem unknown in
Mainland China, and may well be totally inappropriate in
a country where consumerism is highly controlled, and
where, for the last few decades, there has been a durable
if not unbroken record of similar control of expression
and formation of opinion. On the other hand,
cross-cultural psychology seems to be particularly
flourishing in some of the Asian regions, perhaps because
overcrowded and developing societies find themselves
particularly susceptible to pressures resulting from
ethnic minorities.

Whence comes the impetus for this transmission
eastwards of psychology? This question was not amongst
those explicitly put to contributors to the present
volume, and not surprisingly therefore, they barely

mention it. Clearly the newly trained local generation are pushing hard themselves for the adoption of the discipline and its professional adjuncts. The message of its alleged potential in the cause of "national development" comes out time and again and loud and clear. However Sinha (1983) points out that this is in fact a message of recent origin; psychology, he says, even amongst the social sciences "has been a 'retarded discipline' so far as the area of social change and national development is concerned." Sinha argues that the principle reason for this situation is the predominantly western orientation of the subject, with the inevitable lack of concern amongst researchers of the developed world for the needs of developing countries (Sinha 1983, pp.9-10).

But pushing the issue back a stage, it is obvious from the papers that the West and the USSR have approached all these countries, with the exception of Japan, with a deliberate intent of promoting psychology amongst other systems of knowledge and technology. This has been done by various means, principally by direct intervention by the colonizing powers, by less direct transmission from a colonized country to its neighbours (India to Nepal, Australia to Papua New Guinea), and by the neo-imperialist infiltration of international agencies and twentieth century powers. Whether it has been done unthinkingly or not, whether there has been a blind disregard for the traditional psychology of Asia, Melanesia and Polynesia and an unquestioning esteem for the values of First World psychology, are questions which this volume has been put together to raise rather than to answer.

CONSUMER SATISFACTION

Psychologists on the Silk Road have reached a cross-roads. Along one route echoes what Yogesh Atal (UNESCO Regional Adviser for social and human sciences in Asia and the Pacific) memorably terms "the call for indigeniz-ation" (Atal 1981). Down the other sounds a plea for the continuation of cloning of foreign models, and for an expanded contribution to "world psychology" by means of programmes of so-called fundamental (usually laboratory) research.

The call to indigenize may be interpreted as part of a protest against neo-colonialism, against cultural

subordination and even contamination. But it is not a
simple concept. In Asia and Oceania psychology, at least
from the perspectives of this volume's contributors, has
multiple visages. In Thailand it is regarded as a
technology which may assist in preventing inroads by
westernization and changing social structures on
traditional manners and moral systems, whilst casting
illumination upon the latter. In the very recently
independent nations of Papua New Guinea and Fiji, where
psychology has only a precarious foothold, its exponents
naturally represent it as a new technology, useful both
in assisting social planning in a changing milieu and in
understanding traditional and local mores. In Pakistan
there exists a movement towards the Islamization of
western knowledge wherein psychology is presented as a
belief system threatening locally accepted religious
truths. But the Pakistani psychologists themselves are
understandably more inclined to argue for a compromise
position, rather than for outright rejection of their own
hardwon relatively new establishment. A less challenging
countenance is seen in China (both Mainland and Taiwan),
where it is simply argued that "sinification" will enrich
the imported systems. This process apparently is to
include both the incorporation and development of
traditional concepts of Chinese philosophy within modern
psychology, and the application of psychological
techniques to local social problems, particularly within
the realm of social change. In Japan some such process
has already been undergone. In this, that country in Asia
where modern psychology has been longest established,
whilst there has been investigation of certain traditional Japanese concepts, the overall patterns of
development have been modelled on those of the United
States, with some variations as regards areas of emphasis. In India on the other hand, where psychology had
been well established under the rule of the British,
discontent dates back to Independence in 1947. Durganand
Sinha considers the juxtaposition of the new consciousness of national identity with the world-wide growth
post-war of psychology to have been especially significant in bringing about an adaptation of western psychology to the Indian context. Certainly such a state of
affairs as he describes in Indian-oriented psychological
research in the fifties seems to predate similar changes
elsewhere, as does likewise the intensive development in
the sixties of applied psychology in the cause of
national development. In Australia and New Zealand there

is of course no question of cultural incompatibility with psychology, this being as it is only a tiny part of an entire social and intellectual system derived from the British model.

The metaphor used to date has compared the development of contemporary psychology in the East with the purchase of a consumer commodity. Perhaps it can be stretched to accommodate the concept of a dialogue between purchasers and suppliers. Certainly some sort of modified transaction is being demanded by an increasing number of psychologists of varying cultural backgrounds and religious persuasions in the region under consideration. In such demands, psychologists are accompanied by a wide range of social scientists.

Writing in the context of social sciences in general, Krishna Kumar identifies three forms of indigenization:

(a) structural - "defined with reference to the institutional and organizational capabilities of a nation for the production and diffusion of social science knowledge;"
(b) substantive - "the content focus of the social sciences. The essential premise is that the main thrust of these disciplines in a country should be on its own society, people, and economic and political institutions;"
(c) theoretic - "a condition in which the social scientists of a nation are involved in constructing distinctive conceptual frameworks and metatheories which reflect their world views, social and cultural experiences, and perceived goals" (Kumar 1979, pp.104-5).

Advocates of all three of these levels of indigenization can be located amongst our contributors. All would appear to favour the structural variety; an explicit plea for this comes even from the authors of the papers on Fiji and Papua New Guinea, where the university system as such is very new. Probably most as well would support substantive indigenization; certainly a number of them outline research that has been done by psychologists in their countries on culture-specific phenomena and current problems. The third level in Kumar's categorization, that of theoretic indigenization, is current ground for dispute amongst the psychologists of the eastern countries.

The present volume has not taken the shape of a

debate even though one could well be constructed to do so, as the titles of many of the recent utterances of psychologists in the region indicate. The most conspicuous representative of the indigenization lobby within the present volume is Virgilio G. Enriquez, with his vigorous and unequivocating paper on "Decolonizing the Philippino psyche: impetus for the development of psychology in the Philippines." Enriquez not only defends what he states to be the sixty-year-old Philippine objection to the uncritical importation of western models, but discounts the view that Philippine psychology was an American creation in the first place. Notable examples published elsewhere are Malik B. Badri's The dilemma of Muslim psychologists (1979), and a paper by Ashis Nandy, "The non-paradigmatic crisis of Indian psychology: reflections on a recipient culture of science" (Nandy 1974).

Emanating from "the Muslim world" rather than from our particular region, Badri's book has nonetheless made a considerable impact on Asian Muslims, as outlined in Colleen Ward's paper on Malaysia. Its dedication sets the tone:

> This study is dedicated to the Muslim pioneers who broke the chains of mental slavery to Western theories and practices of the social sciences...These pioneers have exposed the atheistic and Judaeo-Christian background of Western social sciences and their distorted concept of human nature. They have thus paved the way for the new generation of emancipated Islamic social scientists (Badri 1979, p.v).

Ashis Nandy's paper has been multiply republished since 1974. After trenchant criticism of characteristics of contemporary Indian psychology, its "baroqueness" (art for art's sake), "the gambit called relevance," and "the deification of numbers," Nandy utters "a plea for an alternative culture of psychology in India," to replace "the attitude of dishonesty and subservience being fobbed off as the scientific temper of the Indian psychologist" (Nandy 1974, p.2). Specifically, he calls upon Indian psychologists to participate actively in a reconstruction of the philosophical basis of psychology, to foster an atmosphere of professional debate, and to generate new theories and data which are culture-sensitive rather than culture-free. Nandy's plea bears some resemblance to the programme for the sinification of psychology outlined in Joseph S. Z. Hsu's paper in this volume, on the history of psychology in Taiwan. Whether programmes sufficiently detailed for implementation will be spelt out from these platforms remains to be seen.

One field where changes may possibly occur in the fairly immediate future is that of clinical psychology. Several contributors (Singapore, Papua New Guinea, Fiji) remark that clients in their countries generally seek out traditional forms of assistance from such as witchdoctors, faith-healers and fortune-tellers before consulting psychiatrists and clinical psycho-logists, and this situation would seem likely to provoke interaction. Such a development would be acceptable to a commentator such as Sinha who, whilst acutely aware of the social context of psychological science, retains a high esteem for the concept of the universality of knowledge. Sinha writes:

> If one pleads for psychologies along the lines of specific countries or nations, nothing could be of greater disservice to the cause of universal science. However, if the topic brings to the fore the fact that contrasting his-torical and socio-cultural factors have dominated the development of science in oriental and occidental traditions, and that scientific enterprise is rooted in the preva-lent world-view of the community, and also that psychological knowledge in each country has certain distinctive character, then I feel that the discourse is taking us in the right direction (Sinha 1981, p.1).

A question that does not seem to have been much addressed to date by the Asian proponents of indigenization is the extent to which any distinctive concepts evolved in their countries may be taken over by others. The notion seems to be of a regional reworking of western and/or Russian systems, taking the imported concepts as a working basis. The notion of a dialogue between partners who both stand to profit is not yet conspicuous in Asian utterances. Indigenization is a one-way process. Whilst dissatisfaction with unqualified adoption of western or Russian models is apparent, primacy in the field is unhesitatingly conceded to them. This situation may well change however; it is ten years since Nandy's paper first appeared, and his is no longer a lone voice.

From another viewpoint, of course, all this may be seen as a storm in a rice bowl. Though psychologists are certainly active in the region, in proportion to its swelling population they are far from numerous, with the notable exceptions of Australia, New Zealand and Japan. (See Rosenzweig 1982, Table 2, p.125 for an estimated number of psychologists per million of population in the forty-four member countries of the IUPS.)

THE FINAL PRODUCT?

The foreseeable future holds a range of possible shapes for psychology in Asia and, to a lesser extent, Oceania, though of course there will be no real finality to this product, any more than to any other cognitive style. Three major alternatives for the next couple of decades seem to be indicated directly or indirectly by this set of papers.

Firstly, psychology in Asia and Oceania may continue to aspire to the same standards as those of the West, the USSR or a combination of both (as presently displayed in Mainland China). Within such a scenario it may well be that lack of funds will prevent the poorer countries from establishing and stabilizing costly research machinery, so that their models will continue to be, as it were, cut out of cheaper cloth, and their contributions to be peripheral, tangential or slight. A more definite if indeliberate fractionation in terms of style may occur in consequence of a combination of rising regional consciousness and aspiration, already evidenced by a proliferation of local journals as well as by the conference activity mentioned earlier. This of course will just be an extension of a similar form of separatism already extant amongst British, European, North American and Soviet psychologists.

Secondly, psychology may simply die out in those countries which do not become industrialized. Such a prognostication would be the outcome of basing an analysis of the material in the volume on the premise that modern psychology, at least in this region of the globe, very largely serves the function of a technology rather than providing a set of concepts for organizing beliefs about the nature of human beings and their social interactions. On the former basis, this prognostication is supported by the fact that psychology appears to have possibly flourished better in both Fiji and Papua New Guinea closer to the time of colonial rule, as is suggested by the closure in 1976 of the Psychological Assessment Unit jointly sponsored by the government and university in Fiji, and of the Psychological Services Branch of the Papua New Guinean Public Service in 1982. Fiji gained its independence in 1970, and Papua New Guinea in 1975; neither country is on the march towards high industrial or urban concentration. On the other hand, it is obvious from Barry Richardson's paper on Papua New Guinea that the government there is experiencing a need for psychological consultants now that it has disbanded its civil service source of these. And the recent emergence of psychology in Nepal, a country never colonized and with an economy almost entirely agricultural, is difficult to explain in these terms – though M. P. Regmi clearly admits that psychology is not exactly thriving there. The latter matches up with Bangladesh, where Hamida Akhtar Begum makes plain the connection between poverty and lack of expansion in psychological services.

Thirdly, the fairly immediate future may hold a fractionation both definite and deliberate, within as well as between local psychologies. The present level of debate between the pro- and anti-indigenization lobbies, which seems currently to be particularly vociferous in the Philippines, India and China, is highly unlikely to be resolved by a total victory for the pro- party, which would need to achieve general adherence not only to the policy of developing an idiosyncratic brand of psychology, but to a particular programme for such. Within any one country a partial victory would however result in a situation where one set of conservative psychologists continues to follow foreign leaders along a well-beaten route, while another proceeds amid argument and uncertainty to blaze a new trail or trails. Such trails may not be restricted to within national boundaries, but may draw along them psychologists of the same broad ethno/cultural backgrounds and religious persuasions, with the result that we get such phenomena emerging as a Chinese or Muslim system of psychology. Within this scenario, it is conceivable that we may get forms of psychology transmogrified out of most resemblances to the parent forms.

Then again, all countries may not follow the same route of future psychological development, and various combinations of the above are conceivable. Over and above the aforesaid possibilities however, looms yet another prospective scenario. Psychology may fail to prove its usefulness in impoverished societies with enormously expanding populations and a rate of social change inconceivable to the West, and simply expire. Naturally such a prospect is not contemplated by the present writers in this book, who are all, in one sense or another, participant in and therefore protagonists of modern psychology. Certainly the history of the discipline elsewhere has shown it to be capable of transforming to a multitude of guises. Chameleon-like, it flourishes today in the United States in at least three major groupings of these, popular, humanistic and academic. The major ideological shift that occurred after the 1917 revolution in Russia is impressive evidence of the capacity of academic psychology to survive basic transformations consequent on social change external to itself. But the rate and scale of transformation currently being experienced by some Asian countries is so overwhelming that it does not seem unreasonable to ask whether psychology, a discipline already with a history of identity crises elsewhere and with a costly and readily abused set of technical devices, can contribute to the survival of these new civilizations and thus itself survive.

REFERENCES

AGAHI, C. & SPENCER, C. Psychology in pre- and post-revolutionary Iran, Bulletin of the British Psychological Society, 1982, 35, 99-100.

ATAL, YOGESH (ed.) Social Sciences in Asia, Abhinav Publications, New Delhi, 1974.

ATAL, YOGESH. The call for indigenization, International Social Science Journal, 1981, 33, 89-197.

BADRI, MALIK B. The dilemma of Muslim psychologists, MWH London Publishers, London, 1979.

BLACKLER, F. (ed.) Social psychology and developing countries, Wiley-Interscience, New York, 1983.

BLOOM, L. Applying psychology in the Third World, Bulletin of the British Psychological Society, 1982, 35, 143-146.

BUCK, P. American science and modern China, 1876-1936, Cambridge University Press, Cambridge, 1980.

BUSS, A.R.(ed.) Psychology in social context, Halsted

Press, N.Y., 1979.

COAN, R. W. Toward a psychological interpretation of psychology, _Journal of the History of the Behavioral Sciences_, 1973, 9, 313-327.

JACOBSON, E. & REINERT , G.(eds.) _International Directory of Psychologists_, North-Holland Publishing Company, Amsterdam, 3rd edn.,1980.

JAHODA, G. Psychology and the developing countries: do they need each other? _International Social Science Journal_, 1973, 25, 461-474.

KUMAR, K. Indigenization and transnational cooperation in the social sciences, in K. Kumar (ed.) _Bonds without bondage_, East-West Cultural Learning Institute, Honolulu, 1979.

MACLEOD, R. On visiting the "Moving Metropolis": reflections on the architecture of imperial science, _Historical Records of Australian Science_, 1982, 5, No. 3.

NANDI, ASHIS. The non-paradigmatic crisis of Indian psychology: reflections on a recipient culture of science, _Indian Journal of Psychology_, 1974, 49, 1-20.

RAHIMI, WALI M. Afghanistan, in Yogesh Atal (ed.) _op. cit._, 69-86.

RIEBER, R.W. & SALZINGER, K. (eds.) _Psychology: theoretical-historical perspectives_, Academic Press, New York, 1980.

ROSENZWEIG, M. R. Trends in development and status of psychology: an international perspective, _International Journal of Psychology_, 1982, 17, 117-140.

SINHA, D. Psychology and the problems of developing countries: an overview, _International Social Science Journal_, 1973, 25, 461-474.

SINHA, D. Non-western perspectives in psychology: why, what and whither? _Journal of Indian Psychology_, 1981, 3, pp.1-9.

SINHA, D. Applied social psychology and problems of national development, in Blackler, F. (ed.) _op. cit._, 1983.

WOLMAN, B. B. (ed.) _International Directory of Psychology: People, Places and Policies_, Plenum, New York, 1979.

ACKNOWLEDGMENT

I am grateful to Erik Kvan for his thoughtful comments on a draft of this paper.

1

Development of
Modern Psychology in Pakistan

S. M. Moghni

THE BACKGROUND

As a new state, Pakistan came into being on 14th August 1947 but its culture and civilization date back to at least 3000 B.C. Its first civilization, named after its largest river, the Indus, developed around the cities of Mohenjodaro in Sind, and Harappa in the Punjab, between approximately 2500 and 1500 B.C. (Dani, 1967).

The Indus civilization was destroyed by the Aryans who hailed from the northern parts of Pakistan. Their most sacred books were the four Vedas, the earliest of them being the Rig-Veda (1400 B.C.). This is the beginning of the Aryan or Hindu civilization. The Vedic or Hindu religion was followed by Buddhism, named after its founder Gotama Buddha (564-484 B.C.). Buddhism was born in the Gangetic plain but, some three centuries later during the reign of the great Mauryan emperor Ashoka (269-233 B.C.), it spread to regions which now comprise Pakistan. It was some three centuries after Ashoka's death, during the reign of Kanishka (approximately 78 A.D. - 101 A.D.) of the mighty Kaushana dynasty, that Buddhism got a fresh lease of life (Dani, 1967). But Buddhism, the religion of the people, could not withstand the ruthless Brahminic onslaught for long, and took shelter in other lands.

The first real challenge to Hinduism, which left a permanent mark on the South Asian subcontinent,[1] came from Islam. According to the generally accepted view, as a conquering force Islam first came by sea-routes to Sind at the time of Umayyad Caliph al-Walid (705-715 A.C.). After two further waves of conquest there followed the long Muslim rule in India through a series of dynasties, the last of which was that of the great Mughuls who originally comprised Chaghtai Turks (Rashid, 1967). The most eminent amongst these was Akbar the Great. The 800-year old Muslim rule in India, particularly the

Moghul rule, was a great landmark in Indian history.

Muslims, unlike the British who succeeded them, did not merely conquer and rule India; they also made it their home, and partook of the joys and sorrows of its people. In the process of interaction with the Hindus, they developed certain social norms, a code of ethics, and even a common language, namely Urdu, which is still the most commonly spoken language of the entire sub-continent.

Another cementing bond was provided by the Muslim saints, the Sufis, who spread the light of Islam in the farthest corners of the sub-continent by their love, piety and selfless service, and in so doing generally kept themselves aloof from the affairs of the state. One index of their popularity is that millions, of every caste or creed, almost year round still throng to their shrines to pay homage. A psycho-social study of the institutions and legends which have developed around these shrines, and the needs and purposes of individuals and groups which they fulfil, would indeed be a very rewarding experience. In brief, the Sufis played a great role in giving a spiritual and moral dimension to the social and political integration which India achieved during Muslim rule. Notwithstanding this integration, Hindus and Muslims have, to this day, continued to constitute two separate streams, their waters sometimes commingling while nevertheless retaining distinct religious identities. For political reasons, the British also added to this hiatus.

The final blow to Muslim rule in India was admin-istered by the British in the Rebellion of 1857 which was a joint struggle of both Hindus and Muslims against British domination. The story of the so-called "mutiny" is now too well-known to be retold. Suffice to say, the British won, and the Indians lost. But the frustration caused by this defeat was far greater among Muslims than Hindus, perhaps because the former had developed closer identification with their ruling co-religionists than the latter. Moreover, privilege which comes with power often breeds laziness and indifference towards work. Unlike the Hindus, the Muslims lacked an active middle class. The Hindus therefore were the first to take advantage of western education, trade and commerce while the Muslims generally developed a negative attitude towards every-thing western, until reformers like Sir Syed Ahmad Khan, founder of the Aligarh School, induced them to accept the reality of British rule and take advantage of it as best they could. In this, he initially met stiff opposition from the conservative and orthodox sections of the Muslim community who thought that by so doing they would be destroying their own identity.

The oxthodox class established its own seminaries to protect the faith and culture of the community. These seminaries mostly taught Quran, Hadith, Muslim jurisprudence, and some history and philosophy, but no modern learning, science, arts or crafts. They generally provided free education, maintained themselves on private charity, and avoided government patronage. Some of them, particularly the Deoband School, were even positively anti-British.

On the other hand, western education as introduced by the British, in which Aligarh played a pioneering role, was largely secular, state-supported, taught modern disciplines, carried power and prestige, and ensured a reasonable means of livelihood through government service, the professions, trade and commerce. This being the case, the latter won the day, although the orthodox class has continued to exist and has had considerable impact on the cultural, social and even political life of the people, particularly among the poorer classes. Mosques and monasteries have been its power base. Not infrequently, therefore, and as a matter of political expediency, the westernized ruling elite even today makes use of this base to serve its own ends and purposes but genuine, intellectual interaction between the two classes is still lacking.

Attempts at reconciliation between the demands of science and religion, reason and faith, individual and society, which began with Sir Syed, have not, as yet, produced the desired synthesis in the educational and social systems of Muslims, but efforts in this direction are still under way throughout the Muslim world. In the Muslim renaissance, Iqbal, the poet philosopher of the subcontinent, played a very distinct role (1958).

British rule in India, by common consent of the major political parties, the Indian National Congress, the Muslim League and the British Government, came to an end in the middle of August, 1947, and was replaced by the independent sovereign states of India and Pakistan. Etymologically, the word "Pakistan" in Urdu means sacred or holy land. Politically, historically and ideologically, its usage expressed the Muslim desire for a separate homeland, where Muslims could govern themselves according to the tenets of their faith, and live their social, political and economic life, unhindered and unthreatened by the Hindu majority, of which they had a rather bitter experience during the period of limited self-rule granted by the British under the Government of India Act, 1935. At least, this was how the Muslims perceived it. Another potent factor in the demand for Pakistan, for which Iqbal had prepared the groundwork (1970), was the Muslim belief in the inseparability of religion and politics. The establishment of an Islamic social order has always been a part of Muslim idealism, which is activated sometimes by pan-Islamic sentiments and sometimes by nationalistic ones. In the demand for Pakistan, one finds a mixture of both. In the language of motivation, "socialized power" (McClelland, 1975) has often been a key variable in the Muslim revolutionary movement since it is part of the Muslim belief and value system. The latest example of it is the Iranian Revolution under Imam Khomeini, which is a source of inspiration for many Muslims. The Afghan resistance against the Soviets could perhaps be cited as another example.

PSYCHOLOGY IN PAKISTAN

Universities and Colleges

Until the early forties, there were perhaps only two universities in the subcontinent which had separate departments of psychology, one in Calcutta in eastern India and the other at Mysore in southern India. At least, they were the oldest and best known ones. Elsewhere, psychology was generally taught as a part of philosophy or education. The situation, however, changed after the Second World War and with Independence. By the late forties more universities began giving separate M.A./M.Sc. degrees in psychology but teaching was still generally done in philosophy departments, mostly by philosophy teachers. This was particularly so in Lahore. For some time, even before Pakistan came into being, the Government College and the Forman Christian College at Lahore undertook collaborative teaching in psychology at the Master's level (Aslam, 1975). From all accounts, the bias was heavily psychoanalytic, but a small laboratory was also functioning. (Professor Aslam, for long associated with Government College, Lahore, was not a psychoanalyst, however. He was a graduate from Cambridge, and his inclinations were more philosophical than psychological.)

As a consequence of the partition of the sub-continent into India and Pakistan, large-scale migrations took place on both sides. Many were killed on the way, and those who succeeded in crossing the borders took years to find new homes. Among the migrants were many talented and skilled persons whose absence from their jobs created a void in the institutions where they were working. Pakistan was the greater loser because there were more Hindus and Sikhs who held these positions than Muslims available to replace them. Institutions of higher learning were the worst sufferers, and the void took long to fill. At the time of partition Pakistan had only two universities, one in her western wing, namely the University of Punjab in Lahore, and the other in her eastern~ wing (now Bangladesh), namely the University of Dacca in Dacca. The University of Sind in Karachi had just come into being. (This later moved to Jamshoro and in its place was founded the University of Karachi). At the time of partition, neither Punjab nor Dacca possessed separate psychology departments. Whatever psychology was taught was mostly done in philosophy departments or Colleges of Education.

It may be added that the University of Punjab, almost until Independence, was only an affiliated examining body. The teaching of most subjects including psychology, even at the M.A./M.Sc. level, was done in certain selected colleges, and not in the university as such, which is not the case now. Among these colleges, the Government College in Lahore stood out as one of the premier institutions in the subcontinent. Its staff, finances and administration were the responsibility of the provincial goverment of the Punjab, but its syllabi and examinations were the responsibility of Punjab University. Those who taught psychology were generally philosophy graduates, who had later specialized in psychology. The psychology in which they specialized and taught usually had a British impress. This was true of almost everything. Anything worth learning or worth doing had to be 'British-like'. And so was it with psychology and psychologists.

It was only after the Second World War that American influence began to penetrate all walks of life. American trained teachers, textbooks, training programmes and the like filtered into Pakistani educational institutions. Psychology certainly gained by this injection for it then presented a more composite picture.

It was not until the mid-fifties, however, that psychology in Pakistan came out of the fold of philosophy and steered its own independent course, although this was by no means an easy task. Philosophy's grip on psychology was still strong (Moghni, 1958); syllabi and text-books, a continuation of the British days, were rather old-fashioned and there was no experimental tradition in either basic or applied research. The only organized applied use of psychology on any significant scale was to be found in the selection procedures of the Defence Forces of Pakistan, a continuation of the British practice. They, with the assistance of some academic psychologists, also helped introduce it into the Central Superior Services (civil) of Pakistan.

However, with the return of a small number of newly trained psychologists from abroad and the slowly growing public awareness of the usefulness of psychology as an applied discipline, the philosopher's hold on psychology began to loosen. Philosophy first reacted like an over-possessive mother (Moghni, 1958), but eventually absorbed the shock although this widened the cleavage between philosophers and psychologists. Sometimes departments within departments began to grow as was the case with the Government College, Lahore. However, in the early sixties the split between psychology and philosophy was formally recognized, with Dr. Ajmal heading the Department of Psychology and Dr. Hamiduddin that of Philosophy. It is interesting to note that both these men were qualified in both disciplines, and the doctorates of both were in psychology -- Dr. Ajmal's from London, and Dr. Hamiduddin's from Columbia. But one opted for psychology and the other for philosophy, perhaps because this made the split easier or at least less traumatic.

In the fifties, two other departments of psychology also came into being in the west wing of the country, one at the University of Sind in Jamshoro, and the other at the University of Karachi. The the eastern wing was not so lucky. Dacca did not have a department of psychology; it had a small laboratory attached to the department of philosophy. It was left to the new university at Rajshahi to establish, in 1956, a separate full-fledged department of psychology which the present author was called upon to head. (At that time he was in Aligarh, India). The Rajshahi Department of Psychology, starting with a tabula rasa, lost no time in introducing modernized syllabi of courses with a reasonable blend of British and American traditions, and this gradually led to similar changes in other universities of Pakistan. It was not uncommon to see among the M.A./M.Sc. textbooks William McDougall's Outline of Psychology (1923) and Outline of Abnormal Psychology (1926), prescribed for General and Abnormal Psychology respectively, and Freud's Group Psychology and the Analysis of the Ego (1922) in Social Psychology. Similarly, laboratory work was confined to a few classical experiments on sensation, attention and memory, with strong emphasis on "introspective" reports, and statistics restricted to means and standard deviations.

With the change of emphasis in scientific training, Rajshahi laboratories soon began to hum with experiments on learning, stress behaviour, perceptual and social psychological problems, as a part of the routine teaching at the Honours and Master's levels. Some research was also introduced. By 1961, a centre of research in psychological testing and student counselling had been added to the department.

With the help of fresh graduates from Rajshahi, the Philosophy Department at Dacca, which already had two psychologists on its staff, started Honours and Master's classes in psychology. Eventually, as elsewhere, psychology in Dacca separated from philosophy to steer its own independent course. That part of the world is now a separate country by the name of Bangladesh.

As mentioned earlier, the oldest centre of psychology in Pakistan is the department of psychology in Government College, Lahore. Several eminent names are associated with it - the latest one being Dr. Mohammad Ajmal, a Ph.D. from London, a psychoanalyst by training and a great advocate of Sufi doctrines and practices in psychotherapy (Ajmal, 1969). The department has a number of promising young psychologists, and also publishes a journal, Psychology Quarterly. Its present head is Syed Azhar Ali Rizvi.

In the early sixties a department of Applied Psychology was established by the Punjab University in Lahore headed originally by Dr. Ghulam Jilani and later Dr. Rafia Hassan, whose interests relate to comparative studies of Pakistani bilingual and monoglot schoolchildren's performances on verbal and non-verbal tests. Recently it has introduced a postgraduate diploma course in clinical psychology. At Punjab University, the American-influenced Institute of Education and Research has been doing psychology in the areas of testing, measurement and guidance. Lahore has other professional groups of psychologists too, mostly doing clinical work. Some of them are working in the Fountain House, a half-way rehabilitatory house for mental patients, headed by a psychiatrist M. Rashid Choudhry.[2] With two departments of psychology in the province of Sind, and two in that of Punjab, it was only natural that a fifth one should have been established at the University of Peshawar in the North-Western Frontier Province of Pakistan. This has had the added importance of being the gateway to the sub-continent since time immemorial. In 1964, the University of Peshawar established a department of psychology and called upon the present author to head it.[3]

The National Institute of Psychology at Islamabad, established by the Ministry of Education, Government of Pakistan, in the mid-seventies, has now moved to Quad-e-Azam University, Islamabad, to become a centre of excellence with Dr. Z. A. Ansari, formerly at Peshawar, as its director. It has an ambitious research programme with work on applications of Piaget's theory at the primary level, rural women's profiles, criminal behaviour, and guidance in schools. A sister institution at Islamabad, Allama Iqbal Open University, is offering certain introductory courses in psychology to those who cannot afford formal education. Its present Dean of Basic and Applied Sciences is Dr. Iftikhar N. Hassan, also president of the Pakistan Psychological Association 1983/84.

Psychology outside academia

The Armed Forces of Pakistan have been using psychology in their selection procedures, a continuation of the British days employing psychologists for this purpose. On the non-academic side, the armed forces of Pakistan are the main employers of graduates.

Another government body which makes use of psychology in selection procedures for the central superior civil services is the Federal Public Service Commission of Pakistan. Some of the mental hospitals and psychiatric institutes also employ psychologists for this purpose or for research. The use of narcotics is one area in which psychologists could play a useful rule, while child guidance, student counselling and psychiatric social work are others. However, the actual employment of psychologists in these areas is far from significant. They need to develop a stronger power base and better public relations. Yet their claims sometimes exceed their accomplishments. A lot more effort needs to be injected into their training programmes.

Professional bodies, conferences and seminars

Despite the large annual turnout of psychology graduates (that is, M.A.s and M.Sc.s) from different universities, it was not until the mid-sixties that psychologists had an exclusive forum of their own. Previously they had a joint section of Psychology and Education in the Pakistan Philosophical Congress, and similar sections in the Pakistan Association for the Advancement of Science, and the Scientific Society, Pakistan.

The first All Pakistan Senior Psychologists' Seminar was held in Peshawar in October 1966. This consisted of only senior academicians and professionals who sat with their counterparts in the related fields of psychiatry, social work and mass communication with the purposes of identifying the areas in which Pakistani psychologists, by virtue of their specialized knowledge and skills, could contribute their best to national welfare and prosperity, and suggest future directions for psychological teaching and research.

They produced a fairly exhaustive report which served as a stimulus for future thinking on academic and professional matters in psychology (Moghni, 1969). Their recommendations ranged from the introduction of new syllabi to the formation of new research and professional bodies, such as the National Council of Psychological Research and Services and the Pakistan Psychological Association. Some of the recommendations have been implemented, such as the formation of the Pakistan Psychological Association and the establishment of the National Institute of Psychology at Islamabad, while others have been under consideration at one level or another.

The Pakistan Psychological Association held its first session in Dacca in March, 1968, and the latest one in Islamabad in May, 1982. The next one will be held in Peshawar in the winter of 1984. For a variety of reasons, it has not been possible to hold its conventions regularly.

The title of the general presidential address of the first session held in Dacca was "Role of Motivation in National Development." It concluded:

> In brief, what I wish to emphasize is that understanding man, his motives and capacities, his relations to physical and social environments and how he organizes them, is basic to the formulation and execution of any plan of national development; that economic behaviour in the final analysis is itself determined by psychological factors; that targets of economic development are much easier to reach if they are understood and treated as goals of purposive behaviour of man. And it is here that we psychologists have some role to play (Moghni, 1970).

The second session of the Pakistan Psychological Association was held in the People's Open University (now called Allama Iqbal Open University), Islamabad, in November, 1975. The theme of the session's general presidential address, which was delivered by Dr. Mohammad Ajmal, pertained to the role of the psychologist in relation to his own people and culture. Psychologists were advised " ... to climb the walls of their neat and tidy disciplines and acquaint themselves at first hand with the poor, illiterate and diseased people of their country." The address concluded with the following observations:

We should be aware of studies made in the West,
but should also be aware of our own spiritual
heritage, and the condition of our people
today. It is in the light of this awareness
that we can perhaps make a creative contribution to the resolution of crises and con-
fusions which beset our people to-day (Ajmal,
1975).

The third session of the Pakistan Psychological
Association was held in the Univeristy of Punjab, Lahore
in May, 1978. Its general presidential address was
delivered by Dr. Syed Matiur Rahman, a psychologist in
the Ministry of Defence, Government of Pakistan, Rawal-
pindi, and its title was "The Proper Image of Man and the
Social Responsibility of Psychologists." He made a strong
plea for social psychological research in Pakistani
society, and concluded:

If we did honestly attempt to apply our
knowledge of the processes of internalization
of values, Pakistani society would not be in
the tragic predicament as it is now. Have we
explored the psyche of our own nation? Is it
not regrettable that in spite of the best ethos
and norms of behaviour ever known to mankind,
we are so hopelessly impoverished for lack of
operationalizing them in our national character
and conduct? (Rahman, 1978).

In May 1982, the Inter-Services Selection Board of
the Armed Forces of Pakistan took the rather unusual and
highly laudable step of holding a two-day seminar at
Kohat, to which they also invited civilian psychologists
from the universities and other institutions. Its main
themes were selection and motivation. The seminar was
inaugurated by the President of Pakistan, and this
obviously gave much-needed publicity to the psychologists. Foremost among the problems discussed were
selection procedures by means of objective and projective
tests, Ideology, and National Character.

Journals

The three professional journals published in
Pakistan (Pakistan Journal of Psychology, Psychology
Quarterly, Pakistan Psychological Studies) appear
irregularly. The difficulties are partly financial and
partly lack of standard research material. From time to
time, newsletters are also published by the National

Institute of Psychology and the Pakistan Psychological Association.

FUTURE DIRECTIONS OF PSYCHOLOGY IN PAKISTAN

It is difficult to predict what directions psychology in Pakistan will take in the future because there appears to be a lack of planning in the social sciences. So far, developments have taken place largely as a function of individual interests. By and large, the students even at the M.A./M.Sc. level are not very sure of why they are doing psychology. Sometimes it is their second or third choice with little opportunity for suitable employment, on the one hand, and the academically demanding nature of the psychology syllabi, on the other. The problem of jobs haunts the male students more than it does the female students, the majority of whom eventually settle down as housewives. This and perhaps also their high expectations of psychology as the solution to life's riddles or as providing the means to play the "game of power" that life will confront them with, bring women in much larger numbers than men to psychology departments all over the country. Although Peshawar is a relatively more conservative region of the country, we have had some of the best women students of the university admitted in psychology over the past twenty years. This is probably true of other Pakistani universities as well.

The preponderance of women among young psychology graduates has created another problem in Pakistan, if this could be called a problem. Male psychologists, both in academia and the professions, are on the way out, and women are taking their place. In some university faculties in psychology, women already outnumber men. What kind of psychology in Pakistan this phenomenon is going to give birth to, it is difficult to say. One distinct direction women seem to be taking is clinical psychology.

Personally, however, I find great merit in developing a "behavioural medicine" approach, a combination of learning theory, abnormal and social psychology, sociology, cultural anthropology, religion, physiology and medicine to problems of mental and physical health and hygiene. This would have great social and cultural relevance for a country like Pakistan with both curative and preventative value. It would provide a large number of people with varied interests opportunities for operating on a much larger canvas, and greater scope for research, at both basic and applied levels. Such an approach would be inclusive of clinical psychology, not exclusive of it. It would also help to generate multidisciplinary and cross-cultural research programmes.

One very lucrative area for Pakistani psychologists is that of testing and measurement. The one thing to which they, particularly the statistically minded ones, could give immediate attention is the construction, with the help of subject-matter specialists, of a good battery of Achievement tests for the Intermediate/Higher Secondary level, because here the conventional public examination has come in for considerable criticism and yet is in vogue because there is no suitable substitute. Efforts have been made a number of times to change this but old attitudes die hard as the vested interests reinforce them. Child-guidance, and student and marriage counselling along scientific lines, are some of the other areas in which psychologists can play a very useful role. However, they can also bring their profession into disrepute by practising their subject without proper training and experience, and the tendency to this effect does exist in some quarters.

Learning and cognition are so fundamental that every university psychology department should accommodate experimental studies of these topics and relate them to individual and social life. Unfortunately, the "flight from the laboratory" has become rather common in Pakistan. Equally unfortunately, not enough importance is given to measurement, the sine qua non of science. However, lately things have begun to change, and it is to be hoped that this shortcoming in our graduates will become a thing of the past.

Last but not least, I am convinced that social psychology in general, with its problems of leadership, communication, group dynamics and the like, and motivation in particular, will have a central place in the future development of psychology in Pakistan. The reason for my conviction is that I find no way of mobilizing our vast human resources for the benefit of the individual and society except through the application of those scientifically tested principles of social motivation. This has to be combined with the equally tested principles of learning and cognition. Adoption of programmed instruction and its derivatives is one way of meeting the shortage of teachers, and supplementing the present conventional class room instruction in many subjects at the primary, secondary and higher secondary levels (Moghni, 1965, 1969). For a developing country like Pakistan with scarce material resources but fast growing population, it is Man with his abilities and motivation who should play a key role in economic development and educational and social progress This brings the psychologist to the centre of the stage.

How psychology will be integrated into Pakistani society is a question which is very difficult to answer at the moment. Modern psychology, wherever it is, cannot and should not be cut off from its western scientific moorings. In all probability, Pakistani psychology will eventually revive its links with psychology in India and Bangladesh because developments there are in many respects relevant for Pakistan. Similarly, Pakistani psychology and Pakistani psychologists are already interacting with psychologists and thinkers from other Muslim and Third world countries. There is also a powerful intellectual movement of Islamizing knowledge including psychology (Al Faruqi, 1982). Furthermore, Sufi doctrines and practices are beginning to have an impact on psychology in Pakistan. Besides, there is a constant flow of new ideas from outside through scholars, books and journals. With all these forces at work, the shape of things to come is difficult to predict but it is certainly going to be worth watching.

Pakistani psychologists must learn to interact with those who have drunk deep from the wells of their own culture, learned men of religion and Sufi orders, literature, philosophy and history. They must, with equal humility, meet the common folks of Pakistan, the ones who need their help and care most, and from whom they can learn their first lessons of bare human existence. They must, however, equip themselves thoroughly with all the tools that science can offer them, and the western and Islamic legacies of their discipline. Only then will Pakistani psychologists be able to develop indigenous models and constructs, study their own people, society and culture, and direct their efforts to solving their problems.

NOTES

1. The term 'subcontinent', more properly called the 'Indian subcontinent' is a geographical region which includes India, Pakistan, Sri Lanka, Bangladesh and Nepal. More recently it has come to be classified as "South Asia", which is the term adopted in the table of contents of this book (Eds.)

2. The Department of Psychology in Karachi Univerity was headed in the beginning by Professor Qazi Aslam who had then retired from Government College, Lahore. It made considerable progress in the sixties under the leadership of Haseenuddin Zuberi, who trained in North America and later returned there, and S.M. Hafeez Zaidi, a Ph.D. from London who left for Nigeria in the mid-seventies. They have been succeeded by Farukh Z. Ahmad and Afzal Imam.

The emphases in Karachi appear to be clinical, learning, occupational and non-reactive methods. The Department also publishes a journal called the Pakistan Journal of Psychology. A post-graduate diploma course in clinical psychology has been recently introduced in Karachi, with Dr. Ahmad heading it. Among the textbook writers (in Urdu, the national language), Mr. Mohammad Faiq of Urdu College, Karachi comes to mind first. Some textbooks are written in the national language, Urdu, and in regional languages such as Sinohi in Sind. However, most are written in English, the common second language and language of instruction at the tertiary level. In Sind University, Jamshoro, where psychology started in the fifties, Professors Razia F. Karim and Ali Ahmad, both trained in North America, have been holding the fort. The interests of the former lie in childrearing practices, and marriage role preferences and value systems among university students, and those of the latter in perception and personality. A third senior teacher, Mr. Abdul Haque, has been working on social stereotypes.

3. We started with a strong experimental bias and with "learning" as our focus of attention soon progressed to correlational studies. The author gradually became more and more involved in social motivation, (Moghni,19-69) following the lead given by McClelland in his books , Achieving Society (1961), and Power: the inner experience (1975) and this has led him to the study of the 'national character' of Pakistan and the 'collective character' of Muslims, Millat or Ummah (Moghni, 1979,1981). In pursuit thereof, a programme of research on motivational thematic analyses of popular Pakistani adult's and children's literature was begun. Thus the department now has a correlational mix, with intelligence, creativity and scholastic achievement occupying the attention of some, and motivation, cognition and communication, that of others. Both basic and applied interests are being catered for, although financial constraints are there. What the department lacks most is a regular supply of first-rate foreign journals. The need here is more acutely felt because it is the only one in the country which runs regular Ph.D. and M.Phil. programmes, and has, at the moment, about a dozen students on rolls. It also publishes a monograph, Pakistan Psychological Studies, but this is far from regular.

REFERENCES

AJMAL, M. Muslim Traditions in Psychotherapy. Pakistan Psychological Studies, 1969, Vol 1.

AJMAL, M. General Presidential Address. Proceedings of the Pakistan Psychological Association, Islamabad, 1975

ALFARUQI, ISMAIL RAJI. Islamization of Knowledge: General Principles and Workplan, International Institute of Islamic Thought, Washington, D.C. 1982.

ASLAM, Q. M. Fifty years of psychology. Pakistan Journal of Psychology, December, 1975.

DANI, A.H.A short history of Pakistan, Book One Pre-Muslim period, (Gen.Ed. I.H. Qureshi.) University of Karachi Press, Karachi. 1967.

IQBAL, M. Six Lectures on Reconstruction of Religious Thought in Islam, Mohamman Ashraf, Lahore. 1958. (First published in 1930).

IQBAL, M. Presidential Address. 21st session, All-India Muslim League, Allahabad, Dec. 29-30, 1930. In Syed Shariffudin Pirzada Foundations of Pakistan Volume II (1924-47), National Publishing House, Karachi. 1970

KABIR, M. A short history of Pakistan, Book Two, Muslim rule under the Sultans, (Gen.Ed. I.H. Qureshi.) University of Karachi Press, Karachi. 1967.

McCLELLAND, D. C. The Achieving Society, Van Nostrand Co., New York. 1961.

McCLELLAND, D. C. Power: The Inner Experience, Irvington, New York. 1975.

MOGHNI, S. M. My submission as a psychologist. Sectional Presidential Address, Psychology & Education, Pakistan Philosophical Congress, 1958. The Pakistan Philosophical Journal, 1959, vol. II, No. 3.

MOGHNI, S. M. A new technology of education and some related problems. General Presidential Address, Pakistan Philosophical Congress, Lahore 1965. Pakistan Philosophical Journal, 1965, vol X, No. 1

MOGHNI, S. M. Report of the All-Pakistan Senior Psychologists Seminar, Oct. 1966. Pakistan Psychological Studies, 1969.

MOGHNI, S. M. Research into the Millat character of Muslims: a proposal and framework for an international study. Pakistan Psychological Studies, 1979, vol. 3. Also in Derasat (Arabic) Journal of the College of Education, Riyad University. 1981

MOGHNI, S. M. & RUSSELL, R. W. Application of new educational technologies to literacy training in Pakistan: A research project. International Journal of Psychology, 1968, Vol. 3, no.3.

QURESHI, I. H. General Editor's Note. In A. H. Dani's A short history of Pakistan Book One Pre-Muslim period, University of Karachi Press, Karachi. 1967.

RAHMAN, S. M. The proper image of man and the social responsibility of psychologists. General Presidential Address. <u>Proceedings of the 3rd Session of Pakistan Psychological Association,</u> Lahore, 1978.

RASHID, SH. A. <u>A short history of Pakistan Book Three. The Mughul Empire,</u> (Gen.Ed. I.H. Qureshi), University of Karachi Press, Karachi. 1967.

2

Psychology in India:
A Historical Perspective

Durganand Sinha

TRADITIONAL INDIAN PSYCHOLOGY AND MODERN PSYCHOLOGY

India has a rich treasure house of psychological knowledge in the ancient philosophical and religious texts. The ancient seers and philosophers were greatly interested in understanding the dynamics of human behaviour. Almost every system of philosophy and important religion had its own view of man, his nature and behaviour. But psychology as enshrined in the ancient text has certain distinctive features (Sinha, 1965). It was distinct in approach, orientation and methodology. Firstly, philosophy, religion and psychology did not stand asunder but formed an integrated whole. Although development in each of these three took place, they maintained intimate ties. In ancient India different-iation did not amount to divorce and psychology never branched off from philosophy. Modern psychologists, on the other hand, tend to guard the frontiers of their discipline jealously and have shown a distinct rebelli-ousness against philosophy to whose apronstring it has been tied for a long time. Secondly, ancient Indian psychology was entirely practical in orientation. Its outlook was that knowledge is not for its own sake but for the liberation of the individual. Like philosophy, psychology did not primarily take its rise in wonder or curiosity as it seems to have done in the West; rather it originated under the pressure of a practical need to eradicate the presence of physical and moral evils in life. Indian thinkers developed psychological and philosophical explanations for evils and suggested ways of eradicating them. Knowledge was not for its own sake, but for the highest purpose for which man can strive, that is, liberation. Thirdly, psychology in India was based on speculation and intuition and not on systematic observation and experimentation. As such, it remained somewhat esoteric and was handed down from the seer to his disciple and did not entirely meet the criteria of objectivity and repeatability which are considered vital for being called a science.

Due to these basic differences, when psychology from the West was introduced to India it was not easily integrated or assimilated into the existing system of knowledge. Political dominance of the West prevented its rejection by the indigenous system. On the other hand, the dominant western system more or less replaced the Indian tradition in psychology almost entirely, at least among the scholars who had received modern western education. Therefore, rather than being integrated or assimilated, the kind of psychology that was prevalent in the West began to be imbibed and emulated in India. Those who still continued to profess the ancient Indian psychology were looked down upon with a certain amount of contempt by modern scholars who became indifferent, if not hostile, to ancient learning. Therefore, what happened was a complete transplantation of an alien discipline on the Indian scene. As a result, in early phases of the discipline in the country, the kind of research activity that occurred was almost entirely replicative and imitative of the West (Sinha, 1972).

THE INITIAL PHASE OF MODERN PSYCHOLOGY IN INDIA

Modern psychology is a recent phenomenon in India. It was introduced from the West as a part of general transfer of knowledge - from the dominant West to the subservient East. The beginning of it can be traced to 1905 when Sir Ausotosh Mukherjee, who was the Vice-Chancellor of Calcutta University, included psychology as an independent subject in the postgraduate course. Sir Brojendra Nath Seal, who was at that time the George V Professor of Mental and Moral Philosophy in Calcutta University, drew up a syllabus in experimental psychology after consulting the syllabi of different universities in Europe and America. But for some unknown reason it was ten years later that the first laboratory of psychology was eventually started and the post-graduate teaching in the subject began the following year under Dr. N. N. Sengupta. He had worked in Harvard University under Professor Hugo Munsterberg, studying the Wundtian tradition of experimental psychology but also became aware of the application of psychology to problems of life and society, an area in which Munsterberg had made a significant contribution. It was because of these two influences on Dr. Sengupta - pure and applied - that from its very inception psychology in India had an applied slant. Dr. Sengupta also visited Cornell where Titchener

had been active and adopted his experimental techniques.
Thus the programme of study and research that was started
in Calcutta and rapidly spread to other centres in India
was very much along the lines of study initiated by Wundt
and Titchener whose textbooks were widely used. As Sinha
(1980c, p.3) points out "Thus, by following Cornell, the
researches that were first initiated in the sphere of
scientific psychology in India, came under the orbit of
influence of Leipzig." In selection of research topics
during the early phases the emphasis was upon the
experimental work related to the classical studies of
Wundt, Kulpe, Fechner, Ebbinghaus and others. As Professor S. K. Bose (1979, p.5) remarks, "The object was
either to supplement these studies by further experimentation or to examine some aspects of it from a new angle.
In laying down the experimental procedure, the techniques
of the structural school were mostly followed." This
trend is very clearly evident in the early publications
in the Indian Journal of Psychology, the official journal
of the Indian Psychological Association established in
1926, and in the account of the first twenty-five years
of the subject prepared by Professor G. Bose (1938).

Besides the "mental chemistry" of the structural-
ists, psychoanalysis and mental testing became popular.
The Indian Psychoanalytical Society, affiliated to the
international body, was founded and training in psychoanalysis became popular. Similarly, assessment of
intelligence and of special abilities as initiated by
Binet and early pioneers like Terman, Spearman and
others, gained popularity and many psychologists began to
use various psychological tests current in the West,
sometimes making only minor modifications to suit the
Indian population. Work on mental hygiene and child
guidance also started and in some centres clinics and
institutes were established. Thus within the course of a
decade or so, Indian scholars started to function in most
of the areas in which psychologists operated in the West.
As western degrees and training had a high premium and
became a recognised means for entry and advancement in
Indian academia, scholars in increasing numbers went to
important centres of research in Europe, U.K. and U.S.A.,
such as Leipzig, London, Cambridge, Edinburgh and
Harvard, and on their return they jealously followed the
lines of work of their teachers. In the classroom also
these was complete dependence on western textbooks. It
may be added that Indian scholars did not display much by
way of innovativeness but more or less adopted the
techniques of research or tests which had been popular in
the West. As has been observed, this was a phase of
replication and imitation of studies conducted in the
West with minor variations and little originality. The

subject was imported as "a ready made intellectual
package" (Nandy, 1974, p.7), and remained as "a photocopy
of psychology as it existed in western countries during
the early years of this century" (Ramalingaswami, 1980,
p.48).

THE POST-INDEPENDENCE PERIOD

With the gaining of Independence in 1947, there was
not only a growth of national pride but a distinct change
which took place in the attitude of scholars. It was
characterised by a conscious-ness of new identity. As far
as psychology was concerned, this period coincided with
the tremendous development and diversification in the
subject that occurred during the Second World War and the
years immediately following. There has been a great
upsurge in research in India since the time of Independence and studies have ramified in different branches and
directions. The rapid growth that occurred in industrial
psychology typifies what generally happened in other
branches. As the review of the area for the period 1915
up to 1969 in the first ICSSR Survey of Research in
Psychology (Mitra, 1972) reveals, no less than 96 per
cent of the studies have been conducted since Independence. There was also a rapid increase in the number of
universities and student enrolment in the subject. At the
time of Independence psychology was taught up to post-
graduate level in only three universities. By 1960 the
number had increased to 19, and by 1982 to 57. Similarly,
at the time of Independence the total post-graduate
enrolment in psychology was hardly a hundred per year but
jumped to 1122 by 1960/61 and to over 4,000 by 1980/81.
Similarly there were very few doctoral degrees awarded in
the subject at the time of Independence. By 1961/62 the
number rose to 12 per year, and by 1981 had swelled to
96. Thus, there were more trained personnel available in
the discipline and demand for its application in industry, hospital, school, the defence services and the like
could be met.

In the field of research there was tremendous
expansion and Indian scholars took up topics which were
popular at that time. Maintaining the framework borrowed
from the West and studying almost the same topics, they
tried to investigate them in the Indian seting to see if
similar factors were operating. A few instances of the
studies conducted during the period bring out the point
clearly. Rorschach, TAT, Picture-Frustration Test and
other projective techniques were very popular at that
time in the West. Indian scholars went on developing
Indian norms or adapting them to the Indian setting with

only minor variations. The same was true with regard to psychometric measures of intelligence, abilities and personality. Direct translations and crude adaptations with only minor modifications were common. As Nandy (1974, p.3) points out, the studies remained "innumerable half-hearted replications, unending streams of adaptations and readaptations of western scales and tests".

Such replicative studies were common in almost all the fields of psychology. A few illustrative examples reveal the main foci of interest of Indian scholars. In educational psychology factors related to occupational preference, vocational guidance, analysis of study habits, factors underlying academic achievement, improving reliability and objectivity of examination were the major concerns. In the area of experimental psychology research on topics such as estimation of temporal intervals, factors governing perception, memory, retroactive inhibition, and the role of reward, punishment and some personality factors in learning were conducted. In clinical psychology, anxiety scales were developed along the lines of Taylor and correlates of anxiety were analysed. Hypnosis and suggestibility, which had gained popularity in the West, were studied. In matters of stardardization of diagnostic testing, studies of psychological disorders and therapy, Indian psychologists followed the footsteps of their western counterparts. In the area of industrial psychology, topics like selection and training, accident, impact of illumination and noise on output, psychological analysis of absenteeism and job satisfaction, worker's attitude, morale and incentives were favourite ones for study. As in the West, leadership in industry and organizational problems also began to receive attention. Indian scholars followed the lead given by western psychologists in ergonomics and human engineering and started to look at human factor problems in design of aircraft displays, the influence of speed and load on signal operators, and other problems in the man-machine system.

Personality and Social Psychology presented a similar picture. Construction and adaptations of various kinds of psychometric and projective tests purporting to measure different aspects of personality became a common pastime of psychologists. There was little effort made towards conceptual clarity or making suitable the measures appropriate for the socio-cultural characteristics of the population. Attention was also focussed on leadership qualities and the authoritarian personality, taking over wholesale the western model. Social Psychology was mainly concerned with measurement of attitude and opinion on diverse objects mostly with ill-developed questionnaires and interview schedules, so much so that the branch has often been labelled as "questionnaire psychology" (Sinha, 1980a, p.162). Other important topics received only a scant attention. There were some studies on prejudice and social distance drawing inspiration from Gardner Murphy's (1953) publication In the Minds of Men which resulted from investigations commissioned at the insistence of the government of India into the various kinds of social tension that are so characteristic of Indian society. Caste and national stereotypes were also frequently investigated.

One of the chief weaknesses of the research conducted during this period was the absence of any sound theoretical base. In fact, Indian scholars seldom bothered to develop their own theoretical model or enunciate any theory based on their findings. While investigating rumours during an earthquake (Prasad, 1935) or behaviour during a catastrophe resulting from a landslide (Sinha, 1952), the investigators came surprisingly close to a new theory of cognitive functioning. But they fought shy of formulating the same while Festinger (1957) utilised their findings as the grounds for his famous theory of cognitive dissonance.

A casual look at the research indicates that Indian investigators closely followed along the lines of their western counterparts. Publications in foreign journals carried tremendous prestige in academic circles and helped greatly in appointment and promotion. The academic community was concerned more about recognition of their research by western scholars rather than by their relevance to the needs of the country. This factor was greatly responsible for the dependence of Indian scholars on the West. As a result, what they investigated was frequently a repetition of what had already been done elsewhere. Such research has been characterised in derogatory terms as "Unitedstatean", "victims of adaptology", or "Euro-American product" (Sinha, 1977, p.3). There was, however, a difference from what was the case in the twenties and thirties in the sense that in the earlier period a distinct effort was made to interrelate the work to Indian social reality. Thus, while studying problems like absenteeism and job satisfaction, for example, some factors peculiar to the Indian setting were investigated. In this sense a search for new identity had begun.

THE PHASE OF INDIGENIZATION

There was a distinct change in the sixties which could be said to mark the period of a new orientation. Firstly, scholars began to feel the shortcomings of their studies in a number of ways. They became conscious of the limitations of the use of theoretical approaches, models and tools forged in the West - a warning sounded by Myrdal (1968). A feeling began to grow that those working in developing countries could not afford to depend upon such indiscreet borrowings and there was a felt need for theories, concepts, models and tools that were realistic and relevant to the countries where research was being conducted. Secondly, there was a distinct orientation towards problem-oriented as distinct from purely theoretical research. As J.B.P. Sinha (1973a, p.103) pointed out, "all kinds of problems keep bombarding us into an inescapable position from where we do not have any alternative except to address ourselves to them". Thus, to a country which had launched itself on the experiment of rapid social change and national development through planned effort, the topic of social change posed a new challenge even to the psychologist (Sinha, 1966). Earlier than in other countries, Indian psychologists entered the arena of social change and national development. This phase of the discipline in the country represented the real beginning of the effort on the part of the Indian psychologists to select topics for research which were of special interest to national development, analysing them with the help of existing psycho-logical techniques and principles. It marked the beginning of indigenization of the subject and gave it a new direction, at least in so far as the content was concerned, which was distinct from what had become the fashion in the West.

Before getting into the details of this phase, it is to be noted that the post-1960 period is marked by very rapid and vigorous expansion of research activities in almost all the fields of psychology. In fact the sixties can be regarded as the decade of the great spurt in research. Mitra (1972) observed that 62 per cent of all publications listed were produced from this period. The ramifications of the discipline in the country can be judged the variety of themes on which the second review of psychology for the period 1971-76 centred (Pareek, 1980a). They included psychological theory and research methods, culture and personality, developmental and cognitive processes, deviance and pathology, counselling and therapy, communication and influence, organisational dynamics, psychology of work, political processes and behaviour, environmental psychology and social issues such as poverty, inequality, population and family planning, dynamics of social change, and the question of relevance. Thus, it was a period not only of rapid growth but also of diversification.

The lines of study prevalent in the fifties were continued with greater vigour and some new areas began to emerge and became prominent. In almost all areas, as is clear from the two surveys of researches sponsored by the Indian Council for Social Science Research (ICSSR), western influence was still very marked, though there was a distinct tendency towards dissatisfaction with the same, and effort to develop new lines more relevant to the needs of the country. The dissatisfaction latent in the studies conducted in the fifties became more articulate and complaint was made about the 'foreignness' and irrelevance of the bulk of research conducted in psychology. The members of the Standing Committee for Psychology of the ICSSR "voiced concern about the foreignness of social science research in India today - in the field of psychology in particular" (ICSSR 1973, p. 43). Consciousness of this limitation generated in turn a strong desire to make research topics relevant to the Indian setting and the outcome relevant to contemporary problems. This tendency is most clearly illustrated in the fields of social psychology, organizational psychology and clinical psychology, though the impact can be discerned in almost every field.

The following examples taken from different fields illustrate this trend towards indigenization:

(a) Psychology and rural development

India being a predominantly agricultural country, psychology there, despite its usual urban orientation, entered the domain of rural development. Taking the lead from McClelland's (1961) work on the key role of the need for achievement in the process of development, Sinha (1969) made a psychological analysis of certain Community Development blocks to identify motivational and attitudinal components associated with agro-economic development. The strategy of study set by him of comparing contrasting groups of villages in terms of development and motivation became popular and it stimulated a large number of studies on villagers' aspirations and motivations. Analysis of the sequence of adoption of new farm practices became a popular topic among some psychologists. Under the general direction of Everett Rogers of Michigan State University, a number of large-scale studies on diffusion of innovations in rural society were undertaken and psychological and social factors that prompted the villagers to modernise their agriculture were isolated.

Gains of economic development are often offset by rapid increases in the population. Health and family planning are, therefore, other components of development programmes. Many psychologists concentrated on the nature of effective communication and factors underlying adoption of family planning practices. Effects of radio and other media were also studied. The strategy of KAP studies (knowledge, attitude and practice), which have been found useful in West, was also adopted by Indian social scientists and a number of studies in this direction were conducted. Another significant area of research concerned the analysis of changes in attitude and behaviour related to rural development as a result of viewing television programmes - a project related to the Indian Satellite Instructional Television Experiment (SITE). These studies not only represented a new ramification of the subject in the country but also marked the beginning of a new sub-discipline by Indian scholars of rural psychology.

(b) Psychological Dimensions of Poverty

Poverty constitutes another area where Indian psychologists have shown interest because of the direct relevance of the subject. With more than 50 per cent of the population living below the poverty line and poverty eradication programmes being an integral component of our recent Five-Year Plan, poverty constituted a new challenge. Psychologists who had long neglected the topic came into the arena in a big way and began to analyse its psychological concomitants. In studying poverty psychologists have generally regarded it as a deficit and have developed an ecological perspective for understanding the phenomenon in the Indian context. The effects of poverty on cognitive and perceptual processes, linguistic development, academic achievement, motivation and personality, personal style and orientation, nutritional aspect and impact on mental health, crime and delinquency have all been investigated (Sinha, Tripathi and Misra, 1982). The main conclusion that emerges from these studies is that though poverty has its origin in the economic system and social structure it has harmful psycholological consequences which render the individual less capable of coping with the problem.

(c) Study of Socialization

In developmental psychology the striking feature has been the gradual setting aside of the Freudian framework and the acceptance of the social learning model for understanding the process of development. In studying socialization investigators have often adopted "near ethnographic" approaches and have focussed their attention on development and handling of aggression in different cultural groups, and the socialization of competence in children belonging to families practising different crafts (Sinha, 1981). Adoption of this approach has enabled due weight to be given to socio-cultural influences operating on development. Another significant aspect has been the realisation of the role of elaborate system of rituals and practices prevalent in Hindu society which provide not only the context but enormous guidelines for the education and rearing of the Indian child (Kakar, 1978).

(d) Prejudice and Secularism

India is committed to goals of religious tolerance and secularism. These, however, have remained elusive ideals and the contemporary society is displaying growing tensions along intercaste, interreligious and inter-communal lines, frequently resulting in orgies of communal and inter-caste violence and riots which have shaken the very foundation of our society. Psychologists shifting from their earlier studies of social distance and intercaste stereotypes and inter-group attitudes have began to go deeper into the roots of prejudice and anti-secular tendencies. Development of religious identity and prejudice have also been investigated (see for example, Hasan, 1982, Paranjpe, 1970, and A.K. Singh, 1981.)

(e) Clinical Psychology

In clinical psychology and psychopathology, societal in-fluences on pathology and epidemiological studies of morbidity have come into prominence. For example, it has been observed that not only are personality disorders rarely identified as deviant in Indian society but there is community support and high social and familial tolerance for conditions such as simple schizophrenia. Similarly, drug use has not always been perceived as serious. Further, surveys on the incidence of mental disorders have been widely conducted and their differential associations with caste, illiteracy, poverty, rural-urban background, type of family and other demographic variables investigated.

The period also marks a sudden upsurge of interest in indigenous modes of health measures and realisation of the basic differences in western and Indian approaches to psychotherapeutic procedures (Kakar, 1982). The nature of healing practices is linked with the Indian world view and the concept of the psyche. As distinct from western society, there is the involvement of the family and even the community in the healing processes. Relational and contextual aspects are stressed as vital factors in healing. Many Indian psychologists have emphasized the collective and contextual features determining personality and behaviour as against the individual and textual aspects that characterise western society.

Scholars have suggested that typical Indian patterns for psychotherapeutic transactions developed in the western cultural setting may not be appropriate in the Indian cultural context, and a guru-chela (preceptor-pupil) relationship has been suggested as being the more appropriate paradigm (Neki, 1976). In the same manner, there is renewal of interest in Yoga and the practices recommended by it for mental health. Not only therapeutic benefits of asana (Yogic posture), meditation and relaxation methods have been brought out but they have been studied using the latest physiological and psychological techniques.

It has also been observed that in the early fifties and sixties there was a distinct revivalistic tendency among some psychologists in India who tried to extol the merits of psychology as contained in ancient texts, and made a plea for Indian Psychology as diametrically opposed to western psychology. Luckily, such uncritical revivalism was never accepted in the cultural ethos of psychologists who frequently referred to it in pejorative terms. On the other hand, it is a healthy sign that there is a distinct effort being made towards integrating the two traditions (Sinha, 1965), scientifically analysing Yogic and other traditional techniques as well as examining the psychological concepts and theories contained in ancient texts.

(f) Culturally Appropriate Tests

Indiscriminate borrowing of western psychological tests has been criticised in the past and the need for the development of both psychometric and other tools appropriate to the Indian setting, especially the unsophisticated rural population, has been widely felt by many clinical psychologists and psychiatrists who have tried to develop suitable health questionnaires and tests. In other spheres too, tools for data collection appropriate for the socio-cultural context have been developed. Special problems are encountered in data collection in the Indian context and efforts have been made to forge culturally appropriate measures, for example of level of aspiration and motivation (Sinha, 1969), psychological differentiation (Sinha, 1978), and

50

risk-taking (Chaubey, 1974).

OVERVIEW

A brief review of some of the new trends in the subject reveals that what Pareek (1980b, p.ix) calls the "growing crisis in psychology" is its failure to make a thrust in the national life, to find a distinct "trend to outgrow the alien framework" (Sinha, 1980b) and to take up problems that are real and relevant. This new trend has widened the frontiers of psychology and is tending to make it more and more problem-oriented and interdisciplinary. It is largely due to the initiative and effort of some Indian psychologists that the area of psychology and national development has become recognised on the international scene. Though the talk of social relevance has sometimes been called a "gambit" which has only produced an "insipid watery brew which neither contributes to the growth of psychology nor proves useful to the policy-makers" (Nandy, 1974, p.8), Pareek (1980b) is right in pointing out that it has enabled psychology to come out of the narrow groove in which it had got stuck and assume a new role in both the development of theory and the searching for effective solutions to practical problems.

REFERENCES

BOSE, G. Progress of psychology in India during the past twenty-five years. In B. Prashad (ed.) The progress of science in India during the past twenty-five years, Calcutta, Indian Science Congress Association, 1938, pp. 336-352.

BOSE, S. K. First psychological laboratory in India: a peep into the past. Calcutta University, Psychological Alumni Association, 1979.

CHAUBEY, N. P. Motivational dimensions of rural development: a study of risk-taking, risk-avoidance, and fear of failure in villagers, Allahabad, Chaitanya Publishing House, 1974.

FESTINGER, L. A theory of cognitive dissonance, Evanston, Ill., Row, Peterson, 1957.

HASAN, M. K. Prejudice in Indian youth, New Delhi, Classical Publication, 1982.

ICSSR A report on Social Science in India: retrospective and prospective: Vol. I. New Delhi, ICSSR Review Committee Report, 1973.

KAKAR, S. The inner world: a psychoanalytic study of childhood and society in India, Delhi, Oxford University Press, 1978.

KAKAR, S. Shamans, mystics and doctors: a psychological inquiry into India and its healing traditions, Delhi, Oxford University Press, 1982.

McCLELLAND, D. C. The achieving society. Princeton, Van Nostrand, 1961.

MITRA, S. K. Psychology Research in India. In S. K. Mitra (ed.), A survey of research in psychology, New Delhi, ICSSR, and Bombay, Popular Prakashan, 1972.

MURPHY, G. In the minds of men, New York, Basic Books, 1953.

MYRDAL, G. Asian drama: an inquiry into the poverty of nations, Vol.I, New York, Penguin Books, 1968.

NANDY, A. The non-paradigmatic crisis in Indian psychology: reflections on a recipient culture of science. Indian Journal of Psychology, 1974, 49, 1-20.

NEKI, J. S. An examination of the cultural relation of dependence as a dynamic of social and therapeutic relationships: I. social developmental. British Journal of Medical Psychology, 1976, 49, 1-10.

PARANJPE, A. C. Caste prejudice and the individual, Bombay, Lalvani Publishing House, 1970.

PAREEK, U. (ed.), A survey of research in psychology, 1971-76, Parts I and II. New Delhi, ICSSR, and Bombay, Popular Prakashan, 1980(a) and 1981.

PAREEK, U. Preface, in U. Pareek (ed.), A survey of research in psychology, 1971-76, Part I, New Delhi, ICSSR, and Bombay, Popular Prakashan, 1980(b).

PRASAD, J. The psychology of rumour: a study relating to the great Indian earthquake of 1934. British Journal of Psychology, 1935, 26, 1-15.

RAMALINGSWAMI, P. Psychology in India: challenge and opportunities. New Delhi, Prachi Prakashan, 1980.

SINGH, A. K. Development of religious identity and prejudice in Indian children. In D. Sinha (ed.), Socialisation of the Indian Child, New Delhi, Concept Publishing Company, 1981, pp.87-100.

SINHA, D. Behaviour in a catastrophic situation: a psychological study of reports and rumours. British Journal of Psychology, 1952, 43, 200-209.

SINHA, D. Job satisfaction in office and manual workers. Indian Journal of Social Work, 1958, 19, 39-46.

SINHA, D. Integration of modern psychology with Indian thought. Journal of Humanistic Psychology, 1965, Spring, 6-21.

SINHA, D. Psychologist on the arena of social change. Presidential Address, Section of Psychology and Educational Sciences, Indian Science Congress, Chandigarh, January, 1966.

SINHA, D. Indian villages in transition: a motivational analysis, New Delhi, Associated Publishing House, 1969.

SINHA, D. Industrial Psychology. In S. Mitra (ed.), A survey of research in psychology, Chapter 5, Bombay, Popular Prakashan, 1972.

SINHA, D. Orientation and attitude of the social psychologist in a developing country: the Indian case. International Review of Applied Psychology, 1977, 26, 1-10.

SINHA, D. Story-Pictorial EFT: a culturally appropriate test for perceptual disembedding. Indian Journal of Psychology, 1978, 53, 160-171.

SINHA, D. Social psychology in India: a historical perspective. Psychological Studies, 1980(a), 25, 157-163.

SINHA, D. Towards outgrowing the alien framework: a review of recent trends in psychological researches in India. Paper presented to the symposium on History of psychology in various countries, XXII International Congress of Psychology, Leipzig, GDR, 1980(b).

SINHA, D. Wundtian tradition and the development of scientific psychology in India. Paper presented to the symposium In memoriam W. Wundt, XXII International Congress of Psychology, Leipzig, G.D.R., 1980(c).

SINHA, D. (ed.), Socialization of the Indian child, New Delhi, Concept Publishing Company, 1981.

SINHA, D., Tripathi, R. C. and Misra, G. (eds.), Deprivation: its social roots and psychological consequences, New Delhi, Concept Publishing Company, 1982.

SINHA, J. B. P. Methodology of problem-oriented research in India. Journal of Social and Economic Studies, 1973, 1, 93-110.

3

Historical Development
of Psychology in Nepal

M. P. Regmi

THE LAND

　　Nepal (the Gorkha-country) is an independent Kingdom, situated on the central southern slopes of the mid-Himalayas. It is located between $80^{0}4'$ and $88^{0}12'$ East longitudes and $26^{0}12'$ and $30^{0}27'$ North latitudes (the same latitude as Florida and Egypt). It is famous for having the highest snow peak in the world, Mount Everest. It has an area of 147,181 sq.km. The average length from the Mechi river in the east to the Mahakali river in the west is 885 km. (K.C. 1982). The geo-political importance of Nepal lies in its strategic location between two giant nations, China and India. India is twenty-two times and China seventy-five times bigger than Nepal in size. Nepal is a land-locked country, the nearest sea-coast being 1120 km. away, in India. Sometimes it functions as a peacemaker, at other times as a buffer and even as arbitrator, which role is appreciated by both these countries. It has a relatively rich endowment of natural resources like Ceylon, Columbia, Peru and Indonesia (Gaige 1975). About ninety-three per cent of Nepalese derive their livelihood from agriculture.

THE PEOPLE

　　In 1981 the total population was 15,020,451, with a population growth rate of 2.67 per cent. Fifty-six per cent of the population is distributed in the hills and mountains and forty-four percent in the terai lands. The average density of population per square kilometer is

106.

Linguistically, Nepal is a land of diverse ethnic groups. Its national language is Nepali, with Devnagari script. About thirty-six dialects are spoken in the country (Malla 1980). The percentage distribution of the languages spoken is as follows: Nepali (52), Maithili (11), Bhojpuri (7), Tamang (5), Tharuwani (4), Newari (4), Sherpa, Gurung, Rajbansi, Sunwar, Satar, Danuwar, and Santhali (17).

The hilly regions constitute eighty-three per cent of the total land area, and the terai form only seventeen per cent of the total land area of the Kingdom. The Tibeto-Burmese races (Tamangs, Newars, Magars, Thakalis, Rais, Limbus and Gurungs) are settled among the mountains and hills, the Newars live in Kathmandu Valley, while the Tharus, Danuwars, Majhis, Darais, Rajbansis, Bodas, Dhimals and Satars are the indigenous inhabitants of terai (Bista 1967). The Chepangs, Kushundas and the Hayus are unpopular minority ethnic groups. Ninety per cent of the population are Hindus (Indo-Aryan speakers), while ten per cent are Buddhists (Tibeto-Burmese speakers). The highlanders (Tamangs, Sherpas and Gurungs) are the followers of Lamaist Mahayan Buddhism, and the terai people (Brahmin and Chhetris) follow Hinduism. The Nepalese culture and religion exhibit a unique syncretic character (Malla 1980).

Nepal is rich in natural resources but very poor in its economy. Much poverty still exists in Nepal, the annual per capita income averaging only approximately a hundred and twenty dollars Australian. Its people have very low motivation for intellectual activities, their state being characterized by poor living conditions and mediocre thinking. They are optimistic even in hardship, but because of widespread illiteracy among the high hills and remote areas they are not motivated to change their situation. In general the Nepalese exhibit high emotionality and sentimentality (Regmi and Asthana, 1981), being poorly motivated to think critically because of their unfulfilled basic needs. But Nepalese generally show valour, courage, friendship, cooperation and hospitality (Mojumdar 1973). Their personalities are shaped by mythology, religion and rituals.

HISTORY AND PUBLIC ADMINISTRATION

The historic consolidation pattern of Nepal is

similar to that of Germany. Like Bismarck, the first King Prithvi Narayan Shah in 1769 consolidated the country into a nation from a host of feuding principalities. Land-locked Nepal shows a historic similarity with sea-locked Egypt in the development of national consciousness and integrity.

Nepal's Zone of Peace proposal[1] shows its foreign policy to be based on goals of mutual trust, friendship, co-operation, nonalignment and neutrality. Now Nepal is an independent country with independent relations with more than fifty countries of the world (Rana 1982).

In 1951 Nepal overthrew the century-old Rana oligarchy with the help of King Tribhuvan Bir Bikram Shah Dev, and in 1955 became a member of the United Kingdom. Panchayat Democracy came in 1960 (Chatterjee 1977). The constitution of 1962 was amended in each of 1967, 1975 and 1980. Thirty-five districts were re-organized into seventy-five development districts and fourteen zones headed by a Zonal Commissioner. Now the country has twenty-nine town panchayats. The Panchayat System is made up of three tiers - the village or town panchayats at the bottom, and above these the district panchayats and the national panchayat, which consists of one hundred and forty members. There are four thousand Village Panchayats in the Kingdom (K. C. 1982).

EDUCATION IN NEPAL

Nepal suffered from two dark periods, seventy-eight years of educational neglect (1768-1846), and a hundred and four years (1846-1950) of opposition to education. Thus for nearly two centuries Nepal kept itself aloof and isolated from the world (Uprety, 1962). There has been marked progress in education since the fall of Rana rule. In 1947 there were only one College and four High Schools in Nepal, in 1948 only seven people holding Bachelor's or Master's degrees, forty-eight undergraduates and fourteen with Sanskrit degrees. Literacy has increased from twelve per cent in 1961 to twenty-three per cent in 1980. Adult literacy programmes also include agricultural activities and health education. An integrated non-formal education strategy has been adopted as well. In 1971, a new education system was introduced, which popularized education and promoted the socio-economic status of the common people. Decentralization of educational facilities was emphasized.

The school system of education is as follows:

Level	Enrolment	Grades
Primary	1,143,000	One through five
Lower Secondary	415,000	Six through seven
Higher Secondary	114,000	Eight through ten

The primary education level emphasizes basic knowledge and use of the three R's, and the secondary level vocational, general and sanskrit education.

HISTORY OF UNIVERSITY EDUCATION

In 1959, the Tribhuvan University[2] was founded at Tripureshwar, Kathmandu. Before that, all educational activities at college level were affiliated to Patna University in India. The university was shifted to Kirtipur in November 1966. The university buildings were erected in co-operation with friendly countries like India and the U.S.A. There are ten institutes where post-secondary level (post-graduate) programmes are operating. Higher education comprises four levels - Proficiency Certificate, Bachelor's Degree, Master's Degree and Research. It takes four years after high school to complete the B.A. degree and two more years to complete M.A. degree courses.

Tribhuvan University remains the only university in the country, with different institutes of higher learning. At present there is a total of one hundred and three campuses including thirty-eight private campuses. In 1981-2 the enrolment was 60,296 including students on private campuses. In 1982-3 the estimated student number was 53,578 excluding private campuses.

The following table shows the enrolment in higher education by institutes:

Enrolment By Institute, 1980/81

Institute	Students Enrolled
1. Education	2,826
2. Medicine	1,293
3. Engineering	1,504
4. Agriculture and Animal Husbandry	1,040
5. Forestry	277
6. Applied Science and Technology	4,043
7. Humanities and Social Science	15,715
8. Sanskrit	504
9. Management	9,182
10. Law	2,066
Total:	38,450

The language used in university teaching is English, but recently Nepali (the native language) has been used as a medium of instruction for undergraduate classes. Entrance requirements are based on academic achievement only, though in medical and engineering classes there are formal admission tests as well. An entrance test used to be a regular feature of the Tribhuvan University as envisaged by the New Education System Plan 1 (1971-6). A battery of tests was prepared under the names General Aptitude Test and Special Aptitude Test, and a core committee was formed in 1975-6 for the development of these tests to serve the educational placement of students entering the Institute of Science, Humanities, Commerce, Medicine and Engineering. But at present entrance tests are no longer used in the selection procedure for general education.

The methods used in teaching are lectures, demonstrations and projects. Students are not very capable of thinking critically and independently because of family and economic pressures; boys feel more free than girls. A reception technique is preferred to a discovery technique students are passive and the teacher active. Community support and concern for education are gradually decreasing. Nepalese culture is relatively static, time-free. Students are dependent on teachers, textbooks, and teacher's notes (or handouts) given in the class rooms. Only ten per cent of students pass their examinations, with failure maximum in English and Mathematics. Students may repeat courses as they choose.

The NDS has been made compulsory at the postgraduate level, inserting a year of development service between the two years of academic study at the Master's level. This will involve some 400-450 students per year.

HISTORY OF PSYCHOLOGY IN NEPAL

Psychology in the University

The history of psychology goes back to 1947, when the teaching of the subject first began at Trichandra Campus, Kathmandu. Psychology was introduced at the I.A.[3] level, and gradually, in 1956 and January 1980, for the B.A. and M.A. levels respectively. Since 1980 psychology has had a separate department at the university, though Trichandra Campus is the only campus where post-graduate classes of psychology are conducted. On Padma Kanya Campus the teaching of Psychology was started in 1956 for I.A. and 1964 for B.A. levels. In Ratna Rajya Laxmi Campus, the subject was introduced gradually in 1964 and 1966 for I.A. and B.A. respectively. Apart from these three campuses (T.C., P.K. and R.R.) of Kathmandu Valley, psychology is also taught at Biratnagar and Janakpur Campuses. Psychology is not yet a popular subject in Nepal.

The greatest impetus for the development of a Psychology Department came from the inititative of the students and the efforts of psychology teachers and of the Vice-Chancellor of Tribhuvan University, supported by the hearty co-operation of the Embassy of India at Kathmandu. The Indian Embassy donated books, and 27576 Rs.(N.C.) for laboratory apparatus, and the Indian Government has provided a reader under the Colombo Plan Scheme for full-time teaching in the department. At present there are ten teachers in the Psychology Department, of whom one is now on study leave for three years under the faculty development programme, while another is on a year's sabbatical leave. Almost all university teachers are native born. The first generation of Nepalese psychologists was trained in Indian universities (Patna, Calcutta, Banaras and Saugar), and the second in Nepal itself. Promotion of teachers depends on both research and teaching experience.

Very few students take psychology because it has low job opportunities. The scope of psychology is still not developed. The ratio between males and females is 1:3 for psychology, as compared to 4:1 in university courses generally. The quality of students is decreasing from one generation to another. Classes of Psychology run in three shifts - morning, day and night. The teaching loads at the I.A., B.A. and M.A. levels are 18, 15 and 12 periods per week respectively.

Psychologists sometimes interact with anthropologists, sociologists and educators. Local psychological conferences are occasionally held by the Nepalese Psychological Association (NPA), which was founded in 1982 and is run by the psychologists of Trichandra Campus. But the NPA is still in its infancy. Rules for membership are conservative and underdeveloped; there is no foreign affiliate status. Moves are however being contemplated which may result in increasing international contact. But lack of money is a severe handicap.

The overriding preference of Nepalese psychologists is for cross-cultural and clinical psychology, mental testing and parapsychology. Psychologists believe that orientals differ considerably from occidentals in their way of life, time-space perspective, culture, personality, mythology, ecology and religion. A right time has come to develop the psychology of specific socio-cultural groups. The social psychology of the east needs to be quite different from that of the west because of phenomenological differences in the concepts, value systems, perceptions and cognitions of those regions.

Contact with International Psychology

Psychology is taught in the Institutes of Education and of Medicine, at the Village development training centre at Jawleakhel, and at police training centres. Psychological testing is used by the Public Service Commission for the selection of administrators. Workshops on Guidance and Counselling for teachers have been organized since 1971 in co-operation with the University of Southern Illinois. Now these workshops are organized by H.M.G.'s Curriculum Development Centre, Harihar Bhawan, Patan.

On sabbatical or study leave teachers either stay at home as required by their research, or more usually they join a university in India or the U.S.A. Psychologists from the U.S.A. and India visit Nepal sometimes as tourists or examiners. Mostly they came from India. No opportunity for collaborative research projects has occurred with psychologists from elsewhere. Psychologists of this country have not yet received any opportunity so far to attend conferences, do research, or to teach in foreign countries. Publication in international journals is also almost nil. The journals of psychology to which Tribhuvan University's library subscribes are the British Journal of Medical Psychology and Contemporary Psychology, both in English. However, this library does have other journals relating to science and literature. Foreign published textbooks are available in Nepal, but these are costly.

Parity or equivalence in degrees is maintained with specific reference to Indian Universities. The system of external examiners also helps in maintaining links and equivalence generally with Indian universities. Psychologists from this country sometimes participate in the Indian Science Congress.

Research and Applied Psychology

At Tribhuvan University there is a Research Division (1973) which finances, conducts and coordinates research projects in various disciplines. Thirty-nine research projects have been undertaken by this division. A number of foreign researchers are affiliated through this 'Research Division' to various research centres and institutes, which are solely for the purposes of research (see Appendix). But psychologists are not employed in any of them. Nor is psychological research at all financed by the private sector.

Research by psychologists in Nepal is mainly problem oriented, exploratory, field-based and uses the survey method. Theory building research is not undertaken here, thus research is at the primary formative stage (simple project form). Few social researchers are assessing the problems of landlessness, destruction of natural resources, population growth, distribution of power, and social history.

Anthropological fieldwork on the other hand is well under way. The efforts of nineteenth century British scholars such as Hamilton, Francis Buchanan and Hodgson resulted in some valuable accounts of the various ethnic groups. Their work has been followed in the twentieth century by Vansittart, Furer-Haimendorf and Macdonald. In the 1960's anthropologists began the study of the character of particular ethnic groups of Nepalese.

There is little in the way of applied psychology in Nepal. The government has a separate training college for administrative staff at Pulchowk, Patan. Social scientists are only very occasionally consulted by the government. At present six psychologists are working in the ministry and public service commission offices.

Psychology and Local Beliefs

The impact of modernism is high on Nepalese psychologists, who are also Hindus by religion. Lord Krishna and King Janak could be said to have been the pioneer Yoga psychologists, whilst Chanakya could be named as a famous political psychologist, and Chyawan Rishi and Charak as undoubtedly fine psychopharmacologists. Hindus are concerned themselves with myth, rituals, spirit-possession and mantras. Ritual cure still prevails in Nepal. Nepalese Hindus show a Buddhist value system, with strong interest in peace, brotherhood, cooperation, coexistence and non-violence. They have more faith in creation and construction than in destruction.

Religion and modernity co-exist symbiotically in Nepal. Undoubtedly, the study of psychology will contribute to change by transforming people into more analytical and critical human beings.

APPENDIX

Research Centres at Tribhuvan University

1. Research Centre for Nepal and Asian Studies (CNAS).
2. Research Centre for Economic Development and Administration (CEDA).
3. Research Centre for Applied Science and Technology (RECAST).
4. Research Centre for Educational Innovation and Development (CERID).
The goals of the Research Division are as follows:

1. To assimilate research work on Nepal.
2. To conduct research on issues related to education in Nepal.
3. To encourage and promote research activities and provide opportunities for researchers to publish their work.
4. To evaluate research work.
The Division has an annual budget of four lacs (one

lac being approximately equivalent to 6500 Australian dollars) for funding research projects.

Other Research Agencies

Central Panchayat Training Institute, Jawalakhel; Department of Mining and Geology, Lainchaur; Nepal Remote Sensing Centre, Maligao; Department of Food Agricultural Marketing Services, Bagbazar; Ministry of Panchayat and Local Development, Pulchowk; Trade Promotion Centre, Lal Durbar; Forest Survey and Research Office, Babar Mahal; National Council for Science and Technology, Kirtipur; New Era, Maharajgunj; East Consult (P.) Ltd., Kathmandu; Gautam Research Centre, Siddharthanagar; Integrated Development Systems, Dillibazar; Samsodhan Mandala, Wotu, Sabal Bahal; Vegetable Development and Seed Production Centre, Khumaltar.

Research projects have been financed by different agencies - DROG, World Bank, CIDA/Canada, USAID-Nepal, GTZ/Germany, ADB/Manila, UNDP/ILO, DCS/Butwal and others. The Royal Nepal Academy and Royal Science Academy are also independent institutions for research.

NOTES

1. His Majesty King Birendra Bir Bikram Shah Dev declared the proposal that Nepal be accepted as a Zone of Peace on February 25, 1975. At present thirty-eight countries have accepted this proposal.

2. The word "Tribhuvan" symbolizes the good name of late king Tribhuvan, the grandfather of the present king.

3. The I.A. (Intermediate Arts) level is the mid class (12th grade), ranging between 10 years of age at high school and 14 years at graduation for the Bachelor's degree.

REFERENCES

BISTA, D.B. People of Nepal. Kathmandu, Department of Publicity, H.M.G., 1967.

CHATTERJEE, B. Nepal's experiment with democracy. New Delhi, Ankur Publishing House, 1977.

GAIGE, F.H. Regionalism and national unity in Nepal. Delhi, Vikas Publishing House, 1975.

KHATRI CHETRI, R.B. Facts about Nepal. Kathmandu, Ministry of Communications, 1982.

MALLA, K.P. Nepal: A conspectus. Kathmandu, H.M.G. Press, 1980.

MOJUMDAR, K. Anglo-Nepalese relations in the nineteenth century. Calcutta, Firma K.L. Mukhopadhyay, 1973.

RANA, B. The evolution of Nepal's peace zone proposal. Kathmandu, Ministry of Communications, 1982.

REGMI, M.P. & ASTHANA, H. S. Cross-cultural study of Nepalese and Indian optimism, Contributions to Nepalese Studies, 1981, 8, 83-96.

UPRETY, T.N. Financing elementary education in Nepal. Unpublished Ph.D. Dissertation, University of Oregon, 1962.

4

Psychology in Bangladesh

Hamida Akhtar Begum

Bangladesh is a new nation which became independent in 1971. Following the partition of the Indian subcontinent in 1947 it was part of Pakistan, prior to which it had been under the rule of the British in India for two centuries, at which time it was known as East Bengal. In consequence, the history of psychology in Bangladesh partakes of that of India and Pakistan.

As in many Asian countries, psychology in Bangladesh is one of the most recent sciences to have been introduced into universities and colleges as a separate academic discipline. For many years it was taught in the Department of Philosophy at the University of Dhaka, established in 1921 and the oldest university in the country. In those days psychology constituted a paper or course in philosophy at the Bachelor's and Master's levels. This position continued until 1955, when the second university of the country, Rajshahi University, was set up, with a separate department of psychology.[1] In the University of Dhaka, psychology achieved the status of an independent department in 1965, although a Master's degree in the subject had been offered by the Department of Philosophy and Psychology since 1962.

Although the introduction of separate departments marks the formal recognition of psychology as a scientific discipline, scientific psychology in fact had its beginnings in 1927 when the first psychology laboratory was established in Dhaka. This laboratory was set up by Professor K. C. Mukherjee from Karachi University, and was equipped with apparatus for experiments on sensation, association, reaction-time, imagery, psychophysics and attention; experiments designed by Titchener, Whipple, Drever and Collins were popular. Along with this experimental trend a keen interest in psychoanalysis prevailed, Professor M. U. Ahmed being a well-known practising analyst.

In the late fifties and early sixties, modern laboratories started to develop in both Rajshahi and Dhaka. Professor Moghni, the head of the Department of Psychology, who did a doctorate in the U.K.,Dr. G. Jilani, likewise trained in the U.K., and Dr. G. C. Deb, head of the Department of Philosophy and Psychology and a renowned local philosopher, took the leading roles here. Remarkable changes occurred in the Department of Philosophy and Psychology in the sixties. Early in the decade, an American psychologist Oscar V. Rouck and two recent psychology graduates from Rajshahi, B. Anam and A. K. A. Rahman, joined the department, and as a result of their efforts the psychology laboratory at Dhaka acquired a considerable amount of modern apparatus and tests imported from the U.S.A. and the U.K. Other scholars, both local and foreign, joined the department in the next few years, among them Mrs. Linda Rouck, Mrs. Vallery and Mr. H. Schuman from the U.S.A., and Dr. M. K. Ali from Dhaka as Director of Guidance and Counselling. All the teachers worked closely together to develop the subject, and the first batch of students graduated with Master's degrees in 1963. The present author was one of them, and joined the Department immediately upon graduation, thereafter sharing the responsibilities of building this academic discipline. In 1964 a former lecturer from the department, Dr. Mir F. Zaman, returned after completing Master's and doctoral degrees in the U.S.A., and under his leadership psychology was separated from philosophy into an independent department.

Initially both universities of Bangladesh taught psychology at the post-graduate level, offering Master's degrees. Subsequently, Honours courses in psychology were introduced in Rajshahi in 1962, and in Dhaka in 1967, and nowboth universities offer Honours, Master's, M.Phil. and Ph.D. degrees. Currently there are sixteen teaching staff at the former and twenty-eight at the latter. Approximately a hundred students complete Master's degrees annually from each university, but to date only five in all have completed M.Phil. and doctoral degrees. Three of these were women. It appears from numbers seeking admission to psychology courses that the subject is gaining popularity, particularly among women students.

Until the end of the sixties, the medium of instruction was English. After independence Bengali, the national language spoken by the people, was introduced at all levels of education. Psychologists have commenced writing textbooks in Bengali, but very few of these have appeared yet. Like others, students of psychology are still dependent on books written in English, mostly in the U.S.A. or U.K., though most of them write their assignments in Bengali.

In the 1960's, psychology was introduced at the undergraduate level in a few colleges below the universities. The number of such colleges did not however increase as had been expected, mainly because of lack of awareness of the need for this branch of science, and the poor economic condition of the country. At present psychology is being taught in approximately less than four per cent of the total number of colleges. Among other institutions where psychology courses are included are the Institute of Education and Research, the Institute of Social Welfare and Research, the Institute of Post-graduate Medicine and Research, and various training institutes such as teacher training colleges and personnel management centres.

Over the last two decades, psychologists in Bangladesh have formed various professional organizations to promote the cause of their discipline. Of these organizations, the Bangladesh Psychological Association, to which almost all psychologists in the country belong, was the first to be set up, in 1972, immediately after independence. It originated in the Pakistan Psychological Association, which was formed in Dhaka with Professor Moghni of Rajshahi University as President and Dr. Zaman of Dhaka University as General Secretary. In all the conferences organized by this national body, psychologists have been trying to impress upon the people and the government the need to introduce the subject to all colleges and universities, and to provide opportunities for psychologists to work as professionals in different fields such as schools and industry.

Among other professional organizations are the Association of Clinical Psychology, the Society for Care and Education of Mentally Retarded Children, and the Bangladesh Association for Research, Training and Education of Mental and Developmental Disabilities. In these groups psychologists have met together with psychiatrists, educationists, social workers and other related specialists. As well, these bodies urge governmental and non-governmental agencies to help expand the scope of their work by providing financial assistance and creating favourable conditions for the development of psychological services. Such appeals have not been altogether fruitless. The Society for Care and Education of Mentally Retarded Children, for instance, with assistance from both the government of Bangladesh and abroad, established an Institute of the Mentally Retarded. This organization has also been able to introduce special education classes for backward children into some regular schools. On the whole however, there has been little opportunity for psychologists to offer their services in the task of development. A handful of them have been engaged in the selection of military personnel and of public servants, two or three have been appointed as industrial psychologists, and there are as yet no positions for school psychologists.

Two journals of psychology are published annually, the Dhaka University Journal of Psychology from 1968, and the Bangladesh Journal of Psychology, brought out since 1972 by the Bangladesh Psychological Association. The former contains research articles from Dhaka University, and the latter publishes the research work of all members of the national association, including some from overseas. Other media of publication for Bangladeshi psychologists are the Dhaka University Studies, Rajshahi University Studies and similar productions of various bodies.

Since psychology developed in Bangladesh in the hands of a few scholars trained in the west, particularly in the U.S.A., North American psychology has had a powerful influence on the nature of this subject in Bangladesh. This has been reflected in interest in and emphasis on applied psychology. Much research activity tends to be applied rather than basic (see for example Begum et al., 1980, 1981; Zaman et al., 1980) and to be initiated by the government. Both government and private organizations ask for psychological tests for personnel purposes, and two tests have been developed locally, one (a personality test for the selection of managers) by Rowshan Jahan from Dhaka University, and another (a performance test of intelligence) by Amjad Hossain Shan from Rajshahi University.

The funding agencies of the country also encourage applied research, as there is a pressing need for psychologists to help solve the many social problems, the foremost of which is population control.[2] Consequently, theory development has been neglected and, as in many other Asian countries, there is a reliance upon western models. Researchers are mostly concerned with testing the validity of western theories, and adapting various tests and instruments developed in western countries for use in Bangladesh. There is however an increasing awareness amongst local psychologists of the shortcomings of their work, and this may enrich future research activities.

In conclusion, it may be said that psychology in Bangladesh is still in its infancy. The main feature of its history has been the effort to acquire recognition as an independent scientific discipline, and thereby to develop services in various fields. Although this effort and the pressing needs of society have stimulated the research activities of psychologists from the 1970's onwards, no distinct psychology has as yet developed which could be called Bangladeshi psychology.

NOTES

1. In 1947, Dhaka University had to take up affiliation and control of about fifty-five intermediate and degree colleges that had hitherto been affiliated to the Calcutta University. Besides the creation of fully-fledged universities of agriculture and engineering, three more general universities were established after 1947; these were the universities of Rajshahi (1952), Chittagong (1968), and Jahangirnagar (1970). The two latter, and the University of Dhaka, have instituted faculties of social sciences, though psychology at Dhaka is in the Faculty of Biological Sciences. Until 1982, "Dhaka" was spelt "Dacca" (Eds.).

2. Psychologists have done some work on issues such as sterilization, among them M. R. Ali, Nihar Ranjan Sorcar, and Sultana S. Zaman.

REFERENCES

BEGUM, H. A., JAHAN, R., BEGUM, R. & AFROSE, D. An opinion survey of corruptions among the government employees in Bangladesh, Bangladesh Journal of Psychology, 1980, 6, 15-27.
BEGUM, H. A., JAHAN, R., ZAMAN, S. S., & ILYAS, Q. S. M. Examining and improving selection and promotion procedures for managers in nationalized industries of Bangladesh, ILO-UNDP Assistance to the National Management Programme, Bangladesh Management Develop-

ment Centre, Dhaka, 1981.

ZAMAN, S. S. et al. Attitudes towards work among women in Bangladesh: a pilot study, <u>Bangladesh Journal of Psychology</u>, 1980, 6, 29-66.

5

Social History
of Psychology in Thailand

Duangduen Bhanthumnavin

INTRODUCTION

Thailand appears on the map shaped like an axe embedded in Southeast Asia. In size it is the same as France, and its population numbers fifty million. Eighty-five per cent of the Thai people are Buddhist, and have a distinctive language and cuisine. The country has enjoyed more than seven hundred years of Chinese rule.

Thai culture has two principal but complementary and mutually reinforcing aspects: classical court culture, which includes Buddhist art, and popular or village culture. Until the twentieth century education was restricted to monks and royalty, but with the establish- ment during the early part of this century of a wide- spread bureaucracy, staff were required with a modern education. The first university, Chulalongkorn Univer- sity, opened in 1916, and education became compulsory for all children in 1921.

Fifty years ago psychology was introduced into the academic arena in Thailand. A general history of psycho- logy in this country until 1979 has been well narrated by Malakul (1979), while the history of that branch with the longest history and the most students, educational psychology, has been documented by Suvannathat (1979). The present article aims at presenting a social history of psychology in Thailand, which may largely be organized around the area of socialization. The term "sociali- zation" is used in the broadest sense of the word to refer to the process whereby individuals throughout their life cycles acquire the knowledge, skills and dispo- sitions that enable them to participate as effective members of groups and of society (Goslin 1969, p.2).

It is intended to demonstrate that the past, present
and future of psychology in Thailand involve first and
foremost the promotion of human development. It is
noticeable that the increase in the number of well-
trained psychologists in Thailand has been relatively
slow so that substantial contribution over a wide range
of areas is virtually impossible. The area of socialization however permits multi-disciplinary approaches to
research and application (Zigler and Child, 1969; Goslin
1969; Baumring 1980). In Thailand as well as in the
United States, there has been group effort by psychologists in the area of socialization in addition to support
from other social scientists and educators, with a
resultant substantial impact on Thai society.

IMPETUS FOR THE DEVELOPMENT OF THE PSYCHOLOGY OF SOCIALI-
ZATION

The development of other areas of psychology in
Thailand was in fact spear-headed by the development of
the socialization area, originating in child or developmental psychology, later joined by educational and social
psychology and other social sciences. The need for
general psychology in Thailand was first felt more than
fifty years ago by members of other disciplines such as
educators and psychiatrists (Bhanthumnavin 1975), especially as related to the areas of developmental, social
and learning. At first, most psychological knowledge was
necessarily imported, and it was only when a strong
determination occurred to apply the content of psychology
to the people of Thailand that an impetus for research
developed.

In Thai culture, children are the most valued
possessions, believed to be an extension of the parents'
own selves. High aspirations for their children's future
are held by many less fortunate parents, and thus great
investment is put by the family into the child's education. Anthropologists report a great variation in child-
rearing practices among different sub-cultures in
Thailand (Smakarn 1976, pp.217-225). Until after World
War II Thai parents seemed to be highly successful at
raising their young, but then everything happened at
once. First, modern technology became more widely
available. Second, the war was followed by a baby boom.
Third, economic pressures were more strongly felt and
Thai mothers had to work harder and for longer hours.

During the early fifties, the burden of raising and educating children became more evident. Traditionally Buddhist monks had taught male children to read and write and were responsible for their moral upbringing; when the task of education was shifted onto the schools, Thai parents believed that the teachers would completely replace the monks. Since teachers have far more personal responsibilities than the monks, this belief was quite mistaken. Teachers have to support and raise their own families, whereas the monks had already cut off their family ties. The monks could care for the boys as if they were their own, and the children lived in the temple grounds. Now, with all children required by law to go to school but girls not allowed to study at the temples, only a small proportion of children overall was being educated by the temples. Thus the educators were the ones who felt the need of a science of child development.

Thirty years ago, the importance of child study in education and national development was felt and acted upon by influential figures in the Ministry of Education (Malakul 1980). The need to establish the first child study centre was strengthened by the international demand to produce empirical data for the purpose of cross-cultural comparisons (Wall 1980). As a result of financial and academic cooperation between the Thai government and UNESCO, the first child psychology research centre, the International Institute for Child Study, was established in Bangkok in 1955. The first group of the Institute's staff members were Thai educators (five Master's and one doctoral degree holders), who had received further training in psychological research at the famous Child Study Center in Toronto. Assisted by numerous UNESCO-funded overseas psychologists from such places as Switzerland, Denmark and Australia (Sorattada 1980), the new centre concentrated on training Thai and foreign students first in developmental and later in educational psychology. From 1973 to 1976 the institute offered Master's degree programmes in these two areas as well as in social psychology. Its name was changed in 1963 to the Bangkok Institute for Child Study, and again in 1974 to the Behavioral Science Research Institute.

RESISTANCE TO THE DEVELOPMENT OF PSYCHOLOGY

In Thailand, a great number of people still believe that it is impossible to measure, to understand and to try to change human beings. On the other hand, a greater number believe that what it takes to change the character or behaviour of a child is only an external magical power or a simple instruction. The first group is the more literate of the two. Thai psychologists have the task of trying to convince both these groups, in opposite directions.

Resistance in Thailand against the development of psychology has been mostly indirect and unintentional. Thai people are mostly open-minded and can easily accept most types of academic knowledge. Buddhism, the religion of eighty-five per cent of the population, is rather flexible and permissive. Factors relevant to this indirect resistance have been: the late recognition of the importance of the human factor in national development, competition with other disciplines, and the problem of maintaining a concentration of academic staff resources.

Until ten years ago psychology, as well as other disciplines in the behavioural and social sciences, received relatively less attention from the public than the applied biological and physical sciences such as medi-cine, engineering and agriculture. This was partly due to the fact that the Thai government had not ade-quately recognized the importance of human factors in the process of national development. This assertion is supported by an examination of the National Plans. The first of these, covering the years 1961 to 1966, had no specific policies regarding child development, and in consequence new graduates in the social sciences, humanities and education at that time started at a lower salary level than other graduates. Attention was given to the educational and nutritional aspects of child development by the Second National Plan, 1967-1971. Only in the third National Plan, for 1972 to 1975, was the need for development of the psychological qualities of Thai children stated clearly. However, more detailed and long-term planning for different groups of Thai children and youth (up to fourteen years of age) came out five years ago (Office of the National Education Commission, 1979). This publication also suggested research topics in the area of child development and policy-making for Thailand.

When psychology first came to Thailand, it was still similar in nature to philosophy, and was not well accepted until its emphasis on empirical research became more apparent. Only when it is shown that psychology can supplement the more traditional fields of philosophy and religion has its value been recognized. Its being imported knowledge from the West added strength to the resistance to the acceptance of psychology in Thailand. When local research findings are added to the original subject-matter, the importance and usefulness of the discipline have been more widely recognized.

The third source of resistance can be identified as factors which have prevented Thai psychologists from attaining higher academic development during the in-service period, and the changing of jobs such that psychological knowledge is no longer directly applicable.

Most psychologists in Thailand have a Master's degree, though before 1970 many did not major in psychology as undergraduates. In that year the first batch of Master's graduates was produced from the first local group of psychology undergraduates, the first undergraduate programmes having begun simultaneously in 1963 at two universities, Thammasart University in Bangkok and Chiengmai University in the north. Since there was no doctoral programme until Chulalongkorn University began one in Educational Psychology in 1974, students had to go abroad to take doctorates; about twenty per cent of Thai psychologists have had this opportunity. But though Thailand produced her first Master's graduates in Developmental Psychology in 1959, it was not until the seventies that psychology had had the time to make a real contribution to local society.

One factor which has prevented an increase in the number of academic psychologists is job-mobility. Many psychologists have been lured away into other positions in which their psychological training is not directly useful. It is a traditional practice of the Thai government to send people to receive higher training for administrative positions; as most colleges and universities in Thailand are run by the government, this practice extends to that sector as well. In more detail, Thai psychologists with a higher degree were recognized as being better educated than most of their co-workers, on top of which, even before continuing their education at the Master's level, these people had already worked in their organization for several years. When they returned to resume work, after a few years most of them were promoted to an administrative or other position, where psychology was of little use.

Even before this, individual research and personal academic development were nearly impossible for teachers in colleges or universities, due to a heavy teaching load and inadequate research facilities. Psychologists were thus put in a vicious circle. First they had difficulty proving themselves useful to the public, and thus received less recognition and support from society. However, before sufficient psychological knowledge could be accumulated to be of any use, a certain amount of investment in the form of research funds, facilities and personnel had to be forthcoming. Thus the content of psychology originally taught in Thailand was not much different in character from that of philosophy or religion, and Thai policy makers and practitioners found it of very limited use.

Thirty years ago, the idea of conducting psychological research on human beings was not widely understood, and research psychologists had to struggle alone to get financial support. In the process of national development Thailand has recently made a sudden turn towards the application of knowledge from the behavioural sciences. This was due to the greater number of locally qualified academics, some of whom had acquired power through their administrative positions. But it is apparent that the country still needs more research personnel and output for these areas to be of service to society.

PSYCHOLOGY OF SOCIALIZATION: PRESENT CONCERTED EFFORTS

Fifteen years ago the biggest group of psychologists in Thailand were in educational psychology and counselling, and more concerned with practical rather than research work. However, many Master's theses were conducted under their supervision, thus laying the groundwork for the psychology of socialization in Thailand. During the seventies many Thai psychologists with high overseas qualifications returned home to work, many in areas such as social psychology, psychometrics and human development as well as in those of educational and counselling psychology. So during the seventies, Thailand witnessed an expansion of psychological work, and many high-quality studies in socialization were accumulated during this period. Towards the end of the decade enough had been reported to enable Thai psychologists to introduce social policies, orientations and technologies, most of which were related to socialization and child development.

An outline will be given of how different types of psychologists have joined forces in the teaching and studying of socialization, how the government and private sectors have given support to the area, and how knowledge in the area of socialization has become more applicable and has begun to gain increased public acceptance. Many other areas of psychology are being taught in Thai universities and colleges as well.

Teaching orientations

The independence of psychology in Thailand began with the offering of a Master's programme in developmental psychology by the International Institute for Child Study (now the Behavioral Science Research Institute), together with the Graduate College of Srinakharinwirot University, in 1955. In 1968 Master's level courses in educational psychology were added to the programme; the College of Education of Chulalongkorn University had been running such courses since 1963.

More than a hundred and thirty students have now graduated from the B.S.R.I., though the programme has been twice interrupted by a shift in emphasis, between 1968 and 1972 to educational psychology, and between 1973 and 1975 to social psychology. But the major emphasis, on the psychology of socialization, has not changed. At the Institute psychology, sociology and anthropology as well as education are represented among the staff, and this institution has been the major centre for research and teaching in socialization in Thailand.

Bachelor's courses were introduced in 1966 in experimental psychology, and industrial and school psychology, by Thammasart and Chiengmai Universities respectively. About 1972 Ramkhamhaeng University began a Bachelor's programme emphasizing social psychology, in 1974 Kasetsart University started an undergraduate programme with developmental psychology as a main area, and in 1978 Srinakharinwirot University through its psychology department offered first degree courses in developmental and social psychology. In total, eight universities and colleges now offer degree courses in psychology, with fifteen different programmes, eight of which are directly related to the topic of socialization

(Office of University Affairs, 1978).

Prospective expansion will be mainly at the graduate level. Between 1982 and 1987 it is anticipated that nine new Master's programmes will commence, among them three in organizational-industrial psychology, one in developmental psychology and one on applied behavioural science. Under the Fifth National Education Plan two doctoral programmes will be available as well, one in clinical psychology at Mahidol University and another in applied behavioural science at Srinakharinwirot University (Office of the National Education Commission, 1982, pp.324-339).

This rapid expansion of teaching programmes could not be staffed by the number of available psychologists, and a variety of scholars had to help out, with a certain amount of confusion regarding course content in consequence. The heavy teaching load also meant that the academic psychologists did not have the time to devote to the Thai Psychological Association which was established in 1965, and the activities of this organization have therefore declined over the last decade. As well, teaching and administrative burdens have retarded the accumulation of high-quality research.

Research trends

The needs and forces that have created psychology in Thailand derive from the problems of personal development, and the development of human resources, in a changing society. Studies of socialization in Thailand have been handicapped by the need to await new knowledge and techniques from abroad, unless psychologists are pushed into conducting research on an inadequate basis. But there is a very strong confidence in the capacity of research to solve all problems. There is however a form of national consciousness among some well-educated Thais, who are against the use of terminology, theories and assessments borrowed from abroad, and some psychologists have responded to this by trying to carry out research into basic processes, only to find mountainous work with inadequate support.

About seventy per cent of research reports in Thailand are the work of graduate students. This is because most academics have lacked the time and funding to carry out their own research, as well as appropriate incentives to do so. Since 1976 however the situation with respect to the latter has altered, with a change in the promotion system such that promotion now depends on producing high-quality research reports. Teaching loads are still very heavy, much more so than in the physical sciences. The supply of research facilities and personnel is still quite inadequate, and many organizational barriers impede success. Most universities have no research centre, and the B.S.R.I. remains the only one of its kind, with about twenty behavioural scientists employed there. A few psychologists are attached to more general research centres at other universities.

The B.S.R.I. has therefore been a leader in research in the area of socialization in Thailand. Earlier studies were concerned with the investigation of various aspects of Thai children's development, such as cognitive, social, value and moral development. More recently, the emphasis has been on child-rearing practices and child development. Various techniques have been developed such as a Piagetian type of cognitive training (Suvannathat et al., 1976). Techniques for the stimulation of the development of moral reasoning, the adopting of a future-oriented perspective, and belief in the relation-ship between effort and results, have also been success-fully tried out in experimental studies (conducted by graduate students under the present author's super-vision). Research contributions have also been made by other institutions, such as the Colleges of Education at Srinakharinwirot and Chulalongkorn Universities, and Kasetsart University. Socialization research activities in Thailand have been well depicted in three review articles (Bhanthumnavin and Suvannathat, 1979; Suvannat-hat 1978; Office of the National Education Commission of Thailand, 1982).

In summary, research on socialization in Thailand has flourished as a result of the efforts of many types of psychologists, but especially the educational, developmental and social psychologists. Many sociologists and anthropologists have also added their contribution. Political socialization will be an important area of research in the near future.

National policy and research support

In 1963 the Thai government set up a research centre to investigate problems of youth, and ten years later (1973), the first Thai youth policy was announced.

However, political change and instability were such that inadequate attention was paid to these activities (Office of the National Education Commission and National Youth Support and Coordination Committee, 1981, Section 1, pp.14-15). In 1977 the psychology and education sub-divisions of the National Research Council announced a long-term research policy in support of many areas of research into socialization, in addition to which, in order to stimulate more research in this area, the National Research Council has chosen the topic of socialization as one of the areas of research concentration for the last three years (Annual Report of the National Research Council, 1980-2).

It was not until 1979 that the first national policy and long-term planning for Thai children (aged up to fourteen years) were announced by the National Education Committee. This was a result of the efforts of many sectors of the Thai government, especially the universities. Professor Saisuree Chutikul, an educational psychologist, was an important coordinator of this work. It was recognized in this endeavour that a great deal of research on Thai children needs to be carried out so that the next national plan will rely less on the personal experience of the planners and more on research information. However, in 1981 the first national policy and long-term planning for Thai youth (ages fifteen to twenty-five years) was announced. In these two publications explicit research suggestions were given, and these will hopefully lead to more research support and activity in the area of socialization.

With strong encouragement from some government sectors, private organizations have started to give support to selected research activities. For example, one of the well-known banks of Bangkok gave a substantial amount of money to a research project on the tolerance and patience of the Thai people, and one newspaper gave financial support for publication of a research report in educational administration.

Thus it is only during the last five years that Thai national policies on socialization research and application have become more concrete and substantial, a fact which appears to give a great deal of encouragement and to heighten the morale of Thai psychologists.

Social application and acceptance

Social acceptance of psychological knowledge has been appraised differently by different groups of psychologists in Thailand. The teaching psychologists feel that aside from lecturing to students, their connection with the other public sectors is not something to be boasted about. On the contrary, the applied psychologists, especially those in the area of sensitivity training, feel that they have received a considerable amount of public confidence. Research psychologists have also felt an overwhelming public acceptance during the last five years. At present, highly educated Thai people are too enthusiastic about research, some of them believing that this can solve all problems. There is an obvious danger in such a belief. Research funds have been distributed to people who lack sufficient training in research methodology and adequate research consciousness. Thus a certain amount of money of this relatively poor country is being wasted each year. However, greater danger and more permanent damage comes from the findings thus accumulated, and consequently the credibility of future research in Thailand is at risk. This craving for research can be satisfied with less danger to society and to psychology by producing more qualified researchers and by giving more in-service training on research methodologies.

The consumers of socialization research in Thailand can be divided into three groups. The first group consists of the various national councils of Thailand who have requested the service of research and applied psychologists in their various programmes, including the National Research Council, the National Council of Parent-Teachers Associations, the National Council of Social Welfare, the National Council of Women, and the Office of the National Education Commission. Other governmental sectors such as the Office of Cultural Affairs and the Department of Community Development have also requested the service of socialization psychologists. Services of Thai psychologists to such high-level organizations are in the form of a membership of permanent committee, advice in development of national policies and plans, being project director or criteria developers as well as research consultants and guest lecturers.

The second group of research consumers are schools, universities and other governmental units, such as the division of mental health in the department of School Health or the Academic Division of the Department of Secondary Education. Services of Thai psychologists to this group are usually in the form of group lectures or the writing of articles on topics such as moral development, moral education, appropriate techniques for child-rearing, importance and measurement of Thai values, mental health in the home, cognitive development and training school achievement.

In Thailand, conferences and symposia on psychology have become more numerous during the last five years. Before this some research institutes such as the Behavioral Science Research Institute had hosted many research conferences which put emphasis on findings from the institute. Then the National Research Council and the Office of the National Education Commission had the responsibility of holding national conferences and symposia. However, more recently Thailand hosted the Second Asian Workshop on Child and Adolescent Development in February, 1982, with Professor Chancha Suvannathat (Director of the BSRI) as chairman. There were 40 presentations and 300 participants from 17 countries. Research interest among Thai people has been greatly stimulated by these conferences and symposia.

The third group of research consumers is the general public. The channel of communication between the Thai psychologists and the public is usually in a written form. Research psychologists in Thailand are hard workers. Once they have finished a study, they usually write a full-sized research report, an English research summary, a few journal articles and also give a presentation at a symposium. In addition, sometimes they are asked to write an article for a popular magazine. Textbooks and handbooks have also been published.

During the last few years, one of the most popular topics for research has been "moral development". Kohlberg's theory of the development of moral reasoning has been widely investigated, and Thai psychologists have found that their research on this topic has supplemented many parts of Buddhist belief and practice. Psychology in Thailand has thus brought people closer to the national religion, at least on the topic of morality.

A senior and well-respected psychologist in Thailand, Professor Tui Chumsai (1983), believes that Buddhist religion is still highly influential with the Thai people, and that thus only when psychology becomes more applicable to religious teaching will psychology be

well accepted in Thailand. The present author believes
that socialization psychology will be useful to religious
teaching in the following ways: first, developmental
psychology will make Buddhist teaching more learner-
oriented; second, socialization psychology will supply
new methods for religious transmission or shed new light
on traditional methods; third, socialization psychology
can explain some religious principles and concepts in
scientific terms more acceptable to the modern generations.

Buddhist monks are broad-minded and eager to do
their preaching well. Psychology is now included in the
religious curriculum for some monks. Numerous research
reports on moral development have also been read and
discussed by some well-respected monks. Some monks also
attend lectures on moral development and moral education
delivered at different schools and associations, and
occasionally lecture in classes on morals in elementary
and secondary schools.

The social application of psychological knowledge
can be divided into two, social orientation and social
technology (Hornstein, 1975). Socialization researchers
in Thailand have given their service to society mostly in
the form of social orientation, their best-known contribution being the handbook for child-rearing practices.

Since Thai people love and value children highly,
they often need reliable advice for raising their
children. Since Thai culture and society have changed
drastically due to cultural diffusion from the West and
the changing of educational objectives, Thai parents feel
that they need proper guidance for their parental roles.
Nevertheless, before 1960 there were only one or two
books on child rearing in Thailand and these were written
by physicians. However, in 1961 there was a series of
radio lectures (mainly relevant to modern psychological
concepts) by a highly revered Thai monk (Panyananthamuni
1976) which were later published. In 1962 the National
Research Council sponsored translation and publication of
a book, "Child care and training", by Faegre & Anderson
(1958). The Thai version was printed three times, each
time with 2,000 copies. After these two books were
published family magazines become abundant, and recently
numerous books on child-rearing practices have been
translated.

Another handbook on child-rearing practices in Asia
is in the course of preparation, the writers being mostly
Thai psychologists, and the rest educators, pediatrists

and psychiatrists. This handbook is based on up-to-date research findings and theories, and is sponsored by the WHO and the Behavioral Science Research Institute at Srinakharinwirot University. The first volume of the handbook was published in 1984. The Behavioral Science Research Institute is actively engaged in numerous studies to supply information for the writing of later volumes.

Thai psychologists had experimented with new techniques in cognitive, value, and moral reasoning training, and these techniques have been demonstrated and used in schools all over the country. In addition, social psychologists have also given some training for improving leadership effectiveness (Fiedler, Chemers, & Mahar, 1976) to many groups of Thai executives. However, there are still insufficient psychologists to fill the need in organizational psychology in Thailand (Fiedler, 1980). It is expected that in the near future the handbook for child-rearing practices in Asia will stimulate more systematic intervention for child caretakers in Thailand.

THE FUTURE OF THE PSYCHOLOGY OF SOCIALIZATION IN THAILAND

In the near future, social orientation and social technology will be in greater demand from the Thai society. Before society can advance to the level of application of knowledge, knowledge gatherers or researchers will have to be trained. Now many sectors of the Thai society have become aware of the usefulness of psychological knowledge in their life and work, but there is still a great deal of research to be done locally before a good policy, a reliable plan or a low-risk practice can materialize. The government as well as private organizations are now ready to give research support. Unfortunately it has been found that Thailand lacks a highly qualified group of behavioral scientists to be trusted with money and research projects. This conclusion has been drawn at the close of each research policy seminar for several years in Thailand.

Even though graduate programmes in psychology and other social sciences increased, during the 1970's, most of these have emphasized content rather than methodology. Most universities which do not have research institutes also suffer from inadequate research models. Therefore, with the present limitations in mind, an effective program for producing good researchers should be offered by a research institute. This need has been recognized by the Behavioral Science Research Institute which in the past has produced graduates in psychology. Starting in 1984, a new graduate programme in applied behavioural science emphasizing research methodology and practice will be offered at this research institute in cooporation with the Graduate College of the Srinakharinwirot University.

Psychology as a leading discipline in the Behavioural Sciences

In 1984 psychology became a hard-core training in the graduate programme in Applied Behavioral Science, and other social sciences such as sociology, anthropology, political science, economics, history and education will be closely incorporated in this new curriculum. This integration of many disciplines in the social sciences and education into a unity which is Behavioral Science is precipitated by at least two social forces. First is the need of the society to try to control human and social problems, requiring a training program which is problem-oriented and consequently multidisciplinary. Second, well trained psychologists in the same field are scattered in different Thai universities. Literally, there are still no two academic psychologists (with a doctorate) in the same field in the same university, hence offering a "pure" programme in any field of psychology at any one university is not realistic. Since there is still no effective system of pooling professors from different universities into one teaching programme, the pooling of different types of social scientists in the same university, into a teaching programme of that university is a lot easier to manage.

Socialization research and application will be fully integrated into the Applied Behavioral Sciences curriculum. In this curriculum socialization is represented in its fullest scope, permitting integration among various fields of psychology as well as among the social sciences.

Social application for national development

In Thailand as in other countries, there are many types of people to whom the knowledge of socialization can be of great assistance. Thai people differ not only in age but also in modernity, not only in socioeconomic status but also in normal standing. Such vast differences bring social problems and personal sufferings. Local research findings with the help of modern knowledge and technologies can hopefully fill some of the gaps and prevent or solve some of the problems, and will thus inevitably promote national development.

REFERENCES

BAUMRIND, D. New directions in socialization research. American Psychologist, 1980, 35, 7, 639-652.

BHANTHUMNAVIN, D. The future of social psychology in Thailand, in Position and Direction of Thai Education. The Educational Association of Thailand, 1975, pp. 137-141.

BHANTHUMNAVIN, D., & SUVANNATHAT, C. Psychology and education, in Social Sciences and Education. Office of the National Educational Commission of Thailand, 1979, pp. 186-229.

CHUMSAI, M. L. TUI. Personal communication, 1983.

FAEGRE, M. L., & ANDERSON, J. E. Child care and training. 7th edition Minnesota University Press, 1958. Translated version published by the National Research Council of Thailand, 1962, 1968 and 1975.

FIEDLER, F. E. Organizational Psychology in Thailand. Special Monograph on the occasion of the 25th anniversary of the Behavioral Science Research Institute, 1980, 131-135.

FIEDLER, F. E., CHEMERS, M. M., & MAHAR, L. Improving leadership effectiveness: the leader match concept. N. Y.: John Wiley & Sons, Inc., 1976.

GOSLIN, D. A. (ed.) Handbook of Socialization Theory and Research. Chicago: Rand McNally and Company, 1969.

HORNSTEIN, H. A. "Social psychology as social intervention". in Deutsch, M., & Hornstein, H.A. (eds.) Applying Social Psychology. Hillsdale, New Jersey: Lawrence Erlbaum, 1975, 211-236.

MALAKUL, PRASARN. Psychology in Thailand, Psychologia, 1979, 22, 2, 65-78.

MALAKUL, PIN In Paris, in Special Monograph on the occasion of the 25th anniversary of the Behavioral Science Research Institute, 1980, pp.7-9.

NATIONAL RESEARCH COUNCIL OF THAILAND Annual Report, 1980, p.26.

NATIONAL RESEARCH COUNCIL OF THAILAND Annual Report, 1981, pp. 8, 16, 146.

OFFICE OF THE NATIONAL EDUCATION COMMISSION OF THAILAND AND NATIONAL YOUTH SUPPORT AND COORDINATION COMMITTEE. Policy and long-term planning for the development of Thai youth, 1981.

OFFICE OF THE NATIONAL EDUCATION COMMISSION. The National Education Plan no. 5 from 1982-1987, Office of the Prime Mini-ster, 1982.

OFFICE OF THE NATIONAL EDUCATION COMMISSION. Research Summaries. The symposium on social science research studies which are related to education, September, 1981.

OFFICE OF THE PRIME MINISTER. Thailand into the 80's, Thai Watano Panich Press Co. Ltd., Bangkok, 1979.

OFFICE OF UNIVERSITY AFFAIRS. Summary of fields of study and degrees awarded: Institution of higher education, 1978.

PANYANANTHAMUNI. Proper ways to love children. Thummabucha Book Office, Bangkok, Thailand, 1976.

SMAKARN, S. Family system and the Thai kinship. Bangkok, Bunakit, 1976.

SORATTADA, L. Remembrance of the past, in Special Monograph on the Occasion of the 25th Anniversary of the Behavioral Science Research Institute, 1980, pp.12-16 (in Thai).

SUBCOMMITTEE ON CHILD-REARING PRACTICES AND CHILD DEVELOPMENT. Research review of studies on child-rearing practices and child development in Thailand, National Educational Commission, 1982.

SUVANNATHAT, C. School psychology in Thailand, in Catterall, C. D.(ed.) Psychology in the schools in international perspective. Vol. 3, Columbus, Ohio, 1979, pp. 109-120.

SUVANNATHAT, C. Teacher effectiveness in Thailand. Research Review, International Development Research Center, Canada, 1978.

SUVANNATHAT, C., et. al. An experimental study of teaching Science and Mathematics concepts to young Thai children. Research report no. 20, Behavioral Science Research Institute, 1976.

WALL, W. D. Message to the Behavioural Science. Research Institute, Bangkok, in Special Monograph on the Occasion of the 25th anniversary of the Behavioral Science Research Institute. Srinakharinwirot University, Bangkok, Thailand, 1980, pp. 7-10.

ZIGLER, E. & CHILD, I. L. Socialization, in Lindzey &
Aronson, (eds.) <u>The Handbook of Social Psychology</u>. Vol. 3
Reading: Massachusetts, 1969, pp. 450-589.

6

Some Observations on the Historical Development of Psychology in the Socialist Republic of Viet Nam

Pham Minh Hac

After centuries of foreign domination, Viet Nam achieved its independence on 2nd September, 1945, after which the government of the people, together with the people themselves, began the building of a new Viet Nam. But the building and development of the country faced great obstacles, for once again Viet Nam was invaded by old-style colonialists as well as by neo-colonialists. A war of resistance against foreign aggression took place, and the northern part of Viet Nam was liberated in 1954. After the liberation of the southern part of the country in 1975 the whole country was unified, and the Vietnamese people continue with the building of a socialist society. During the process of the building and development of a new Viet Nam, special attention has been paid by the government to the development of culture, science and education, psychology included.

Psychology has been established and developed according to the daily needs of human beings at certain levels of social advancement and economic development. It is closely linked with the progress of thinking and with the scientific and technical achievements of humankind in general and of each people in particular. During the process of defining its research object, identifying appropriate methods in order to develop, step by step, a universal theoretical system regarding that object, and adopting an explanation that will form the psychological world and thus contribute to the changing of social reality, psychology also determines its own form. So that is what should be considered as the historical development of psychology, with special reference to the stage when it has become an established discipline.

Psychology in Viet Nam over the last fifty years has developed mainly from a discipline taught at teacher training schools and universities. Textbooks on psychology before 1945 were written following French models such as Foulquie's Psychology; French was also the language of instruction. After 1945 the psychological concepts taught at teacher training schools in Saigon were derived from introspectionism, the idealist stream of personality theory and parts of psychoanalytic theory. Since 1950, textbooks of psychology used in both northern and southern parts of Viet Nam have been written in Vietnamese (Hac 1966), and the language of instruction has also been Vietnamese. In this process of teaching psychology in Viet Nam, local as well as overseas research is utilized. Texts and lectures are presented in a way suitable to the intellectual level of the students. The forthcoming curriculum for Teacher Training Colleges, detailed in Appendix 1, exemplifies this; it is a thoroughly objective and materialist curriculum which presents psychology as the indispensable component in human activity, directing and regulating this activity. (For examples of textbooks written in Vietnamese, see Minh, Coc and Xuan, 1960; Hac and Tuan, 1970; Hac 1983. The table of contents of this last is given in Appendix 2.)

Through the process of meeting the special needs of other branches and subjects, psychology very soon found out its position in the cause of social progress. This is also the basis on which psychology should be developed into an established discipline, one of the leading sciences that conducts research on human beings. This process began in 1961-2; research concentrated mainly on child psychology, educational psychology and to a lesser extent on clinical psychology and the psychology of sport. (See Hac et alii., 1964; Gia et alii., 1969; Tuan 1969; Department of Psychology, N.I.E.S., 1975; Hac and Minh, 1973.)

Today psychology is considered as an integral element of the social, natural and technical sciences, occupying a firm position in the classification of sciences in Viet Nam. The very recent leap forward of these sciences has become the impetus for the development of psychology. The more individuals firmly grasp social and natural laws, the more they are able to understand themselves thoroughly, to understand the psychological world of human society, and to understand people as entities of the whole of society.

As well, psychology has to serve the cause of reconstruction and social progress in Viet Nam.

In Viet Nam, human activity, people and their relationships to each other are the focus of all psychological research. Stemming from this, there is a need to study transactional psychology, issues of group relations, group dyanmics, social activity, the social motive and so on. By solving these problems we may come to understand the psychological aspect of new relations of production, a step which is necessary for organizational, social, economic and production management.

Right after the liberation of the North in 1954 psychology, alongside other sciences, was paid much attention by the Government. Simultaneous with the establishment of the Hanoi Teacher Training College, the first psychology department was set up in this school. In order to develop a curriculum and textbooks, people in this department studied extensively the writings of Soviet psychologists. For the first time, the achievements of psychology as represented by Soviet psychologists were introduced in a textbook written in Vietnamese. Also, during the school year 1959-60, a course on psychology and education was conducted in Hanoi Teacher Training College by two Soviet Associate Professors. In order to solve the problems imposed by the shortage of workers in this field, the question of training psychologists received a lot of attention. In 1955, among the students sent abroad to study, two were chosen to study psychology in the Soviet Union.

In addition to the shortage of psychological workers, there was a lack of suitable experimental facilities. To help solve this problem, right from the beginning one of the requirements for psychologists was that alongside their study of general theory and methodology, they must thoroughly understand the use of practical methods in order to conduct experiments successfully. This is regarded as the only way to turn psychology - an established discipline taught at teacher training institutions - into a science and an integral part of the country's scientific establishment. In 1964, for the first time, an article reporting an experiment on the memory of Vietnamese pupils appeared in the daily press. Since then there have been experiments on the thinking, attention and the like of Vietnamese pupils in schools for general education; examples have already been indicated.

There are at present nearly a hundred universities in the country, including Hanoi University, the Polytechnical University, the Medical University, the Pharmaceutical University, the Cultural University and others. As previously mentioned, when newly established the whole northern part of the country had only one department of psychology and pedagogics, but now at the faculty of educational psychology at the Hanoi Teacher Training College alone there are three sections for psychology. At the National Institute of Educational Science (N.I.E.S.), set up in 1961, there is a department of psychology with five sections, regularly conducting psychological experiments and research. In addition, at the Institute there is an Experimental Department of Children's Psychology and Pedagogics. At the Institute of Philosophy in the Commission for Social Science, there is a department of psychology. Hanoi Teacher Training College, which is of university status, has the only faculty in Viet Nam which trains researchers and teachers of psychology and education at a tertiary level; students there study a wide range of areas over a much longer period than in the other training colleges. Since 1979, both this College and the National Institute of Educational Science have been conducting post-graduate courses in psychology as well.

Within the teacher training system there are teacher training colleges or universities, and nowadays at all hundred and forty-six training institutions from the upper secondary to the tertiary levels, including eight pedagogical institutes, there is at least one section of educational psychology. At all levels within the teacher training system, students of all the natural and social sciences are required to study psychology for two semesters, for a total number of eighty-five class hours. The Appendices present the curriculum which will be used for this purpose, beginning in the 1984-5 school year, as well as the table of contents of one of the textbooks available to accompany it.

At present there are about five hundred people working as psychologists in Viet Nam. These include two people with doctorates and about thirty at the Master's level. Two of the latter took their degrees in Viet Nam, while the others were trained in the USSR, DDR, Czechoslovakia and France. At present the number of higher degree candidates in Viet Nam itself is increasing, and this year (1984) three of them will defend their theses. The majority of psychologists work as teachers, though some are employed in branches of government such as the Ministry of Health, the General Department of Vocational and Technical Education, and the General Department of Sport and Games, where there are special psychological sections. But there are not enough trained people to satisfy the growing need in many divisions for research on people in modern society (as opposed to those in the previous semi-feudal and colonial regimes), directed towards the production of higher labour yields. To resolve this situation, there should be a programme to mesh together all the different specialized branches of the subject.

An Association of Psychologists will be set up in the near future, and at present twenty-five psychologists representing all branches of psychology in the country have been brought together in a Contemporary Executive Commission. Some local conferences have been held, the sixth in 1982.

Vietnamese psychology has made itself known in the international arena. At the 21st International Congress of the IUPS in 1976, the Socialist Republic of Viet Nam sent a psychologist for the first time; I read a report entitled "Behaviour or activity?" (Hac 1976). At the 22nd International Congress of Psychology in 1980 in Leipzig, a delegation of five Vietnamese psychologists was invited, and I gave a lecture (Hac 1980). In 1978, at the first psychological conference of the socialist countries held in Potsdam, DDR. I was invited to present a paper "On the goals of Marxist psychology" at the plenary session, and four other reports were read by my colleagues at symposia.

In addition, Vietnamese psychologists have been asked to contribute papers to psychological journals of Latin America (Colombia), Asia (Japan), the Soviet Union and the German Democratic Republic. In 1978 I visited Thailand's Institute of Psychology at Bangkok University, and learnt from my colleagues's research much that was of value. And with this short article, we hope to have an opportunity to introduce to readers in Asian and Pacific countries some thoughts about psychology in Vietnam. We also hope that in future cooperation in this region will develop, and that there will be a frequent exchange of information amongst us.

APPENDIX 1

Below is the curriculum of psychology to be given to full-time students of faculties other than psychology and pedagogics, in the four-year system at the Teacher Training Colleges. This curriculum was prepared by the present author, together with Mr. Le Khanh, Mr. Tran Trong Thuy and some others. It was approved by the Ministry of Education of S. R. Vietnam, and will be adopted during the 1984-5 academic year.

CURRICULUM OF PSYCHOLOGY

Part 1: General Psychology

I   Human sciences and psychology

    (a) Man as simultaneously subject and object of educational activities
    (b) Human sciences and psychology
    (c) Psychology and educational activity

II   Activity, relation, psyche and consciousness

    (a) Activity
    (b) Relation (as the necessary condition for psychological formation and development)
    (c) Psychology as the product of activity and the basis of social communication
    (d) Consciousness (as the highest form of psychological reflection)
    (e) Attention (as the focus of consciousness and as the condition for conscious activity)

III   Personality as subject of activity and relation communication

    (a) The concept of personality and its structure
    (b) Personality and its formation for pupils of general secondary schools
    (c) Education and personality
    (d) Activity and personality
    (e) Relation, communication and personality
    (f) Personality and collectivity

IV   Cognitive activity

    (a)   Sensory cognition (sensation and perception)
    (b)   Rational cognition (thinking and imagination)
    (c)   Language and cognition
    (d)   Characteristics of the cognitive activity of pupils in general secondary schools

V   Affective life

    (a)   Affection and personality
    (b)   Laws of affective life
    (c)   The quality of affective life in pupils at general secondary schools

VI   Behaviour and will

    (a)   Behaviour - the unit of activity
    (b)   Will
    (c)   Will as a quality of personality
    (d)   Personality and will behaviour

VII   Memory

    (a)   Processes of memory and its law of evolution
    (b)   Memory mechanisms
    (c)   Memory and personality

VIII   Character and temperament

    (a)   Character
    (b)   Temperament

IX   Tendency and ability

    (a)   Tendency
    (b)   Ability

Part 2: Age Group and Pedagogical Psychology

    X   Age group and pedagogical psychology and education

        (a)   The target audience, responsibility of age group and pedagogical psychology

        (b)   Psychological development in teaching and learning activities

        (c)   The experiential way and the theoretical way of acquiring knowledge; concept formation

        (d)   Some laws of teaching and learning, and methods for teaching pupils of general secondary schools

    XI   Psychology of the teaching/learning activity

        (a)   The nature of the teaching/learning activity

        (b)   Fundamentals of the learning activity

        (c)   The experiential way and the theoretical way of acquiring knowledge; concept formation

        (d)   Some laws of teaching and learning, and methods for teaching pupils of general secondary schools

    XII   Pedagogical psychology

        (a)   Ethics and behaviour

        (b)   The complete personality - agent of ethical behaviour

        (c)   The social/psychological foundations of the formation of ethical consciousness, world outlook, ethical feeling and ethical behaviour

        (d)   The chief activities of pupils in general secondary schools, and the formation and development of their personalities

    XIII Industrial and vocational psychology for general secondary schools

        (a)   Bases of industrial psychology for general secondary schools

      (b)   Psychological foundations of vocational
            education taught at general secondary
            schools

XIV Teacher psychology

      (a)   The teacher as the organizer of the
            pupils's learning activity
      (b)   Teacher/pupil interaction
      (c)   The pedagogical ability and personality of
            the teacher
      (d)   The self-training of the teacher

XV Some methods for researching pupils' psychology

      (a)   Guiding principles
      (b)   Some concrete research techniques

APPENDIX 2

Below is the table of contents for a recently
published introductory textbook written in Vietnamese.

Introduction to Psychology by Pham Minh Hac, 1980,
        Giao Duc Publishing House, Hanoi.

I   What does psychology study?

1.   The first work on psychology (Aristotle)
2.   Socrates and the maxim "Understand oneself!"
3.   A brief survey of the history of psychology
4.   On the object of psychology in the USSR

II   The development of psychology into an independent science

1.   The vital inheritance of pre-Marxist psychology
2.   The year 1879 in the history of psychology
3.   The deadlock of metaphysical psychology

III Trends of objective psychology

1.   Behaviourism
2.   Gestalt psychology
3.   Psychoanalysis

4. The crisis of contemporary psychology: a humanistic, existential or cognitive psychology?

IV The development of Marxist psychology

1. Marxism and objective psychology
2. The first programme for the development of
Marxist psychology
3. Fundamental principles of Marxist psychology

V The systems approach in psychology

1. Major viewpoints in psychological research
2. The structural approach in non-Marxist psychology
3. The systematic approach in Marxist psychology

VI The development of psychology in Vietnam

1. Introspective psychology. The analysis of a
textbook on psychology published in Saigon
2. The experience of Soviet psychology
3. Psychological experimentation
4. Two initial premises
5. Psychology in the service of national construction and defence

REFERENCES (in order of date of publication)

DUC MINH, PHAM COC, NYUGEN THI XUAN. Psychology: a
textbook for teacher training colleges, Hanoi, Giao
Duc Publishing House, 1960.
PHAM MINH HAC et alii. Some data on the mechanical memory
of Vietnamese pupils, Pedagogical Study No. 1, NIES,
1964.
PHAM MINH HAC. On a textbook of psychology in Saigon.
Science report presented at seminar at Hanoi Teacher
Training College, 1966.
PHAM HOANG GIA et alii. Some characteristics of the
thought processes in the perception of concepts in
pupils of the lower secondary level, Psychological
Records, Hanoi, 1969.
TRUONG ANH TUAN. Subject preferences of upper secondary
level pupils, Psychogical Records, Hanoi, 1969.

PHAM MINH HAC & TRUONG ANH TUAN (eds.) <u>Psychology: a textbook for teacher training colleges</u>, Hanoi, Giao Duc Publishing House, 1970.

PHAM MINH HAC & NYUGEN DUC MINH. Initial study on psychological characteristics of lower secondary pupils, <u>Pedagogical Study</u> No. 13, NIES, 1973.

DEPARTMENT OF PSYCHOLOGY, NIES. <u>Some issues relating to the pedagogical and age-group psychology of Vietnamese pupils</u>, Hanoi, 1975.

PHAM MINH HAC. Behaviour or activity, <u>Proceedings of the XXIst Congress of the International Union for Psychological Science</u> Paris, 1976.

PHAM MINH HAC. Approach activity-personality, contemporary psychology, <u>Proceedings of the XXIInd Congress of the International Union for Psychological Science</u>, Leipzig, 1980.

PHAM MINH HAC. Activity, personality, interpersonal relations. Report presented at the Sixth Conference of Psychologists of Viet Nam, Hanoi, 1982.

PHAM MINH HAC (ed.) <u>Psychology for the use of teacher training schools</u>, Hanoi, Giao Duc Publishing House, 1983.

ACKNOWLEDGMENT

This paper was prepared with the assistance of Mr. Phi Van Gung.

7

Appendix:
Notes on Psychology
in the Socialist Republic of
the Union of Burma

Burma covers an area of 262,000 sq. miles and supports a population of 35.6 million people. From independence in 1948, through insurrections from minorities in the fifties, the country achieved a stable (initially military) government in 1962. Led by general Ne Win, the military regime became a one party socialist government with a new constitution in 1974. It has a proclaimed policy in foreign affairs of independence and non-alignment.[1]

TEACHING OF PSYCHOLOGY

Up to the outbreak of the Second World War general and experimental psychology were taught in Burma within the Philosophy Department of the University of Rangoon. It was not until 1952 that psychology was offered as a separate degree subject. In that year, the Department of Philosophy began to recruit staff specifically to teach psychology subjects only. With graduates returning from overseas, expansion of psychology teaching became possible and the Department of Philosophy was then able to offer advanced courses in psychology. In 1957, Hla Thwin was appointed to the first chair of psychology in Rangoon as the Department achieved independent status. A year earlier a group of psychologists were attached to the Department of Philosophy at Mandalay University College to start a separate course in psychology there. In 1958, Mandalay University College became the University of Mandalay and U Sein Tu, an assistant lecturer with a Ph.D from Harvard, was appointed to its first chair of psychology.[2] Both universities now offer psychology as a major subject.

English was the language of instruction in the universities up until 1964 when a new system of education replaced it with Burmese. Accordingly, psychology textbooks have been translated into Burmese (notably S. S. Sargent's Basic teachings of the great psychologists) and are used to teach psychology in basic and advanced undergraduate courses although students are also encouraged to read reference books and learn technical terms in English. Indeed, at the postgraduate level, students must not only read reference books and journals but also write their examinations and theses in English which they study as a minor subject as part of their undergraduate curriculum.

At the universities, psychology is offered only to those intending to major in the subject although at teacher's training colleges and at the Institute of Education, everyone is required to take a course in educational psychology. The Bachelor of Arts curriculum at the two universities is spread over four (without honours) or five (with honours) years. Students majoring in psychology take an introductory psychology course in their first year (with six other minor subjects) two psychology courses in their second, three in their third, and five in their fourth year. For those pursuing honours an additional year of study, including the submission of a thesis, is required. Honours graduates can proceed to a Master's degree of four courses plus a thesis which, at the University of Mandalay, is usually in the field of psychological testing.

Almost all of the academic psychologists working at present in Burma obtained their first degree locally. After graduation the usual path is to study for a Master's degree and work for a while at university to get some experience in teaching. Only later do graduates compete for a scholarship to study abroad. The sponsoring institution is invariably the Ministry of Education although sometimes scholarships offered by foreign governments are available through the Ministry of Education. Most of the academic psychologists now working at the universities have obtained their postgraduate degrees abroad in such countries as the United Kingdom, the Soviet Union or the United States. The average teaching load for staff varies from ten hours per week for Professors to sixteen hours per week for tutors in addition to which they carry out research, supervise student projects, write articles and the like.

No restriction whatsoever is placed upon the type of research that can be done at the university. One can conduct any kind of research in any field. However, there is a greater emphasis on applied rather than basic research. Psychological research at the two universities is funded by the Ministry of Education. Joint research ventures with other scientists from educational institutions, psychiatric and paediatric hospitals, are undertaken from time to time.

There is an annual meeting of psychologists at which research papers are read. Most psychologists and students of psychology attend the meeting.

NOTES

1. Taken from the All Asia Guide (13th ed. 1984), compiled by the editors from information contributed by Far Eastern Economic Review correspondents in the region.

2. See Hla Thwin. Department of Psychology, University of Rangoon, Burma. Psychologia, 1962, 5, pp.107-111.

ACKNOWLEDGMENT

The editors are grateful for the help given by U Khin Maung Than, Head of the Department of Psychology at the University of Mandalay, in the compilation of this appendix.

8

Psychology in the People's Republic of China

*H. Wing Lee
and Matthias Petzold*

BRIEF HISTORY OF DEVELOPMENT[1]

The development of psychology in the People's Republic of China is generally regarded as having undergone five broad periods. The important events of each period are outlined in the following sections.

The Beginnings (1921-1949)

While psychological ideas are apparent in Chinese writings dating back three thousand years and Chinese scholars have been in touch with Western psychology for over a century, psychology did not emerge as an independent discipline in China until about the turn of the present century. The first Chinese translation of a Western psychology book appeared in 1889 ("Mental Philosophy" by Joseph Haven). Psychology courses were first offered in the Tong Wen Guan and Shi Fan Guan, and later in intermediate normal schools during the Qing dynasty. Following the Revolution of 1911, new courses based on Western psychology were made available at institutions of higher learning, and the first laboratory was set up at Beijing University in 1917, followed by the establishment of the first psychology department in Southeastern University in 1920.

A new step in Chinese psychology was taken when the Chinese Psychological Society was formally established in 1921. The ensuing year saw the first publication of a psychological journal, and in 1928 the Institute of Psychology was founded within the Chinese Academy of Sciences. Over ten psychology departments or sections were instituted at various universities, for example, Central University, Qinghua (Tsing Hua) University, Fudan University, Furen University and Daxia University. In 1931 the Chinese Testing Society and, subsequently, the Chinese Mental Health Society and the Chinese Psychoanalytic Society were founded. It was estimated that between 1922 and 1940 some three hundred and seventy books on psychology were published. Of these over forty per cent were translations; the rest consisted mainly of text books based on Western materials and, to a lesser degree, research reports or monographs by Chinese psychologists.

Similar to the situation in Western universities in these early years, the development of the academic discipline of psychology was fairly slow. For instance, even in the case of the former Central University, the first university with a psychology department, psychology graduates in the first fifteen years totalled below fifty, and most of them were unable to find suitable jobs.

Development was handicapped during 1937-1945 while China was preoccupied in her war of resistance against Japan's invasion. As a result, institutions teaching psychology or engaged in psychological research were either closed down or evacuated, while the Psychological Society suspended practically all its activities, including publication.

This initial period of development was dominated by Western schools of thought, since most of the leading Chinese psychologists at that time were graduates from the USA, with a handful from Britain and Germany. Hence, Wundtian psychology, structuralism, functionalism, behaviourism, psychoanalysis and Gestalt psychology were introduced one after another and seemed to flourish equally (Pan, Chen, Wang & Chen, 1980, p.368).

Reorientation (1949-1956)

1949 saw the founding of the People's Republic of China, with a broad programme of socialist-economic construction. During this period there was a general belief that it was necessary to construct a new psychology to replace the Western version which had failed to fit well into the political system and cultural milieu that prevailed. Hence a number of significant steps were taken.

Introducing Marxist philosophy. Before 1949 only very few psychologists were familiar with Marxist thinking, which then became the official political guideline. Thereafter psychologists had to study Marxist writings and were beginning to discuss the relevance of Marxism for building a dialectical materialistic psychology, and it was suggested that psychology should be developed on the basis of Marxism, Leninism, Maoist thought and Pavlovian theory. With respect to epistemology and the mind-body problem, a materialistic monism was adopted. Two primary principles, that psychological phenomena are a product or function of the brain and that mind is a reflection of objective reality in the outer world, were drawn from Lenin's theory of reflection expounded in his Materialism and empirico-criticism and from Mao Zedong's On contradiction and On practice (Jing, 1980). Within such a framework, however, there was no room for social psychology and educational and psychological testing (such as intelligence tests). Sociology was even banned as a scientific discipline in 1957.

Critical review of Western psychology. As a first step towards reorienting psychology under Marxist principles, a discussion on how to evaluate Western schools and theories of psychology was launched, including structuralism, functionalism, behaviourism, Gestalt psychology, Freudian psychoanalysis, social psychology and Thorndikean principles of education. The psychology of James and Dewey received particular attention because theirs had been the prevailing theories in pre-revolutionary Chinese psychology. Parallel to these discussions, new experimental research on basic questions of psychology was carried out.

Orientation toward Soviet psychology. In the belief that the Soviet Union was more advanced in the field, political leaders in China advised the psychologists to study Soviet psychology almost exclusively. Soviet works such as Kornilov's Advanced psychology, Teplov's Psychology and Smirnov's Psychology as well as Pavlov's Lectures on conditioned reflexes were translated into Chinese and used as teaching materials in universities and colleges in the early 1950s (The Executive Committee of the Chinese Psychology Society, 1982, p.128). Soviet psychologists began lecturing at Beijing Normal University and their audience consisted of psychologists from many different cities. At the same time, about twenty Chinese students received postgraduate training in the Soviet Union (Xu, Jing & Over, 1980). Pavlov's theory of conditioned reflexes became the official foundation of psychology as well as of biology and medicine. However, this political guideline was not followed by all of the psychologists. Most of the leading psychologists had graduated in Western oriented psychology, and one of the Russian advisors complained about the "bourgeois attitude" of Chinese psychologists in his report on his activities in China (Petrushevski, 1956).

Debate on the scientific nature of psychology. In the course of critically reviewing Western psychology and studying Pavlov's theory, differences of opinion arose on the relation between psychological activity and higher nervous activity as well as on the justification of studying underlying processes of behaviour in psychology. At one extreme, psychologists maintained that psychological activity and higher nervous activity are one and the same. At the other extreme, psychological activity was regarded as a higher phenomenon which could not be explained by nervous activity alone. After long discussions, the majority of psychologists concluded that psychological activity is a result of higher nervous activity which has evolved over a long period, and that this activity, being peculiar to humankind, is far more sophisticated than and qualitatively different from that of animals. While there was general agreement that the task of psychologists is to study the human brain, these psychologists stressed that psychological phenomena are reflections of objective reality.

Founding of the Institute of Psychology. Already in 1951 a small laboratory for psychological research was founded in Beijing. Subsequent to the reinauguration of the Chinese Psychological Society in 1955, the Institute of Psychology was formally reestablished within the Chinese Academy of Sciences in 1956. The year 1956 also saw the first publication of the journal Acta Psychologica Sinica.

Growth and Development (1957-1966)

1957 saw a rupture of the formerly close relationship with the Soviet Union, followed by a period when criticism of government policy was forbidden and the scope of scientific research was limited. By 1958 the general consensus was that it was necessary for psychologists to initiate laboratory work and field studies related to practical needs. Accordingly, the period between 1960 and 1966 saw the publication of some five hundred papers. Of these, about thirty per cent were on child and educational psychology, while a similar number dealt with physiological psychology and sensory or perceptual processes. The remainder focussed on clinical, industrial and other applied areas.

A professional committee on educational psychology was formed in 1962, and plans were subsequently made to launch a five-year research project on children's psychological characteristics at different ages. Professional courses in psychology were offered at Beijing University, Beijing Normal University, East China Normal University and Nanjing College of Education, which contributed to the education and training of a group of professionals. As well, three psychology texts were compiled to meet the special pedagogic needs of the nation. These were General psychology, Child psychology and Educational psychology (The Executive Committee of the Chinese Psychological Society, 1982).

Another feature of this period was that research work was no longer oriented to the Soviet tradition and developed in a more independent and international fashion, freely taking in useful ideas from both the East and the West. However, because of the internationally political status of the People's Republic of China no international exchange was possible in this decade.

In August 1964 the Chinese Psychological Society began publication of a new quarterly entitled Information on Psychological Sciences. Membership of the Society rose to an all-time high of 1,087 in 1965, and there were twenty-three regional branch societies (Zhao, 1980b).

Havoc and Destruction (1966-1976)

The so-called Cultural Revolution had a devastating effect on scientific work, especially that of psychological investigation. The attack on psychology started in October 1965 with an article in the leading newspaper by the Communist Party's chief of propaganda, Yao Wen-yuan, who used the pseudonym of Ge Ming-ren (revolutionary man). Yao argued, among other things, that psychologists who perform experiments by the abstraction and manipulation of a few variables are approaching problems that are nonexistent in reality; such psychological studies are therefore scientifically absurd. He added that psychological problems should, instead, be approached exclusively by the method of social class analysis, since people from different social classes have different laws for their mental activities and there are no common psychological laws for the whole human race. He therefore condemned experimental psychology as a pseudo-intellectual activity and a politically harmful pseudo-science because, in the guise of a scientific discipline, it is actually trying to do away with the Marxist principle of the class nature of society (see Yao, 1965). Following his ascent to power, Yao mounted a full-scale campaign against psychology. As a result, free scientific discussion was suppressed, research as well as teaching was suspended, laboratories were closed, Acta Psychologica Sinica and Information on Psychological Sciences both ceased publication, and receipt of overseas literature was discontinued.

This period is aptly depicted by Jing (1980, p. 1087):

> ... in the years between 1966 and 1973, psychology in China was completely liquidated. Senior psychologists who disagreed with Yao were called bourgeois, reactionary, academic authorities and were subjected to persecution. Younger staff workers had to turn to other tasks or work as farmhands or factory workers. The Institute of Psychology was closed from 1969 to 1972, and teaching and research practically ceased for almost ten years (1966-1976).
> The power exercised by the Gang of Four had such a devastating effect on our nation that economic, cultural, and educational institutions were in a state of chaos. The country was on the brink of destruction. In science and technology a decade without recruitment resulted in a lost generation.

However, even at this darkest moment of misfortune, some psychologists still braved all threats of imprisonment and adversity and steadfastly carried on their research, translation and writing on psychology (The Executive Committee of the Chinese Psychological Society, 1982, p.129).

Revival and Expansion (1976 to the Present)

Psychology in China took a new turn soon after the death of Mao Zedong and the fall of the Gang of Four in October 1976. The Central Committee of the Communist Party of China treated scientific development as a matter of great urgency, one result being that psychologists have been working with renewed vigour and zest ever since, in an attempt to make up for the precious time lost in the previous ten gloomy and catastrophic years.

PRESENT STATUS

The task of reviving and developing psychology is currently being organised at different levels by the Chinese Psychological Society, the Institute of Psychology, and Universities and Colleges (Xu, Jing & Over, 1980).

The Chinese Psychological Society

In August 1977 the Chinese Psychological Society resumed its functions, with a mandate to bring together psychologists from all parts of the country to work actively on the promotion of psychological research and the popularization of the discipline, and to develop psychology with a view to contributing to the modernization of industry and education. A national assembly was subsequently convened in Beijing to work out a blueprint for reconstruction and development. Nine months later, a larger academic conference was held in Hangzhou at which over one hundred representatives from practically all provinces reported on their current research and teaching projects as well as on plans for future development, with special emphasis on the importance of developmental, educational and theoretical psychology for the reconstruction of the educational system. The Society's 1978 annual meeting took place in Baoding in December, with two hundred and thirty participants and two hundred and forty eight papers. Parallel sessions were run over four areas: developmental and educational psychology, general and engineering psychology, medical and physiological psychology, theoretical and historical psychology. The next annual meeting followed in Tianjin a year later, and was attended by three hundred and fifty people who submitted over four hundred papers. In 1980 the Society became a member of the International Union for Psychological Science.

To mark the sixtieth anniversary of the founding of the Chinese Psychological Society, the third national representative assembly and academic conference was held in Beijing in December 1981 with over three hundred representatives and over four hundred and fifty papers. Invited overseas delegates included psychologists from Australia, Hong Kong, India, Japan, the USA and West Germany as well as representatives from the International Union for Psychological Science and the International Association of Applied Psychology (Acta Psychologica Sinica's Specially Invited Correspondent, 1982).

The Society now has twenty-eight regional branch societies and a total membership of more than two thousand. However, only about eight hundred are graduate members (Zhao, 1980b). To be eligible for graduate membership one must be a graduate in psychology or a related discipline from an approved educational institution, and have worked for not less than two years in psychological practice or research. More than half of the present members specialize mainly in developmental and educational psychology, and the rest in clinical psychology, physiological psychology, general psychology and engineering psychology.

To accomplish its multifaceted task, the Society has, since 1978, established committees on developmental and educational psychology, basic theoretical studies in psychology, medical psychology, physical education and sports psychology, general and experimental psychology, industrial psychology, physiological psychology, standardization of psychological terms, scientific popularization of psychology, and the edition, translation and publication of psychological literature. As well, there is an editorial board for each of the Society's journals, Acta Psychologica Sinica and Information on Psychological Sciences, which resumed publication in August 1979 (with a circulation of 10,000 copies) and June 1980, respectively (Jing, 1980; Zhao, 1980b). As part of the plans for the scientific popularization of psychology, a proposal was made to publish in 1985 a series of books entitled Contemporary psychology (Zhao & Ho, 1980).

Social psychology is now given room in Chinese psychological research and in spring 1983 a new society, the Chinese Society for Social Psychology, was founded. This society coordinates research on such questions as juvenile delinquency, social customs, family planning and the education of the only child. A new <u>Journal of Social Psychology</u> is also scheduled for publication.

The Institute of Psychology

The Institute of Psychology, which is located in Beijing and forms part of the Chinese Academy of Sciences (rather than of the Academy of Social Sciences), is a specialized research centre and, as such, the largest in the country. It has an establishment of about one hundred researchers plus support staff. Research staff are appointed at one of four levels: apprentice for research, assistant research fellow, associate research fellow, and research fellow. Apprentices are recruited from recent graduates through competitive examinations and their appointment is initially for one year on probation. After a further four or five years, they have the option of either leaving the Institute to take up teaching appointments elsewhere or of remaining behind to become assistant research fellows. Promotion above the level of assistant research fellow is based primarily on research productivity or leadership. Current research is being conducted in four main areas, described below (Jing, 1980).

Developmental psychology. Research topics include development of the concepts of class, number, space, orientation, colour, form, time, causality, and partwhole relationships as well as language and moral development in children of different age levels, and the development of gifted as well as mentally retarded children. A rating scale has been developed for diagnosing the intellectual behaviour of mentally retarded children who visit clinics, and for determining whether the various treatments given have resulted in any progress. In recent years the division has undertaken research into the developmental characteristics of the psychology of only sons (Liu, 1984). The scale assesses behaviour in five categories: gross motor skills, fine motor abilities, self-care, language, number concepts and mathematical operations; each category is related on a 6-point scale. Methods of remedial work for the mentally handicapped have also been explored.

Perception. The focus in this division has been on applied issues such as illumination and colour vision so as to meet the demands for industrialization. Topics studied include the luminous efficiency function of Chinese eyes and colour standards for use in colour television and colour photography (tolerance of Chinese facial skin colour, tolerance of commonly seen object colours, memory of colours and the like). Recently, however, there has been a shift of direction within the perception division, with leanings towards fundamental research. Areas currently under investigation include colour and spatial vision, pattern recognition, perceptual aftereffects, and haptic perception.

Physiological and Medical Psychology. Extensive research efforts have been made to study brain mechanisms underlying learning and memory, and a team of specialists in neuropsychology has been formed to look into aphasia. Investigations have also been made to identify the basis for pain control and to determine which variables predict acupunctural analgesia. Psychologists, in collaboration with medical practitioners, study emotional changes before, during, and after surgical operations and their relation to physiological and biochemical changes. Hypnosis has been tried in mental hospitals, while biofeedback and behavioural therapy are also being studied.

Theoretical Studies in Psychology. At the 1978 annual meeting of the Chinese Psychological Society, twenty-nine papers were presented on theoretical problems. After much debate, it has now been generally agreed that Marxist dialectical materialism will remain the guiding principle in all psychological research and instruction, and that psychology, being a discipline which has the characteristics of a social as well as a natural science, may be studied in any way so long as contact with reality is maintained. Mental testing and social psychology, formerly forbidden, are now open to research for the first time. Some psychologists have already started revising the Wechsler Intelligence Scale for Children (WISC) for use. Sociology has been re-admitted into the family of science, and social studies in psychology departments have recently been introduced.

Universities and Colleges

At present psychology is taught as a major discipline at Beijing University, Hangzhou University, East China Normal University and Beijing Normal University. The areas of specialization at these institutions are, respectively: experimental psychology, ergonomics, educational psychology, and developmental psychology. Other institutions that offer psychology at a sub-departmental level include Nanjing Normal College, Central China Normal College, South China Normal University, Southwestern Normal College, Northeastern Normal University and Shanxi Normal University. In short, psychology is a compulsory course in at least one institution of higher learning in each province. There is a college of education in almost every province offering psychology as a compulsory course in an attempt to provide in-service professional training for teachers and educational workers (Brown, 1981; Liu, 1984).

Until 1978 psychology had the status of a sub-division or speciality in such departments as education or philosophy. Beijing University was the first to have an independent department of psychology, followed by Hangzhou University, East China Normal University, and Beijing Normal University (The Executive Committee of the Chinese Psychological Society, 1982).

Beijing University. The first intake to the new department at Beijing University was limited to twenty-seven students selected by examination from applicants from all provinces. The undergraduate programme extends over four years, during the first two of which students complete common subjects. These include general psychology, English, advanced mathematics, biology and human physiology, politics and physical education in the first year, and experimental psychology, physics, neuroanatomy and neurophysiology in the second. In the last two years the concentration has been on psychology, with a thesis being required in the fourth year. In addition, senior students can choose to work in one or more such specialist areas as abnormal, engineering or physiological psychology. Teaching is supplemented in advanced courses by practical experience in factories, hospitals or schools.

Beijing Normal University. Beijing Normal University resumed its teaching of psychology in 1978, and in 1979 there were thirty-three undergraduate students and four postgraduate scholars. The four-year undergraduate programme includes courses in general psychology, child psychology, educational psychology, statistical techniques, experimental psychology and history of psychology. Courses planned for the future include thinking in children (with special reference to the work of Piaget), the history of child psychology, computer-assisted instruction, instructional psychology, and Marx's and Lenin's views on psychology. Great emphasis is placed on students' need to study political theory, the history and philosophy of the Chinese Communist Party and the struggle of international communism, along with economics, physiology, neuropsychology, logic, physics and mathematics (Brown, 1981).

East China Normal University. An immediate goal of East China Normal University when it resumed operation in 1978 was to train teachers in a two-year programme as an emergency measure to make up for the losses incurred during the period of the Gang of Four. The programme was therefore designed for teachers, and for those likely to work in research institutes. It covered physics, mathematics, psychology and education. In addition, seminars were given on learning in industry and on medical psychology.

Research has also begun on the way young children learn languages, on the early identification of children with special talents, and on ways to improve kindergarten training. Further planning includes work on the transfer of knowledge, the deduction of principles without specific teaching, and the relation between different intellectual abilities and learning. As well, a section has been established concerned with foreign literature in psychology, especially with theories of learning, moral development and the teaching of school subjects, and will publish a journal of translations from foreign literature.

Hangzhou University and Nanjing Normal College. At both of these universities, emphasis is placed on industrial psychology, child development and educational psychology. The former offers professional training in engineering psychology and educational/ developmental psychology.

Shanxi Normal University. Psychology is taught within the Department of Education, although an Educational Science Research Institute has now been established to teach a basic course in psychology to students of education. Those in the institute have all been teachers, and their current research relates to the teaching of mathematics, examining, psychological testing, and the place of psychology in kindergartens.

Central China Normal College. The first class of thirty students was admitted in 1978, with another thirty the following year. The programme is basically educational and covers theory, history, general psychology, child psychology and educational psychology. General psychology involves philosophical foundations, physiology, feelings and emotions, and personality. Despite what they see as limited manpower, the staff (thirteen in all) would like to do research on the fundamental processes in psychological development, human needs and motivation, the characteristics of personality and the development and measurement of ability.

FUTURE PROSPECTS

Thus the development of psychology in China over the past thirty years has experienced many ups and downs. By surviving their long years of storm and stress, however, Chinese psychologists have also learned a number of invaluable lessons, which may serve as their guidelines for the future. Some of these lessons have been courageously and explicitly articulated by most of the psychologists and scholars previously referred to in this paper. On the one hand, they have pointed to the futility of citing quotations from Marxist writers as evidence in scientific research, the folly of treating different scientific viewpoints as political issues, and the danger of blindly harbouring antagonistic and hostile attitudes towards foreign sources. On the other hand, they have stressed the importance of and need for practice and experimentation in scientific investigations, free and democratic discussions of scientific matters, and exposure to and exchange with a much greater number of different theories of psychology and psychologists overseas (Jing, 1980; Wang, 1980).

Writing in more specific and action-oriented terms, Xu (1979b) maintains that Chinese psychologists should now direct their efforts to the following five areas: (i) personnel training, especially in science and technology, with a view to modernizing education via psychological research and making foreign things serve China; (ii) productivity-raising -- by tapping creative capacities and establishing a scientific system of enterprise management which may help to provide prototypes for the invention and manufacture of automatic equipment; (iii) research on physical and mental health; (iv) development of social psychology -- so that public opinion can be gauged quickly and accurately and the leadership provided with the most effective methods to organize, mobilize, influence and lead the masses, and (v) research in basic theory, covering such areas as sensation, perception, brain chemistry, neuro-endocrinology of agitation and depression, and aiming at provision of new ideas for designing new electronic computers, machine translation and for architectural science. The overall goal is to ensure that psychology does serve the nation's four modernizations of industry, agriculture, science and technology, and defence.

Wang (1980) aspires to the establishment by the end of the twentieth century of a Chinese system of psychology which is (i) unique in basic theory and methodology, being guided exclusively by dialectical materialism; (ii) typically Chinese, fully revealing and elevating those rich psychological thoughts in Chinese history, and fully reflecting the true spirit of the Chinese people on their march to the four modernizations in an era of socialism; (iii) a perfect combination of natural and social aspects without overemphasis on one or the other; (iv) character-istic of its own era, making full use of modern theories of science and technology in the study of psychological issues, and (v) a true union of theory and practice.

Besides endorsing Xu's (1979b) idea of making foreign things serve China and Wang's ambition (1980) of establishing a Chinese system of psychology, Pan (1980) stresses the importance of open-mindedness and collective effort as well as the need to study psychological thoughts of ancient Chinese thinkers.

Finally, as a collective decision and declaration, the Executive Committee of the Chinese Psychological Society (1982) urged that Chinese psychologists should (i) make a complete and systematic study of Marxism and Mao Zedong Thought in order to guide and direct all endeavours in psychology; (ii) further raise standards in basic theoretical research; (iii) attach importance to and strengthen fundamental research; (iv) broaden and deepen research in applied areas; (v) strengthen profess-ional teaching and raise professional standards; (vi) strengthen popularization of psychology qualitatively as well as quantitatively; (vii) promote and improve international academic exchange; (viii) thoroughly implement the "Double Hundred Policy" (that is, the policy of "letting a hundred flowers blossom simultan-eously and a hundred schools of thought contend at the same time," or, in other words, allowing for or even encouraging free and spontaneous expression of a multi-plicity and diversity of ideas, (ix) increase quantity and quality of scientific equipment and output of publications, and (x) strengthen unity and collaboration.

Bridging the Human or Professional Gap

The urgent need to produce and nurture young psychologists has been generally recognized (Zhao, 1980a; The Executive Committee of the Chinese Psychological Society, 1982). Two national meetings were held between 1979 and 1981 to discuss and decide on ways and means of popularizing psychology. Extensive use was made of the mass media, television and radio in particular, and of different types of study groups and seminars, reaching an estimated audience of some six hundred thousand. According to preliminary reports from ten provinces/cities, sustained effort was partially reflected in the conduct of two hundred and thirty-nine short courses and the publication of over twenty different kinds of reading materials.

A nationwide appeal has been made to solicit help and support, professional as well as material, for existing university departments of psychology. At the same time, active measures have been taken to increase the number of both compulsory and elective courses, and to improve equipment, instructional material and teaching methodology. Individuals of demonstrated excellence and/or of high potential have been sent abroad to pursue further studies.

The year 1982 saw the first batch of graduates from the four universities that offer psychology as a major discipline (see p.7 above). While the number is small relative to the total population, it signifies a great leap forward.

Research on Psychological Thought of Ancient Chinese Thinkers

The first reported attempt to study the psychological thought of thinkers in ancient China was made by Chen (1963). Pan's (1980) appeal seems to have stimulated much activity in this area. To date, ten such studies have been reported in the Acta Psychologica Sinica (Lin, 1980; Yan, 1980, 1981; Xu, 1980; Zeng, 1980; Chai, 1981; Wei, 1981; Lei, 1982; Chen, 1982; Zhu, 1982). It may therefore not be too far wrong to expect this line of research to continue for a while.

SOME PERSONAL IMPRESSIONS

These impressions have arisen from the experience acquired by the first author (Wing Lee) while taking part in the 1981 Annual Scientific Conference of the Beijing Psychological Society and his subsequent contacts with interested or concerned scholars passing to and from China.

The Conference was the very first of its kind the Society held in the past eighteen years. It was also the Society's very first conference to which psychologists outside China were invited. The latter point is perhaps particularly significant in that it served to confirm that psychologists in China really are anxious to establish and promote academic and professional contact and exchange with their colleagues elsewhere.

The papers presented at the various sessions in which the author participated were, on the whole, of a reasonably high standard in spite of the general lack of technical and material facilities. One particularly noteworthy feature was the "thematic approach" adopted in their research efforts. In most cases, the researchers operated as members of a team such that, while each piece of research was individually and independently carried out, it formed an integral part of a wider concerted effort directed towards the attempt of finding a plausible solution to a major and more complex problem.

There seemed to be a fairly acute shortage of material resources (for example, equipment, textbooks, journals and the like) and, perhaps to a lesser yet more serious degree, human resources among the younger generation. Those currently at the helm are mostly in their late fifties or over and, their having been completely cut off from active research and the outside world for so long, it may take considerable time before they can be truly abreast of the times. There is a vacuum in the twenty-five to forty range.

It therefore appears that China is now faced with two pressing needs: first, to provide opportunities for her senior or key psychologists to meet and cross-fertilize ideas with their overseas colleagues; second, to somehow bridge the human or professional gap brought about by one lost generation. In point of fact, active measures have been taken in recent years in an attempt to meet such needs.

These observations are based on only a few days' experience. Besides, the scope and complexity of the present state of the art are so great that one could hardly see beyond the tip of the iceberg even after a long period of personal observation and intensive study in the land. The first author, while admitting his limitations, would like to sound an optimistic note. Given time and politico-social stability, much can be expected to emerge from a nation of one billion people.

NOTE

1. Much of the material for this section was taken from the following sources: Che & Guo, 1979; Department of Education, Shanxi Normal University, 1979, 1980; Xu, 1979a; Chen, 1980; Jing, 1980; Xu, Jing & Over, 1980; Kuang, Luo & Liu, 1980; Li, Xu & Kuang, 1980; Lin & Fang, 1980; Pan, 1980, 1982; Pan & Chen, 1959; Pan, Chen, Wang & Chen, 1980; Peng, 1980; Brown, 1981; The Executive Committee of the Chinese Psychological Society, 1982, 1983.

REFERENCES

ACTA PSYCHOLOGICA SINICA'S SPECIALLY INVITED CORRESPOND-ENT The third representative assembly and academic conference in commemoration of the 60th anniversary of the founding of the Chinese Psychological Society, Acta Psychologica Sinica, 1982, 14 259-261 (in Chinese).

BRITISH PSYCHOLOGICAL SOCIETY Monthly report, Bulletin of the British Psychological Society, July 1981, 34, 294-295.

BROWN, L. B. Psychology in contemporary China. Oxford, Pergamon, 1981.

CAO Ri-chang (TSAO Jih-chang) What does psychology investigate? Acta Psychologica Sinica, 1959, 4, 244-249 (in Chinese).

CHAI Wen-xiou Thoughts of sport psychology in ancient China, Acta Psychologica Sinica, 1981, 13, 124-128 (in Chinese).

CHE Wen-bo, & GUO Zhan-ji. 30 years of Chinese theoretical psychology, Acta Psychologica Sinica, 1979, 11, 267-280 (in Chinese).

CHEN Zhong-gang. Some psychopathological thoughts in the Book of Tso Chuen, Acta Psychologica Sinica, 1963, 2, 156-164 (in Chinese).

CHEN Da-rou. Thirty years of physiological psychology in China: A historical retrospection and some basic problems, Acta Psychologica Sinica, 1980, 12, 22-29 (in Chinese). English transln. in Chinese Sociology and Anthrology, 1980, 12, 78-96.

CHEN Yan-gu. On Confucius's thoughts on educational psychology, Acta Psychologica Sinica, 1982, 14, 466-472 (in Chinese).

DEPARTMENT OF EDUCATION, SHANXI NORMAL UNIVERSITY 30 years of Chinese psychology, Acta Psychologica Sinica, 1979, 11, 255-266 (in Chinese).

DEPARTMENT OF EDUCATION, SHANXI NORMAL UNIVERSITY. 30 years of Chinese child and educational psychology, Acta Psychologica Sinica, 1980, 12, 127-134 (in Chinese).

EXECUTIVE COMMITTEE OF THE CHINESE PSYCHOLOGICAL SOCIETY Retrospect and prospect of 60 years of psychology in China, Acta Psychologica Sinica, 1982, 14, 127-138 (in Chinese).

EXECUTIVE COMMITTEE OF THE CHINESE PSYCHOLOGICAL SOCIETY Sixty years of Chinese Psychology: Retrospect and prospect, International Journal of Psychology, 1983, 18, 167-187.

GUAN Lian-rong. The delegation of American psychologists visits China, Acta Psychologica Sinica, 1981, 13, 243-245 (in Chinese).

INTERNATIONAL COUNCIL OF PSYCHOLOGISTS News of members, International Psychologist, 1982, 23, 17-18.

JING Qi-cheng (CHING, C. C.) Psychology in the People's Republic of China, American Psychologist, December 1980, 35, 1084-1089.

KUANG Pei-zi, LUO Sheng-de, & LIU Shan-xun, 30 years of physiological in China, Acta Psychologica Sinica, 1980, 12, 144-151 (in Chinese).

KUO You-yuh. Psychology in Communist China, The Psychological Record, 1971, 21, 95-105.

LEI Yan-hu & LI Ji-bai. On the psychological thought of Han Fei, Acta Psychologica Sinica, 1982, 14, 311-317 (in Chinese).

LI Xin-tian, XU Shu-lian, & KUANG Pei-zi. 30 years of Chinese medical psychology, Acta Psychologica Sinica, 1980, 12, 135-143 (in Chinese). Engl. transln. in Chinese Sociology and Anthropology, 1980, 12, 97-123.

LIN Chuan-ting. A sketch on the methods of mental testing in ancient China, Acta Psychologica Sinica, 1980, 12, 75-80 (in Chinese).

LIN Zhong-xian, & FANG Zhi. Thirty years developments in Chinese experimental psychology, Acta Psychologia Sinica, 1980, 12, 9-15 (in Chinese). English transln. in Chinese Sociology and Anthropology, 1980, 12, 43-61.

LIU Fan. Preliminary viewpoints regarding the subject matter of psychology, Acta Psychologica Sinica, 1959, 4, 250-255 (in Chinese).

LIU Fan. Developmental psychology in China, International Journal of Behavioural Development, 1982, 5, 391-411.

LIU Fan. Personal communication, 20 January, 1984.

OVER, Ray. Chinese psychologists trained in the United Kingdom. Bulletin of the British Psychological Society, 1980, 33, 130-131.

PAN Shu. On the subject matter of psychology and related problems, Acta Psychologica Sinica, 1959, 4, 227-233 (in Chinese).

PAN Shu. On the investigation of the basic theoretical problems of psychology, Acta Psychologica Sinica, 1980, 12, 1-8 (in Chinese). English transln. in Chinese Sociology and Anthropology, 12, 24-42.

PAN Shu. A summary of 60 years of experience, Open a new stage of development in psychology in China - Opening speech of the third representative assembly and academic conference in commemoration of 60 years of the founding of the Chinese Psychological Society. Acta Psychologica Sinica, 1982, 14, 139-142 (in Chinese).

PAN Shu, & CHEN Da-jou. Ten years' developments in Chinese psychology, Acta Psychologica Sinica, 1959, 4, 191-203 (in Chinese).

PAN Shu, CHEN Li, WANG Jing-he, & CHEN Da-rou, Wilhelm Wundt and Chinese psychology, Acta Psychologica Sinica, 1980, 12, 367-376 (in Chinese).

PENG Rui-xiang. Thirty years of industrial psychology in China, Acta Psychologica Sinica, 1980, 12, 16-21 (in Chinese). English transln. in Chinese Sociology and Anthropology, 1980, 12, 62-77.

PETRUSHEVSKI, S. A. On the status of psychological science in China and the development of scientific contacts with Chinese psychologists, Voprosy Psickologii, 1956, 2, 102-108.

PETZOLD, M. Entwicklungspsychologie in der VR China. Saarbruecken & Fort Lauderdale, FL: Breitenbach, 1983. English transln. Cambridge, Cambridge University Press (in press).

124

TANG Yue, On the subject matter of psychological study, Acta Psychologica Sinica, 1959, 4, 234-236 (in Chinese).

WANG Ji-sheng. On the modernization of psychology in China: Fundamental theoretical viewpoint and methodology, Acta Psychologica Sinica, 1980, 12, 30-36 (in Chinese). English transln. FBIS-REPORT Joint Publications Research Services, No. 76133, 1980, 103-114.

WEI Mao-rong. On the psychological point of view of Dai Zhen - an 18th century Chinese thinker, Acta Psychologica Sinica, 1981, 13 (4), 386-393 (in Chinese).

XU Lian-cang (HSU Lien-tsang). Some psychological investigations in the People's Republic of China, Australian Psychologist, November 1978, 13, 359-367.

XU Lian-cang (HSU Lien-tsang) The road is tortuous; the prospects are bright - 30 years' development of Chinese psychology, Nature Journal Yearbook, 1979, 1, 136-143 (in Chinese), (a).

XU Lian-cang (HSU Lien-tsang)Psychology in the service of the four modernizations, Acta Psychologica Sinica, 1979, 11, 22-28 (in Chinese), (b).

XU Lian-cang (HSU, L. T.), JING Qi-cheng (CHING, C. C.), & OVER, Ray. Recent developments in psychology within the People's Republic of China, International Journal of Psychology, 1980, 15, 131-144.

XU Qi-duan. A study of psychological thoughts in the ancient Chinese writer Wang Chong's work, Acta Psychologica Sinica, 1980, 12, 377-384 (in Chinese).

YAN Guo-cai. Xun-Zi's exposition on feeling, desire and nature, Acta Psychologica Sinica, 1980, 12, 212-219 (in Chinese).

YAN Guo-cai. A comment on the psychological thought of Huai Nan-zi, Acta Psychologica Sinica, 1982, 14, 285-293 (in Chinese).

YAO Wen-yuan, Is there a scientific method and correct direction for studying psychology? A question for psychologists, Guang -ming Ri-bao, 28 Oct. 1965, p.3. English transln. in Survey of Chinese Mainland Press, No. 3587, 1965, 9-18.

ZENG Li-ge. A research into the psychological thoughts of an ancient Chinese writer Xunzi, Acta Psychologica Sinica, 1980, 12, 385-389 (in Chinese).

ZHAO Li-ru. Third academic annual meeting of the Chinese Psychological Association, Acta Psychologica Sinica, 1980 (a), 12, 244-250 (in Chinese).

ZHAO Li-ru. The past and present status of the Chinese Psychological Association and its activities, <u>Acta Psychologica Sinica</u> 1980 (b), <u>12</u>, 473-481 (in Chinese).

ZHAO Li-ru, & Ho Jin-xa. The Chinese Psychological Association and its local societies, <u>Acta Psychologica Sinica</u>, 1980, <u>12</u>, 116-123 (in Chinese).

ZHU Yong-xin, Research on the thoughts of Cheng-ying and Cheng-yi, <u>Acta Psychologica Sinica</u>, 1982, <u>14</u>, 473-479 (in Chinese).

ZHU Zhi-xian (CHU Chih-hsien). Some view-points concerning the subject matter of psychology, <u>Acta Psychologica Sinica</u>, 1959, <u>4</u>, 237-243 (in Chinese).

9

The History of Psychology
in Taiwan

Joseph S. Z. Hsu

Taiwan, also known as Formosa ("beautiful island", so called by the Portuguese mariners who chanced across it in 1583), is an island 13,808 square miles in extent, situated off the southeastern coast of the Chinese mainland. Traditionally a province of China, between 1895 and 1945 Taiwan was occupied by the Japanese. When the communist party took over control of Mainland China in 1949, the previous Chinese leadership with the support of General Chiang Kai-shek moved its government to Taiwan, from whence it continues to assert its right to control all China. The United States played a very substantial role in the post-war reconstruction and economic build-up of Taiwan, whose living standard is now one of the highest in Asia. The national language is Mandarin. The form of government is that of a republic, with manhood suffrage; the founding party of the 1949 government, the Kuomintang, has remained in power throughout the republic's existence. [1]

THIRTY-FIVE YEARS WITHOUT TRADITION

Psychology in the universities

Although psychology was quite firmly established in the universities on the mainland during the twenties, this tradition had very little direct influence on the emergence of the discipline in Taiwan, because of the domination of that country by the Japanese for half a century until the end of World War II. Taipei Imperial University (now called National Taiwan University) had lectures on psychology in its Faculty of Literature at

128

that time, and substantial reminders of this were left behind after the war, in the form of approximately four thousand books of psychology, one thousand five hundred volumes of journals, and a hundred and fifty pieces of laboratory apparatus. Because of this, the head of the Philosophy Department, Professor Tong-mei Fong, suggested to Professor Hsiang-yu Su, who was teaching psychology in the Faculty of Literature, that he should establish a department for the discipline, based on the scientific method and the experimental approach. In 1949 this came about, in the Faculty of Science.

Although only thirty-five years have passed since the establishment of this first department, there are now seven departments of psychology or psychology-related disciplines in Taiwan. A second psychology department was established at Chung Yuan Christian College of Science Engineering in 1966, and a third at National Cheng-chi University in 1971. As the importance of psychology to education, student guidance and industry became recognized, a Department of Educational Psychology was established in 1968 at National Taiwan Normal University (formerly Taiwan Provincial College of Education), and a Department of Applied Psychology at Fu-Jen Catholic University in 1972. At the Chinese Culture University there is a Department of Children's Welfare. In 1979, the Institute of Guidance was finally set up in National Normal University to offer degrees in guidance at the Master's level. The latter, National Taiwan University, and Cheng-chi University now all have graduate schools, National Taiwan University having offered training for the M.S. since 1961, and for the Ph.D. since 1971.[2]

Journals and societies

Since 1958 the publication of psychological journals has been increasing, with nearly a hundred research articles now produced annually. The major journals of psychology in Taiwan are Chinese Journal of Psychology (until 1984 known as Acta Psychologica Taiwanica, and published by the Chinese Psychological Association), Psychological Testing (Chinese Association of Psychological Testing), Bulletin of Educational Psychology (National Taiwan Normal University), Journal of Education and Psychology (National Cheng-chi University), Journal of Guidance (Chinese Guidance Association), Bulletin of Counselling (Teacher Chang's Centre), and Mental Health

Bulletin (Chinese National Association for Mental Hygiene). Major pieces of research are first reported in the annual academic research meeting sponsored by the Chinese Psychological Association and the Chinese Association for Psychological Testing.

The Chinese Psychological Association was born in 1953, in the psychology department of National Taiwan University. Its elected chairman is usually the head of this department. In 1982 the membership of the Association was six hundred and seventy.

The Chinese Association for Psychological Testing was first founded in 1931 in Nanking by Professor Wei I. After the war, when the Nationalist government moved to Taiwan, Wei I re-established the Association in 1951 in Taiwan, mainly within the Department of Educational Psychology of National Normal University. The first issue of Psychological Testing was published in 1953. Up to 1983, this journal has published approximately three hundred research papers, including theoretical and methodological studies in testing and measurement. Hundreds of tests and measures have been introduced to various applied fields -- educational, police, criminal, clinical, military, industrial and so on. In the meantime, construction, standardization, revision and modification of tests have been taking place, widely applied to both research and practical purposes. All tests revised and published before 1978 have been included in a booklet published by the Association.

In addition to these two academic organizations, there is a Chinese National Association for Mental Hygiene. Founded in 1937 in the mainland, in 1953 this was revived in Taiwan, its members being psychiatrists and a few clinical psychologists. The Mental Health Bulletin has been published since 1957. Clinical studies of mental illness and behavioural disorder are commonly done by teams of psychiatrists and psychologists, a prime example here being Taipei City Psychiatric Centre.[3]

Professional practice

In 1974 Provincial Mental Health Centres were founded in Taipei and Kaohsiung City; Taichung and Tainan later followed suit. Centres are composed of part-time psychiatrists and full-time psychological counsellors, social workers and nurses. Although the main aims are preventative, they provide diagnosis and treatment for outpatients, and also play the role of coordinator in the operations of various mental health related organizations such as general and mental hospitals, counselling centres, social service bodies and so on. Both budget and organization are still at the trial stage. With the rapid changes Taiwan has been experiencing in its social structures in recent years, such Mental Health Centres are of great importance.

A Student Counselling and Guidance Centre was first established in National Taiwan University in 1964, and the next year a similar centre was set up in Tu-dan high school. At the present time most schools in Taiwan, from elementary to university level, have counselling and guidance services for students. These aim to provide students with educational and vocational guidance, and with counselling for adjustment problems encountered during school life; as well, they collect mass data about students for purposes of research. Where the university has a psychology department, this will be responsible for the counselling centre.

During the 1960's there were only a few psychologists pioneering the clinical field, but since 1970 the number has increased rapidly. There are sixty psychologists distributed around the island engaging in clinical work, in mental hospitals or psychiatric divisions of general hospitals, in psychosomatic medicine within general hospitals, in rehabilitation centres, community mental health centres, and counselling and guidance centres. In 1980 the Chinese Association of Psychology set up a clinical psychology group. This group has been actively engaging in and advocating research work, and discussing the status of clinical psychologists and training programmes. In 1983, the question of how to get official government recognition was taken up.

APPLIED PSYCHOLOGY AND RESEARCH

Psychological testing and measurement

Since the establishment of the Chinese Association for Psychological Testing in 1951, about a hundred testing and measurement tools have been constructed and revised in Taiwan. Not only practical but also methodological studies are done; most of the tools however are based on the modification of instruments of U.S. origin. Nevertheless, the application of psychological testing and measurement in various fields is widely accepted, and supported by the government. The use of psychological tests in Civil Service Examinations was initiated in 1964 and continued until 1966, when a different form of examination (Examination Yuan) was introduced.

Armed Services. In 1947, China Air Force began to use psychological tests for the purposes of personnel classification. In 1951, the National Defence Department set up a research section for psychologists to construct and revise many kinds of tests, and established a confidential research and personnel classification system. In 1952, both Navy and Army also set up their own Psychological Research sections, and the application of tests in the personnel area became very common. In 1956, the U.S. government appropriated a grant of forty million U.S. dollars to assist the Chinese government with the discharge of fifty thousand soldiers. Many psychologists were called in to interview and evaluate the soldiers with respect to their intelligence, aptitude, personality and the like, for purposes of vocational placement. In addition to these personnel practices, planning and research are undertaken in the area of psychological warfare.

Police. In 1954, analysis of the personality traits of the Criminal Police was begun by the Principal of Central Police. This move emphasized the important role of psychological research in police work, and was supported by the government and Division of Provincial Police. By 1957 many kinds of tests had been constructed for the analysis of personality traits of police officers, criminal police, prisoners and juvenile delinquents. Tests for the following are applied in the selection of police officers: Reading and Vocabulary, Arithmetic Reasoning, Spatial Relations, Physical and Chemical Information, Clerical Aptitude, Leadership, Social Aptitude, Legal Aptitude, Security Information and Localization.

Education. Since the 1950's revision and construction of numerous tests has been taking place for the evaluation of students' ability, aptitude, personality and achievement motivation, as well as of teaching methods. These results have been applied for the purposes of school counselling and guidance.

Clinical psychology

Since 1958 there has been a close relationship

between the the psychiatry and psychology departments at National Taiwan University, and the publication of joint research. Whilst the main role of the clinical psychologist in the hospital has been diagnosis by psychological instruments, and experimental research, in recent years behaviour therapy has been studied as well. In 1970 the child mental health centre was established, attached to the department of psychiatry (Medical College), and this has concerned itself with intensive therapy for autistic children, and treatment of neurotic symptoms such as phobias, tics and enuresis, along Eysenckian lines. (Professor Su-ken Yang studied these methods in England.) Neither psychoanalysis nor phenomenological concepts have been introduced in any systematic way to psychology students. Psychotherapy is still not at all common in Taiwan, the exception being behaviour modification which is practised extensively in several mental hospitals.

Clinical psychology began with the work of Professor Fa-yu Cheng, who had been teaching psychology to medical students in the Medical College of National Taiwan University. Psychiatrists were adopting a psychological approach to mental illness from 1960, and thereafter Professor Dr. Yung-ho Ko has devoted his efforts in the mental hospital of National Taiwan University to the advancement of diagnostic testing (Ko 1963, 1964). In particular he has revised the Bender-Gestalt test and the MMPI, and has developed Ko's Mental Health Questionnaire. Numerous other tests have also been revised for local use, but still not in a thorough and systematic way.

Experimental psychology

During the thirties and forties Japanese psychology was dominated by the Gestalt school, with the result that the early stages of experimental research in Taiwan, until the late fifties, were mainly concerned with problems of perception. By the early sixties however, the first generation of students to take degrees in the U.S. were returning to Taiwan and beginning their own research. In particular they pursued problems in learning theory which was so topical with American psychologists in the thirties and forties. Studies on processes of conditioning, generalization, reaction time and the like took place, mostly performed on laboratory animals. As English is a required language course throughout high

school and university years, American textbooks and their
translations inevitably became the main source of
teaching materials.

By the late sixties however, the interests of researchers, as in the U.S., were moving to the higher
mental activities of the human mind - verbal behaviour,
analysis of language and processes of language acquisition, problem solving and other cognitive processes.
Whilst mainly human subjects were used for this research,
even the learning of sign language by chimpanzees was
investigated. Since the mid-seventies the growth of the
computer industry in Taiwan has been extremely rapid, and
knowledge of computers is now the norm amongst academics.
In consequence, just like psychologists in the U.S.,
psychologists in Taiwan have also begun computer simula-
tion of human mental activities; the information processing model has become the chief concern of experimental
psychologists.

Personality and social psychology

Initially, research in these areas consisted mainly
of the application of tests and statistical analysis to
the investiga-tion of the traits of the aboriginal people
and of students. However, during the 1970's more intensive work began along a number of lines, taking a more
dynamic approach. In consequence, a variety of social
phenomena have been studied, oriented toward practical
problems in the social environment. The major areas are
the following:

Industrialization. Problems of interpersonal
conflict, and phenomena of change in the Chinese character during the process of industrialization.

Modernization. Change in individual social orientation and psychological needs resultant on modernization
in the social environment.

Urbanization. Studies in individual adjustment and
adaptation in an urbanized social structure.

Population. Problems of residential crowding in an
urban society, related to interplay of high-density
dwelling conditions, interpersonal value systems and
ideal family size.[4]

Problem behaviour. Analysis of the influence of
factors of family, school and social environment on
psychological needs; reaction to success and failure;
increase in crime rate in a changing society.

Business organization. The relationship between the working environment and morale, personality traits and feelings of satisfaction in the employee.

Aerospace medicine. Studies in correlation between the personality of Chinese pilots and flight accidents.

Immigration. Mental health problems of Asian immigrants in the United States.

Cross-cultural. Comparison of the motivation, temperament, character, aggressiveness, competitiveness and cooperativeness of overseas Chinese with those of the people of Taiwan.

Educational and developmental psychology

Much research on education and student behaviour has been done by both National Normal University and National Cheng-chi University; the results are published in the Bulletin of Educational Psychology and the Journal of Education and Psychology.

Since the 1950's, various psychological tests for the guidance and evaluation of teaching methods in schools, such as science teaching and teaching by television, have received nationwide use. Contingency models for predicting the teacher's effectiveness and desirable characteristics, and new methods for learning foreign languages as well as model curricula have been constructed. In the 1970's the parent-child relationship has received special attention. Recently, problems of special education for such groups as the mentally retarded, physically handicapped, children with learning disabilities and gifted children are under discussion.

Although a range of aspects of child development has been studied, systematic long-term observation like that of Gessell have only recently been undertaken in this area and are yet to appear in print, while theoretical investigations such as those of Piaget have not yet been attempted.

RETROSPECT AND PROSPECT

Although only thirty-five years have passed since the establishment of the first independent department of psychology in Taiwan, now more than two hundred students graduate each year from seven departments, and a hundred research works are published annually. For almost any undergraduate course of psychology, there is now a textbook written in Chinese.

Unlike most western countries, Taiwan has developed psychology in the absence of any traditional concepts of philosophy or religion, lacking even a scientific background from physiology and biology. Academic psychology here has simply adhered to the mainstream of American scientific psychology, adopting a methodology of laboratory experimentation and quantitative measurement. Arguments being advanced elsewhere against psychology's status as a science have had practically no impact in Taiwan.

On the other hand, there have been quantitative studies in behaviour, and the application of psychological tests in an attempt to resolve more practical problems, as central concern has shifted from basic theoretical issues. This has resulted in some criticism of the generality and validity of those psychological methods and tools borrowed from Western countries and applied to the Chinese people. Consequently, there is now an emphasis on indigenous psychology based on Chinese tradition and culture, that is, the so-called policy of sinification (or sinicization) of psychology in Taiwan. But no matter how psychologists in Taiwan advocate the sinification of their discipline, they are still adamant in their adherence to the empirical stance, to objective data, and to the operational definition of concepts. Thus the results of any such policy would be limited to changes in <u>content</u>, without innovation in basic concepts and methods.

In fact, since 1980 new areas of interest have opened up, covering Chinese language and various social problems, while the number of cross-cultural studies has increased. The following issues are being advocated by academic psychologists as being of central concern in the sinification of psychology (Yang and Weng, 1982):

* Translation of psychological concepts or terms into the Chinese language; use of textbooks written in Chinese by Chinese psychologists; encouragement of the publication of psychological books or journals in Chinese.

* Basing of academic research dealing with the problems of human nature on notions of traditional Chinese philosophy, which is both quite distinct from Hellenistic thought and highly developed.

* Application of principles of western psychology to the Chinese, in order to find out the extent of their generalizability.

* Identification of culture-specific mental phenomena and unique behaviour patterns in Chinese mental life (for example "Face," "Pao," "Yi," "Shiu," "Yuang").
* Revision or creation of new psychological theories based on Chinese native philosophy.
* Modification of methodology to produce experimental designs or new practical research methods suitable to the Chinese situation.

Physiology brought to the new scientific psychology its empirical methods applied to the questions of philosophy, and modern cognitive psychology was originally a part of epistemology. Nevertheless, a broad under-standing of human psychology with objective data and biological underpinnings is not enough. As long as mind is understood as the totality of immediate conscious experience of mental life, both philosophically and methodologically psychology must be based on phenomenology.

Account must also be taken of the essential differences between the social and the natural sciences. In general, physical sciences can only have one paradigm at a given time, whereas in the case of the social sciences there may be several paradigms. Moreover, psychic phenomena fail to occur in the sterile environment of the laboratory. Psychologists are in the difficult position of having to locate themselves between the social and the natural sciences. In the 1980's, Chinese psychologists in Taiwan have become aware that one cannot contemplate the psychology of organisms without knowing about biology and physiology on the one hand, and the social environment, cultural traditions, institutions, value systems and conscious experience on the other. Consequently, there is a questioning of a narrowly legalistic "scientific" method, and an opening up of new and broader prospects via a pluralistic approach.

The Chinese have a history for the investigation of human nature which dates back five thousand years. In recent years some western scholars, such as the American clinical psychologist Carl Rogers and the British psychiatrist R. D. Laing, have been applying Chinese philosophical concepts to the explanation of human mental phenomena (Rogers 1965, Laing 1976). Japanese psychiatrists have developed a system of Oriental psychotherapy based on the thought of Zen, the so-called Morita therapy. (Much has been published on Morita therapy; for examples see Caudill 1959; Kelman 1959; Kora 1965; Reynolds and O'Hara, 1967.) Psychoanalysis of the

Japanese mentality has produced a concept of "Amae," supposed to be a uniquely Japanese characteristic. The crisis of contemporary psychology requires conceptual evolution, but not the collection of new data. Why do not Chinese psychologists try to look into their classical world, and learn something from the wisdom of their ancient philosophers?

NOTES

1. This introductory section was written by the editors on the basis of information contained in a booklet issued by the Chung Hwa Information Service, Taiwan, "141 Questions and Answers about the Republic of China," 1974-75 (Eds.).
2. In 1982 there were twenty-five universities and colleges in Taiwan, some under state and some under private control, as listed in The World of Learning 1982-83, 33rd edn., 1982 (Eds.).
3. The International Directory of Psychologists (3rd edn., 1980) lists in addition the Chinese Association of Special Education, the Chinese Guidance Association, the Chinese Association for Mental Testing, and the Chinese National Educational Association (Eds.).
4. The Statistical Yearbook of the Republic of China for 1982 gives the population of Taiwan as just over eighteen million. The rapidity of urbanization is indicated by the fact that whereas in 1960 28.9 per cent of the population lived in localities of 100,000 or more, by 1981 48 per cent were doing so (Eds.).

REFERENCES

CAUDILL, W. The cultural content of Japanese psychiatry, in M. K. Opler (ed.) Culture and mental health. Macmillan Co., New York, 1959.
KELMAN, H. Psychotherapy in the Far East, Progress in Psychotherapy, 1959, 4, 296.
KO,Y. The relation between Bender-Gestalt performance and intelligence and personality, Psychological Testing, 1963, 19, 122-126.
KO, Y. The item analysis of the Ko mental health questionnaire paranoid scale, Acta Psychologica Taiwanica, 1964, 6, 21-27.
KORA, T. Morita Therapy, International Journal of

Psychiatry, 1965, 1, 611

LAING, R.D. _The facts of life - an essay in feelings, facts and fantasy_. Pantheon Books, New York, 1976.

REYNOLDS, D. & O'HARA, K. _Morita therapy and attempted suicide_. Suicide Prevention Center, Los Angeles, 1967.

ROGERS, C. A humanistic conception of man, in R. E. Farson (ed.) _Science and human affairs_, Science and Behavior Books, 1965.

YANG, KUO-SHU & WEN, CHUNG-I (eds.) The sinicization of social and behavioral science research in China, _Institute of Ethnology Academica Sinica Monograph Series_, B, 10, 1982.

ACKNOWLEDGMENT

The editors wish to acknowledge the comments on points of detail in this paper made by Professor In-mao Liu of the Chinese University of Hong Kong (formerly of National Taiwan University), and by Dr. Chao-Ming Cheng of National Taiwan University.

10

To Know the Heart:
Psychology in Hong Kong

Geoffrey H. Blowers

INTRODUCTION

Psychology in its western sense has been late coming
to Hong Kong but 'principles of the heart' (sum leih hok,
the romanised form of the spoken Cantonese equivalent)
has been understood since the days of the Sung dynasty.
While this understanding resides within the hearts of the
southern Chinese peasantry that make up the vast majority
of Hong Kong's population (conservatively estimated at
5.3 million[1]), attempts to shift the anatomical origin of
the psyche (from heart to head) by its educators have not
been altogether successful. In spite of their good
intentions, the history of western psychology in the
unique place that is Hong Kong may turn out to be a study
in failure in what otherwise has been a series of
successes both in the educational and economic sectors of
the community. To understand this better, it is as well
to look at some historical background to Hong Kong's
social, political and educational structures.

HISTORICAL BACKGROUND

Colonial influence in Hong Kong can be said to have
begun with the occupation of the island by the British
during the first opium war with China (1839-1841) –
Britain having been keen to maintain the lucrative trade
in Bengal opium monopolised by the East India Company as
a means of restoring the trade imbalance with China begun
over a century beforehand. Under the Nanking Peace Treaty
of 1842 Hong Kong Island was ceded by the Chinese. Under
the Convention of Peking in 1860, China ceded part of the

Kowloon peninsula after the second opium war. In order to increase the size of its property and to strengthen the crown colony, Britain in 1898 obtained a 99 year lease of the New Territories mainland terrain and some 235 islands making up an area of 366 square miles in all. Thus Hong Kong Island and the Kowloon peninsula are theoretically, British in perpetuity while the bulk of the New Territories where thrives most of Hong Kong's modern industry and (hence means of livelihood) is due to revert to China on July 1st 1997. Talks between London and Peking since 1982 resulted, on 26th September 1984, in both sides initialling the draft text of an agreement on the future of Hong Kong. The conditions of the agreement indicate that Britain will renounce sovereignty after July 1st 1997, and Hong Kong will become a Special Administrative Region of the Central People's Government of the People's Republic of China. It will enjoy a high degree of autonomy and self government except in foreign and defence affairs which will become the responsibilities of the Central People's Government. However the further implications of this development have yet to be spelled out in detail.

Hong Kong has lived with uncertainties throughout its 144 year existence. An ever increasing population has been not only the major motivating force behind Hong Kong's development but also its plague, hindering the provision of a genuinely better quality of life for its people. From 1851 until 1931 the population rose from 32,983 (31,463 Chinese) to 878,947 (859,425 Chinese). By the end of the Second World War it had fallen to 600,000, but by 1947 had risen again to 1.8 million. In 1948-49 with the fall of the Nationalist Government, Hong Kong received an influx unparalleled in its history. Approximately three quarters of a million people - mainly from Guangdong province, Shanghai and other commercial centres - entered the territory during 1949 and the spring of 1950. By the end of 1950 the population was estimated to be 2.3 million, since when it has continued to rise.

These pressures have placed an enormous strain upon the resources of the city in terms of housing, education and welfare. Although more than two and one quarter million people now live in some form of public housing managed by the Housing Authority, there are still many who live in 'squatter' huts - illegal dwellings on the side of hills and on rooftops which are tolerated while the building programme continues to provide 35,000 houses every year (Parsons, 1984). Educational needs have been more problematic given the different types of school and variation in language of instruction, but to date the government has seen fit to provide compulsory education for the first nine years of the pupil's school life. This means that secondary school places are available for every student up to the age of 15. However with just two universities, two polytechnics and an upgraded post secondary college, the opportunities for tertiary education, in spite of recent expansions, is limited. This situation produces a fiercely meritocratic system with a heavy emphasis placed upon examinations and ability to use English. Many of those who fail to make the grade into the local universities apply to go abroad to study in Britain, Australia, Canada and the United States.

Psychology is primarily a tertiary educational subject although it was introduced into the sixth form curriculum in the mid-seventies to a few schools who were willing to take it on. The opportunities for its study and practice at graduate level are few and far between although there are now well developed relevant curricula in each of the two universities.

INTRODUCTION OF PSYCHOLOGY AT THE UNIVERSITY
OF HONG KONG (1939-1967)

Psychology courses were first taught in 1939 in teaching programmes within the Faculty of Arts at the University of Hong Kong (Harrison, 1962a). This is the older of Hong Kong's two universities, originally founded in 1911 as a teaching institution to furnish the indigenous Chinese population, as well as scholars from the mainland, with a thorough grounding in western-based knowledge in the professions of Medicine, Law and Engineering. However, after the overthrow of the Imperial regime in China in the same year as the University's founding, few scholars from China found their way to its doors since the new republic was more preoccupied with militaristic than with educational matters (Harrison, 1962,b).

The University's degrees are equivalent to those awarded in British universities. This equivalence is ensured by a system of appointing external examiners from outside of Hong Kong who make periodic visits (usually once in every three year appointment) to Hong Kong for 'on-site' inspection. With the exception of the department of Chinese, teaching is normally conducted in English, although there has been a steady increase in the amount of teaching through the medium of Cantonese in the past decade.

The war interrupted work in the faculty, but in 1948 courses in Arts were resumed. Initially, they were organised around groups of studies: letters and philosophy, economics and politics, and Chinese studies. In the 1951/52 academic year, teaching was organised on a departmental basis and two types of degree for differing periods of study were conferred - the three year Pass degree and the four year Honours degree. Two years later, both degree curricula were of four years duration, but in late 1954, concurrently with the introduction of advanced level requirements for matriculation, they were amalgamated and shortened to form a single three-year B.A. Honours degree which remains in force today. The view of psychology as a Liberal Arts subject prevailed until the late sixties when further thought was given to its role as a social science and to the possibility of offering postgraduate professional training in a new Faculty of Social Sciences.

It was in the early post-war period however, that the University advertised its first full-time lectureship in psychology -- a post designed to provide a teacher of psychology for philosophical studies. Dr. J. C. Tsao took up the position and became the first psychologist appointed to the University. Tsao came to Hong Kong by way of China and England. Having obtained his first degree in psychology from Tsing Hua University in China in 1935, he was actively connected for the next five years with the Mass Education Movement led by Dr. James Yen. He became a lecturer in psychology at South West University, Kunming, during the war, and in 1945 went to the Psychological Laboratory at Cambridge where he did research for a Ph.D. on time intervals in learning and memory, under Bartlett. He was appointed to HKU in July 1948 on a one year contract which was renewed for a further year, the university's financial position at this time being very precarious. Ironically in 1950, when Senate reconsidered the status of lecturers in the Arts faculty along with reorganisation of its subjects, Tsao, who had been invited to apply for one of the new lectureships, left rather suddenly to take up a post as Deputy Director of the Institute of Psychology at the Academica Sinica in Peking under the newly formed Communist Government in China.

The teaching of psychology was then continued by a part-time lecturer, Wu Hei-tak, from the Education Department of the Hong Kong Government, who resigned in late 1952. Following his resignation, Erik Kvan, at that time a residential hall warden at HKU, took up the teaching in early 1953. Kvan, a Dane, had been working in Hong Kong since 1946, initially at the Tao Fong Shan Christian Institute, established for the purpose of conducting studies in comparative religion and of providing a meeting place for Eastern and Western thought. He has been the University's longest serving teacher of psychology, having also been twice head of department. The first of these occasions was in 1966 as head pro temp of Philosophy prior to its splitting off from psychology as a separate department (a move which came very late to Hong Kong - 1967), and then in the department of psychology as Senior Lecturer and Head for a four-year period from 1976 until his 'retirement' in 1980. He continues to be active in the teaching and supervision of students of psychology in a number of different departments throughout the University in which the subject is now taught.

The terms of Kvan's initial appointment were rather typical for the day. The university had little money for the provision of 'full' terms of service, that is those on which serving expatriate government officers were employed (regular monthly salaries, subsidised housing and assisted passages), and so employed many people on a part-time basis. This meant that they were paid by the hour for lectures with the university having no other responsibilities towards them. In the early post war years many of those recruited in this way were Jesuit priests who were highly qualified and were working in religious institutes throughout the colony. Another group were expatriate wives of Government officers and businessmen, who were in many cases also well qualified but who had sacrificed a job in their mother countries for the sake of their husbands' career advancement. Although the terms of service for all people employed in higher education have steadily improved over the years and the number of staff employed on full terms has risen proportionally to those employed on a part-time basis, the tradition of employing part-timers remains. Psychology in HKU has been a particular beneficiary of this arrangement.

Kvan's influence has been pervasive. From his broadly liberal eclectic perspective he has endeavoured to foster an attitude of positive agnosticism in generations of students (Blowers & Wong, 1983). This perspective has led to the absence of overspecialisation in one or two specific areas of psychology that marks many departments in the West. Whilst each staff member is free to pursue research in whatever area he or she wishes (subject to financial constraints), and indeed are usually appointed to posts advertising particular specialities, the very nature of academic duties in this part of the world, where one is called upon to teach a variety of undergraduate and possibly postgraduate subjects and engage in some community service such as answering queries from the media, writing occasional articles for the local press, giving public talks and serving on the management committees of voluntary welfare agencies, ensures that one remains a generalist. At the same time this perspective has not prevented the department from launching specialist postgraduate programmes in Clinical and Educational psychology. In the early fifties however, with few professionals at work in the psychological field, the scope of research and practice was limited.

One of Kvan's early interests was in assessing the potential for development of facilities for the mentally and physically handicapped. In 1953, he, along with Marie Clements, a lecturer in the Education Department of the University, joined Dr. Irene Cheng, then an inspector of schools in the Government Department of Education and a handful of people from other professions, notably teachers centred on True Light Middle School, interested in the general area of 'mental health', to form a study group. This led to the formation in January 1954 of the Hong Kong Mental Health Association. For many years this Association looked to the Department of Philosophy and Psychology for logistic support. It defined as one of its objectives the promotion of "the advancement of a mental health programme in Hong Kong in its broadest medical, educational and social aspects concerning the needs of both the mentally ill and the mentally retarded" (Wong, 1976, p. 1). Later that same year approval was given for the setting up of a Child Guidance Clinic and Marie Clements, Kenneth Priestly, the head of the university's education department, Beryl Wright and Anita Li were granted permission to engage in consultation work within it.

The other main psychological development in the early fifties was the psychological research carried out by Kvan and Clements on the reading ability of matriculation students (Clements and Kvan, 1954; Kvan, 1956). These studies demonstrated that students who came into the university never progressed much beyond what they had achieved during their middle school years. The upshot of these findings was for Kvan and Clements to institute a series of reading courses in connection with the department of English which eventually led, in later years, to other departments within the university (most notably the Language Centre and the Student Counselling Unit) setting up courses of study methods and the like. These activities were fuelled by a general concern for declining standards in English amongst the student population as a whole and form a part of the continuing language debate in Hong Kong.[2] Much of this debate revolves around considerations of the relative merits of learning English as opposed to or in addition to a first written Chinese language and spoken Cantonese - the commonly spoken dialect (for which there is no official written equivalent) or Putonghua (Mandarin). Indeed, making the language of instruction a student's second language has been a colonial artefact difficult to shake off. While other research in this area has looked at the problem from a number of perspectives, such as measuring people's attitiudes to second language learning (for example, Cheng et al, 1973), very little of the research has been concerned to view language as it is embedded in the total life experience of the individual (Kvan, 1969; 1976).

The language problem originated within the secondary school system where historically two quite separate types of school developed: the Anglo-Chinese secondary school in which all subjects (except Chinese) are taught in English, and the Chinese Middle School where the medium of instruction is Cantonese. Before 1948 programmes of the Chinese Middle Schools were related to those of China and students completing courses looked to China for their higher education. With the Communist takeover there in 1949 many students who would otherwise have sought a university in China looked closer to home. At the same time there were large numbers of refugee students from the Mainland who desired to continue their studies (Fulton Report, 1963). Neither group was sufficiently versed in English to meet the University of Hong Kong's entrance requirement of a pass in Use of English at Matriculation level. This led to the unfortunate situation of only the exceptional students from the Chinese Middle Schools being accepted into HKU - many capable students being rejected because of the second language requirement. It was against this background that the Keswick report of 1952, examining the future of tertiary education in Hong Kong, recommended the removal of the English language requirement and making Chinese the language of instruction in Hong Kong University, while at the same time suggesting that all students be required to pursue some form of English language training within the University whether or not this formed part of their formal training. However the relevant authorities could not agree on what form of Chinese (that is, Mandarin or Cantonese) should be taught nor what would be appropriate texts. The deliberations over language in higher education eventually led in the early sixties to the setting up of a second university, The Chinese University of Hong Kong, in which the principal language of instruction was Chinese - both Cantonese and Mandarin. Ironically, psychology, in which research studies done in Hong Kong have indicated some of the difficulties of second language ability, is taught principally in English.

From 1948 until 1967, psychology was taught initially as one and subsequently as three courses in the philosophy department. According to the 1952 Calendar, the three papers were listed as General Psychology, Differential Psychology and Social Psychology. By 1962 the listings were Experimental Psychology, General (including Social) and Philosophical Approaches to Psychology. The psychology papers were externally examined in 1961 for the first time by a psychologist, N.S. Sutherland, at that time of Magdalen College and the Laboratory of Experimental Psychology at Oxford. Prior to his appointment, the practice had been for psychology papers to be examined by the appointee for the philosophy papers - an arrangement which proved to be less than satisfactory to one examiner, I.M. Crombie (also of Oxford) who was instrumental in getting the system changed.[3]

Crombie's comments in his written reports often revealed the persistent differences which existed between the teaching styles at HKU and Oxford and which frequently made examining difficult. While not unsympathetic to the educational system at HKU, his reports revealed the gap between the Oxford system and the realities of teaching in a culture where students are taught in a second language and are weaned on rote learning in the secondary schools. The differences have not been resolved to this day and form part of the continuing debate on education in Hong Kong.

DEVELOPMENT OF PSYCHOLOGY (1967-1986)

Psychology at the University of Hong Kong

In 1967 J.L.M. Dawson, (now Binnie-Dawson) an Australian, was appointed to the first chair of psychology in the newly formed department which offered courses in both the faculty of Arts and the newly created faculty of Social Sciences and Law. The latter faculty had been formed in May of that year following recommendations made in the Tress Report. The Vice Chancellor at the time had wanted the faculty and was keen to have a department of political science and a department of Law - a subject which had been taught up till then as Ll.B. courses for the London University external degree in the Extra-mural department. Economics had one person teaching political science part-time, and another teaching Sociology. Social Work also came under the umbrella of Economics. Tress recommended that these be separate subjects under a new faculty, and that psychology and philosophy be allocated to both faculties so that psychology might eventually be offered as a degree in its own right within the faculty (Tress, 1967). In spite of staffing limitations this was achieved, and the first graduates in psychology emerged in 1970.

Dawson, having a strong anthropological background, saw Hong Kong as a natural laboratory for cross-cultural psychology (Dawson, 1970) and soon established a course in his particular speciality, bio-social psychology, within the undergraduate curriculum and set about promoting the subject (Dawson, 1971) and encouraging visitors from abroad to spend sabbaticals and do research in his department. In the early seventies academic visitors from overseas were few and far between, but in the eighties, with the opening up of the People's Republic of China, the department has entertained a constant stream of people passing through. Most stop briefly to give a seminar but the occasional visitor has stayed for three months or even a year - long enough to comment and make reflections on research possibilities (Ripple, 1983). Partly as a result of Dawson's interests and intentions, the International Association of Cross-cultural Psychology was formed in 1972 and held its first conference in August of that year, hosted by the Department of Psychology at HKU. The Department also hosted the first Asian regional conference in 1979. There are presently twelve full-time members of staff of lecturer grade or above.

Psychology teaching at other institutions

Following recommendations made in the Fulton Report (1963), the Chinese University of Hong Kong was inaugurated in September 1963 as a federal university from three pre-existent colleges.[4] Psychology was first taught only through elective courses within other disciplines, most notably sociology. In 1973 a 'psychology section' was formed within the department of sociology at Chung Chi College under the headship of Jennie Lee-Ng. As a section it taught psychology only as a minor subject, students being offered a range of courses but being allowed to take only a sufficient number to make up two papers. The Chinese University is modelled after the American University system with a four-year degree programme, entrance to which may be sought by passing an examination after a student has completed a sixth year of Chinese Middle School or the HKU Advanced Level Examination. In 1982 the psychology section was granted full departmental status with a professorial chair established for the purpose. Its first incumbent is Professor Liu In-mao, formerly of National Taiwan University. It now offers a broad range of courses at the undergraduate level and allows students the opportunity to take the majority of their papers in the subject, and has plans to launch its own Master's programme in clinical psychology in the near future. There are presently seven full-time members of staff and relations between the department and that at HKU are very cordial.

Other tertiary education institutions comprise the Hong Kong Polytechnic, the new City Polytechnic and the post-secondary colleges, Baptist College, Shue Yan College and Lingnam College which offer courses in psychology within social work, sociology and business studies but none of them is a degree awarding body as yet, nor are they able to teach psychology as a major subject. A growing number of secondary schools is now offering psychology as an 'A' level course so that candidates may take it as a matriculation subject for entrance to university. The teaching of psychology as a major discipline at undergraduate degree level remains the sole prerogative of the two universities. Since entry to post-graduate courses in psychology in Hong Kong and Commonwealth universities requires a certain level of undergraduate experience (not only in terms of the class of degree but in number and type of courses taken), these departments are the only available source for that experience in Hong Kong. To further facilitate entry to professional training, HKU offers a Certificate in Psychology course[5] which enables graduates with insuffi- cient psychology in their first degree to acquire the necessary prerequisites for postgraduate courses.

Postgraduate research degrees by thesis, at first M.A., later M.Phil. and Ph.D., have been offered for many years in HKU. Amongst other things, they constitute a form of training for those seeking employment as teachers particularly in institutions of tertiary education. In the early seventies the first postgraduate course for training graduates to the profession of clinical psycho- logy was launched. In order to understand how that came about it is necessary to examine the roles played by Hong Kong's professional society for psychologists.

The Hong Kong Psychological Society

In the late sixties the small but growing number of psychologists in Hong Kong felt it was important to put the "development of professional psychology on a proper footing from its inception. With this in mind, the Hong Kong Psychological Society was formed in February 1968" (Ho, 1971). The initial proposal from Professor Dawson was for an overseas branch of the British Psychological Society (which had been the status of the society in Australia, for example, until the formation of its own society in 1965) but this was not possible without the approval of twenty Fellows and Associates of the BPS (which Hong Kong did not have at the time) so the Hong Kong Psychological Society was begun, to "get things going".[6] From the beginning the Society and the BPS established reciprocal membership rights for their members. The Hong Kong Psychological Society is the only professional psychological organisation in the world to have this arrangement with the BPS. By 1970 the Society boasted of forty members and in 1984 had over 170. Its principal aims have been to "encourage growth of psycho- logical activities...and the development of an appropr- iate professional environment to facilitate the main-

tenance of professional standards for psychologists"
(Dawson, 1970, p.65).

To begin with, the Society worked entirely from
within Dawson's department where most of its original
members were employed. Over the years it has spread its
wings as more and more of its membership has been
recruited from graduates of the department of psychology
at HKU who retain an interest (but who do not seek
professional training) in their subject, and from the
professional sphere which has itself been slowly expanding in the community. Excluding the academic members, the
number of professional psychologists working in Government and subvented agencies is approximately 60 with one
or two working in private practice. Throughout its short
history the Society has looked to its founding department
for leadership and technical support, but in recent years
it has gradually become more independent.

Adopting the principles of organisation of the
British and Australian Psychological Societies a number
of categories of membership were devised in order to
identify professional qualifications and number of years
of experience of its members. Following some revisions,
the present constitution lists three grades of professional or full membership: Fellow, Associate and Graduate
and one non-professional grade: Affiliate. Professional
membership is normally granted to anyone who possesses
one of the following qualifications: 1. an honours degree
for which psychology is the main subject or 2. a post-
graduate qualification in psychology awarded by a
responsible authority or 3. such other qualifications in
psychology as the Council shall accept. Alternatively an
applicant may be granted membership by passing a qualifying examination. The Society acts in an advisory capacity
to Government and other organisations and formulates
guidelines for private practice in Hong Kong. It sponsors
an annual conference, a number of scientific meetings,
seminars and workshops throughout the year given by local
professionals and overseas visitors. It also publishes a
journal, the Bulletin of the Hong Kong Psychological
Society which appears twice a year and is devoted to
issues of theoretical and practical concern to psychology
in Hong Kong.

The question of 'professional' membership however
has been and continues to be a matter of some debate.
While professional membership is normally granted to any
applicant holding an honours degree in psychology from
HKU or an 'equivalent' qualification from another

university as determined by the Council, the equivalence has, in some instances, been difficult to determine. This is particularly the case where the content of the degree is not clear or where the manner in which the subject has been taught departs from the pattern established in British and Commonwealth universities. The need for equivalence arises out of the links that the Society has forged with the BPS, which acts as overseer of standards of professionalism by monitoring the structure (but not the content) of courses taught within the departments of psychology at Hong Kong's two universities. At the undergraduate level there has been a need to ensure that certain 'fundamental' subject areas are covered (such as learning, perception, cognition, statistics, experimental design, social psychology), and students are given the opportunity to pursue a research project in an independent manner under supervision and to present the findings in a thesis. Above and beyond these fundamental requirements students are free to choose from a variety of courses offered within the curriculum. In the UK, entrance to most postgraduate courses in applied psychology areas such as clinical, educational and industrial psychology is dependent upon a student having a 'recognised' first degree in psychology. Without this the postgraduate courses would not be recognised by the BPS and graduates of such courses would probably find it difficult to further their careers in the profession. The BPS thus fulfils its function in the UK of acting as a liaison between prospective employers of psychologists and the educational institutions which train them. Essentially it legitimates the functions of both by monitoring their standards.

The Hong Kong Psychological Society is keen to function in much the same way. It has met with some success in its dealings with Government over the employment and terms of service of clinical psychologists, although the task has not been easy. As David Ho pointed out in 1971:

In Hong Kong psychologists are something of a rarity (and sometimes looked upon as something of an oddity) among a population of four million; the impact of psychological science has hardly made itself felt on intellectual life or on society as a whole. For, while the attention and resources of society have been directed mainly to the sphere of economic

activity, the development of psychology is
inhibited by an attitude of indifference and
even scepticism. (p.39)

While the population has risen by more than a
million since then, the general resistance to psychology
has remained. Nevertheless there were sound arguments
advanced both in that paper and in others for the
government to employ individuals with psychological
skills - arguments to which the government has slowly
warmed.

The rise of clinical psychology

In 1969 an informal study group comprising representatives of the department of psychology at HKU, the Hong
Kong Psychological Society and various government
departments carried out a survey of existing psychological services with a view to establishing what future
requirements government would have in terms of trained
personnel.[7] The results of the survey revealed amongst
other things that while there were a few psychologists in
service there was a lack of procedures for appointing and
establishing certain psychological posts and related
ancillary staff. In some instances services were non-
existent or carried out by non-psychologically trained
government officers. Also "some social service agencies
indicated that they offered clinical services but in all
cases these were provided either by social workers or
unqualified volunteers. These workers offered advice on
psychological problems. However in no case was a qualified psychologist employed in these activities which is a
matter for considerable concern" (p.5).

From the report it appeared that Government recognised the lack of adequately trained personnel and the
need to expand its recruitment. The problem was, where
would suitable persons be found? Until that time there
had been a reliance on recruiting individuals trained
overseas who were in some cases expatriates. There were
obvious advantages to training psychologists in Hong
Kong. Students selected from the local population which
is predominantly Cantonese speaking would not be handicapped by language or cultural barriers in their work.
Furthermore the fact that students would receive their
practical training in local clinical settings would
render their overall training more relevant to local

needs and conditions. These realisations led to the initiation in 1971, within the department of psychology, HKU, of a graduate training programme leading to the degree of Master of Social Science in the field of clinical psychology. This course was overseen by the BPS, approved provisionally at the time and formally approved by it in 1980 after two on-site visitations in 1973 and 1979.[8]

Since the first five graduates of the course emerged in 1973 the number of applicants has exceeded the number of places and numbers of both applicants and places have risen each time the course has been offered, that is, every second year since 1971. The employment of many of the graduates within the Government is beginning to have significant effects upon the initial resistance to such activities from 'rival' and more dominant professions already established within the Civil Service machinery (such as psychiatry in the Medical and Health Department and social work in the Social Welfare department). At the same time, the Correctional Services (formerly Prisons) Department has been very appreciative of the need for psychological services, and has done much to foster the Government's recognition of the autonomy of clinical psychology as a profession distinct from social work and other related professions.[9] However the continuing practice and development of clinical psychology is not without its problems. At the 1980 Annual Conference of the Hong Kong Psychological Society four clinical psychologists offered varied accounts of their professional duties and spoke of their expectations and suggestions for the future practice of their discipline.[10] These included changing the attitude of both clients and administrative superiors, the recruitment of additional staff to ease workloads so that the time can be allocated to research, and the specification of a concrete division of labour within the profession itself. At present, most clinical psychologists are working in isolation and are called upon to perform a wide range of clinical duties. If however they were organised in departments of clinical psychology specialising in a range of skills for which there was sufficient manpower to carry out their duties effectively, a more efficient and productive division of labour, so it is argued, would occur.

Whether this is likely to develop will depend in part upon Government's resources for such expansion measured against its need to improve other areas of the 'helping' professions, as well as its recognition of the need to employ psychologists as opposed to other professionals. This need arises because of the necessity for implementing certain specific skills in response to social problems such as mental testing and other forms of psychological assessment, individual and family counselling.

Recent developments

After several years of protracted negotiations between the department of psychology at HKU, the University and Polytechnic Grants Committee and the Education Department of Government, a one year Master's degree course in Educational psychology was offered for the first time in 1981 with the Department (later School) of Education providing a considerable input to the teaching. Pressure for the course had come five years earlier from Ms. J. E. Rowe, Education Officer for the Special Education Unit. It was her wish to have the University of Hong Kong provide a psychological training course for members of the Special Education Unit to enable them to develop more specialised skills in testing and assessment of children. At the outset the realisation that most members of the unit lacked even a basic training in psychology led the department of psychology in 1978 to introduce a one year Certificate course leading to a qualification (Certificate in Psychology) equivalent to that of undergraduates majoring in psychology. This has subsequently become a popular programme for many students lacking an undergraduate education in psychology but wishing to pursue postgraduate professional training in the subject. Meanwhile the Educational Psychology Master's programme has expanded to two years and has become the sole responsibility of HKU's Department of Psychology.

Although this programme has signalled an increase in both the supply of and demand for appropriately trained psychology personnel in the educational sector, clinical psychologists have been quite the largest single group of members within the Hong Kong Psychological Society and generate most of its activities. Those within the group who are employed directly by government have formed a professional association,[11] and a smaller number have set up a consulting agency[12] which offers free clinical psychological services on an experimental basis to some agencies and government departments who require them. In addition the 'Mental Testing Workshop', operating under the aegis of the Society and comprising nearly all clinical psychologists in Hong Kong, has been an umbrella for a range of activities. In response to these a division of clinical psychology was formed in early 1982, and certain protectionist measures designed to safeguard the interests of psychology's practitioners have been instituted. These include a change in registration from the Societies to the Companies Ordinance Cap. 32 – the Hong Kong Psychological Society is now a company limited by guarantee and not having a Share Capital.[13] This means that individual members have some protection (albeit limited) against any possible malpractice suits and the Society can operate as a agent for the distribution for psychological tests (and hence monitor their use). There is the further issue of whether or not psychologists should be licensed since this is currently under debate in the British Psychological Society (see for example, Watts, 1980; BPS Steering Committee on Registration, 1984), and until it is resolved there, the Hong Kong Psychological Society is unlikely to move for fear of jeopardising the arrangements that exist for reciprocity of membership with the BPS[14] as well as being uncertain at this time about the role of psychologists in the constitutionally changed form of government existing in Hong Kong after the renunciation of sovereignty in 1997.

THE FUTURE

The transition of psychology from a liberal arts subject to a qualification in professional training in the short space of less than twenty-five years must be seen against the background of political uncertainty about the future administration of Hong Kong after China has regained sovereignty. While statements from various officials in the People's Republic have strongly implied that its Government is keen to maintain Hong Kong as a highly autonomous self-governing city state, the precise way in which this will be achieved has yet to be spelled out in any detail. The large outflow of capital from the colony, taken with the fall in property market prices in recent years and the general indifference of the local population towards long-term developments, have all been significant indicators of the lack of confidence with which Hong Kong has recently been struck.

These symptoms, which have erupted before, most notably in the late fifties and sixties, have subsided to some extent since Beijing and London made formal announcements on the results of their protracted negotiations. With the realisation that they will no longer be able to rely on British support after 1997, the people of Hong Kong have begun to develop a hitherto unknown political consciousness. Within the professional realm, social workers seem to have taken the lead in community activities designed to show publicly their allegiance to Beijing, and to promote confidence in the populace about the role they can play in a sophisticated Chinese city state. However such concerns would appear to be developing hand in hand with a disturbing parochialism. Less attention would appear to be directed at maintaining international links and being receptive to innovative ideas from abroad.

Psychologists, on the other hand seem preoccupied with status and international recognition, the price for which has been a lack of acceptance at the grass roots level of Hong Kong social life. Of course psychologists are in much smaller numbers than social workers, but the success of their efforts at expansion may well depend upon how far they are able to infiltrate deeply rooted traditional views of help-seeking in the culture.

Chinese typically present 'psychological' problems as the expression of bodily symptoms, a process known as somatisation which has been widely reported and documented (see for example Cheung, 1982). This tendency leads them, if they seek western style help at all, to a medical doctor in general practice. Only at a later stage might they be referred to a psychologist. It is also the practice for potential clients/patients to 'shop around' when obtaining such help, seeking confirmation of a diagnosis in the private sector. Also, in government clinics the tendency appears to be for doctors to make only the most elementary notes, thus making it harder (if not impossible) for doctor B for example, to know what doctor A prescribed for the patient a week ago. The effect of these practices is for there to be very little continuity of medical (and by implication, psychological) care.

A further problem resides in the psychologists themselves. Suspicions abound to the effect that when practising forms of non-directive counselling in psychotherapeutic practice, the Hong Kong Chinese psychologist assumes the role of 'master' and imposes an authoritarian structure upon the relationship s/he has with a client.[15] The possibility of this occurring is being studied by investigating whether a Taoist model of man lies behind the practice of much clinical psychology (Koo, 1986).

The replacement of values implicit in western psychology (particularly those associated with the ideology of individualism) by collectivism to fit a Chinese mould (see for example, Ho, 1984) is not consciously experienced by students of psychology during their training here. One reason advanced for this has been that few of them have been in a crisis situation themselves for which they might find their western psychology inadequate for their needs. In other words the shift in symmetry of the client-therapist relationship from equality to dominance by the therapist by virtue of his/her supposed authority, is a process that takes place largely at the unconscious level.

These speculations are clearly in need of further investigation and hopefully this will be achieved by the practioners themselves. In the meantime it would appear that for the vast majority of people in Hong Kong, sum, - the source of traditional principles of morality - remains the barometer of temperament for which habitual consultative visits to the local temple (whether Taoist or Buddhist) are made[16]. Here it is the temple soothsayer who is likely to provide the solace, support and direction that the people need without committing themselves to the teachings of gwailo[17] psychological doctrines from the West.

NOTES

1. Ninety-eight per cent of the population are Chinese. There is a British community of 19,700 excluding military forces, 12,800 Americans and 84,400 other western expatriates. About seventy per cent of the population is Hong Kong born. (Figures taken from All Asia Guide - 13th ed. 1984 - compiled from information contributed by Far East Economic Review correspondents in the region.)

2. This issue is elaborated in 'The Language Debate' in G.H. Blowers and T. W. Wong (eds.) Questions of Psychology: interviews with Erik Kvan, Bulletin of the Hong Kong Psychological Society, July 1983 - January 1984, 11/12.

3. Crombie objected to examining papers in psychology because he did not feel qualified to do so. His objections led to the appointment of Dr. Sutherland, and the two of them split their fees in proportionate quantity for the period of their appointment. In 1963 however, under the University's general policy of one external examiner per department, the previous arrangement was reverted to upon the appointment of Sir Karl Popper as external examiner of philosophy and psychology. Popper's relationship with the department for the duration of his three year appointment (including his one visit to Hong Kong in 1963) proved to be a turbulent one as the correspondence between the University administration and Joseph Agassi (a former student of Popper and then Head of department) makes clear.

4. New Asia (founded by Dr.Ch'ien Mu and a small group of refugee scholars in 1949), Chung Chi (founded by Hong Kong Protestant churches in 1951) and United (created by the amalgamation of five 'refugee' colleges, which decided to pool their resources, in 1956).

5. This curriculum extends over one year full-time or two years part-time and comprises eight B.Soc. Sci. courses in psychology plus a thesis.

6. Taken from a departmental circular written by Professor John Dawson 3rd January 1968.

7. Report of the Study Group on Social Science Co-ordination of Psychological Services in Government. Unpublished manuscript, Department of Psychology, HKU. 1969

8. Approval in 1980 was granted following the submission to the BPS Executive Council of the report by the its Professional Affairs Board, the UK body responsible for approving courses in clinical psychology for the National Health Service (via the Whitley Council) in Britain. The report recommended a de-emphasis of training in testing and a greater emphasis on behavioural procedures, and encouraged the enlistment of teachers from allied disciplines and of clinical psychologists offering direct supervision in the field. The course organisers are in the process of implementing these changes and subsequent correspondence with the BPS and a further on-site visit in 1984 has ensured approval until 1989, at which time a further visit by examiners will enable a subsequent re-asessment and recommendation to be made. This form of continuous assessment is identical with the manner in which the BPS monitors the standard of courses offered in the UK.

9. However, although autonomous in terms of duties, clinical psychologists in Government service are answerable to seniors from other professions: to prison officers in the Correctional Services Department; to social workers in the Social Welfare Department; to psychiatrists in the Medical and Health Department. Except for the appointment of a senior clinical psychologist in Correctional Services, there is no working hierarchy for psychologists in the Government.

10. These reports are published in the Bulletin of the Hong Kong Psychological Society, January 1981, 6.

11. The Association of Government Clinical Psychologists.

12. The Institute of Psychological Services - formed in September 1980.

13. This took place in April 1981 when the revised constitution was finally approved by the Registrar of Companies.

14. The issue of reciprocal membership with the BPS may have to be raised again and reapproved with the recent change in their membership regulations in 1978.

15. See in particular the section 'Issues in professionalisation and practice' in G. H. Blowers and T. W. Wong (eds.) Questions of psychology: interviews with Erik Kvan, Bulletin of the Hong Kong Psychological Society, July 1983- January 1984, 11/12. Also, Li Chin-keung, Tools for investigating the relationship between the clinical psychologist and the client: A case study, Bulletin of the Hong Kong Psychological Society, July 1982, 9, 27-38

16. The majority of Hong Kong's religious believers are Buddhist or Taoist, or a mixture of both. They worship on any day at one of over 360 temples. There are also nearly 600 Christian churches and chapels which are attended by about nine per cent of the population; three mosques where more than 30,000 followers of Islam worship; a Hindu temple for the 10,000 members of the Hindu community; and a Jewish synagogue with about 500 members (Savidge, 1977; Parsons, 1984)

17. Romanised Cantonese popular slang term for 'foreigner' (literally 'ghost man').

REFERENCES

BLOWERS, G. H., and WONG, T. W. (eds.) Questions of psychology: interviews with Erik Kvan, Bulletin of

160

the Hong Kong Psychological Society, July 1983 -
January 1984, 11/12.
BPS STEERING COMMITTEE ON REGISTRATION, Recommendations
for the registration of psychologists, Bulletin of
the British Psychological Society, 1984, 37, 1-7
CHENG, N. L., SHEK, K. C., TSE, K. K. AND WONG, S. L. At
what cost: instruction through the English medium in
Hong Kong Schools, Shum Shing Printing Company, Hong
Kong. 1973
CHEUNG, F. Somatisation amongst the Chinese: a critique,
Bulletin of the Hong Kong Psychological Society,
1982, 8, 27-35.
CLEMENTS, M., and KVAN, E. Silent reading: a preliminary
survey with the 1953 Matriculation classes in Hong
Kong Research, Journal of Education, 1954, 13.
DAWSON, J. L. M. Psychology in Hong Kong, Australian
Psychologist, 1970, 5, 59-68.
DAWSON, J. L. M. Theory and Research in Cross-cultural
psychology, Bulletin of the British Psychological
Society, 1971, 24, 291-306.
FULTON, J. S. (Chairman) Commission to advise on the
creation of a federal-type Chinese University in
Hong Kong, Hong Kong Government Printer, Hong Kong.
1963.
HARRISON, B. The faculty of Arts. In B. Harrison (ed.)
The University of Hong Kong: the first fifty years,
University of Hong Kong Press, Hong Kong. 1962.
HARRISON, B. The years of growth. In B. Harrison (ed.)
The University of Hong Kong: the first fifty years,
University of Hong Kong Press, Hong Kong. 1962.
HO, D. Y. F. The role of psychologists in mental health
in Hong Kong. In W. H. Lo, W. Chan, K. S. Ma and A.
Wong (eds.) Aspects of Mental Health in Hong Kong,
Mental Health Association of Hong Kong. 1971.
HO, D. Y. F. Cultural values and professional issues in
clinical psychology: implications from the Hong Kong
perspective. Submitted for publication. 1984.
KESWICK, J. (Chairman) Report on Higher Education in Hong
Kong, Hong Kong Government Printer, Hong Kong. 1952.
KOO,J. H. C. The Taoist conception of Man as an explan-
ation of social behaviour, Submitted Ph.D. thesis,
University of Hong Kong, Hong Kong. 1984.
KVAN, E. Increasing the rate of reading: report on an
experiment, Journal of Education, 1956, 14.

KVAN, E. Problems of bilingual milieu in Hong Kong: strain of the two language system. In I. Jarvie and J. Agassi (eds.) Hong Kong: a society in transition, Routledge and Kegan Paul, London. 1969.

KVAN, E. Bilingual education: a socio-psychological perspective. In R. Lord and B. T'sou (eds.) Studies in Bilingual Education, Heineman, Hong Kong. 1976.

PARSONS, M. J. Hong Kong 1984: a review of 1983, Government Information Services, Hong Kong. 1984.

RIPPLE, R. Reflections on doing psychological research in Hong Kong, Bulletin of the Hong Kong Psychological Society, 1983, 10, 7-23.

SAVIDGE, J. This is Hong Kong: Temples, Government Information Services, Hong Kong. 1977.

TRESS, R. C. The Social Sciences in the University of Hong Kong, University of Hong Kong, Hong Kong. 1967.

WATTS, F. N. The legal registration of psychologists: some questions and answers, Bulletin of the British Psychological Society, 1980, 33, 77-79.

WONG, C. L. A brief history of the Mental Health Association of Hong Kong. In W. H. Lo, W. Chan., K. S. Ma, A. Wong and K. K. Yeung (eds.) Perspectives in Mental Health, Mental Health Association of Hong Kong. 1976.

ACKNOWLEDGMENTS

The author is grateful to Veronica Pearson, Erik Kvan, and Duncan Hunter for their thoughtful and perceptive comments on an earlier draft of this chapter.

11

Psychology in Korea

Jae-Ho Cha

Until the end of the 19th century, Korea was a kingdom ruled by what is known as the Yi Dynasty. Toward the end of the century, foreign powers came into the country and clashed militarily in order to have exclusive control over the Korean peninsula. Japan defeated China and Russia, and in 1910 formally annexed Korea, ending the five hundred year rule of the Yi Dynasty. Japan's colonial rule of Korea came to an abrupt end in 1945 when all the Japanese in Korea withrew to the Japanese mainland as a result of Japan's surrender to the allied forces.

Two years after this liberation, Korea emerged as a new independent nation with a modern democratic government. But even before Korea was liberated, the allied countries had drawn up a line across Korea, dividing it into North and South Koreas. A year after the South Korean government was established, the communists in the northern part of Korea set up a communist government. A massive military incursion by the North Korean forces of South Korea only two years later started the Korean War (1950-1953), which devastated a new nation that was still smarting from the wounds inflicted by the Japanese colonial rule, World War II, and the political chaos following liberation.

What is written here is the story of psychology in South Korea. From its very beginning, South Korea (to be called simply Korea henceforth) came under the influence of the United States. In the years immediately following liberation, the United States had occupation forces stationed in South Korea. During the Korean War, it had a large troop fighting together with the South

Korean Army as a part of the United Nations Forces.
During and after the war, Korea became heavily dependent
on foreign economic and other types of aid, and much of
the needed assistance came from the United States. Thus
the United States came to influence the economic and
cultural life of the Korean people profoundly,
particularly in the years immediately following the war,
which wiped out whatever little traditional culture was
left of Korea after the rigour of thirty-six years of
Japanese colonial rule. Only in the early 1960's, when
Korea had regained some social stability and achieved a
degree of economic development, did the American
influence begin to taper off and Korea begin to assert
its identity.

A few words concerning the academic traditions of
Korea as pertaining to psychology are in order. Until
the demise of the Yi Dynasty toward the end of the 19th
century, the prevailing academic tradition was Neo-
Confucianistic. In the 16th and 17th centuries, some of
the finest Korean scholars of this tradition wrote and
debated extensively on the nature of Yi (reason) and Ki
(something roughly equivalent to energy or drive), and
their mode of interaction. Their writings also touched
on the different kinds of human emotions and feelings
that could be found. Their arguments were mostly
rational with little empirical grounding, but the issues
tackled were clearly psychological, and not philosophical as was often supposed. This tradition should be
a part of Korean psychology, but modern psychology in
Korea has developed without being influenced by its
ideas.

The break from Korea's academic tradition was caused
by the introduction in the 19th century of modern or
western education in Korea. Modernization or westernization of the educational process in Korea was actually
led by two forces, the American (and some European)
missionaries and the Japanese colonial government. The
former opened up the private schools in Korea, and the
latter organized the public schools. Just prior to the
outbreak of the Pacific War in 1938, the Japanese
government deported all Americans and Europeans from
Korea, and banned the use of the Korean language in all
public and private schools in Korea either as subject
matter or as a language of instruction. Upon liberation
Korea regained its language, but the traditional
scholarship written exclusively with Chinese (as distinct
from Korean) characters did not return easily.

THE BEGINNING AND GROWTH OF PSYCHOLOGY IN KOREA

The first Korean psychologists were educated at various Japanese universities in the thirties and forties. Particularly important among them is Keijo (Seoul) Imperial University, which was the last of the six imperial universities established throughout Japan and at the same time the only regular university in the Korean peninsula. When it was started in 1924 psychology was an area of concentration within the Department of Philosophy, which in turn was a part of the Division of Law and Humanities. It had a large psychological laboratory, reputedly the best that could be found anywhere in the Far East and perhaps Asia. (It is said that Kurt Lewin had a hand in the design and planning of the laboratory.) Keijo Imperial University is important in the history of Korean psychology primarily because it produced five of the first nine Korean psychologists who were to found Korean psychology.

The first Korean student to major in psychology was Im Sok-Chae, who graduated from Keijo in 1930 (Tokyo and Kyoto Imperial Universities had their first Japanese psychology students graduate in 1905 and 1909, respectively (Umemoto & Hoshino, 1981)). By the time Keijo University was closed in 1945, it had produced seven Korean and eleven Japanese psychology majors. Of the seven Korean graduates, only five were physically present in South Korea when the country was liberated, and thus available to play a role in the building of Korean psychology.

The missionary-supported private colleges in Korea could not produce psychologists because, not being fully-fledged universities, they did not have departments of psychology or any concentrated courses in psychology. But these schools did teach psychology. The first instructors to teach psychology were American missionaries, and at Ewha Woman's College psychology was taught as early as 1917.

It is convenient to follow the post-liberation development of Korean psychology in five stages.

The founding period (1945-1953)

When the Japanese adademics left Korea in 1945, there were only nine Koreans who could be recalled to create new departments of psychology. All but one or two were holding nonacademic jobs at that time, and only one had a Master's degree. None held a professorship, but a few of them had worked at Keijo's Psychological Laboratory as assistant at one time or another after their first degrees.

These founders established the first departments of psychology in Korea. The first was established at Seoul National University in 1946. The first national university of Korea inherited the physical facilities of Keijo University, but unlike Keijo Seoul National University had an independent department of psychology. In the next year a second department of psychology was established at Chunag'ang University, and a third was established in 1951 at Ewha Woman's University right in the middle of the Korean War, at its campus in refuge in Pusan. Back in Seoul in 1953, a department of educational psychology was established at the College of Education of Seoul National University, a break away from the Department of Education. The first-generation psychologists of Korea, namely those who entered college before the outbreak of the Korean War, were produced by these first three departments. They number about ten if we consider those who are still active, and most of them were produced by the department at Seoul National University.

What the first-generation psychologists learned as students was mostly an American variety of psychology with occasional exposure to German books written by Gestalt psychologists. Japanese books were available but too intermittently, and American books were much more readily available. They were largely self taught, particularly after their first degrees. Thus from the very beginning the Japanese education of the colonial period had little influence on the development of Korean psychology.

The nine psychologists referred to earlier might be called the founders of Korean psychology. They are Im Sok-Chae (Keijo 1930), Yi Chae-Wan (U. Oregon? year unknown), Yun T'ae-Rim (Keijo 1931), Yi Chin-Suk (Keijo 1933), Yi Ui-Ch'ol (Keijo 1938), Song Paek-Son (Waseda 1940), Yi Pon-Yong (Keijo 1941), Pang Hyon-Mo (Tohoku 1941), and Ko Sun-Dok (Rikkyo 1943). These people were responsible for educating all of the first-generation psychologists and some of the second-generation psychologists. On February 2, 1946, seven of them gathered and launched the Korean Psychological Association. The first president was Im Sok-Chae, the first psychologist of Korea. The presidency passed in 1959 to Yi Chin-Suk, for many years the chairman of the department of psychology at Seoul National until his death in the early 1960's. During the Korean War Korean psychology lost two of its founders, Yi Pon-Yong and Yi Chae-Wan, to North Korea.

By 1950, Korea had two psychologists with Master's degree from American universities. Ko, one of the founders, returned in 1950 with a Master's degree in psychology and resumed teaching at Ewha and Seoul National. The other was Chong-Bom-Mo, who returned in 1952 with a Master's degree in educational psychology and began teaching and organizing what turned out to be a highly active psychometric laboratory at the College of Education, Seoul National University.

The recovery period (1954-1962)

The post-war period was characterized by a relative inactivity in research. During this period, only a few papers were published each year with no evidence of increase over the years (Cha, 1976). It was also a period in which the first-generation psychologists, educated by Korean professors, were fed into the departments. Only a few of them had Master's degrees when they entered the profession. As a matter of fact, the first Master's degrees in psychology were given in 1954, one at Seoul National (to Chong Yan-Un) and another at Ewha (to Chu Tong-Hye). By the end of this period, about half of them had a Master's degree. In Kim Ki-Sok came back from the United States with a Ph.D. in education, the first psychologist in Korea to have a doctorate.

Two more departments were added during this period, a department of psychology at Songkyunkwan University in 1954 and a department of educational psychology at Korea University in 1959 (to be remodelled in 1963 as a department of psychology). Then in 1961, in accordance with the Ministry of Education's university restructuring plan, the department of educational psychology at Seoul National was absorbed by the department of education, and the department at Ewha, which was a part of its college of education, was made a department of educational psychology (these two departments still remain that way today). This left three departments of psychology and two departments of educational psychology.

Graduate programmes in psychology were mostly created during this period. Seoul National University opened its graduate school in 1946, the first psychology major being admitted in 1950. Ewha Woman's University opened its graduate programme in psychology in 1952, Chung'ang University in 1963, Songkyunkwan University in 1958, and Korea University in 1963.

In the last year of this period, the Student Guidance Centre at Seoul National University was established. This centre is of some importance historically because for a time it served as the only training centre and clearing house for graduate and postgraduate students in all areas of psychology. Being the first major organization staffed largely by psychologists, it drew researchers and trainees from all departments of psychology and educational psychology. The centre was also instrumental in training the first generation of counselling psychologists (who came from the second-generation Korean psychologists), and in stimulating similar centres at other universities.

The period of take-off (1963-1973)

This third period was marked off purely on the basis of a new trend in research output. Starting from 1963, the number of papers published by psychologists began to grow at a phenomenal rate. From the previous base line of about four papers a year, the annual output increased to sixty-two papers by 1973, more than a fifteen-fold increase over the initial level (Cha 1976, p.79). In 1960 Korea was rocked by two major political upheavals, the April Student Uprising which brought down the civilian government of Sigman Rhee, and the May Military Revolution which ushered in the military regimes. It is not clear at all what caused the sudden turn in research output by Korean psychologists. One possible cause was the accumulation of scholars with a Master's degree. Master's theses constitute a significant portion of total research output in a country where the established scholars do not publish much, and thesis-based articles could easily appear in printed form via numerous college or department reviews and journals.

Other factors could be cited. The government began doling out small research grants to academics, hoping to stimulate research. Another factor could be the many research organizations which sprang up during this period. Toward its end no less than twelve research or service centres utilizing psychological knowledge were in existence in Korea. Most impor tant of all, life in Korea was regaining a degree of normalcy, and Korea itself was undergoing an economic "take-off" in the mid-sixties.

There were other developments marking this period. Second-generation psychologists of Korea arrived on the scene to teach at colleges and do research at newly established research centres. These were ten to fifteen years younger than the first-generation psychologists, nearly all already with a Master's degree, and many of whom went on to work for a doctorate. It was from this group that the first psychologists with a doctorate in psychology appeared, the first of whom graduated in West Germany in 1966. The first Korean psychologist to receive an American doctorate and return to Korea did so in 1971 (a few Koreans had received American doctorates in psychology in the sixties but not returned to Korea). At the start of this period, only two (both educational psychologists) held a doctorate, and fifteen held a Master's degree. At the end of the period twenty held a doctorate (six in psychology and fourteen in education), and sixty-four a Master's degree. Clearly, then, there was a large change in manpower in the profession of psychology at this time.

It took the second generation psychologists on the average fifteen years after the Bachelor's degree to become permanent faculty members in psychology departments of any kind (in Korea all teaching positions are tenured from the very beginning), whereas the first generation psychologists achieved the same status in the relatively short time of four to five years. The reason for the delay is obvious; despite the growing number of graduates holding a Master's degree or doctorate, the number and size of the faculty of departments of psychology stood still until 1977. There were only four departments of psychology (excluding two departments of educational psychology, one of which was established in 1971) through out the period.

The third period is also to be remembered as a time during which the first generation of applied psychologists was trained. These also came from the ranks of Korea's second generation psychologists. The first counselling psychologists received the necessary experience and training at various student guidance centres on college campuses, the first industrial psychologists at various research institutes and counselling centres recently established, and the first clinical psychologists at several medical schools. All received experience and training outside the schools they attended. In the case of clinical psychologists, they either became assistants in departments of psychiatry or entered a graduate programme in a medical school after their Bachelor's or Master's degree in psychology. These latter eventually received appointments as psychologists in the psychiatric wards of large hospitals. By the end of the 1970's, all of them had become full-time professors of psychology in the departments of neuropsychiatry in medical colleges. In this process of securing a place for themselves, they received little help from the main body of psychologists.

The period of diversification (1974-76)

The number of psychologists with advanced degrees continued to grow, and by 1976 Korean psychology had some thirty-four doctorate holders (of whom twenty-two had foreign degrees - nineteen from the U.S., two from West Germany, and one from France) and seventy-four Master's degrees. The remaining forty-two (of the members of the KPA 1976) had only a Bachelor's degree (Cha, 1976). This meant that one hundred and eight psychologists held advanced degrees in 1976, an increase of twenty-four since 1973. The number of psychologists holding full-time teaching positions in college stood at seventy-five in 1976 as compared to twenty-nine in 1965 (the figure for 1973 is not available). Since the number of psychology-related departments or the size of their faculty had not changed significantly, it means that psychologists found their way into departments other than psychology related departments.

The period of expansion (1977 to the present)

Until the end of 1976 there were only six departments of psychology (including two departments of educational psychology at two of the women's universities). Then in 1977 a new department of psychology was established at Pusan National University. This was the first department of psychology to be established in a so-called "regional" university, that is, a university located in a province and outside the capital city of Seoul. No-one was aware at the time that this was the start of a great wave of new departments. In the short duration of the next four years, no less than twelve new departments of psychology were created. Then in 1982 a department of educational psychology was added and in 1983 three more departments of psychology, making the total number of psychology-related departments in Korea up to twenty-three (nineteen departments of psychology, three of educational psychology, and one of industrial psychology). Korea now had four times as many departments related to psychology as in 1976. The number of full-time faculty members in that time rose from twenty-eight to almost eighty. The number of undergraduate major students rose from 582 in 1976 to more than 3,096 in 1983. The number of graduate students doubled, from 53 in 1976 to 199 (149 in the Master's and 50 in the doctoral programmes) in 1983, even though the number of graduate departments did not increase during the period.

This explosion in the number of departments and the number of students majoring in psychology was the result of a sudden turnabout in policy on the part of the Ministry of Education, which authorizes the creation of new departments in universities and sets quotas for the number of students to be admitted to a college or univerisity each year. It had been keeping a tight ceiling on the quotas for many years, thus allowing the number of high school graduates rejected by colleges to grow to such an extent that they threatened to become a social problem. The sudden shift in policy was part of an attempt to defuse the problem, part of a larger plan to cope with increases in the number of high school graduates seeking admission to college, and not a result of the influence of any particular individual or individuals. In 1980, for example, the Ministry allowed the national admissions quota to increase by as much as two hundred per cent in some universities. (The national quota was 50,395 in 1971, which was increased to 95,795 in 1976 and then to 305,264 in 1981.) Iin response to this many universities proposed to create new departments of psychology as a way of accommodating an increased influx of students, and the Ministry simply approved these proposals.

Whatever may have been the reasons for this change in the attitude of the Ministry of Education, psychologists in Korea were unprepared for it. The sudden increase in the number of departments and consequent demands for

full-time teaching personnel made a considerable impact
on the dynamics of Korean psychology. First, Seoul
ceased to be the uncontested centre of activities of
Korean psychologists. Though the city still harbours a
disproportionately large number of departments of
psychology (ten out of a total of twenty-three), now
other cities or regions are ready to compete with it as
centres of psychological activity. The city of Taegu is
a case in point, with as many as five departments within
its city limits and vicinity. Second, the role of the
Department of Psychology at Seoul National University as
the principal supplier of faculty members for departments
of psychology was threatened. More than ten of the new
positions created in recent years were filled by
graduates from the department of psychology at Korea
University. The department at Chung'ang University also
made some headway in this respect. Third, there was a
large influx of younger psychologists among the ranks of
full-time faculty members.

Many of the newly arriving academics were third-
generation psychologists of Korea and came with a minimum
of preparation to teach the specialities to which they
were assigned.   Many were brought back from applied
fields, and others came fresh out of Master's programmes.
According to the writer's count, sixty-four per cent of
the faculty members at these newly created departments
did not have a doctorate, whereas in the six older
departments only twenty-three per cent did not.

As the younger psychologists landed in the new
departments, the last of the founders of Korean
psychology still living in Korea retired as a professor,
in 1979. Two others are already dead and two lost to
North Korea, while two are still active in the
profession.

KOREAN PSYCHOLOGICAL ASSOCIATION

Since its establishment in 1946, the Korean
Psychological Association (KPA) remains the sole national
organization for all psychologists in Korea today. Its
membership size as of August 1983 stands at 248. A
Master's degree in psychology is the minimum
qualification for full membership. Exceptions are made
for those who are currently teaching psychology at
college or who can show evidence of experience in
psycholgogical research.

The increase in the number of psychologists holding graduate degrees inevitably led to diversification of the research interests of Korean psychologists. Because of the large size of the group attending its meetings and the increasing difficulty psychologists were experiencing in understanding others' research, the Korean Psychological Association (KPA) decided in 1974 that all paper-reading monthly meetings should be held separately by appropriate divisions instead of by the KPA itself as had been the practice until then. The following year, the KPA established two new divisions, the Division of Social Psychology and the Division of Developmental Psychology, making a total of four (the other two, the Divisions of Clinical Psychology and Industrial Psychology, had been established in 1964).

The KPA has five divisions, Clinical and Counselling Psychology, Industrial Psychology, Social Psychology, Developmental Psychology, and Experimental and Cognitive Psychology. At the latest count, these five divisions had 54, 41, 29, 18, and 16 registered members, respectively. Membership of the KPA is sufficient qualification for membership of any one of these divisions.

The Association holds an annual convention in October, at a different site each year. It also holds a Spring Symposium of Psychology each year, and more recently it has been conducting what have come to be called Winter Workshops, a series of lectures aimed at introducing the professionals to new developments in different areas of psychology.[2]

Twice yearly, the KPA publishes the Korean Journal of Psychology, its only official academic journal, with articles in Korean or English. Its English abstracts are carried by Psychological Abstracts. Another official publication of the KPA is the KPA Newsletter, published bimonthly in Korean. Although not an official journal of the KPA, the Division of Clinical and Counseling Psychology publishes an annual Journal of Clinical and Counseling Psychology.

Currently the KPA and the Division of Clinical and Counseling Psychology are jointly operating a licensing examination system under which qualified clinical and counselling psychologists are licensed. Because of their preponderance among its membership, the KPA is run mostly by the academics. So far, it has not developed a code of ethics, although there exists a standing committee on professional and ethical standards. It is affiliated with the International Union of Psychological Science and

is a member of the Korean Social Science Research
Council.

THE PRESENT STATUS OF PSYCHOLOGY IN KOREA

The KPA encompasses practically all active psychologists in Korea excepting perhaps a handful who do not
have an advanced degree but are active in certain applied
areas. The KPA membership size thus serves as a fairly
accurate estimate of the total number of psychologists in
Korea. As of August 1983, there were 298 names on the
KPA membership roster, of whom 50 were either inactive,
have left the profession, emigrated to another country,
or were otherwise not reachable. Of the remainder, 21
have a Bachelor's degree, 168 a Master's degree, and 71
(or 29 per cent) a doctorate. The breakdown of the KPA
members according to area of specialization shows that
the areas of clinical psychology (49) and counselling
psychology (37) represent the largest groupings. Next
largest are developmental psychology (28), industrial
psychology (26), social psychology (23), and educational
psychology (20). Next is the area of experimental
psychology (17), while the smallest areas are measurement
(8) and personality (8). (The remaining 32 could not be
placed in any of the above categories.) When compared
with the figures for 1976 (Cha, 1976), the figures for
such areas as clinical, counselling, developmental,
experimental (particularly cognitive), and social represent large increases since the previous year. The
increase is most dramatic for the area of clinical
psychology, which shows a net increase of 37 following
the production by graduate programmes in clinical psychology of a steady flow of clinical psychologists in the
latter seventies. The other five areas show an increase
of 7 to 16 over the same period.

The occupational breakdown of the Korean psychologists (the KPA members) shows by far the largest
single occupational group to be full-time college
instructors (152), followed by mental hospitals (20),
part-time college instructors (16), full-time researchers
(16), government officials including military officers
(6), psychological specialists in private firms (3),
nonprofessional employment in private firms or self-
employed (4), graduate students or unemployed (18), and
secondary school teachers (1). (The remaining 12 could
not be classified.)

Of the total of 71 doctorates, 36 came from a department of psychology (as contrasted with departments of education or educational psychology or other departments). Exactly half of the 36 psychology degrees came from a Korean university, and another 18 came from a foreign university (11 from the U.S., 5 from West Germany, one from France, and one from Canada). Of the other 35, 11 came from Korea, 23 from the U.S., and one from Japan.

Relatively large numbers of doctorates are represented in counselling, educational, social, developmental, and experimental psychology. This is to be expected in view of the large number of psychologists working in these areas. There are anomalies though. Although there are as many as 49 clinical psychologists, only 4 hold a doctorate, none from a foreign university. Likewise, although there are 26 industrial psychologists, only two hold a doctorate and none from a foreign university. All but one of the nine degrees in the area of experimental psychology were received since 1976. Despite the large increase in the number of doctorates, there are as yet no doctorate holders in Korea in such areas as physiological psychology, cognitive psychology and biopsychology. The nine doctorate holders in the "experimental" area all fall under the broad category of cognitive psychology (perception, memory, and verbal learning).

PSYCHOLOGY EDUCATION IN KOREA

At the undergraduate level, a concentration in psychology basically begins in the second year of college although a student's major is determined at the time of admission. Instruction relies heavily on lectures. In many cases textbooks assigned are in English, but this varies depending on the quality of the student body. There is likely to be a course specifically designed to train entering psychology majors to read psychology textbooks or articles written in English, and the student is introduced to this course at the earliest possible opportunity. This stress on English was partly a practice taken over from the post-liberation era when textbooks in Korean were scarce. Even today, there are not many introductory textbooks for specific areas of psychology written in Korean although there has been a rush to publish textbooks by Korean psychologists in the past five years.

Because of the stress on English, students at a more competitive department will have a good command of written English by the time they are in the third year of school. They may also study a second foreign language as part of a liberal education, but a textbook in a foreign language other than English is almost never used at any level of psychology instruction.

Students are encouraged to think independently, but they tend to be dependent and passive in their study partly because they find it very difficult to depart from the textbooks and read other materials, and partly because they have been brought up in an authoritarian culture.

Until now, especially at the more elitist departments of psychology, undergraduate education has been geared to preparation for an academic career. For example, the Department of Psychology at Seoul National University admitted only ten students to its undergraduate programme each year until the late 60's (in 1982 it began admitting 53 students). But many commencing students do not see much in the career of a psychologist. In other words, psychology is unpopular, particularly among male students for whom getting into a secure job which will also bring them wealth and high social position seems to be all important. For high school graduates, psychology as a vocational area is an unknown quantity. There is a high degree of ignorance about what psychology is on the part of general public. Furthermore, psychology has to compete with such traditionally valued areas as law, commerce and economics, the areas the general public think are conducive to becoming a high ranking government official, for long the ambition of both traditional Koreans and Japanese.

Among female students, psychology is quite popular. They feel less parental pressure to be in more traditional vocational areas, therefore there tend to be more female students in departments of psychology than in other departments. The figure varies from thirty to seventy per cent of all students in a department depending on the department. The less competition there is, the greater the proportion of female students in the department. The department of psychology at Pusan National University now has 66 male and 115 female students (it has no graduate students). At the graduate level, the sex ratio is more evenly balanced, and this is true for all graduate departments (except Ewha which admits only female students). The latest trend has been for more female students to seek graduate degrees. For example, of the seventeen doctoral students currently at the Department of Psychology at Seoul National University, seven are women.

At Korean universities, the Master's and doctoral programmes are completely separate. An applicant to the Master's programme has to pass an entrance examination, and performance here is the sole consideration for admission. The examination consists of a series of achievement tests and does not include ability tests of any kind. The applicant is required to submit undergraduate records, but these records rarely influence admission. The entrance examination typically includes tests on foreign languages, usually English and one other language (typically French or German). The make-up of the entrance examination for the doctoral programme is basically the same but has more difficult questions. Once admitted to the Master's programme, students have to complete course requirements (which can be done in three semesters), pass a qualifying examination, and write a thesis. The entire process is repeated at the doctoral level. These processes are very much similar to those used in American universities except that in Korea the two programmes are separated. Since the process is repeated, a graduate student has to go through four qualifying examinations including two entrance examinations, a thesis and a dissertation before getting a doctorate. The titles of the degrees given to a student of psychology are Master of Letters and Doctor of Letters.

The Master's programme is run more rigorously than the doctoral programme. The Master's candidates are generally full-time students, guided through a well-developed curriculum. But once in the doctoral programmes they are soon employed elsewhere outside their schools, in many instances at some other university or at a research institute. Two factors contribute to produce this situation, lack of study grants to enable doctoral students to become full-time students, and shortage of teaching personnel in Korea. This shortage may continue for another five years and is not limited to the field of psychology, although the situation for psychology has been made worse by the unexpected sharp increase in the number of new departments of psychology in the last five years.

Another reason why the doctoral programme cannot be carried out at a more intensive level is the relative small number of staff in a typical department of psychology with a graduate programme. The modal size is four or five professors, with the largest department (at Seoul National University) having eleven. As the doctoral students cannot study full-time, the number of doctoral students in the departments is high. For example, the Department of Psychology at Seoul National University has seventeen doctoral students, some in their sixth year in the doctoral programme (which means about nine years in the graduate programme). The department has lately been granting an average of only one degree a year, but is still admitting new students.

ACADEMICS IN KOREA

A professor is expected both to teach and to do research, but the teaching load is heavy so that it is very difficult to expect highly original research. A professor is required to teach at least three courses a semester, which means at least nine hours of teaching a week, but many have to teach as many as five courses a semester, which means fifteen hours of teaching a week. Naturally, the load carried by a professor is heavier in smaller departments and for junior members.

The number of years served within the university where he or she is currently employed is the single most important factor determing a professor's promotion. A lack of a minimum of research work may delay a professor's promotion, but any amount of research will not speed up the process. Evaluating a professor on the basis of research is still considered too subjective and difficult a task. Research is funded by the government or by private foundations; research support is quite readily available in Korea so that it is possible to have a research grant almost every year. However, money from private foundations has become scarce during the last two years. The sex balance in a faculty varies from department to department. Some departments maintain an all male faculty whereas some other departments of psychology have one female professor in their faculty. Departments at women's universities, and all departments of educational psychology, have more female professors among their faculty. In all, 19 per cent (15 out of 79) of all faculty members at the departments of psychology and related areas are female; almost of them arrived in their present faculty positions after the mid 1970's. The sudden increase in the faculty positions available in recent years considerably assisted women to make inroads into the profession.

Departments of psychology and other related departments in Korea are almost exclusively staffed by Korean professors, but they are quite open to foreigners desiring to lecture, say for a year or so. The universities in many cases have funds available to cover salary and housing. The Fulbright Commission in Korea also has programmes supporting American scholars in Korea for a fixed period. A scholar who is not native to Korea may also become a faculty member, particularly at a private university. In either case, a good academic background and fluency in English would be important. Fluency in Korean would also be highly desirable, but we know that it is unrealistic to expect this from a foreigner.[3] To date there has been no case of a foreigner staying as a lecturer in one of the departments of psychology in Korea although foreign guest speakers do speak at seminars or colloquia from time to time. Their short visits to Korea, ranging from a few days to a week, are often supported by university funds in the form of an honorarium and airfare to and from Japan. Guest speakers so far come from the U.S., West Germany, Canada, Japan and India.

For obvious reasons, there is as yet no fully-fledged sabbatical system in operation in Korean universities. But there are many other ways in which a professor can leave teaching for a year or less and do research. One is through a professor exchange programme controlled by the Ministry of Education, whereby professors in the Seoul area and those in the outlying areas trade their place of work for half to one year. If the departments and the professors involved find such an exchange agreeable, the professors move to each other's department, teaching probably one course only. A second way is to become a temporary research professor, the term being usually one year, and the openings quite limited. Those selected will be freed from normal teaching obligations while being fully paid. A third way is to be on the Ministry of Education's programme under which professors are sent out to various countries to study and do research for a year, with accommodation and travel expenses paid in addition to normal salary. Priority is given to those professors who have no experience of studying abroad and are under fifty years of age, or to professors with a doctorate from a foreign university who have not been abroad in the last ten years.

Professors in Korea rarely interact intellectually with professors in other areas. Primary obstacles to such interaction seem to be the heavy teaching load and the other many duties thrust upon the professors. Nor do psychologists attend international conferences often, though small groups have attended three international conferences, twice in Japan and once in Taiwan. Visits by Korean psychologists to another country for attending research seminars are more frequent, but such visits are limited to the very few who have a good command of one or another foreign language. There has been very little collaborative research with psychologists from other countries. In the few cases where this has occurred it was with American psychologists, with one recent case of collaboration with a psychologist in Hong Kong.

The larger among the Korean universities take all major international journals, including all the American Psychological Association journals. But often the issues before the early 1970's are not available. The composition of the psychological journals drawn is heavily weighted toward those published in English and originating from the U.S. So far, very few Korean psychologists have published articles in international journals.

Now that Korean psychology is nearing its fortieth year, the handful of founders who saw it through the difficult days of its beginnings have all but passed away from the scene. Though temporarily stunted in growth in the early fifties because of the war, psychology in Korea has shown itself resilient, keeping up a steady rate of growth until the late seventies when it achieved a phenomenal growth spurt. Today, it has four times as many departments of psychology and educational psychology, six times as many students majoring in the subject, and three times as many faculty members as it had before 1976. In the same period, the membership of the Korean Psychological Association has nearly doubled, and now stands at almost 250, a size comparable to that for any other national social science organization in Korea. At least in size, Korean psychology has come of age. Soon, Korean psychologists may be able to play a significant role in the development of the science of psychology.

NOTES

1. During the turbulent years immediately following liberation, both professors and students on every campus were split into warring pro- and anti-communist camps. Yi Pon-Yong was one of the few academics who did not flee during the brief period at the beginning of the war when North Korean forces occupied Seoul and the university was under communist control. When the North Koreans were forced to evacuate, the small group of leftist professors, as well as those others who fell into the hands of the communists, were marched to the North. Having been an active communist during the occupation, it would not have been safe for Professor Yi Pon-Yong to have remained even had he wished to do so. Yi Chae-Wan was the only one of the founders to become a teacher with a degree from an American university, but it is known he returned from the USA with an anti-American sentiment. He too remained in Seoul during the occupation, but whether he went over to North Korea, and if so under what circumstances, is not certain.

2. These workshops, begun by a group of young professionals not acting under the auspices of the KPA, have been an enormous success, and the Association now organizes them on an annual basis. It seems that in a country like Korea where well-trained specialized professionals are few in number, such workshops are a good way of pooling resources.

3. The best language programme specially designed for foreigners is at Yonsei University in Seoul, but Korean is a difficult language to acquire for a person whose native tongue is Indo-European.

REFERENCES

CHA,J.-H. History and present status of Korean psychology and possible directions for interdisciplinary research among social sciences, _Social Science Journal_ (The College of Social Sciences, Seoul National University), 1976, 1, 61-100 (in Korean).

CHA, J.-H. Korean psychology: A study of a science and profession, _Social Science Journal_ (Korean Social Science Research Council), 1978, 5, 142-184 (abridged English version of the above).

CHA, J.-H. Psychology (Academic traditions of Korea. 11), _Choson Monthly_, November 1982, 331-357.

UMEMOTO, T., and HOSHINO, M. Historical development of psychology in Japan. Paper presented at Joint IACCP-ICP Asian Regional Meeting, Taipei, Taiwan, August 10-12, 1981.

ACKNOWLEDGMENTS

The writer wishes to express his gratitude to the many faculty members of various departments of psychology who willingly cooperated in supplying the needed information. They are too numerous to be mentioned by name. He is especially grateful for the information provided by Dr. Sun-Dok Ko. Sok-Chae Yi, in the early stage of this study which started several years ago, Chang-Hyon Song, and Song-Hi Kim, in the later stage of the study, assisted in the collection of data, and their help is gratefully acknowledged.

The writer is also grateful to Ch'ung-Hui Chong of the Ministry of Education for clarifying the nature of the policy change regarding the establishment of new departments of psychology.

12

Japanese Psychology: Historical Review and Recent Trends

Akira Hoshino
and Takeo Umemoto

HISTORICAL SKETCH

Being an country of four main islands which make up its bulk (Honshu, the main central island; Hokkaido in the north; Shikoku bordering the inland Sea; and Kyushu in the south) with an area of 142,800 sq. miles, Japan has not been susceptible to invasion. As it is rather close to the Asian mainland it has had fairly easy access to advanced foreign cultures. This has given it many points of contact with other Asian cultures while simultaneously enabling it to develop a highly independent one of its own.

Shinto is the natural indigenous religion of Japan. All natural objects and phenomena are considered as having Kami, shinto gods. Gradually its practice extended to the worship of ancestors. From the nineteenth century, it was regarded as the national religion, and the Emperor became deified. After the First World War the practice of religion and the functions of the state were separated. Buddhism was introduced in the sixth century via China and Korea and, until the twelfth century, was the religion of the aristocracy. From the thirteenth century it became popular among the common people. At this time Zen Buddhism also became popular among the warrior class. Buddhism has been the principal religion of the Japanese people since that time.

In 1549 St. Francis Xavier introduced Christianity to Japan. At first, some of the ruling class were interested in western culture and were friendly towards the propagation of the Catholic religion. Later, it was considered a danger to the feudal shogunate and was repressed by power groups. After Japan established diplomatic relations with the West in the nineteenth century, propagation of the Christian faith again began to flourish. At present there are about three hundred and seventy thousand Catholics and four hundred and ninety thousand Protestants in Japan.

In the seventeenth century, the feudal shogunate embarked on a period of isolation from the rest of the world although they continued to trade with China and Holland. The main elements of this policy were the exclusion of Catholic missionaries and traders whom, it was thought, might bring military forces to invade Japan from their homelands of Spain and Portugal. A conservative political and social system founded in the early seventeenth century was preserved until the middle of the nineteenth century. During this period levels of domestic manufacturing and commerce developed, producing a period of prosperity, also marked by rapid cultural and educational advances.

The arrival at Uraga in 1853 of Commodore Perry from America finally broke Japan's period of isolation, and this event led to the resumption of overseas trade and international relations. In 1868 a new imperial government was formed with Emperor Meiji as its head after the Tokugawa shogunate collapsed suddenly under pressure from local lords and warriors.

By the end of the nineteenth century, Japan's industrial revolution was flourishing. The military rose to political prominence and gained control over both domestic and international policies. Japan by this time had begun a quest for world power which was to include conquests in Korea, Manchuria, China and finally Southeast Asia. Defeat in the Second World War put an end to the country's aspirations in that direction. In 1945, after the emperor's decision to surrender right after the bombing of Hiroshima and Nagasaki by the American Air Force, Japan experienced its first taste of occupation by foreign military forces. During the occupation, a wide range of social and educational reforms were made to implement equal rights for the people.

Today, as Asia's dominant economic power, Japan has begun to emerge from under the protective wing of the United States. Reversion of the Ryuku Islands from the US to Japan in 1972 was symbolic of the nation's total post-war recovery by then.[1]

THE EARLY PERIOD OF PSYCHOLOGY IN JAPAN

Psychology in the western sense of the word has roots in Japan that go back over a hundred years. Records indicate that it was taught as far back as 1874 at the Kaisei Sho, the predecessor of the Imperial University of Tokyo, but the beginning of psychology in Japan is taken to be the translation and publication in Japanese of Joseph Haven's Mental Philosophy (1869) in 1875 by Nishi Amane (1826-1894). He was the first Japanese scholar to study philosophy and social science formally in the West, and he introduced these subjects to Japan after his return home.

Knowledge, technology and other aspects of western civilisation were substantially introduced during the eighteenth and nineteenth centuries before the early Meiji period. Both the author and translator of the above mentioned book sought, for the first time, a scientific knowledge of human nature and mind set apart from moralistic or metaphysical speculation. The word "psychology" was translated by Nishi into Shinrigaku and has since been used widely, not only in Japan, but in China.

There was, of course, psychological thought and speculation in Japan before the 19th century. One will find some psychological insights wherever there is some thought given to human beings, and Japan is no exception. Almost all the literature of Buddhism has some psychological insight especially the excellent writings by Kukai, Dogen and several of the Zen monks.

In the Edo period (1603-1868), Ishida Baigan (1685-1744) founded a school of Shingaku ("Heart Learning"), a conventional morality, which became a popular psychology among citizens at that time. Also Kamada Ryuo Hosai (1754-1821), a Shingaku scholar, tried to invigorate this school of thought with his knowledge and understanding of western Science and of Buddhism.[2]

The first modern Japanese psychologist was Motora Yujiro (1858-1912), who received a Ph.D under Stanley Hall at Johns Hopkins and became the first lecturer in psychophysics at the Imperial University of Tokyo in 1888. He built the first laboratory of psychology in Asia in 1903 and attempted to clarify the fundamental problems in psychology, theoretically as well as experimentally.

Dr. Matsumoto Matataro (1865-1943), who was one of the first Japanese to receive his training in psychology in Japan (under Motora), also received a degree under Edward W. Scripture at Yale and later moved to Leipzig, where he studied under Wundt. After his return home he was appointed to the first chair of psychology at the Imperial University of Kyoto. He built there the second laboratory of psychology in Japan. In 1913 he was appointed professor of psychology at the Imperial University of Tokyo as the successor to Motora, and stayed there until his retirement in 1926. In 1927 Matsumoto became the first president of Japanese Psychological Association and founded the Japanese Journal of Psychology. Motora and Matsumoto were both directly or indirectly influenced by Wundt and were therefore responsible for the Wundtian tradition (structuralism) taking root in the academic world of psychology in Japan.

We may call the roughly fifty year period from 1878 to 1925 the period of enlightenment in psychology because, during this time, textbooks and research articles from such countries as Germany, England and the United States were imported and partly translated into Japanese. University chairs in psychology were established and psychological laboratories were built not only at the national universities but also at several private universities such as Keio, Waseda, Doshisha, Kanseigakuin and Nihon Universities.[3]

In 1905, the department of psychology at the Imperial University of Tokyo graduated the first seven psychology students in Japan. This was followed by three students graduating from the Imperial University of Kyoto in 1909. There were two other national universities, the imperial universities of Tohoko and Kysusho, from which the first psychology graduates appeared soon after 1927. Besides the imperial and private universities, there were several national colleges and normal schools where university graduates could find teaching positions, although only a few found positions in academic institutions. Others went to child guidance centres, advertising agencies, reform homes for delinquent boys, and so on.

Dr. Matusmoto himself was very much interested in not only experimental but also applied fields of psychology. His works on "Psychocinematics" in 1910 and "Intellect" in 1914, stimulated young students in the Taisho era (1911-1926) into organising a "society on human efficiency." In 1909, Matsumoto established the "Society of Popular Psychology" with Drs. Motora and Fukurai Tomokichi, and the first popular lecture series was held at the Imperial University of Tokyo on such topics as "colours of Kimono (Japanese dress)", "a man of quick response and slow response," "the lies of children," and the like. It was recorded that more than four hundred people attended the lectures and many people could not even enter the full auditorium at the university. When similar lecture meetings were held in local cities such as Nagano, Niigata, Sendai, Yamagata and others, more than one thousand people attended each time.

However, an unhappy incident occurred. Professor Fukurai of the Imperial University of Tokyo became involved in the study of extra-sensory phenomena after he completed his doctoral dissertation on hypnosis. As the department of psychology was trying to adhere strictly to a scientific approach to the study of psychological phenomena, he was accused of non-scientific deviation by some of the younger scientists and forced to resign his position in 1913.

Nevertheless, popular or applied psychology has been a continuing trend running parallel to academic Japanese psychology throughout its history. Among the thirteen hundred or so articles of psychology published in the period from 1874 to 1932, over seven hundred were in applied fields.

Changes in the trend of academic psychology in the first twenty years of the Showa era (1926-1945) were evident in the impact made by young psychologists returning from study abroad. At that time there were thirty-three Japanese psychologists who took advanced degrees in psychology after studying in Europe or America. The "Psychological Register", published in the United States in 1931, contained forty-six names of Japanese psychologists who had specialised in the studies of sensation, emotion, animal behaviour, intelligence of children, teaching, and problems in industry.

Dr. Kuwata (1882-1967), one of the first graduates from the Department of Psychology, Imperial University of Tokyo, introduced Wundt's "Volkerpsychologie" as well as his experimental psychology and established the Research Institute for Oriental Culture on the campus. Professor Masuda Koreshige, who once studied at the University of Chicago, taught animal psychology and seriously concentrated his efforts on establishing empirical methods of psychology until his death in 1933.

ADVENT OF GESTALT PSYCHOLOGY AND INDIGENOUS PSYCHOLOGY

One of the most important events in the Showa period (1926-1945) was the advent of Gestalt Psychology. A number of Japanese psychologists were greatly influenced by Gestalt Psychology which was first introduced in Japan by Takagi Teiji who had studied under Titchener. In 1923, Onoshima and Sakuma visited Germany, worked under Kohler and Lewin and after their return openly espoused the theory. As a result there was a tendency for Japanese psychologists to be strongly motivated toward research in the field of perception. Their studies featured minute surveys of each concrete perceptual phenomenon, and this kind of minuteness, in surveys and meticulously detailed experimental exploration, has been one of the character-istics of Japanese psychological research to this day.

However, not all psychologists contented themselves with explorations of only the perceptual process as such. A few took a critical attitude toward this new school and there were severe debates over the merits and defects of Gestalt Psychology. Also in the period, pioneering attempts were made at developing the psychology of memory, learning, children's social behaviour (such as social facilitation and competition), and human group organisation.

After the First World War there was an increase in the number of psychologists who studied abroad, partly because of the temporary improvement in Japan's economic situation due to the rise in value of the currency. Changes in academic psychological trends were evident through the efforts of those students returning home. After returning, they became the leading Japanese psychologists of their day and this practice continued right up to the fifties with a break during the Second World War. Among those returning from abroad, Yatabe Tatsuro, who studied under Pieron at the Sorbonne, established his own system of psychology, and wrote volumes on the psychology of thinking and the history of conative psychology; Kanae Sakuma, who studied at Berlin and worked with Kohler and Lewin, established the foundations of Japanese phonology; Koga Yukiyoshi, who studied at London under Spearman, introduced psychometric methods to the Japanese; and Takagi Sadaji, who studied in Clark under Titchener, introduced experimental methodology to Japanese psychology.

There were several psychologists who made pioneering attempts to analyse the psychological concepts indigenous to Japanese culture. Kuroda Ryo did experimental research on the concept of kan,[4] intuition or sub-consciousness, and published two books in 1933 and 1938. Chiba Tanenari studied the concept of koyuishiki, consciousness proper, in 1935. Tachibana Kakusho studied the concept of sabi[5] in 1938.

In 1957, Sato Koji, a professor of Kyoto University and a representative of Japan at ICP from 1959 to 1970, established the journal Psychologia: an International Journal of Psychology in the Orient, wherein he published several articles on Zen Buddhism and attracted much interest from around the world in oriental psychology.

During the Second World War many young and able psychologists were forced to do military service and military research (such as personnel selection, aptitude surveys and testing for aviation). As the war became more intense it became practically impossible to perform fundamental studies and this unfortunate situation prevailed for nearly ten years. However, studies such as those on individual differences, intelligence levels measured by means of the translated Binet and Stanford-Binet Scales, and studies of personality measured by the Introvert-Extrovert test and the Uchida-Kraepelin performance test, were carried out during wartime and in the immediate post-war period. Some pioneering works were even done on clinical studies of psychosis, aphasia and problem children during the pre-war period.

In the late twenties, the thirties and the first half of the forties psychology courses were taught not only in established national universities but in at least five private universities such as Waseda, Keio and Nihon in Tokyo, Doshisha in Kyoto and Kansei Gakuin near Kobe, as well as in twenty higher schools (liberal arts or prep schools for university).

TRENDS IN EDUCATION AND RESEARCH

Traditionally education in Japan as elsewhere has been the prerogative of the ruling class, but, after the Meiji restoration, the Government established a formal education system from elementary school to university. In 1872 the first compulsory educational system was introduced. Later the French educational system and, after the Second World War, elements of the American curriculum were also incorporated into the Japanese educational system. From the end of the Second World War until the seventies, Japan was strongly influenced by American culture and education[6] which spread to all aspects of living and knowledge. However in spite of foreign influence the language of instruction has remained

Japanese even at colleges and universities except at a few private universities where some foreigners teach classes in other languages. Most Japanese students can read English or another foreign language but most of them cannot speak it since the formal entrance examinations[7] do not require them to listen to or speak it. Most textbooks are written in Japanese although some English material is used in advanced seminar classes. In spite of the plethora of universities, competition for the top ones is severe with something like three to five students competing for each place. Ironically the competition for the middle and lower ranked universities is even higher since many students apply to these as a form of security while biding their time until they obtain the qualifications necessary to make them eligible for entrance to one of the higher ranked ones.

Psychology has been no exception to foreign influences and has been confronted with rapid developments in American concepts, theories and methodologies, especially in the fields of social, applied, and clinical psychology. This influence has also been strong in the field of experimental psychology. The changed characteristics of Japanese experimental and applied psychology can be summarized in the following seven statements:

(1) In experimental psychology, the weight of research which has lain for the most part on perception and cognition has continued in this area whereas studies in learning, motivation and physiological psychology have greatly increased.
(2) New laboratory experimental methods have been introduced, utilizing electronic devices such as macro computers. By such means, studies in such areas as the nervous system and social group response patterns has become more effective.
(3) In various fields of psychology, statistical methods have been introduced and data from laboratory experiments and social surveys have been analyzed in terms of their distribution, significant differences, correlation and cluster. This was achieved at first by use of the abacus, then by hand-calculators and finally by electronic computers.
(4) A remarkable transition in theories of personality has been observed. This has gone from "typology" through "trait theory" to "dynamic theory"; the work of Gestalt psychologists such as Lewin, and analytic scholars such as Freud and Jung have become especially popular as has

the translated works of Gordon Allport and Hans Eysenck.
(5) In more applied areas such as clinical psychology,
Wechsler's intelligent scales, the Rorschach test, TAT,
Doll play, Sand Play, Baum (Tree) Test and other projective techniques have been utilized by standardization of
the questions, and making the scoring and interpreting
procedures suitable for the Japanese. Various methods in
counselling and psychotherapy including group approaches
have been utilised with clients, patients, psychology
students in training and schoolteachers and nurses.
(6) A section of Experimental Social Psychology have been
added to the department of psychology in some national
universities such as the University of Kyushu and the
University of Tokyo probably because of its significance
for the post-war democratization of Japanese social
systems, with its potential for assessing public opinion,
group dynamics and interpersonal communication. This is
regarded as the new area of expansion in scientific
psychology.
(7) The reformed educational system in post-war Japan
brought tremendous opportunities in jobs for psychologists and instructors of psychology. Seven national
universities of education as well as faculties of
education in more than forty universities were established in the fifties and sixties. Each university or
faculty was allowed to employ more than two psychologists. Since educational and/or adolescent psychology
courses are required for the secondary school teachers'
certificate, many psychologists have been given opportunities for working on teaching and research on child
development, learning and teaching, adjustment and mental
health, group structure and processes.

We may add to these trends the expansion of job
opportunities in the area of correctional psychology. The
Ministry of Justice and the Family Courts opened positions for Bachelors in psychology at its central and
local (governmental) classification offices, correctional
institutions for juvenile delinquents, and family courts
through a qualifying examination at the national level
held once a year. It is estimated that more than three
hundred psychologists are now working for correctional
institutions in Japan.

Japan has no licensing arrangements for psychologists at the present time nor diploma or equivalent
course for professional training. However, further
education in psychology is possible by way of M.A.,

M.Ed., Ph.D. and Ed.D. programmes in graduate schools. Psychology is recognised as a profession only within the grounds of academia. However this has not prevented the flourishing of professional academic psychological associations.

PSYCHOLOGICAL ASSOCIATIONS

In 1983, at least fourteen nationwide professional associations were in existence, some of them only recently established. They have offered opportunities for presenting papers and for publishing research results. Most of them have annual meetings at least once a year and publish a journal regularly or occasionally. The oldest and leading association is the Japanese Psychological Association. An official committee meeting with representatives from each of the ten associations established before 1980 is held monthly for purposes of coordinating and cooperation. The function of the committee is to exchange professional information and discuss problems in the overall psychology world. A newsletter called Saikologisto is edited and published occasionally by the coordinating committee and the number of subscribers to this newsletter is, at present, seven thousand, equivalent to the total number of psychologists in Japan.

CURRENT PROBLEMS AND PERSPECTIVES

As Shirai Tsune, Professor Emeritus of Tokyo Christian Women's University, pointed out at the 3rd Asian Cross-Cultural Psychology Convention in 1981, the status of female psychologists in Japan has not been well recognised. Although the number of female psychologists has increased in every professional organization and paper reading, the number who hold positions in the established universities and research institutions has not kept pace. Many female psychologists are working either on a part-time basis, or full-time but at a lower level of the academic hierarchy (such as instructor/assistant) or in the applied areas as, for example, a child guidance counselor or play therapist. Among the more than twenty members of the board in each professional association, less than fifteen per cent are female psychologists. This means that the psychological world in

Japan is, as in other countries, dominated by males. However, not only the number but the quality of psychological research studies and practice by female psychologists in Japan may be expected to increase.

Two further related problems concern the lack of professionalisation in the practice of psychology. Both authors are of the opinion that curricula and type of instruction in psychology in Japan are far from satisfactory because of a lack of professional training when compared to counterparts in the United States and Europe. The present two and a half years of coursework in psychology offered in most liberal arts colleges, faculties of letters or education are not sufficient to qualify a graduate of one of these institutions to do research. Even at the Master's level with the writing of a thesis there is insufficient space in the curriculum reserved for the study of basic and advanced general psychological knowledge, so that potential candidates for higher degrees find that they have to engage in further preparatory study in many areas before embarking on postgraduate research. This kind of problem is caused not only by insufficient funds and a lack of personnel with adequate professional training but by insufficient foresight in planning curricula and application in seeing them carried out.

Related to this is the problem of sectionalism or sekushonarisumu. Most psychology departments are concerned only with the welfare of their own members including their graduates and not with the profession as a whole. This mentality filters even into the psychological associations which have, until very recently, been more concerned with academic matters and publishing journals than with the interdependent nature of research, teaching and practice. Thus while great advances in specialised areas of perception, physiological psychology and learning have taken place amongst the groups of psychologists concerened with those activities, they have occurred at the expense of the development of a recognised profession communicating effectively with all of its members.

Another problem is that we have not greatly contributed to the development of psychology in the world at large or even in Asia, except with the publication of individual papers in international journals and in the English-language publication Psychologia. Japan did however host the twentieth International Congress of Psychology in Tokyo in 1972.

CONCLUSIONS

After reviewing the trends in psychology in Japan what kind of work should be done next? As sensible and responsible Asian psychologists what should we do now? The following three proposals have been made by Hoshino (1979):

(1) To edit and publish a volume of collected papers in English, choosing from among the great contributions in Japan and other countries, those past scientific and clinical achievements of each country, in order to make a contribution and share it with people of similar and differing viewpoints in Asia.
(2) To increase the exchange of ideas and information, and get acquainted with the people of other countries in order to better understand their ways of feeling, thinking, motivation and interpersonal relationships.
(3) To promote cross-cultural or inter-cultural studies, collaborating on an equal basis with other cultures, including the sharing of financial costs in appropriate proportions.

More than the above, we ought to strengthen our partnerships and set a firm foundation for joint ventures in psychology in Asia as much as in other regions of the world.

NOTES

1. Part of the information in this section was gathered from the All Asia Guide (12th ed. 1982), compiled by the editors from information contributed by Far Eastern Economic Review correspondents in the region.
2. The term shingaku was originally used to refer to a school of Chinese philosophy developed by Lu Xianshan (1139-92) and Wang Yangming (1472-1529). It combined elements of the teachings of Shinto, Confucianism and Buddhism into doctrines aimed at the moral edification of the common people and well suited to the growing merchant class (Kodansha Encyclopaedia of Japan, pp.111-112).
3. In 1980 there were 93 national universities, 34 prefectural and municipal universities, 319 private universities and 520 junior colleges.
4. Kan is an important concept referring to intuition, the so-called "sixth sense", premonition, a knack

of doing things, inspiration and sudden realisation. Kuroda Ryo's experimental work on Kan in the thirties discerned two distinct aspects. The first is an intuitive power revealed in cognition and judgement while the second is _kotsu_ (a knack or physical skill) which manifests itself in the handling of objects or in other voluntary acts. It is _kotsu_ which Japan's artists and artisans have traditionally sought to attain in their works and performances. In common parlance however, the two nuances of _kan_ are not distinguished.

5. _Sabi_ is an ideal expressed in the poetic form of _haikai_ (or _haiku_ consisting of seventeen syllables arranged in lines of five, seven and five). It points towards the medieval aesthetic combining elements of old age, loneliness, resignation and tranquillity yet the colourful plebeian qualities of the Edo culture are also present (_Kodansha Encyclopaedia of Japan_ vol. 6, p.361).

6. Following the American system compulsory education for the first nine years, which did not become available to all children until 1947, was introduced.

7. As part of the entrance examination system, students are required to take a _Kyotsu Ichiji_ (common primary) achievement test, the results of which are sent to each university for which the student applies, and this is taken into account along with other (secondary) achievement tests set by each university. Private colleges and universities set their own criteria for entrance – usually a combination of achievement tests, an essay test and/or interview using a documentary screening system.

REFERENCES

AKISHIGE, Y. (ed.) Psychological Studies on Zen, part I. _Bulletin of the Faculty of Literature Kyushu University_, 1968.

AKISHEGE, Y. (ed.) Psychological studies on Zen, part II. _Bulletin of the Zen Institute of Komazawa University_, 1977.

HIDANO, T. Trends in researches of Educational psychology. In _Collected Papers for the 41st Annual Convention Japanese Psychology Association_, 1977, p. 87-90 (in Japanese).

HIDANO, T. (ed.) _Trends in current psychology in Japan 1946-1980_. Kawashima Shoten, Tokyo. 1980 (in Japanese).

HOSHINO, A. Current trends in psychology in Japan. _Psychologia_, 1979 Vol.XXII, pp. 1-20.

HOSHINO, A. Psychology in Japan. In _Kodansha Encyclopaedia of Japan_. Kodansha International, Tokyo. 1980

OGOSHI, T. Recent trends in clinical psychology in Japan. In S. Mizuyama and Y. Emi (eds.) _Clinical Psychology_. Fukumura Shuppan, Tokyo. 1978 (in Japanese).

OYAMA, T. Trends in research of experimental psychology. In _Collected Papers for the 41st Convention Japanese Psychological Association_, 1977, pp.99-102 (in Japanese).

REISCHAUER, E. O. _The Japanese_. Harvard University Press, Massachusetts. 1977.

SAGARA, M. Presidential address. _Procedings of the XXth International Congress of Psychology_, 1972, pp. 11-15

SATO, K. Zen from a personological viewpoint. _Psychologia_, 1968, 11, pp.3-24.

SUKEMUNE, S. Recent Trends in Child Psychology. In T. Fujinaga _et al._ (eds.) _Annual Review of Child Psychology_. Kanekoshobo, Tokyo. 1978 (in Japanese).

TANAKA, Y. The status of Japanese experimental psychology. _Annual Review of Psychology_, 1966, 17, 233-272.

THE JAPANESE SOCIETY OF SOCIAL PSYCHOLOGY. _Social Psychology in Japan: a brief guide_. 1972.

THE 20TH CONGRESS OF JAPANESE EDUCATIONAL PSYCHOLOGY PUBLICATION COMMITTEE. (eds.) _Symposium on Educational Psychology: History and Perspectives 1959-1978_. Kawashima Shoten, Tokyo. 1980 (in Japanese).

YOSHIDA, M. The research trends in each country - Japan. In T. Suenaga (ed.) _Koza Shinrigaku vol. 1: History and Trends_. Tokyo University Press, Tokyo. 1972 (in Japanese).

WAGATSUMA, H. Major Trends in social psychology in Japan. _The American Behavioral Scientist_, 1969, XII, pp.36-45.

13

Appendix: Notes on Psychology in Macau

INTRODUCTION

Macau is situated about 60 kilometres to the west of Hong Kong and consists of six square miles (including the islands of Taipa and Coloane). It is a Chinese territory with a Portuguese administration and a community of 400,000, ninety-seven per cent of whom are Chinese. It presents itself to the world as a colourful and dynamic entertainment and resort attraction, the major source of livelihood of the people being derived from the tourist industry.

Macau is developing commercially and socially at an exceedingly fast pace. It is experiencing what Hong Kong had previously encountered but on a much more intensified scale. Unlike Hong Kong, which has a high degree of influence from the West superimposed on a Chinese population with highly flexible and adaptive abilities, Macau has been under the simultaneous influences of the West, Portugal in particular, and Mainland China. Most of the Chinese inhabitants were either born locally or immigrated from nearby Chinese provinces. Whilst those who live in fairly remote areas and engage themselves in agricultural pursuits still conduct their lives in a traditional Chinese manner, those who live in urban districts have, in many aspects, taken up the western style of living. One pervasive western influence has been the infiltration of Portuguese culture. Portuguese priests and merchants were in Macau as long ago as 1557, but intense Portuguese cultural impact was not felt until 1887 when Portugal formally acquired political sovereignty over Macau from the Chinese Government. The pervasive and subtle Portugese enculturation was partially channelled through or accomplished by its highly centralized form of colonial government. However, in 1984 the Legislative Assembly was dissolved by Portugal at the request of the governnor, Vasco Almeida e Costa, and new electoral laws were introduced with a view to making the assembly more democratically representative. It is not yet clear whether Portuguese administration will be brought to an end when British rule ends in Hong Kong.[1]

The population of Macau can be said to be a "young" one, with relatively few old people, but a fairly large proportion of young people and children. The large number of young people has long posed an extremely keen demand for the establishment of a university as a centre for advanced learning. It is partly in response to this need that the University of East Asia, the first University in Macau, came into existence in 1981. The University is a private one and aims ultimately to establish itself as a centre of research and learning. At present it is divided into three schools, social sciences, arts, and business management, which serve not only the people of Macau but also those in the East Asian region and beyond. Over eighty per cent of the students are Chinese from Hong Kong while the other twenty per cent are made up of Chinese from Macau, Singapore and Malaysia. A handful are Portuguese. The University has been well received by the local community and turned out its first graduates in June of 1984. All of these have been able to find respectable jobs in the local community. Further, a variety of evening service courses for the local community have met with favourable reactions.

THE TEACHING OF PSYCHOLOGY

The study of psychology in the formal sense of controlled observation and experimentation did not exist in Macau until the establishment of the University. At the present initial stage of the establishment of the University, psychology is taught in the school of social sciences to some two hundred and fifty students in three academic years. Three undergraduate psychology courses are being offered: "Psychology: Human Behaviour and Experience", "Psychology of Language and Communication", and "Developmental Psychology". These are elective courses as at present there is no offering of a major in psychology. The University has one instructor on its staff who is responsible for teaching these three courses, who obtained his M.Sc. in psychology from United States. However, in line with the overall established plan of the University of East Asia, the faculty is expanding in phases, and in future other psychology courses will also be offered. The emphases of these three courses are on concepts and principles developed from studies performed in the West, but cross-cultural psychology is greatly stressed. Issues and problems significant to this region are also being explored. Occasionally, psychologists in Hong Kong and other regions are recruited to act, on a part-time basis, as academic supervisors to students taking such courses. The University is hoping to offer a new graduate programme of study in psychology in the future which will involve the completion of a research project and will lead to the degree of Master of Social Science.

The Institute of Social Work of Macau in collaboration with the Hong Kong Polytechnic provides training courses to students intending to go into the field of social work. In that programme, two psychology courses are being offered: one is an introductory course taught by a Catholic Father while the other is developmental psychology taught by a lecturer associated with the Hong Kong Polytechnic. The near future will witness the development of a comprehensive programme in the study of psychology when other planned courses are given.

General and Developmental Psychology are also taught at post-secondary level in training courses offered to nurses at the Escola Technica Dos Servicos de Saude and at Corde de Sao Formuario Hospital. Similar courses are given to kindergarten teachers trained at the Escola de Magisterio Primario, given by Macau's only Portguese-trained clinical psychologist.

Whilst the contents of the presently-offered courses are based on the system developed in the West, emphases on the development of an indigenous psychology and cross cultural comparisons are greatly stressed. In crude terms, students are encouraged to investigate how various psychological terms and constructs are defined by local inhabitants, to derive methods of study relevant and appropriate to the local culture, and to compare results of their studies with those performed in the West. In the short run, efforts are being made to forge institutional linkages between the psychology programme at the University and educational, social work and mental health centres in Macau. In the recent past the University has organized for the second time an in-service training programme for primary and secondary school teachers in Macau on major psychological proceses involved in the system of school education.

Psychology is so much in touch with other disciplines that it holds tremendous promise for the betterment of individual and social welfare. While the study of psychology in Macau could be said to have been virtually nonexistent a few years ago, the University has begun an intensive effort to make it a socially relevant discipline.

NOTE

1. Some of the information in these paragraphs is taken from the All-Asia Guide (13th ed. 1984), compiled by correspondents to the Far East Economic Review. Further information on Macau may be sought from the following two sources: Almanac of Macau Economy, Jornal Va Kio, 1983, and Austin Coates' readable book, A Macao Narrative, Hong Kong, Heinemann, 1978.

ACKNOWLEDGMENTS

The editors are indebted to Professor K. E. Shaw, and Mr Cheuk Wai-hing, lecturer, both of the School for Social Sciences, University of East Asia, Macau, for their help in the preparation of this appendix.

14

The Historical Development and Current Status of Psychology in Malaysia

Colleen Ward

Psychology as a discipline and profession in Malaysia is still in its infancy. Despite general industrial, technological, medical and educational advances, at present there are no more than thirty-five qualified psychologists, some imported, to fill the needs of Malaysia's growing population of fourteen millions and to provide input for mental health programs, social and rehabilitation services, counselling, industrial development, education and university teaching and research. Impediments to the discipline's development, fostered by socio-cultural pressures and academic traditions and reflected in the scarcity of independent academic departments and inadequate standards of public psychological services and facilities, have left psychology the Cinderella of the social sciences - primarily exploited to suit the needs of other disciplines and professions, notably medicine, education and social work. Psychologists themselves, working under constraining conditions, are most often isolated from each other, creating further obstacles to the establishment of a professional body which could advance the status of psychology and lend direction and cohesion to the discipline's development. The goals of Malaysian psychology, "to share knowledge and skills in the service of society", as proposed by Professor Wan Rafaei Abdul Rahman (Abdul Halim Othman and Wan Rafaei Abdul Rahman, 1980), the founder and head of the Department of Psychology at the Universiti Kebangsaan Malaysia (UKM), have not yet been fully realized. Until fairly recently, the government has largely ignored the potential contribution of psychologists to social services and policies, further demeaning the relevance and value of psychology in the

Malaysian context.

   With such a background, this paper gives a brief
socio-political overview of Malaysia and attempts to
trace the evolution of psychology in Malaysia, to analyze
critically its present scope and status and to put
forward suggestions and recommendations for its future
role in Malaysian development.

SOCIO-POLITICAL OVERVIEW OF MALAYSIA

   After more than a century of British colonial rule,
Malayan and Borneo territories were granted independence
in 1957 and formed the Federation of Malaysia, including
Singapore, in 1963. In 1965 Singapore withdrew from the
federation and became an independent republic. The
present Federation of Malaysia is composed of two
geographical regions - Peninsular Malaysia and East
Malaysia (states of Sabah and Sarawak).

   Malaysia is a multi-ethnic society although the
racial composition differs in the Eastern and Western
regions. On the peninsula, with approximately eleven
million, Malays represent a slight majority (53%), but a
significant proportion of Chinese (36%) and a lesser
number of Indians (10%) may also be found. Eastern
Malaysia's smaller population differs considerably, being
composed predominantly of tribal peoples (such as Dayaks
and Kadazans), and a Chinese population which exceeds
that of the Malays (Tham, 1981). The peninsula is the
more developed and populous of the two regions, and the
national capital Kuala Lumpur is located in this area.
East Malaysia is often perceived as the poorer sister of
the West, whose resources are exploited but whose
development is not given overall priority.

   Malaysia is a rapidly developing country, although
still primarily rural and subject to extensive poverty.[1]
In terms of economic development, rubber and tin have
been the mainstay although palm oil, timber, petroleum,
pepper and manufactured goods are becoming increasingly
important. The historical development of the dual economy
of the former colonial system, subsistence agriculture
and export-oriented commerce, has divided Malaysians
further along occupational and geographical lines in
addition to the existing ethnic distinctions. The Malays,
with the lowest per capita income, have traditionally
been concentrated in subsistence agriculture such as rice
cultivation and inshore fishing. The Chinese, by con-

trast, have been dominant in commerce and manufacturing and enjoy the most favorable financial position. Economically, the Indians occupy an intermediate position and have been largely associated with rubber plantations, railways and public works (Marimuthu, 1981). Consequently, urban centres have been identified with the Chinese and to a lesser extent the Indians while rural communities are composed primarily of Malays and other indigenous groups.

Despite economic disadvantages and rural origins, the Malays retain the political power in the ruling National Front through the United Malays National Organization (UMNO).[2] Current and recent administrations have concentrated their efforts on the introduction and implementation of national policies which are aimed generally at broad social and structural changes and in particular at the redress of socio-economic imbalances in Malaysian society. An outstanding policy of this type has been the New Economic Policy (NEP) which attempts to eradicate economic inequality by redistributing equity participation, employment and incomes to allow greater economic benefits to Malays. The legislation has provoked a negative reaction from the non-Malay community (Muzaffar, 1983), and while undoubtedly moving quickly to diminish economic imbalances has had the undesirable consequences of upsetting ethnic sensitivities and increasing feelings of suspicion, distrust and alienation by the implementation of economic favouritism (Oo, 1982). Discontent of the non-Malay population has also been increased by the National Language Act (1967), making Bahasa Malaysia the sole official language, and the National Cultural Policy, establishing indigenous culture as its base and emphasizing the contribution of Islam, the national religion.

Recent educational trends in Malaysia are of great interest. The educational system has undergone considerable revision in the past twenty-five years, inheriting the basic characteristics of a British system but initiating innovation after Merdeka (independence). Under colonial rule Malay, Chinese, Tamil and English schools operated separately and independently. While no attempt was made to build a unified curriculum at that time, the post-independence era saw the merger of disparate systems into one national educational programme with a Malaysian oriented syllabus. Bahasa Malaysia was gradually introduced as the sole medium of instruction, a project completed in 1983 when all strata through to the tertiary level implemented the national language. Although school enrolments are steadily increasing some aspects of education, particularly university admission, are still contentious. Recent attempts to establish an independent Chinese university were unsuccessful although Malaysia has lately founded a new international Islamic university.[3]

Socio-culturally, Malaysia is particularly interesting not only because of its blending of ethnic communities and traditions but also because of its modernization process and influence of the Western media - music, fashion, television, film, entertainment and even fast food restaurants. While exposure to Euro-American culture is widespread, this cultural imposition is strongly embraced by a certain segment of society, more critically evaluated by most and totally rejected by others. Most Malaysians, including those educated abroad, are reluctant to assimilate "Western decadence", yet an undercurrent of a "foreign-is-better" attitude may still be found. Despite a certain ambivalence, Malaysia remains a relatively conservative Asian society and maintains traditional Asian values, strong family bonds and considerable religious devotion.

Malaysia's economic future is undoubtedly bright and growth trends for all major sectors are healthy. The future of Malaysia's development in social and political terms is not so clear. A large portion of the population is still resistant to legislation on education, religion, culture and economic development, and current Islamic rivalism has increased the anxiety of the minority communities who fear potential assimilation. As Tham (1981) has noted, the future of Malaysian development depends not only on external economic progress but also on the proper management of the competing interests of the major Malaysian communities.

PSYCHOLOGY - PAST AND PRESENT

Psychology in Tertiary Education

The discipline of psychology is a relative newcomer to Malaysian universities. From its inauguration it has been viewed predominantly as a service subject, either subsumed under a department of anthropology and sociology or channelled toward supplying appropriate and relevant courses for schools of medicine or education. In contrast to other former British colonies such as India and Pakistan, where psychology was initially linked to the philosophy curriculum at the tertiary level, the subject was first formally introduced at the Universiti Malaya in the early sixties within the Faculties of Education and Arts, with an emphasis on educational and social psychology (Wan Rafaei & Abdul Halim Othman, 1974). Later, when Universiti Malaya's Faculty of Medicine was formed, clinical psychology was included in the curriculum (Tan & Wagner, 1971). With the exception of the Universiti Kebangsaan Malaysia where a Department of Psychology was set up in 1979, psychology (in Universiti Malaya and Malaysia's other three newer universities) remains as a contribution to education, sociology, anthropology, social work, counselling and medicine.[4]

The foundation of Universiti Kebangsaan Malaysia's Department of Psychology was not without its problems. With the establishment of the university in 1970 came the proposal that psychology should be considered as a separate discipline and eventually be established as an independent department. In practical terms however there were many obstacles to the policy's implementation. First and foremost was the shortage of qualified Malaysian psychologists as the university necessarily required staff who were trained abroad, willing to return to Malaysia, and fluent in the national language for teaching purposes. By 1972 there were only two lecturers in psychology, and these concentrated their efforts on the social psychology component of the Anthropology and Sociology curriculum. A major turning point occurred in 1973 with the organization of a Conference on Psychology and Related Disciplines in Malaysia, and the discussion of psychological contributions to developing societies. Adbul Halim & Wan Rafaei (1980) noted that the conference resulted in a greater support of the expanding role of psychology and the acceptance of interim assistance from Peace Corps volunteers and Indonesian colleagues in the department's development. The expansion and transformation of a psychology component within the Anthropology and Sociology curriculum and the establishment of an independent psychology department in 1979 occurred largely as the result of the hard work and dedication of UKM's two original psychologists, Wan Rafaei and Abdul Halim. This is particularly significant in light of the fact that past plans for psychology departments at other Malaysian universities, notably Universiti Sains Malaysia, have gone awry.[5]

This department, within the Faculty of Social Science and Humanities, is now staffed completely by Malaysians, with fourteen posts filled and six of these staff currently away on study leave.[6] The instruction is largely concentrated on applied psychology, particularly industrial psychology and organizational behaviour, counselling and psychometrics. The curriculum also includes a wide variety of courses in cognition, personality, statistics, psychology of economic development, ergonomics, tests and measures, developmental, experimental, social, physiological and cross-cultural psychology, with plans for clinical, environmental and community psychology. A fourth year honours programme is available to selected students. In addition, the department offers a diploma of counselling with the Ministry of Education, in-service training of clinical psychologists for the Ministry of Health and post-graduate qualifications in organizational behavior. Overall, the curriculum has been designed and implemented with four major objectives:

1) to equip students with the knowledge of psychology and related fields,
2) to study psychological processes related to society and cultures, in particular the local society and cultures,
3) to advance psychological knowledge through teaching and research, and
4) to provide the basic training for professionals who will be applying the knowledge of psychology and related disciplines to their careers (Abdul Halim Othman & Wan Rafaei, 1980).

The educational system is largely British in flavour, with use of external examiners but with some American influences. Teaching is undertaken in Bahasa Malaysia, the national language, although appropriate textbooks are in short supply and the majority of readings are in English. Shortage of textbooks in Bahasa Malaysia is a problem for most university courses. In practical terms students must be bi-lingual as lectures and examinations are in Bahasa but most readings are in English. Many students are disadvantaged by this situation. Malays are more often deficient in English comprehension and have difficulty with readings. Chinese, Indian and Eurasian students typically have more difficulty expressing themselves in Bahasa Malaysia and are disadvantaged in the examination setting. Despite obstacles and limitations, psychology has proved to be quite a popular course among UKM undergraduates with a total enrolment of four hundred and forty-nine students in the 1983/4 academic session. In addition, twenty-five students enrolled for the postgraduate diploma in counselling.

The vast majority of students pass their examinations and obtain formal qualifications. In most universities psychology would be taken either as part of a professional course (education, social work or medicine), or along with sociology. UKM provides a mixture of theory and applied psychology. To some extent the system encourages students to think critically, particularly as theories typically involve some cultural adaptation. On the other hand, lecturers are seriously regarded as sources of authority. UKM has a slight majority (fifty per cent) of females as undergraduates, but not in the post-graduate counselling diploma.

The department has also been active in research pursuits. It is remarkable that a developing department of eight full-time resident staff with teaching responsibilities for more than four hundred students has also had the time and enthusiasm to sponsor workshops on testing and counselling, as well as national seminars on psychology in industry and career guidance. There has been continuing cooperation in research activities with psychologists from the university of Newcastle, Australia. In 1983 the psychology department also played host to the regional meeting of the International Association of Cross-cultural Psychology with the theme of Psychology and Socio-economic Development. In addition, the department has plans to form a national psychological association and to produce a journal of psychology.

The proportion of male to female academics varies among universities although a rough estimate is about sixty per cent male. The staff of UKM is more than three fourths male whilst the majority of Universiti Malaya's staff are female. The majority of psychologists are Malay, and the number of foreign professionals has been steadily dwindling over the years. While research is seen as important, ethnicity is probably the most significant factor influencing hiring and promotion (although there is some variation among universities). This is in line with government policy, and the fact that tenure is relatively freely available to Malay staff tends to discourage productivity. The original generation of psychologists is still working, and the majority of staff are still sent abroad for doctoral studies. The UKM department does however have several Master's students. The universities function on different terms although the average staff load is about twelve hours teaching per week.

Sabbatical leave is available although only to a few senior staff. Foreign visitors have been attracted by some conferences such as the 4th Asian Forum on Child and Adolescent Psychiatry (March 1983), IACCP (May 1983), and the Asian Workshop on Child and Adolescent Development. International journals may be found in the libraries, but the selection is not always very good.

Psychological Research

As with teaching, Malaysian psychological research and publications in the past have been largely applied to the professional practice of medicine, counselling, business and education, with little emphasis on theoretical or methodological issues (Wan Rafaei & Abdul Halim, 1974). The situation has improved in recent years with the UKM Psychology Department boosting research activities with graduation exercises pursued by undergraduates in the areas of achievement motivation, attitudes, counselling, psychological measurement, industrial, developmental and social psychology.

Recent and current research undertaken by local and foreign university staff includes areas such as test standardization, psychology and development, adjustment and counselling psychiatry, sex trait and ethnic stereotypes, culture bound disorders, religious movements and beliefs, concept acquisition and moral development.[7] This list is not exhaustive. The Department of Pedagogy and Educational Psychology at the University of Malaya has ongoing projects in cognitive development, reading disabilities and attitudes toward science courses. Related research has also been undertaken by psychiatrists and anthropologists in areas such as culture-bound reactive disorders (Teoh & Tan, 1976) and indigenous therapies (Kinzie, Teoh & Tan, 1972). With a few notable exceptions the majority of Malaysian psychologists are more prolific in Malay and tend to publish locally. In addition, local and regional conference and seminar presentations are common.

Promisingly, Malaysia has forged cross-cultural links, often with universities where Malaysians have trained abroad but also with contacts established at international conferences. While Australian colleagues, in particular Daphne Keats and Ann Harding with interests in child development, have a well-established association with the UKM department, other cross-cultural contacts and interests are rapidly developing (Ismail & Dyal, 1983) with Canada, Japan and the United Kingdom. The advent of foreign researchers, however, has been met with some ambivalence. While it is viewed favourably as adding to a body of Malaysian research data, it has also raised queries over adequacy of cultural understanding, linguistic knowledge, appropriateness of research instruments and releveance of hypotheses, similar to concerns voiced by academics and professionals in other developing countries (Ciacco, 1981; Hoorweg, 1970).

Various sources of research funds are available from such sources as universities, government and international organisations. While university funds are available for a wide range of topics, the government usually specifies the area of interest. Occasionally, international organizations such as UNICEF or WHO offer funds for interdisciplinary research which includes psychology.[8]

Applied Psychology

Despite the shortage of trained psychologists, demands for such have been heavy in medicine, industry and education. Ironically, while Malaysia has recognized the need to employ clinical psychologists, the country has not seen fit to train them adequately. To date there are only six qualified clinical psychologists in Malaysia, all of whom have been educated abroad. It is obviously impossible for these psychologists to provide adequate services for West Malaysia's two mental hospitals with inmates totalling over seven thousand, five general hospital psychiatric units and three medical schools. The situation is typified by the Universiti Malaya's Department of Psychological Medicine, which retains two clinical psychologists who are burdened with relatively heavy teaching loads and used extensively for psychological assessment of psychiatric patients, leaving little time for therapeutic endeavors or psychological research. This shortage of trained clinicians has left

many vacancies in the Ministry of Health but has also led
to the employment of psychology and sociology graduates
who are not adequately qualified to assume these positions. The UKM in-service training scheme has remedied
this situation to a certain extent.

Malaysia's rapid economic and commercial development
has also prompted private and government enterprise to
rely on psychological consultation in the industrial
setting. Organisational development and employee motivation have been of prime concern, and consultants have
typically adapted group dynamics techniques to the local
environment for the implementation of appropriate
industrial programmes. Psychologists have also rendered
assistance with management selection and training and
attitude change in local factories. While the majority of
programmes have met with short-term success, and Malaysian industry still smiles benevolently on the psychologist, there are no reliable research data available to
assess long-term effectiveness.

In addition, Malaysia has utilized applied psychologists in education, government and sport. In the first
instance, psychologists have played important roles in
translating and standardizing intelligence and achievement tests and designing local test materials for
Malaysian school children. They have also been employed
on a consultant basis in connection with local and
national programmes, such as Project Inspire, designed to
broaden children's experiences and contribute to the
total learning process, reflecting Malaysia's increased
concern for educational development. Within the government Malaysia maintains a division of psychological
warfare which is responsible for a portion of the
national propaganda and liaises with the military. On the
lighter side, psychologists have been utilized in the
sports arena, introducing training and motivating
techniques for Malaysian athletes who participate in
international competitions.

Psychological Associations

To date psychological associations per se have not
met with great success in Malaysia. There has been one
Psychological Society composed predominantly of interested laypersons but this organization has lapsed into
inactivity. Universiti Kebangsaan has proposed a Malaysian Psychological Association to register psychologists

and to provide guidelines on ethics and professional responsibility; this, however, has not yet been instituted.

Malaysia, nevertheless, does lay claim to a Mental Health Association founded in 1968 and composed of psychiatrists, psychologist, nurses and social workers. As the mental health movement is relatively new in Malaysia, the main aims of the MMHA are to promote basic educational programmes and services for the mentally ill. Activities in the past have included joint endeavours with the Churches Counselling Center, participation in public exhibitions, fund raising welfare projects for psychiatric patients, and organization of the Malaysian Conference on Mental Health (Woon, 1980). The association was also instrumental in the recent initiation of a day care centre for rehabilitated mental patients in Selangor. Over the past years the MMHA has gained popularity and now boasts between ninety and one hundred members (Vytialingam, 1980).

Problematic Issues in Malaysian Psychology

Pollution of Professional Psychology. The shortage of psychologists in Malaysia remains a major difficulty and the absence of a professional society creates problems. With no official body to distinguish qualified psychologists and a deficit of trained professionals, the issue of who is a psychologist in Malaysia is still a matter for discussion (Abdul Halim Othman & Wan Rafaei, 1980). Under these conditions Malaysia relies heavily on undertrained personnel. A more significant and detrimental consequence, however, has been the exploitation of the Malaysian situation by entrepreneurs of Western 'pop' psychology. A wide variety of self-improvement courses has gained popularity on the Malaysian market, mostly at considerable expense. In addition to confusing the issue about who psychologists are and what they can do, the programmes are potentially dangerous in their uncritical importation of Western systems and values. With little or no cultural adjustments, utilization of these techniques could result in negative consequences for both the consuming public and the integrity of professional psychology in Malaysia. Professional psychologists have noted these developments with alarm, maintaining that the situation has reached a dangerous level and urging the government to study the impact of these imported programmes in Malaysia (New Straits Times, 1980). Unfortunately, steps have not yet been taken to resolve the difficulties in this area.

Resistance to Psychology in Malaysia. Although modern psychology had its origins in the West, contemporary scholars are moving away from misguided parochialism and recognizing the the need to consider the discipline within a global perspective. This is evidenced by the expanding activities in cross-cultural psychology and increasing efforts to adjust psychological theory and practice to its host environment. However this emerging philosophy has not reached the awareness of many policy makers and educators in Malaysia, who are largely apathetic or antagonistic toward the role and potential contribution of psychology in a developing country. Many hold that psychology means Western psychology, imported uncritically in toto, at best irrelevant and at worst threatening to the Malaysian way of life. In some academic circles, established scholars in social sciences also view psychology as limited to consideration of the individual, and attempts to advance the discipline's status have led to petty academic rivalries and jealousies. A combination of these common misconceptions of psychology has historically impeded its development in Malaysia.

Without a doubt, legitimate queries should be raised about the significance of psychology in the Malaysian context. Allowing for cultural adaptability, there is generally a recognition of a need for psychologists in applied areas such as education, social services and mental health. There is also an overall demand to integrate psychological theory with the interests of national policy makers. More specific demands for psychology in developing societies such as Malaysia, however, may be intrinsically different from those of industrialized, technological nations and former colonizers, which could account for the underlying apathy towards psychology in the Malaysian context. To a large extent psychologists, while aware of these needs, have not addressed themselves to the culture-specific problems characteristic of Malaysia's development. This was illustrated to a certain degree by the 1983 International Association of Cross-cultural Psychology's Conference on Psychology and Socio-economic Development.

While there are some who maintain that psychology is unnecessary in Malaysia, there are others who hold that, with its Western flavour the discipline is potentially subversive, threatening social traditions and religious values. On the social level, emphasis on such topics as the development of individuality, achievement and competition favoured in Western psychologically-based theories of child-rearing and education, may be perceived as antagonistic to Asian values of filial piety or communal responsibility. Likewise, the openness of encounter therapies and sensitivity groups may appear threatening to the Asian who highly values face-saving. These, of course, do not represent fundamental issues or insurmountable difficulties, but are typical examples of objections and misconceptions about psychology in an Asian context.

Often the religious objections are more serious than the social ones in this conservative, predominantly Muslim society. On one level there is the general controversy about intrinsic conflicts between psychological and religious truths which is an oft revived philosophical debate found as well in Western civilization (Miles, 1981). In fact, Zaidi (1976) has contended that education in the British secular tradition is at the heart of this controversy, as it has been aimed at presenting the position that religion, particularly Islam, is anti-scientific. He also argues that Islamic contributions to psychology have been historically ignored. On a more specific level, Islamic psychologists have had to deal with particular issues, such as treatment of homosexuals, which potentially conflict with their faith. With respect to these topics, Malik B. Badri's (1979) <u>Dilemma of Muslim Psychologists</u> seems to have had some impact in Malaysia, as it discusses sensitive areas in the union of psychology with Islam and concludes that there is nothing intrinsically unacceptable about psychology, but that the discipline must be adapted and utilized within the context of Islamic values. While this is the position taken by most Muslim psychologists in Malaysia, unfortunately the reconciliation of psychology and Islam is not widely apparent to all Malaysian professionals, and even less to the general public.

Social and religious objections have underlain resistance to psychology in general, but more specific issues are involved with the acceptance of psychology within the general framework of mental health. Tan (1971) and Kwan (1981) have noted that in Malaysia the mental health profession has not really gained recognition from either the medical profession or the general community.

The origins of psychiatric facilities in peninsular Malaysia date back to the first lunatic asylum in Penang in 1829 (Woon, 1978), whose inmates were a mixture of criminal and psychiatric cases. Three state hospitals existed before 1900, and in 1911 Tanjong Rambutan, the first federal psychiatric facility, was established. Currently, peninsular Malaysia maintains two state hospitals, but on the whole mental health is often viewed as a luxury and has not been given the status or consideration that other medical needs, such as eradication of infectious diseases and prevention of malnutrition, have been accorded by the government.

Other impediments exist to the implementation of top quality mental health services. The shortage of trained personnel in the areas of psychiatry and psychology is obvious (Tan & Wagner, 1971). In addition, cultural adaptation of training received abroad is also necessary. Professional prejudice is often apparent due to misconceptions concerning mental health services and lack of appreciation for the overburdened condition of workers in this area. The general public is also wary of mental health facilities as these are remedial in nature and often perceived as the last resort. Many Malaysians would prefer to seek assistance from native healers available in the Malay, Chinese and Indian communities and to avoid the stigmatization of psychiatric treatment. Kinzie et al. (1972) examined psychiatric admissions and found that thirty-one per cent had previously been to indigenous therapists. With their own indigenous theories of causation, classification and treatment of mental illness, often based on magical rather than on medical, psychological or socio-cultural models, the majority of Malaysians, particularly the rural population, views psychiatric and psychological services as superfluous.

While resistance to psychology has been strongest in the past, complete acceptance has not been gained in the present. The dedication and striving of the UKM department and the recent conference on socio-economic development have served as bright signs for the future. Nevertheless, for the growth and evolution of the discipline, Malaysian professionals must still evoke certain attitude changes and demonstrate psychology's relevance and potential contributions to Malaysian society.

PSYCHOLOGY - DIRECTIONS FOR THE FUTURE

While there are many paths Malaysian psychology could follow for a successful future, it must be directed toward fulfilment of Malayian needs. Because demands are plenty and psychologists few, the first requirement is an increase in the number of trained professionals. Achieving that, psychology may expand in university education, broaden in research and advance its operation in applied areas. It is in these applied fields that psychology is likely to make its most significant contributions to Malaysian development. While the discipline has apparently been functional in industry and education in the past, a look to the future reveals that the most pressing needs are concerned with Malaysia's prolific social problems. Of these, mental health and ethnic relations warrant special precedence.

As the press and media indicate, psychosocial problems and mental health disorders are multiplying in Malaysia. Drug abuse is a major social concern (Choo & Navaratnam, 1980; Spencer & Navaratnam, 1980). Alcoholism is on the rise with the National Union of Plantation workers estimating that one in every three male estate labourers is an alcoholic (New Straits Times, 1980). Suicides are increasing (New Straits Times, 1979). In addition, recent reports highlight an "emotional deprivation" syndrome in Malaysian children resulting in emotional disturbances, psychosomatic complaints and occasional attempted suicides (New Straits Times, 1981). Rural-urban migration also claims many victims, young men and women who arrive in the cities seeking jobs, who find themselves unemployed or underpaid, socially isolated and unable to cope with the stresses of their new environment. Given these problems, and considering that government mental health services are inadequate in urban areas and non-existent in rural localities, psychologists could play a role in the development of mental health programmes or small community clinics to alleviate this human suffering. The call for non-psychiatric personnel to assist with the development of mental health services in Malaysia (Tan, 1971) and the development of community mental health programmes (Kwan, 1981) has been supported by psychiatrists and social workers.

The area of ethnic relations also warrants special attention by applied psychologists. With Malaysia's multiracial composition of Malays, Indians and Chinese, political power and economic control have become sensitive issues. Some of the government's racial policies have caused controversy, and efforts to support a national Malaysian culture, somewhat at the expense of different ethnic traditions, have met with hostile reactions from certain segments of the population. While a relatively harmonious picture of multi-racial Malaysia has been painted, a considerable amount of racial tension has been repressed, and the country remains a potential time bomb for a racial explosion. The tragedy of the May 1969 riots which left hundreds dead attests to the fact that the racial situation in Malaysia has not always been stable. Applied psychologists could certainly make contributions in handling this delicate situation, by working in conjunction with the National Unity Board, increasing research in ethnic relations and developing practical strategies for the achievement of racial harmony and inter-racial unity in Malaysia.

Of course, there are many other areas in which the psychologist's skills and expertise can be utilized, such as test standardization, counselling or sports psychology, but whatever the paths Malaysian psychologists choose to follow, it is most important that they "share knowledge and skills in the service of the community", that they address themselves to significant Malaysian issues and problems and that they adapt themselves to the needs of this rapidly developing country.

NOTES

1. The 1970 census indicates that 49 per cent of peninsular Malaysia's households were considered to be in a state of poverty (R. Chander (ed.) General Report - 1970 Vol 1, Statistics Department of Malaysia).

2. National Front is actually a political conglomeration including the Malaysian Chinese Association and Malaysian Indian Congress.

3. Malays are given preferential treatment and are admitted to university with lower qualifications. The government also intervened with the attempt to found a Chinese university, maintaining it was not in the national interest.

4. Universiti Malaya offers courses in Departments of Sociology and Anthropology, Psychological Medicine, and Pedagogy and Educational Psychology. Universiti Sains Malaysia offers psychology in the School of Social Science (Departments of Sociology & Anthropology, Social

Development and Administration and Management), School of
Education and School of Medical Sciences. Universiti
Pertanian maintains psychology courses in the Faculty of
Educational Studies (Department of Social Sciences).
Malaysia also has a Technology University, an inter-
national Islamic university established in 1983, and
plans for a sixth national university in 1984.

5. In the 1970's Universiti Sains Malaysia employed
local and imported foreign psychologists to assist with
the establishment of a psychology department within the
School of Social Science, but this was abandoned over the
years largely due to internal politics.

6. Currently the department has only three staff
with doctorates, although staff are sent abroad for
further qualifications. Popular training places for
Malaysians include Australia, United States, United
Kingdom, and to a lesser extent Canada and New Zealand.
The majority of psychology staff at Univerisiti Malaya do
hold doctoral degrees, although Masters' degree holders
are now more common at Universiti Pertanian. Universiti
Sains Malaysia has a fairly equal number of Master's and
doctoral degrees among its psychology-trained staff.

7. See for example Abdul Halim & Wan Rafaei, 1980;
Ismail & Choo, 1983; Khare & Upadhhaya, 1983; Abdul Halim
& Wan Rafaei, 1983; Abdul Halim, 1979; Shamshudin Hussin,
1983; Wan Rafaei, Inau Nom, Othman Bakar, Salehuddin
Wahab, Onn Mat Salleh, Mahjuddin Jusoh Johari Mansor,
1983 ; Wan Rafaei & Devandaran, 1983; Chooe, Ward &
Navaratnam, 1980; Ismail, 1983; Ward, 1982; Ward, in
press; Ward & Hewstone, 1984; Lee & Ackerman, 1980;
Ackerman & Lee, 1981; Keats, Keats & Mohammed Haji Yusuf,
1976; Wan Rafaei, 1976, and Chiam, 1982.

8. Examples would be the Kanita project on women and
community development and research on drug abuse at the
National Centre for Drug Dependence Research, both at
UKM. Research which contributes to indigenous theory
building is not conspicuous.

REFERENCES

ABDUL HALIM OTHMAN The identification of adjustment
    problems, life change stress and perceived useful-
    ness of problem solving resource in a Malay student
    sample in the United States. Dissertation Abstracts
    International, Ann Arbor, Michigan, 1979.

ABDUL HALIM OTHMAN & WAN RAFAEI ABDUL RAHMAH Issues and problems related to the teaching of psychology and training of professional psychologists. Paper presented at International Conference on the Role of Universities in Developing Nations, Kuala Lumpur, November, 1980.

ABDUL HALIM OTHMAN & WAN RAFAEI ABDUL RAHMAN Modernity and levels of socio-economic development. Paper presented at Third Asian Conference of International Association of Cross-Cultural Psychology, Bangi, Malaysia, 1983.

ACKERMAN, S. E. & LEE R. L. M. Communication and cognitive pluralism in a spirit possession event in Malaysia, American Ethnologist, 1981, 8(4), 789-799.

CHAIM, H. K. Moral development and moral education in adolescents. Paper presented at Asian Workshop on Child and Adolescent Development, Bangkok, Thailand, 1982.

CHOO, P. K., & NAVARATNAM, V. An overview of dadah (drug) use in a high-risk area. National Drug Dependence Research Centre, University of Science Malaysia, 1980.

CHOO P. K., WARD, C., & NAVARATNAM, V. Personality and drug abuse in Malaysia: A comparison of users and non users in an urban community. Paper presented at Third Asian Conference of International Association of Cross-Cultural Psychology, Bangi, Malaysia, 1983.

CIACCIO, N. V. Cross-cultural studies of personality development in 'Third World' countries. Paper presented at Second Asian Conference of the International Association of Cross-Cultural Psychology, Taipei, Taiwan, 1981.

DITIMAR, M., RATNASINGAM, M., & NAVARATNAM, V. Comparative Analysis of the psychological profile of an institutionalized drug-using population in Malaysia. Paper presented at Third Asian Conference of the International Association of Cross-Cultural Psychology, Bangi, Malaysia, 1983.

HARDING, A. V. Interaction between children of different ethnic groups: Data from Australia and Malaysia. Paper presented at Third Asian Conference of Cross-Cultural Psychology, Bangi, Malaysia, 1983.

HOORWEG, J. Africa - South of the Sahara. In V. Sexton & H. Misiak (eds.) Psychology around the world, Monterey, Ca., Brooks Cole, 1976.

ISMAIL, B., & DYAL, J. Differential effects of ethnicity and sex on cultural affirmation/accommodation by Malay Malaysians and Chinese Malaysians. Paper presented at Third Asian Conference of Cross-Cultural Psychology, Bangi, Malaysia, 1983.

ISMAIL, M., & CHOO, P. The reliability and factorial validation of the Tennessee Self-Concept Scale for a sample of Malaysian university students. Paper presented at Third Asian Conference of Cross-Cultural Psychology, Bangi, Malaysia, 1983.

ISMAIL, Z. Psychiatric patients in private practice. Paper presented at Third Asian Conference on Cross-Cultural Psychology, Bangi, Malaysia, 1983.

KEATS, D. Workshop in the cognitive assessment of social values. Paper presented at Asian Workshop on Child and Adolescent Development, Bangkok, Thailand, 1982.

KEATS, D., KEATS, J., & MOHAMMED HAJI YUSUF Attribution of reasons for religious beliefs in four ethnic groups, Akademika, 1976, 9, 21-28.

KEATS, D. M., KEATS, J., WAN RAFAEI ABDUL RAHMAN Concept acquisition in Malaysian bi-lingual children, Journal of Cross-Cultural Psychology, 1976, 7, 87-99.

KHARE, C.B. & UPADHYAYA, S. A study of life events in two ethnic groups. Paper presented at Third Asian Conference on Cross-Cultural Psychology, Bangi, Malaysia, 1983.

KINZIE, D., TEOH, J. I., & TAN, E. S. Native healers in Malaysia. Paper presented at Conference on Culture and Mental Health in Asia and the Pacific. Honolulu, Hawaii, 1972.

KWAN A. Y. Mental health and social development: Implication for services in Malaysia. Paper presented at Seminar on the Year of the Disabled, Perak Society for the Promotion of Mental Health, Ipoh, Malaysia, May, 1981.

LEE, R., & ACKERMAN, S. The socio-cultural dynamics of mass hysteria: A case study of social conflict in West Malaysia, Psychiatry, 1980, 43, 78-89.

MALIK B. BADRI The dilemma of Muslim psychologists. London, MWH London Publishers, 1979.

MARIMUTHU, T. Education and challenges of national development: the Malaysian experience, Negara, 1981, 5(1), 27-41.

MILES, T.R. A conflict between psychology and religion? Bulletin of British Psychological Society, 1981, 34, 94-96.

MUZAFFAR, C. Has the communal situation in Malaysia worsened over the last decade? Paper presented at the Conference on Modernization and National Cultural Identity, Kuala Lumpur, January, 1983.

NEW STRAITS TIMES Suicide on fairly low increase, July 9, 1979.

NEW STRAITS TIMES Are we boozing too much? 1980.

NEW STRAITS TIMES Study urged on imported motivation techniques, December 29, 1980.

NEW STRAITS TIMES Take care - your child may be on a tightrope, March 27, 1980.

OO, Y. H. Problems and challenges of national unity: Old wine in a new bottle, Negara, 1981, 5(1), 7-15.

SHAMSUDIN HUSSIN Training of Counsellors. Paper presented at Third Asian Conference of International Association of Cross-Cultural Psychology, Bangi, Malaysia, 1983.

SPENCER, C. P., & NAVARATNAM V. Social attitudes, self-description and perceived reasons for using drugs, Drug and Alcohol Dependence, 5, 421-427 (a).

SPENCER, C. P., & NAVARATNAM, V. Patterns of drug use amongst Malaysian secondary school children, Drug and Alcohol Dependence, 5, 3793-391 (b).

SPENCER, C. P., & NAVARATNAM, V. Drug abuse in East Asia, Kuala Lumpur, Oxford University Press, 1981.

TAN, E. S. A look to the future. In N. Wagner & E.S. Tan (eds.) Psychological problems and treatment in Malaysia, Kuala Lumpur, University Malaya Press, 1971.

TAN, E. S. & WAGNER, N. Psychiatry in Malaysia. In N. Wagner & E. S. Tan (eds.) Psychological problems and treatment in Malaysia, Kuala Lumpur, University Malaya Press, 1971.

TEOH, J. I., & TAN, E. S. An outbreak of epidemic hysteria in West Malaysia. In W. Lebra (ed.) Culture bound syndromes, ethnopsychiatry and alternative therapies, Honolulu University of Hawaii Press, 1976.

THAM, S. C. Social science research in Malaysia, Singapore, Graham Brash, 1981.

VYTIALINGAM, N. Report from the Honorary Secretary General, Berita Kesihatal Mental, 1980, 2(2), 2-3.

WAN RAFAEI ADDUL RAHMAN & ABDUL HALIM OTHMAN Peranan dan orientasi psikologi dan ahli-ahli sains social di Malaysia, Peranan dan orientasi sains sosial dan ahli-ahli sains social di Malaysia, Universiti Kebangsaan Malaysia, 1974.

WANRAFAEI ABDUL RAHMAN & M. DEVANDARAN The use of Repertory Grid as a tool for counselling in a drug rehabilitation centre. Paper presented at Third Asian Conference of International Association of Cross-Cultural Psychology, Bangi, Malaysia, 1983.

WAN RAFAEI ABDUL RAHMAN, INAU NOM, OTHMAN BAKAR, SALEHUD-DIN WAHAB, OON MAT SALLEH, MAHUDDDIN JUSOH AND JOHARI MANSOR The problems of adjustment among first year university students. Paper presented at Third Asian Conference of the International Association of Cross-Cultural Psychology, Bangi, Malaysia, 1983.

WARD, C. Sex trait stereotypes of males and females in Malaysia. In R. Rath, H. S. Asthana, D. Sinha, & J. B. H. Sinha (eds.) Diversity and unity in cross-cultural psychology, Lisse, Swets & Zeitlinger, 1982.

WARD, C. Sex trait stereotypes in Malaysian children, Sex Roles, in press.

WARD, C., & HEWSTONE M. Inter-ethnic perceptions and social attribution processes in Malaysia and Singapore. Paper to be presented at VII International Congress of Cross-Cultural Psychology, Acapulco, Mexico, 1984.

WOON, T. H. A history of psychiatry in peninsular Malaysia, 1830-1975, Medical Journal of Malaysia, 1978, 32(3), 258-263.

WOON, T. H. The first decade of Malaysian Mental Health Association. Paper presented at the First Malaysian Conference on Mental Health, Kuala Lumpur, February, 1980.

ZAIDI, S. M. H. Pakistan. In V. Sexton & H. Misiak (eds.) Psychology around the world, Monterey, Brooks Cole, 1976.

ACKNOWLEDGMENTS

The author would like to thank Professor Woon Tai Hwang, (Department of Psychological Medicine, Universiti Malaya), Dr. Wan Rafaei Abdul Rahman (Department of Psychology, Universiti Kebangsaan Malaysia), Professor Chiam Heng Keng (Department of Pedagogy and Educational Psychology, Universiti Malaya), and Associate Professor Shamshudin Hussin (Guidance and Counselling Unit, Universiti Pertanian Malaysia), for their assistance with background information in this paper. However, the views contained in this paper are those of the author. The

majority of background research was done while the author
was a lecturer at Universiti Sains Malaysia.

15

Psychology in Singapore: Its Roots, Context and Growth

F. Y. Long

INTRODUCTION

Psychology in Singapore has had a slow and rather lopsided growth. How it has arrived at this stage must be viewed within the historical framework of Singapore's transformation from a fishing village to a dynamic modern city republic.

The development and growth of psychology in Singapore may be examined and discussed within four historical contexts, namely, the founding of Singapore to the First World War (1819-1914); between the two World Wars (1914-1945); from the Japanese Surrender till Singapore's Independence (1945-1965); and finally from independence to the present (1965-1983).

SINGAPORE : FROM FISHING VILLAGE TO COLONY TRADING CENTRE (1819-1914)

When Stamford Raffles landed in Singapura (lion city) in January 1819 he came upon a Malay settlement of over one hundred houses and other groupings of Chinese and Indians further up river. The settlers had long established themselves and actively engaged in fishing and trade. In fact Singapore was a flourishing trading centre which formed part of the Hindu Javanese empire. In the 14th century, Singapore (then known as Temasek) became a battleground for domination between the Majapahit Empire of Java and the Siamese Ayudhya Empire. Singapore was ravaged in the ensuing struggle between Java and Siam and reduced to a backwater settlement until Raffles arrived. Through a treaty with the Malay chieftain, Raffles established a trading post for the East Indian Company. From that point onwards Singapore grew rapidly to become the administrative centre of the Straits Settlements consisting of Singapore, Malacca and Penang. Because of its harbour which provided sheltered anchorage and location in an area rich in tropical produce, many traders and settlers poured in from China, India and Malacca. By 1824, the island had grown from a fishing village to a prosperous town of at least 10,683 inhabitants (according to the first census there were 74 Europeans, 4,580 Malays, 3,317 Chinese, 16 Armenians, 15 Arabs, 756 Indians and 1,925 Bugis)[1]. In 1867 Singapore became a British Colony.

The new colony was a multi-racial, multicultural society with the Chinese, Malays and Indians well set in their own cultures and religions within Buddhism, Islam and Hinduism. It was in this hardened cultural soil that psychology had to attempt to take root.

Psychology in both philosophical and scientific forms was probably unheard of in this remote colony. There were simply no educational institutions which could receive the new psychological doctrines of Wundt, William James, Dewey or Watson, unlike Europe and America where there were established universities and institutions of higher learning. In places such as in Australia where there were existing universities, psychology seemed to take root quite readily. Taft (1982) clearly shows the historical growth of psychology in Australia to be closely linked with the expansion of university teaching programmes, particularly in philosophy and education.

During the early days, schools on the island of Singapore were nothing more than a few Koran classes for Malay children and several Chinese writing schools. Raffles himself had far-sighted plans for educating the local youths by teaching them in their native languages as well as providing some instruction in English and science. His ambition was to establish a college in Singapore. In fact on 5th June 1823, he laid the foundation stone of his proposed 'Institution'. The Singapore Institution was to consist of a scientific department to be staffed by a professor of natural history and another professor for natural philosophy, a literary and moral department for the Chinese, and a literary and moral department for the Malays and kindred peoples.

Although Raffles had noble intentions and firm convictions, his college could not be realised at this juncture. "The lack of tradition, the attitude of the population consisting of transient immigrants and men with no intention of establishing permanent residence and the fear by the parents of religious conversion worked against the successful establishment of the Institution" (Doraisamy, 1969 p. 9). It was not until 1907 that a medical school, the King Edward VII Medical College, was established. Raffles' own vision of a college, the Raffles College (which later became the University of Singapore) was not realized until 1928 (more than a hundred years after Raffles laid the foundation stone).

Had Raffles succeeded in establishing his college in 1823 one could speculate that psychology might have had a much better chance of taking early roots in Singapore. That could have been the case because the Singapore Institution envisaged by Raffles placed considerable emphasis on the teaching of philosophy, which was a basic discipline in universities in England, Europe and America, and from which psychology was frequently an outgrowth.

Psychology in the lunatic asylum?

Instead of originating from a university philosophy department like many others, psychology in Singapore possibly owes its genesis to the lunatic asylum. The British as early as 1841 had erected a thirty-bed 'Insane Hospital'. It was transferred to a new site and renamed the 'Lunatic Asylum' with 100 beds, in 1862. By 1887 the 'New Lunatic Asylum' was built with 250 male and 50 female beds at the present site of the Faculty of Medicine. It certainly appears that the British were more inclined to build mental asylums than institutions of higher learning at this period. With the opening of this new hospital, the post of psychiatrist was canvassed in England in the same year (Murphy, 1971). Dr Gilmore (Gilbert) Ellis served as Medical Superintendent from 1887 to 1909. According to Murphy (1982),[2] Gilbert Ellis had some learning in psychology in Europe before he assumed the post of psychiatrist and medical superintendent in Singapore.

It is a matter of conjecture whether psychology in any guise was known to the physicians and psychiatrists in the mental asylums. Certainly by 1889 the first legislation relating to detention of persons of unsound mind was introduced to Singapore. The Straits Settlement Ordinance No. VIII of 1889 embodied much of British legislation on the subject and was likely to contain matters of psychological practice in relation to mental deficiency. Following the opening of King Edward VII Medical College in 1907, the first clinical course in Psychological Medicine was given to medical students in 1914. The three-month course, with some content in psychology, was supervised by a trained male psychiatric nurse. In the following year, further classes in psychology were added (Teoh, 1971).

Unlike similar British colonies (Australia and Hong Kong), where psychology was spawned by fathers from academic philosophy, Singapore psychology was ill-conceived by medical forebears, thus giving rise to a warped course of development.

SINGAPORE: BRITISH BASTION TO JAPANESE OCCUPATION (1914-1945)

With the opening of the Suez Canal in 1869 and the advent of steamships and international cable telegraph, Singapore became a vital trade and communication centre on the new Great Marine Trunk Route between Europe and the Orient. The First World War sharpened Britain's perception of Singapore as the 'Gibraltar of the East'. The British soon built an enormous shipyard and also developed Singapore as a naval and military base. In education, the learning of English was emphasised. Government English schools, notably the Raffles Institution, had been established to meet the needs of the British colonial administration. Christian missions also organized schools in both English and Chinese. Various independent Chinese, Malay and Tamil schools were allowed to sprout. The result was a widening gap between an English educated elite and the various other vernacular groups. By 1928, Raffles' College was opened as a college of education offering diplomas in Arts and Science.

The First Singapore Psychological Association

In November 1929, one Dr. P. Fennelly LL.D. arrived in Singapore from England to conduct public courses in 'Practical Psychology'.[3] Dr. Fennelly's credentials in psychology remain uncertain. He appears to have been some kind of itinerant lecturer whose courses aroused considerable interest among the British gentry in Singapore. It was not just because of the contact with home for the British as such. He was billed as a highly qualified person with a rather appealing set of lectures. Nonetheless, his course had a strong 'clinical' bias. Topics for the series of lectures he delivered at the prestigious Victoria Memorial Hall are listed in the Appendix. They included such items as "Science of Life," "Rules for Analysing Others," "Rules for Liberating Hidden Powers,", and "Employing the Hidden Self."

Dr. Fennelly's lectures were enthusiastically received by about fifty colonial officials and members of high society, including businessmen, medical and other professional figures and their wives. A handful of English-educated Asian gentlemen were also in the group. Those who attended the course formed themselves into the Singapore Psychological Association on 12 January 1930.

The Objectives of the Association were:

(a) to afford persons resident in Singapore who are desirous of pursuing the study of practical psychology the opportunity of doing so,
(b) to afford members the opportunity of establishing and maintaining contact with psychologists visiting Singapore and with societies, associations and clubs of the same nature in other parts of the world,
(c) to establish and maintain a library of works on psychology for the use of members.

Mr. C. R. Stuart and Dr. D. Frankel (both well-known names) were elected president and vice-president respectively. The subscription was $10 (Singapore)[4] per annum, a tidy sum indeed in those days. This Association was an active one with regular meetings being held at the then prestigious Adelphi Hotel. A library of about 140 books was in operation. Books by Freud, Jung, William McDougall, J.C. Flugel, J.A. Hadfield, A. Adler, Bertrand Russell, and Havelock Ellis were high on the list.

The Association functioned till 30 June 1939 when the rumbles of the Second World War scattered the various members to different parts of the world. The evacuation of British families of government officials and business leaders as well as a number of favourite local luminaries left the Association foundering.

The British surrendered Singapore to the Japanese army on 15 February 1942. The Japanese Occupation (1942-1945) marked the beginning of the downfall of the British Empire. Both prisoners-of-war and the local inhabitants suffered from the cruelty of the Occupation. Singaporeans till the present day cannot forget the atrocities committed by the Japanese, nor forgive the British for surrendering the Gibraltar of the East so easily. The Japanese Occupation exploded the myth of British invincibility. It contributed to future cynicism towards any suggestion that the British or Western way of thinking could be superior to that of the East. Whether this cynicism has indirectly contributed to the retardation of psychological growth in Singapore remains as an area of speculation.

After the Japanese Occupation and Surrender in 1945 attempts were made to revive the Association, especially by one Mr. Ignatius N. Sumboo who remained in Singapore during the War. Neither Mr. Stuart nor Dr. Frankel returned to Singapore. In 1969 Mr. Sumboo, one of several surviving members of the Association, turned over the funds of the Association (a sum of $546.91 kept in the Post Office Savings Bank had accrued interest amounting to $1,245.43) to the Singapore National Defence Fund, thus marking the demise of the first psychological body.

It is interesting to note that psychology in Singapore at this early phase was presented as something practical rather than as a scientific discipline to be studied in an institution of higher learning. Although Raffles' College had been established a year earlier, philosophy was not included as a course of study. It is not far-fetched to suggest that this early perception of psychology led to the development of psychology as a profession rather than an academic discipline.

POST-WAR SINGAPORE (1945-1965)

Although the British returned as liberators after the War in 1945 the local population of Chinese, Malays and Indians had lost confidence in British colonial power. From being a Crown Colony from April 1946, Singapore became an internally self-governing state in 1959. During this period, Singapore and neighbouring Malaya were engaged in the anti-colonial movement. In 1963 Singapore joined the new Federation of Malaysia, thus ending British rule of this island.

Beginning of Psychological Services in Singapore

It was within this context that psychology reappeared. After the British had re-established colonial rule in Singapore, the first known person to be appointed as a psychologist was V. W. Wilson, D.S.C., M.A., Dip. Ed. Wilson, an Australian, was appointed to the Colonial Medical Service in 1956 on contract from the United Kingdom to build up and incorporate a full psychological service within the mental health programme based at the Woodbridge (Mental) Hospital.

In 1928 when the Woodbridge Hospital (then known as the Mental Hospital) was established, the psychiatric services were run mainly by British doctors and psychiatrists. Custodial care was the mainstay of the day. The Medical Superintendent from 1928-1934 was Dr. E. R. Stone, and from 1935-1950 Dr. B. F. Home. During this time, Electroconvulsive and Insulin Coma therapies were introduced. (From 1942-1945, the Hospital was taken over by the Japanese and became the Japanese Civilian and Military Hospital.) From 1950 till 1958, Dr. J. Browne M.D., D.P.M., F.R.C.Psych. was Medical Superintendent, and he introduced many changes and improvements to Woodbridge Hospital, including the need for a psychological service. The appointment of Wilson was in line with the policy of the time, according to which key appointments were normally filled by British officers.

Just before Wilson's appointment Wong Man Kee, a graduate of Western Reserve University (USA), commenced limited psychological functions as a 'pupil psychologist'. The term 'pupil psychologist' was used to denote that he required further training before he could be deemed "qualified" for professional service, and he in fact left for further training at the Institute of Psychiatry, London.

Upon his appointment on 11 September 1956, Wilson began to construct the basic framework for the development of a psychological service. He proposed that the Psychology Department would function in four main ways:

(1) to provide psychological and clinical services in the medical, social welfare and educational fields;
(2) to plan a programme of basic psychological research into social and cultural influences;
(3) to organise formal courses in psychology for psychiatric nurses and other professional staff whose work brings them into contact with psychological problems;

(4) to make available professional advice to Government bodies, for example on selection and promotion methods.

From the outset, Wilson's proposal for a psychological service, although within the mental health programme, was quite far-reaching, covering medical, social welfare and educational fields as well as providing advisory services to government bodies. Wilson, and later Wong, extended this service to the Shell Petroleum Company in developing Shell's personnel department.

Wilson's contract expired in December 1959, so M. K. ong, who returned at that time, took over his functions. Wilson's departure from Singapore was part of the 'Malayanization' process during which national workers replaced colonial expatriates serving in various government posts. Wong replaced Wilson at about the time when Singapore gained internal self-government.

The new internally independent State of Singapore between 1959 and 1963 was set on seeking full independence and was anti-colonial in outlook. In such an atmosphere, the infant psychological service could not have received the impetus for growth it might have done had it remained under British Colonial administration. Wong was to work alone for the next nine years in nurturing the service until a second psychologist was appointed in March 1968. Wong left the service in 1969.

The slow growth of psychology during the 1960's and early 1970's could be attributed to two factors. At the general level, the newly elected Singapore Government, which a few years earlier had fought for and won independence, was consolidating its authority. Understandably, there was a strong resistance to any foreign interference to its socio-political policies. Two expatriates associated with philosophy and psychology, Professor F. Cioffi and Professor Leonard Cohen[5], at separate periods had open ideological differences with the authorities over certain social issues which stirred the already murky waters concerning foreign interference. Professor Cioffi reportedly debated with certain key supporters of the then newly elected PAP (People's Action Party) Government over sensitive labour and trade union policies. Professor Cohen allegedly took issue with the Government in the press over policies on national (military) service, housing and other matters around 1970-1971. Some of his critical remarks were made in the Singapore Herald, at the height of a controversy over the Government's move to shut down this newspaper after an alleged foreign move to gain control of the paper. It is not too far wrong to believe that academic psychology was thus not held in high esteem by the authorities for a number of years following.

At the more specific level, because psychological services from their very inception came under psychiatric administration they were accorded lower priority and had to play second fiddle to psychiatry. Although the working relationship between psychiatrists and psychologists has all along been cordial compared with the perennial conflict between the two professions in other countries, the domination of psychiatry was an important factor in eclipsing the development of clinical psychology in Singapore.

PSYCHOLOGY TODAY IN THE REPUBLIC OF SINGAPORE (1965 TO THE PRESENT)

On 9th August 1965 Singapore became a fully independent Republic. The chief architects of modern Singapore, Premier Lee Kuan Yew and his colleagues, were totally committed to building Singapore into a viable and progressive modern state. Apart from its multi-racial population[6] and strategic geographic position, Singapore is devoid of any natural and mineral resources. The success story of how Singapore grew in strength and in international stature as a centre for commerce, finance, communications and industry, enjoying political and labour stability, is best told elsewhere (for example, in Time Magazine, January 25, 1982). The main preoccupation of Singapore since independence was (and still is) socio-economic survival and industrial progress.

During the '70's Singapore faced several crises; the premature British pull-out from East of Suez and the oil crisis were just two which could have crippled and even destroyed the young nation. To survive, industries had to be rapidly developed. The British military bases and installations had to be turned into commercial and other useful centres. The drive towards industrialisation was intense and fast. Because of the close association between GNP growth and the standard of engineering and technology, especially as observed in Japan and West Germany, the Singapore Government was committed to technical education in the schools as well as to the training and deployment of scientific and technological professionals at the tertiary institutions. Engineering, architecture and other applied 'hard' sciences were emphasised.

Against this backdrop, psychology re-implanted as a psychiatry-based service was hardly seen as relevant to Singapore's drive towards industrialisation. As an academic subject, psychology was regarded as a 'soft' science involving experiments with rats and the like. The pressing need of Singapore was a technocrat in a factory, not a rat in a Skinner box.

The Teaching of Psychology

The academic aspect of psychology in Singapore is one of identity crisis. Although psychology was taught as early as 1914 or 1915 to medical students, the growth of this subject over the decades has been rather stunted. Psychology as a subject in one form or another is being offered at present in the departments of social work, sociology, philosophy, business administration, and in the faculty of medicine at the National University of Singapore; it has never been accorded the respectability of being a separate department. In 1965, the then University of Singapore Council decided on sociology instead of psychology as an additional department in the Faculty of Social Science.

Psychology was taught in the Department of Social Work as early as 1952 as part of the social work curriculum. Ms. Beryl Wright, an Australian psychologist, taught the implications of both Eastern and Western philosophy for psychology for a year under a Colombo Plan arrangement. After her, the subject was taught by several expatriate part-time personnel who had some qualification in psychology. At present psychology courses are conducted by two full-time lecturers within the Social Work Department, emphasising human growth and development and counselling.

The Department of Philosophy (which became a full department in 1954 after being part of the English Department) did offer some courses relating to psychology. Professor Frank Cioffi (now Professor of Philosophy at Essex University) between 1955 and 1956 introduced a Philosophy of Science course which discussed the theories of Freud, Jung and Adler. At present some aspects of psychological approach to theory and methodology are taught in the Philosophy of Natural and Social Sciences as well as in Logic and Scientific Method courses.

Social psychology and organisational psychology are now being taught in the department of Sociology and Business Administration. In the Faculty of Medicine, general and clinical psychology have been featured since the mid-1950's. The course lecturer has all along been one of the clinical psychologists attached to the Woodbridge Hospital. A full-time lecturer has since been appointed to lecture in psychology within the Department of Psychological Medicine.

Though Nanyang University had offered some courses of study relating to psychology to the undergraduates in the Department of Education prior to 1967, general psychology was only formally introduced to the faculty as an optional course for all first year students in 1969. The following year saw another two courses (social psychology and social statistics) added to the curriculum for the second year students.

Because of the popularity of the courses among the students, the then Nanyang University decided to set up a degree granting unit in 1976 within the Faculty of Arts. It was to be known as the Sociology/Psychology Programme. The programme provided various major courses in sociology as well as in psychology. It was well accepted by the students until the merger of Nanyang University with the University of Singapore into the National University of Singapore in 1980, since when these courses have been discontinued. English remains the language of instruction at the University, so that textbooks are readily available.

Apart from the two universities in Singapore, the other tertiary institution which has offered psychology was the Teachers' Training College. Dr. Lau Wai Har (who later became the College's director) was one of the earliest to teach educational psychology in the early 1960's. Educational Psychology then was only part of the Principles of Education course which also included History of Education. Most of the psychology courses were geared to the preparation of teachers in training. Educational psychology had been taught in the School of Education, University of Singapore, since the 1950's. As the Teacher's Training College developed rapidly, the School of Education was closed down. Today, educational psychology is a prominent subject in the Institute of Education (the new name for the TTC).

234

Research

Since there has never been a separate department of psychology in any Singapore university, there is virtually no active psychological research programme at this level. The present library of the National University of Singapore has a fine collection of books and journals in psychology which can provide reasonable support for any psychological research projects.

Published work in established psychological journals by psychologists in Singapore based on on-going research activities in the country is rare. Various individual psychologists have however published journal articles, in the areas of their own interests, but there is a lack of a well coordinated cross-cultural research programme.

Some of the known published works by psychologists in Singapore include early papers by Wilson (1959, 1960) who conducted studies on juvenile prostitutes and on the use of the Rorschach with Asian people. Boey (1977, 1978) and Elliot (1971, 1972, 1978) have both focussed on perceptual and cognitive psychology. Leong (1978) has made a study on the adjustment of youths in the army while Tai (1981) dealt with the drug menace in the Singapore Armed Forces. Ong (1969, 1970, 19733, 1977) paid attention to the study of university students' attitudes and scholastic achievement. In the area of medical and clinical psychology, Long and colleagues (1972, 19733, 1974, 1977, 1980) have done limited studies in haemodialysis, child guidance, token economy, transsexualism, and traditional healing. Several normative studies have been attempted, by Kadri (1971) of the MMPI, and Long (1973, 1979) of the Raven's Progressive Matrices and the Eysenck Personality Inventory. There have been other normative studies carried out by the Personnel Research and Education Department (Ministry of Defence) on the 16 PF and a range of other psychological measures, but the findings have not been published.

Applied Psychological Services

As earlier indicated, the professional angle of psychology in Singapore has been better perceived by the community than its academic aspect. Even so, there has been a misperception of the role of a psychologist as most Singaporeans, including professionals, have little or no idea what psychologists really do. There has always been the confusion between a psychiatrist and a psychologist. For historical reasons, psychologists have been thought to work only in mental hospitals.

Concepts of mental health in Singapore vary considerably among the various racial and cultural groups and are also strongly dependent on levels of education. All along, most Chinese, Indians and Malays have attributed any form of abnormal behavioural pattern to spiritual causes for which they would consult traditional healers (temple mediums, bomohs, priests and the like). Studies have shown that at least 51 per cent of first admissions to Woodbridge Hospital had consulted traditional healers prior to coming for help at the psychiatric hospital (Tan, Chee & Long, 1980). This figure of 51 per cent is low compared with other reports where 90 per cent of Chinese patients sought traditional healers first before their admission into an acute general hospital (Gwee, A.L., 1969).

Concepts of mental health also vary according to educational level. Those westernized Singaporeans well educated in English are more inclined to accept western concepts, whereas those with low education (primary level or below), regardless of ethnic grouping, tend to follow their respective cultural beliefs regarding abnormal behaviour. Psychology in the main has not exercised any sort of formative role. It is seen more as a set of clinical techniques. There is no interaction or clash of values with any of the major religious tenets. The fastest phase of development of applied psychology in Singapore was during the 1970's in the areas of clinical psychological service and personnel research and evaluation in the armed forces. The clinical psychological service was probably the earliest applied area of psychology to take root in Singapore. At the direction of the then Minister for Health, Mr. Chua Sian Chin, a five year projection for psychological services within the Ministry of Health was submitted in April 1970 by F.Y. Long. It recommended among other things that by 1975 there should be a total of nine psychologists serving the Ministry instead of the existing two. The Ministry of Health Department of Psychology now has the highest number of psychologist, seven in all, serving at the Woodbridge (psychiatric) Hospital, Child Psychiatric Clinic and the Singapore General Hospital. Together they provide clinical services for children, adolescents and adults in both assessment (psychometric, diagnostic, neuropsychological) and therapy (behavioural, supportive, play and group). During 1980, this Department held 2,417 clinical sessions involving 1,786 new cases.

Independence in 1965 was followed by the need for national defence and a fairly rapid build-up of the Singapore Armed Forces. Several psychologists were appointed to these. Yip Weng Kee, trained in educational and industrial psychology, became the first head of the Armed Forces' Education Department, which by 1966 also included psychological services. The main concerns were motivation, morale, conduct and attitudinal adjustment of young national servicemen. A separate psychological unit was formed out of the Education Department. By 1968 the Personnel Research and Education Department had taken over all the psychological and educational functions. This P. R. & E. Department, headed by Lieutenant-Colonel Leong Choon Cheong and later by Lieutenant-Colonel (Dr.) Tai Foong Leong, was to make a major contribution to applied psychology in Singapore. At present five civilian psychologists and a number of military research officers make up its staff. The Republic of Singapore Air Force since 1982 has begun its own separate aviation psychological unit.

Applied psychology in the education area has been largely in the form of vocational guidance and counselling. Before moving to the Ministry of Defence in 1966, Yip Weng Kee was head of the Guidance Unit in the Ministry of Education. His main programme was in vocational guidance and test development. The vocational guidance programme was carried on later by Tan Teng Wai till the mid-1970's when it was phased out by the Ministry of Education. Another Guidance Unit based at the Institute of Education was started in 1975 by Katherine Yip and continues to serve the schools today. The other psychology-related activity in the Ministry of Education was educational research where various test and measurements projects formed part of the Research Division's activities. It was not until 1982 that an Educational Psychology Unit was set up to provide services to the schools, and this is not yet fully operational.

The Ministry of Social Affairs (which caters for general social welfare and welfare institutions) appointed its first psychologist, Dr. John Elliot, in 1974. This Ministry now has two psychologists who provide assistance to the Juvenile Court, Probation and Aftercare Service, as well as a programme of assessment and therapy of individual problem cases. Several voluntary welfare organisations for the blind, retarded and the educationally sub-normal have all recently engaged their own psychologists to carry out their respective welfare programmes.

The Prisons Department within the Ministry of Home Affairs appointed its first psychologist, Loh Yan Poh, in 1973 to draw up a programme of assessment, counselling, and rehabilitation of inmates at the Changi Prison, Reformative Training Centre and Drug Rehabilitation Centre. The Home Affairs Ministry now has two psychologists.

Industrial psychology was quite irrelevant to Singapore's needs during the first half of the 1960's as the drive towards industrialisation was not in full swing until the latter half of the 1960's. It was in the 1970's that the multinational corporations began to make their presence felt. Even so there was no felt need for industrial psychology. Labour was plentiful and cheap and the Singapore workers were, it seemed, naturally hard-working and productive.

Singapore's labour shortage came about with rapid developments in the shipbuilding, petrochemical, electronics, precision engineering and building construction industries. There was manpower shortage in practically every sector as the push towards the upper rung of the technological ladder necessitated a more skilful and productive workforce. It was only in the last five years that the importance of applied psychology was realised.

The current emphasis on productivity in both industrial and service organisations has given a strong impetus to the need for applied psychology. The National Productivity Board, a semi-governmental body which is spearheading the productivity movements in Singapore, has recruited five psychologists to augment its programmes concerning work motivation, performance appraisal, quality control circles, human relations and the like. From time to time well known overseas experts in organisational and industrial psychology have been invited by the NPB to conduct courses and seminars for interested groups.

The Training and Employment of Psychologists

As the universities in Singapore do not have any full teaching programme in psychology all the Singapore psychologists have received their training and qualifications in psychology from overseas universities. In 1967, a meeting with five psychologists was convened by the Public Service Commission to discuss training requirements. The PSC, which is the central training and recruitment authority for the Civil Service, felt then that it was time to deal with social and cultural improvement following a period of rapid technological and industrial change.

The 1967 meeting was chaired by the then Secretary of the Public Service Commission, Mr. Chan Keng Howe. Mr. Chan, in his address to the meeting, stated that Singapore by 1967 had to a large extent successfully dealt with the physical construction phase in terms of building up an infrastructure and the physical amenities of housing, road, bridges, school buildings and the like. The supply of scientists and technologists was considered satisfactory. He stressed that it was now time to focus attention on social and cultural development in the country with emphasis on integrating the various ethnic groups into one nation. It was felt that the contribution of psychologists was essential in achieving this ultimate objective. It was therefore necessary to project the training requirements right away in order to anticipate the "lead-time" taken up by training before qualified personnel would be available. It was intended that scholarships which were hitherto heavily weighted in favour of sciences and technology should be channelled to other areas such as psychology.

Indeed, within a few years a number of scholars were sent to Australia and America for training in psychology. Table 1 presents the countries from which 44 members of the Singapore Psychological Society received their highest qualifications in psychology[8].

Table 1: Countries Where Singapore Psychologists Qualified

Country	Number	Percentage
Australia	18	40.9
United Kingdom	12	27.3
United States	8	18.2
New Zealand	4	9.1
Hong Kong	1	2.2
Canada	1	2.2
	44	100

As can be seen, Australia has trained the highest number of Singapore psychologists, followed by the United

Kingdom and United States. Thus, Australia's influence on psychology in Singapore has been felt from Beryl Wright in 1952 and Wilson in 1956 till the present time.

Not all the graduates in psychology are employed in the capacity of professional psychologists. Only about half are engaged in psychological functions or teaching. Only one or two are in private clinical practice. Most of the rest are not directly involved with psychological work. Table 2 provides a rough classification of work settings where psychology graduates were employed in 1980.

Table 2: Work Settings of Psychology Graduates

Setting	Number	Percentage
Administration/Management	8	18.2
Hospital/Clinic	7	15.9
Armed Forces	6	13.6
Welfare/Social Service	5	11.3
Education	5	11.3
University	4	9.1
Industry	3	6.8
Private Practice/Enterprise	3	6.8
Correctional Service	1	2.3
Journalism	1	2.3
Others	1	2.3
	44	100

The Singapore Psychological Society

The 1930 Singapore Psychological Association was more a social club than a learned society. Those who could afford to attend Dr. Fennelly's lectures qualified as members. There was no examination of any sort. None of the members had any academic qualification in psychology. However, although it was essentially a social club this first Psychological Association, had it not been interrupted by the War, could have developed into a society for professional and academic psychologists.

From the late 1960's several unsuccessful attempts were made by the handful of psychologists to form a professional association. The lack of members was obviously a setback here. It was not until October 1978 that the renewed effort led by LTC C. C. Leong bore fruit. The Singapore Psychological Society was thus inaugurated on 20 January 1979 with forty founding members. The first elected president was F. Y. Long who served two terms followed by LTC C. C. Leong in 1981 and Dr. F. L. Tai in 1982. The present S.Ps.S. was formed along similar lines to psychological societies in the USA, UK or Australia.

The aim of the Society is to advance psychology as a science and as a profession in Singapore. It sets out to promote knowledge in psychology and its application for the benefit of the community. A Code of Professional Conduct modelled very closely on that of the Hong Kong Psychological Society and the Australian Psychological Society has also been adopted.

Full membership of the S.Ps.S. is open to those with a university degree in which psychology is a main or major subject, plus two years of relevant working experience. It is also open to those with a postgraduate qualification in psychology recognized by the S.Ps.S. Council. Associate membership is open to psychology students and to those who have studied the subject to some extent at a university.

Since its inception the Society has established contacts both with local professional and public bodies and various international psychological organisations. Its activities include the holding of regular talks, a community welfare service scheme, publication of a monthly newsletter, a career guidance pamphlet and a professional bulletin[9] (Singapore Psychologist), participation in seminars,[10] workshops and social functions. Some members of the Society have also joined hands with allied professionals in social work and psychiatry to form the Singapore Association for Counselling which was launched in May 1982.

The formation of the S.Ps.S. marks a significant milestone in the growth and development of psychology in Singapore in that it has become widely accepted by other professionals as a distinct professional group. Since its formation the Society has spoken out on the need for a department of psychology at the university and on other relevant social issues in Singapore.

FUTURE DIRECTIONS

The future for Singapore psychology is one of mixed uncertainty. On the one hand, psychology in Singapore is at the threshold of an exciting spurt in growth as Singapore moves rapidly in its industrialisation drive up the high technology ladder. McKinney (1976) observed that psychology grew up in those cultures where there was an emphasis on industry and commerce. He pointed out that the growth of psychology in the US has been greatly influenced by the American culture which places strong emphasis on these fields. Indeed, Singapore is looking towards both Japan and the advanced industrialised Western world (US, UK, West Germany and others) for the transfer of technology and manpower development practices. The human factor in this scenario will undoubtedly require the attention of applied psychology in a significant way.

There are signs that government leaders, administrators and some professionals are beginning to see the importance of applied psychology. The Singapore Government has committed itself to making radical changes to its personnel management philosophy for the whole civil service. The aim is to provide long-term career planning for individuals by identifying their talents and developing their potential to the fullest, and also to bring out the best in them in a good man-to-job match (Straits Times, April 19, 1982). Within this framework, there is plenty of scope for psychologists in Singapore to make a contribution. The President of the Republic of Singapore himself has hinted at the need for psychologists to assess "the strength of character and emotional stability" of potential scholars earmarked for prestigious scholarships and who will serve as leaders in the Civil Service (Straits Times, July 2, 1982).

Apart from its drive towards higher productivity and human resources development in both the Civil Service and private industrial organisations, the Singapore Government is also deeply concerned with educational, social and community development. The present concerns in these areas are the restoration of the traditional extended three-tier family, the inculcation of religious values and Confucian ethics, bi-lingualism in education, reaffirmation of cultural identity for the different ethnic groups, and crime prevention.

Within this context of social change and community development, Singapore psychologists can certainly make a contribution. For instance, the Government has commissioned a team of psychologists (with a sociologist and a psychiatrist) to make an in-depth psychosocial study of Triad secret societies with the view of taking preventative measures to help youths escape the lure of such deviant groups. The team submitted its report in March

1981, since when the Government has taken steps to revive the boys' club movement as a countermeasure against the adverse influence of the Triad gangs (Straits Times, May 6 and 11, 1982).

Most recently, the Singapore Government has also come to grips with an ominous population trend involving unmarried graduates. The Prime Minister in his 1983 National Day speech drew attention to an alarming number of graduates remaining unmarried;[11] those graduates who are married tend to have fewer children than the population norm (1.7 children as compared with 3.5). This situation is confounded by a preference among Singapore male graduates to marry women with lower educational levels, whereas female graduates usually choose husbands with equal or higher qualifications. Statistically, the outcome of this population trend is likely to be skewed, with negative social and economic implications for Singapore's future progress. A team comprising sociologists, doctors, administrators and a psychologist has been appointed to make a close study of the issues involved in order that steps may be taken to counteract the drift.

Other problem areas can be similarly identified where psychologists may be called upon to study and recommend programmes of assistance and prevention. Problems such as crowded group living, multiracial relations, inter-generational relations, ageing, multi-language learning and a host of human factor difficulties in industry can exercise the expertise of social, occupational, clinical and educational psychologists for years to come.

Despite signs pointing to a bright prospect for applied psychology in Singapore, its expected growth may be hindered by the prevailing government decision to freeze all civil service posts for the present in line with the policy on mechanisation and manpower saving. Numerically, the fifteen orso psychologist posts in the Civil Service are not likely to be added to in the near future.

On the other side, academic psychology is likely to remain obscure. It is unlikely that a department of psychology will be established in the next five years at the University although the subject content in psychology has increased in the medical, social work and sociology curricula. From time to time, a visiting professor in psychology may be appointed to a fixed-term chair in one of the large departments, such as the School of Management. But this is far short of a department of psychology. The reason for academic psychology's retarded growth is due to the persistent misconception of psychology as belonging to the psychiatric hospital, and that a university department of psychology must necessaarily produce professional practitioners to serve the mental hospital and welfare institutions.

It therefore appears that the private sector holds a brighter prospect for psychologists to make their contributions, especially in the areas of personnel evaluation and selection, performance appraisal, management role enhancement and the like. At present several psychologists have established themselves in management consultancies, consumers research and clinical practice. There is wider scope for more psychologists to take up the challenge in the industrial and service sectors.

In whichever area they may find themselves, there is no doubt that psychologists in Singapore will be playing a more significant role and making a contribution on their part to help the Republic of Singapore to become a clean, green and cultured nation where its citizens enjoy gracious living.

NOTES

1. The Bugis were an ethnic group from the Celebes Islands, Indonesia.

2. Professor H. B. M. Murphy, at present professor of transcultural psychiatry, McGill University, was a former student health physician at the University of Singapore during the 1950's. Professor Murphy and his wife, a social worker with training in testing, conducted various psychological tests on university students for research purposes.

3. Reference for Dr. Fennelly's visit and lectures was by way of some very old photographs, pre-War (undated) newspaper cuttings and various pieces of papers kept in Mr. Ignatius Sumboo's possession.
Just prior to Dr. Fennelly's arrival, a new Mental Hospital of 24 wards was constructed in 1928. 1030 patients were transferred from the New Lunatic Asylum to this new Mental Hospital (the present Woodbridge Hospital).

4. During this period, this amount of money could buy several hectares of land in Singapore.

5. Professor L. Cohen was a professor in the School

of Commerce at Nanyang University but he usually identified himself as professor of psychology and behavioural science.

6. The 2.4 million population today is composed of 76.9% Chinese, 14.6% Malays, 6.4% Indians and 2.1% Eurasians and other ethnic groups. (Based on 1980 Census in Monthly Digest of Statistics, Department of Statistics, Singapore, August 1982, Vol. 21, No. 8).

7. Following the merger, the former Nanyang University campus has been developed into the present Nanyang Techological Institute. The NTI provides degree courses in the engineering sciences.

8. There were 7 members with doctorates, 21 with Masters degrees and/or Post-graudate Diplomas, and 16 Bachelors (including Honours) degrees.

9. This is published annually. The first issue included such topics as "Singapore Psychologists in Search of a Role", "Psychology as a Profession", "Mental Testing of Brain Damage and Functional Disorders", "Stress, Emotions & Psychosomatic Manifestations", "S.Ps.S. Code of Professional Conduct", and a "Directory of Members".

10. The Society has organised annual seminars on such themes as "Psychology in Education" and "Psychology in the Service of the Disabled".

11. Based on an Inland Revenue Department Survey, there are 30,197 Singaporean graduates (8980 females and 21,217 males). As at July 1983, 54 per cent of 7516 graduates employed in the Civil Service alone are unmarried.

APPENDIX

Topics of lectures delivered by Dr. P. Fennelly in Singapore in 1929

Science of Life - intelligence in the body
Origin and Growth of Individuality - instincts, repressions, complexes, sublimation
Mind, its Growth, Development and Purpose - origin of fear, nerves, rules for liberating hidden powers
Science of Healing - harmonising mental conflicts, origin and cure of inferiority feeling
Defensive Mechanisms and their Amazing Influence on Health Explained - curing colds and influenza, constipation, insomnia, failing eyesight, deafness,

stammering, asthma, nerves, indigestion, rheumatism, neuritis, catarrh and other complaints

Rules for Liberating Hidden Powers - establishing reliable memory, developing power of concentration, cultivating and directing thought and imagination

Reading and Understanding Others - the key to character, distinguishing marks of personality, why some succeed and others fail, how hidden talents and dormant potentialities are discovered and employed

Business Rules - acquiring presence and poise, dominating a situation, influencing by argument and suggestion, preparing, writing and displaying advertisements

Rules for Analysing Others - rules for self analysis, revealing and establishing latent powers, self-realisation, correcting nervous disorders

Neurasthenia, Depression, Inertia - mind wandering, indecision, shyness, self-consciousness

Employing the Hidden Self - overcoming mental conflicts, unifying the mind, establishing personality, creating magnetism

Vibrations, Colour Values - rules for developing will power, force and control, rules for developing power of concentration, rules for developing efficiency

Rules for Developing the Master Mind - establishing memory, character, initiative, self-confidence, self-assurance, directive ability, health, happiness and success

REFERENCES

BOEY, K. W. The relationship between traditional Chinese parental attitudes and the development of cognitive complexity and rigidity. Institute of Humanities and Social Sciences, Nanyang University, Research Project Series, 1977, No. 84.

BOEY, K. W. A cognitive approach to the study of rigidity: a revision. Institute of Humanities and Social Sciences, Nanyang University, Occasional Paper Series, 1977, No. 87.

BOEY, K. W. Cognitive complexity and rigidity measured under task-oriented ego-involved conditions, Journal of Sociology & Psychology, 1978, 1, 9-16.

DORAISAMY, T. R. (ed.) 150 years of education in Singapore. Singapore Teachers' Training College Publication Board, 1969.

ELLIOT, J. M. (with CONNOLLY, K. J.) Evolution and ontogeny of hand function, in Blurton-Jones N. (ed.) Ethological studies of Child behaviour, Cambridge University Press, Cambridge, 1971.

ELLIOT, J. M. (with CONNOLLY, K. J.) Hierarchical structure in motor skills, in K. J. Connolly & J. Bruner (eds.) Development of   Competence, 1972.

ELLIOT, J. M. (with CONNOLLY, K. J.) The effect of visual frame of reference on a judgement of plan stimulus orientation by children, Perception, 1978, 7, 139-149.

GWEE, A. L. A study of Chinese medical practice in Singapore, Singapore Medical Journal, 1969, 10, 2-7.

KADRI, Z. N. The use of the MMPI for personality study of Singapore students, British Journal of Social and Clinical Psychology, 1971, 10, 90-91.

LEONG, C. C. Youth in the army, Singapore: Federal Publication, 1978.

LONG, F. Y. (with KHOO, O. T., LIM C. H. et al.) Three years experience of regular dialysis in Singapore, Annals of the Academy of Medicine, 1972, 1, 13-25.

LONG, F. Y. Note on Psychological Services in Singapore, Australian Psychologist, 1972, 7, 215-219.

LONG, F. Y. (with OON, P. K. & LEE, M. M.) Two years experience of child guidance service in Singapore, Singapore Medical Journal, 1972, 13, 245-248.LONG, F. Y. Some intelligence and personality data of Singapore medical students, Singapore Medical Journal, 1973, 14, 34-36.

LONG, F. Y. (with PHUA, E. C. & TAN, K. H.) Token economy programme in Singapore, Nursing Journal of Singapore, 1973, 13, 103-109.

LONG, F. Y. (with LEE, M. M.) Some psychosocial charact- eristics of sex change requestors in Singapore, Malayan Medical Journal, 1974, 28, 208-212.

LONG, F. Y. (with TSOI, W. F. & KOK, L. P.) Male transsexualism in Singapore: a description of 56 cases, British Journal of Psychiatry, 1979, 31, 405-409.

LONG, F. Y. A study of the RPM and EPI with some occupa- tional groups in Singapore, Journal of Sociology and Psychology, 1979, 2, 36-42.

LONG, F. Y. (with TAN, C. T. and CHEE K. T.) Psychiatric patients who seek traditional healers in Singapore, Singapore Medical Journal, 1980, 21, 643-647.

McKINNEY, F. Fifty years of psychology, American Psycho-

247

logist, 1976, 31, 834-842.
MURPHY, H. B. M. The beginnings of psychiatric treatment in the Peninsular, in N. N. Wagner, & E. S. Tan (eds.) Psychological problems and treatment in Malaysia, Kuala Lumpur, University of Malaya Press, 1971.
MURPHY, H. B. M. Personal Communication, 15th September 1982.
ONG, T. H. Student personnel work in higher education, Malayan Journal of Education, 1969, 6, 66-70.
ONG, T. H. A study of the relationship between study methods and scholastic achievement of university students, Nanyang Digest, 1970, 2, 388-393.
ONG, T. H. A study of general abilities of university students, Malayan Journal of Education, 1973, 10, 23-28.
ONG, T. H. A comparative study of the scholastic achievement between the national service and the non-national service students at Nanyang University, Institute of Humanities & Social Sciences, Nanyang University, Occasional Paper Series No. 67, March 1977.
STRAITS TIMES, April 19, 1982.
STRAITS TIMES, May 6, 1982.
STRAITS TIMES, May 11, 1982.
STRAITS TIMES, July 2, 1982.
TAFT, R. Psychology and its history in Australia, Australian Psychologist, 1982, 17, 31-39.
TAI, F. L. (ed.) Curbing Drug Abuse: The SAF Experience. Singapore: Federal Publications, 1981.
TEOH, J. I. History of institutional psychiatric care in Singapore 1862-1967, in N. N. Wagner, & E. S. Tan (eds.) Psychological problems and treatment in Malaysia, Kuala Lumpur, University of Malaya Press, 1971.
WILSON, V. W. A psychological study of juvenile prostitutes, The International Journal of Social Psychiatry, 1959, 5, 61-73.
WILSON, V. W. The use of the Rorschach method with Asian people, Australian Journal of Psychology, 1960, 12, 199-202.
WOODBRIDGE HOSPITAL. Newsletter: 50th Anniversary (1928-1978) Special Issue, 1978.

248

ORAL HISTORY SOURCES

1. Professor Ho Wing Meng, Department of Philosophy, National University of Singapore.
2. Associate Professor Anne E. Wee, Department of Social Work, National University of Singapore.
3. Mr. Ong Teck Hong, Lecturer in Psychology, Department of Social Work, National University of Singapore.
4. Mr. Ignatius N. Sumboo, Retired Chief Clerk, Former Singapore City Council. (Mr. Sumboo passed away in 1982.)
5. Dr. Lau Wai Har, Retired Director, Institute of Education.
6. Mr. Yip Weng Kee, Deputy Secretary, Ministry of National Development.
7. Mr. Wong Man Kee, Director, Finance Company.
8. Dr. Ong Jin Hui, Head, Department of Sociology, National University of Singapore.
9 .Associate Professor Tsoi Wing Foo, Department of Psychological Medicine, National University of Singapore.

ACKNOWLEDGMENTS

My special thanks to Professor Norman D. Sundberg, Professor of Psychology, University of Oregon, for his most helpful comments and suggestions, and to Dr. Teo Seng Hock, Director, Woodbridge Hospital, for his advice and support.

16

Psychology in Indonesia:
Its Past, Present and Future[1]

S. C. Utami Munandar
and A. S. Munandar

BACKGROUND

Once known as the East Indies, Indonesia consists of some 13,600 islands covering 576,000 sq. miles and supporting a population of about 165 million. The islands are spread in an arc south of the Asia mainland, north and west of Australia and straddling the equator. Indonesia has been moulded by the cultures of the different peoples who have lived there throughout the ages. Most of the present very mixed ethnic population has come from relatively recent migrations (reportedly in the first and second millenia B.C.) from the Asia mainland. Other evidence points to some Melanesian influence from the Pacific Islands.

Until the fourteenth century Hinduism and Buddhism held sway over the ruling Indonesian families whence the last of the Javanese Hindu kingdoms (Majapahit) succumbed to Islam. Two centuries later the Portugese came in search of cloves and spices and a hundred years later were replaced by the Dutch, who began a slow subjugation of Java and the other islands. This process was not completed until the early part of this century, after both the French and English had held possession of the islands in the early nineteenth century. The Dutch fostered economic development through the forced culti-vation of cash crops, while the Chinese migrant popu-lation established a stronghold over the retail trade.

The Dutch were eventually evicted in 1942 by the Japanese; when Japan surrendered they were able to issue the decalaration of Independence in 1945 under President Sukarno, which was not however recognised by the Dutch.

After many vicissitudes, a unitary state was proclaimed in August of 1950. Subsequent rebellions, including an abortive communist coup in 1965, led to the military takeover under general Suharto and the establishment of more conservative political and economic policies designed to save the country from social disorganisation and financial bankrupcy. General elections held in July 1971 resulted in a landslide victory for the Government backed <u>Golkar</u> - functional groups of technocrats and members of the armed forces in non-military functions. Golkar won again in 1977 and 1982.[2]

Psychology before Indonesian Independence (1945)

At the beginning of the 20th century, European psychology was fostered in Indonesia (at that time known as Netherlands-Indie) by the Dutch. In the 1920s there were sporadic studies conducted by Dutch psychologists (Engelhard, 1923; van Schilfgaarde, 1925; Kits van Heyningen, 1925). In these studies psychological tests were administered to Indonesian ethnic groups in order to gain insight into the 'psyche' of those groups. About two decades later, Dubois conducted a social psychological study on the people of Alor (1944), and Margaret Mead studied the Balinese and their child rearing practices (Mead and Cooke MacGregor, 1951; Mead and Wolfenstein, 1955). These and other studies are cited in Koentjaranigrat (1975).

At that time there were no psychologists in Indonesia. The above mentioned studies were conducted by Dutch psychologists and American anthropologists who took their research data back to their respective countries. Although psychology as related to education was taught at the Teacher Training Schools and dynamic depth psychology within medical schools, psychology was not taught as an independent discipline until the early '50s, after Indonesia became an independent nation.

Psychology after Indonesian Independence

After the Japanese surrender at the end of the Second World War, Indonesia proclaimed its independence (August 17, 1945). However, it was not until 1949 that it was recognized by the Dutch. Together with the allied forces, the Dutch returned to Indonesia and established

the NICA (Nederlands-Indisch Civil Administration) in
Dutch occupied areas. After recognition by the Dutch of
Indonesian independence in December 1949 and their
subsequent withdrawal from the country, they left behind
some administrative officers working for the Balai
Psychtechniek under the auspices of the Ministry of
Education and Culture. This institute was founded in
1941 for the purpose of conducting assessments of
schoolchildren in terms of both their intellectual
abilities and their vocational choice. Others remained
with the Dutch Army psychology unit which was handed over
to the Indonesian army, and later became the Army Centre
of Psychology (Pusat Psikologi Angkatan Darat, PSIAD) in
Bandung. Young Indonesian officers were sent from there
to the Netherlands to study psychology, and they later
continued their studies in psychology at German
universities. In the early 1960s, the Army Centre of
Psychology was consolidated with the return of these
graduates and others from the University of Indonesia.
The need for more staff was felt at this time with the
realisation that tasks were becoming more numerous and
more complex.

It was felt that these needs could best be met by
establishing a Faculty of Psychology at the University of
Padjadjaran. This was approved by the Minister of
Education and officially established in 1961 with the
late Professor Dr. Sumantri Hardjoprakoso, psychiatrist
and Head of the Army Centre of Psychology, as its first
Dean. The teaching staff were mainly drawn from
psychologists at the Army Centre of Psychology, who had
received their training abroad. Now both the Centre and
the faculty of psychology at the University of
Padjadjaran have supplemented their numbers with
graduates trained from within the country.

In 1951, the Institute for Psychotechnics was
established within the Ministry of Education and Culture
headed by a Dutch psychometrist, one of the Dutch
personnel left behind after Indonesian independence. Its
main task was to conduct psychometric measurements for
vocational selection and admission into Secondary
Vocational schools. This Institute established a three
year study programme in psychology to produce assistant
psychologists. This was on the initiative of Professor
Slamet Iman Santoso, at that time one of the very few
Indonesian psychiatric neurologists with a keen interest
in psychology and education. The programme was tutored
by Dutch and Indonesian experts and later became

established within the Department of Psychology, under the Faculty of Medicine, at the University of Indonesia in Jakarta, providing a graduate programme in psychology.

In 1960, the department of psychology was given the status of an autonomous faculty, with Professor Slamet Iman Santoso appointed as its first Dean. At that time it was well staffed with psychologists , mostly graduates from universities in the Netherlands and West Germany, and several graduates from the faculty of psychology itself. Apart from graduate study, several applied fields were established in separate departments: vocational and industrial psychology, clinical psychology, child and educational psychology, experimental psychology, and later, social psychology.

Besides the faculty of psychology at the University of Indonesia, Jakarta, and the faculty of psychology, Padjadjaran University, Bandung, a third psychology faculty was established at Gadjah Mada University, Yogyakarta in 1950. This was the faculty of Letters, Pedagogy, and Philosophy which, by 1955, had split into three: Letters, Philosophy, and Pedagogy. The latter faculty developed a section for psychology. In 1964, when the faculty of Pedagogy was integrated in the Institute of Teacher Training, this section became an autonomous department. The faculty of psychology is an outgrowth of this department, formally established in 1965, with Professor Dr. Masrun as its first Dean.

Looking at the development of these three faculties, it can be seen that psychology emerged as an applied science (for military service, selection and vocational guidance, and education) rather than as an academic science as in Europe. The rapid growth of psychology in general after World War II and, more specifically, the extensive use of psychological tests together with the development of test methodology from abroad, considerably affected psychology in Indonesia. The trend has been to educate 'generalists' rather than 'specialists'. Theoretically as well as in their practical training, students are introduced to various fields of psychology: clinical, child and developmental, educational, vocational and industrial, experimental, and social. Such a curriculum benefits a developing country where there is a scarcity of psychologists. Having absorbed a basic knowledge and practised in various fields, graduates may pursue their personal interest in one specific area of psychology but they also have the basic skills to provide services in other fields of psychology when called upon to use them, as is often the case in Indonesia. Yet now, in view of the growth of psychology abroad, the ever widening applicability of psychology in Indonesia and the ever increasing demands of society, there is a need to consider training specialists.

In consequence of these pragmatic considerations, the faculty of psychology at Padjadjaran University recently decided to train specialists rather than generalists. After a student has obtained the 'Sarjana Muda' (equivalent to Bachelor's) degree, an orientation course (which includes theoretical subject matter as well as practical experience) is given in various applied fields followed by specialization in one field of psychology, according to the student's interest and capabilities. In the near future, specialization courses in various applied fields (for example industrial and organizational psychology, child and developmental psychology, clinical psychology) will be conducted regularly in postgraduate programmes alongside the Magister (S2) postgraduate programme.

In 1977, a two-year specialization training programme in child and developmental psychology for staff members of the department of child and developmental psychology was initiated and sponsored by the University of Indonesia and by the Free University of Amsterdam. The programme comprises a theoretical training in Indonesia followed by a practical training in the Netherlands.

THE CURRENT STATUS OF PSYCHOLOGY IN INDONESIA

The Study of Psychology

The Universities of Indonesia, Padjadjaran and Gadjah Mada are all state run. Apart from the three psychology faculties at these universities, two private universities in Bandung (West Java), Maranata University and the Islam University Bandung, have each established a faculty of psychology. The graduates of these two faculties have to take state examinations in order to be recognized as professional psychologists. Because of the great demand both for psychologists and for those wanting to study the subject, other faculties of psychology are about to be established. One will be opened soon at the Airlangga University in Surabaya (East Java).

In Indonesia the activities of higher education are based on the 'Tri Dharma Perguruan Tinggi', the 'Three

Duties' or basic principles of higher education, comprising teaching, research and service to society, all proportional and in mutual harmony with the development of science and culture (Ministry of Education and Culture, 1977). Education in general is oriented toward the national development programme. The system of education in Indonesia involves six years at Primary School, six years in High School and five years at University to obtain a <u>Sarjana</u> (equivalent to Master's) degree. The higher educational institutions do not generally recognise the Sarjana Madda (equivalent to Bachelor's) degree as a completed course of study. Performance of students at examinations is assessed on a ten point scale with six as the passing grade. Since 1942, the Indonesian language Bahasa, has been the medium of instruction (Budiardjo, Assegaff and Soenarto, 1974).

Higher education in Indonesia occurs to various levels (Strata). The basic level, 'Zero Strata'(S_o), is a non-degree programme and is more practically oriented. Students do not obtain a degree, but receive a 'Diploma' (certificate) as recognition of the skills they have learned. The next level of education, called 'Strata one' (S_1) is a Masters degree programme. Having obtained the Master's degree, graduates may continue following a Magister degree programme, 'Strata Two' (S_2), or they may, according to their interests, follow a 'specialization programme' to become specialists in a branch of psychology (such as a Magister in Educational Psychology, or Specialist in Child Psychology). Education on the highest level, 'Strata Three' (S_3), is a doctoral degree programme for those with a Magister degree of outstanding achievement. The specialists can continue following a programme to become 'higher level' specialists.

<u>The study programme.</u>In spite of their diverse historical background, there is a close working relationship between the three faculties of psychology of the State Universities, through the 'Konsorsium Psikologi.' This is an advisory body, represented by the Deans of the three faculties and coordinated by an Executive Secretary whose main task is to think of ways and means of carrying out programmes to enhance the study of psychology as well as increase its services to Indonesian society. All three faculties of psychology provide a Master's degree programme. Additionally the three faculties provide a two year Magister degree programme in various fields of psychology.

Since 1974, a recognized basic curriculum for a Master's degree in psychology has been established by the 'Konsorsium Psikologi'. This comprises five and a half years of study, leading to a Sarjana Muda or Bachelor degree after three years, and to a Sarjana or Master degree after an additional two and a half years.

At the undergraduate level the general subject matter of psychology is taught, as well as an introduction to the various fields of applied psychology, that is experimental, child and developmental, educational, social, industrial, clinical psychology and psychodiagnostics. Beside these, psychology-related subjects such as sociology, pedagogy, anthropology, and criminology are considered relevant and fundamental to the study of psychology. Other disciplines such as philosophy, religion, Pancasila (the State Philosophy), biology, physiology and neurology, are also taught as well as statistics and research methodology which are included in the curriculum to prepare the student for scientific empirical work.

Number of students in psychology. Over the years the number of students in psychology has been increasing. In 1982 there were 1349 students, of whom 63 per cent were female. Although the number of candidates applying to study psychology is increasing annually (from a few hundred in 1969 to several thousand in 1982), the scale of existing facilities (space, equipment, and teaching staff) is not keeping pace.

Number of graduates in psychology. Compared to the annual input of 100 to 110 new students, the annual output of graduates in psychology remains rather low, resulting in an accumulation of students in the final year. A cause of the rather low output is the high number of drop-out students after the first and second year. The number of graduates from the three faculties of psychology in Indonesia up to July 1982 was 1005.

Research

Research is the second basic principle of the 'Tri Dharma Perguruan Tinggi'. Compared with the other two basic principles, education and service to the society, research has not been proportionally represented. Most of the staff's time is taken up with 'educational functions' (giving lectures and supervising the practical training of students as well as Master's theses) and in services to the community (such as the giving of public speeches on request, providing vocational counselling, psychological assessments in schools and industry, clinical counselling and psychotherapy).

Although clinics for child guidance, vocational guidance and clinical psychology are primarily intended only for practical training purposes, in certain situations the staff have to deal directly with clients or patients.

Staff in higher education are expected to organize research projects, conducted by themsleves as well as by the students. The targets of research are the improvement of research skills of the Civitas Academica, the development of science and technology in Indonesia, and assisting the government in solving problems of both national and regional interest.

As is the case with education in general, research is oriented to the national development programme. Basic or fundamental research studies are not getting the attention they deserve. A review of the research studies conducted by the three faculties of psychology shows that almost all comprise applied research even though basic research is considered important.

One research activity is in the area of psychological testing. Quite a number of tests (intelligence, aptitude, projective tests, inventories, situational tests) from abroad have been translated and standardised with Indonesian norms; some have been adapted or modified, and a few tests have been developed specifically for use in Indonesia, such as the T.K.I. (a group intelligence test) and the T.K.V. (a verbal creativity test).

We are aware that what is valid in one culture may not be valid in another. Yet very few cross cultural studies have been carried out, within and acoss the country. Such studies are necessary to test the generality of psychological theories, to allow comparisons between different cultures, to have an understanding of patterns of behavior, attitudes, and values across cultures. Not much research along these lines has been conducted, considering that psychology has been applied in Indonesia for more than thirty years.

Service to the Community

At the faculties of psychology, service to society comprises activities related to education and the giving of professional services. Educating the community includes activities such as the giving of public lectures on practical psychology for special groups, such as parents or managers, and conducting upgrading courses and workshops for managers and employees. Professional services to the community cover activities such as making psychological assessment, counselling, giving psychological advice and psychotherapy.

The department of child and developmental psychology has a child guidance clinic which deals with the diagnosis of children with emotional disorders and learning difficulties, and gives counselling, guidance, and therapy when needed. The department of clinical psychology provides diagnostic and therapeutic services for those who are in trouble and seek professional assistance. The department of vocational and industrial psychology provides services for individuals seeking study and occupational advice, and for organizations requiring consultation on selection, personnel management, training, and the like. Within these departments service to society is combined with the function of education. Services to society are carried out mostly by psychology students who have to do their practical training under close supervision of the staff, and by some institutes and foundations within or attached to the faculties of psychology.

All three faculties have a foundation established to raise funds to support their needs and activities, including research. The faculty of psychology at Gadjah Mada University has a Consultation Bureau and a publishing foundation. At this and at Padjadjaran University the faculties are not allowed to establish their own independent institutes. Those which do exist are directly responsible to the Rector of the University and have an interdisciplinary structure. The faculty of psychology at the University of Indonesia has two institutes, the Institute of Applied Psychology and the Institute for Psychological Research through which it is extending its services to the community. The Institute for Psychological Research was established in 1975, for the purpose of contributing to the advancement of psychology in Indonesia. It has already provided public services by conducting several research projects requested from outside (for example a study about child rearing practices in several villages in Java and a comparative study about cognitive development in urban and rural areas). It has established cooperation with domestic as well as with foreign scientific institutions (Universitas Indonesia, 1978).

The Association of Indonesian Psychologists

The Association of Indonesian Psychologists (Ikatan Sarjana Psikologi Indonesia) was founded in 1959 and is the only professional association for psychologists in Indonesia. At that time there were only about 10 to 15 psychologists in the whole country. In 1983 the Association had branches in 5 provinces of Java, and about 445 members spread thoughout several branches, 208 in the Jakarta, 101 in West Java, 57 in Yogyakarta, 41 in Central Java, and 38 in East Java. There are only a few psychologists working and living on the islands outside Java.

Lack of facilities and lack of available time of its members have constrained the scope of the Association's activities, although since 1979 efforts have been made to improve things. In October of that year, the first Congress of the Association was held in Yogyakarta, and was attended by a few hundred Indonesian psychologists from all over the country. Thirty-six papers were presented, covering topics in industrial and organizational, social, developmental, educational, clinical psychology, and psychometrics. At this Congress the Constitution of the Association was revised and an Ethical Code of Conduct for Indonesian Psychologists formulated and accepted. The Second Congress of the Association of Indonesian Psychologists was held in October 1982 in Bandung, West-Java, and its theme was 'The Role of Psychology in National Development'.

FUTURE PERSPECTIVES

Psychology in Indonesia is rapidly becoming popular and its scope is widening. There is an increasing demand for psychologists and psychological services. All too often, however, more is demanded from psychologists than can be offered. There is a big difference between the 'psychology mindedness' of Indonesian cities and of villages or remote areas where psychology is still unknown. To date, graduates in psychology have had no difficulty in finding suitable jobs. Even before graduation, final year students get ample opportunity to apply their psychological knowledge and skills, such as by assisting practising clinical, school, and industrial psychologists, as test administrators in group selection and group testing procedures, as interviewers or surveyors in field projects, or in giving guidance to children's playgroups. In almost all fields of application, a rapid expansion of psychological services can be observed.

Educational Psychology

The formal school system comprises a six year primary education, a three year junior secondary education, and a three year senior secondary education. For graduates of primary and junior secondary schools there are schools of vocational education at the junior and senior secondary educational levels if they pass the necessary national or institutional entrance examination. Graduates of senior secondary schools may continue to academic institutions, universities or other forms of tertiary education.[4]

Schools in Jakarta and other big cities are increasingly aware of the services to be provided by school psychologists, not only in diagnosing individual cases, but also in giving psychological evaluations of all the pupils in school, identifying their potential and talents. There are schools which request a psychological report before admitting a new pupil. In these schools, yearly psychometric assessments are undertaken in practically all grades. Psychologists also work with children with special difficulties, such as the blind, deaf, physically and mentally handicapped and the emotionally/ behaviourally maladjusted. Currently, a workgroup of the Ministry of Education and Culture, headed by a psychologist (one of the present authors, S. C. U. Munandar), has been given the responsibility of planning and implementing educational programmes for gifted and talented children in Indonesia (BP3K, 1982). Psychological services in education are also applied in a wider context, such as enhancing village women's capacities, re-educating vagabonds and researching leisure activities.

Child and Developmental Psychology

Child psychologists are needed in a growing number of child guidance clinics and in hospitals. In the fifties and sixties, most parents went to child guidance clinics because they were referred by medical staff or by the school, and a great percentage of the cases were problems of mental retardation. Nowadays, many parents seek advice of their own accord. There is also more variety in the type of emotional and behavioural problems brought to the clinic, indicating that parents are more aware of psychological problems and the services that can be offered.

Industrial and Organizational Psychology

Although selection used to be the main activity of industrial psychologists, other aspects of this field have now been recognised as a result of the economic growth of the country. These include developing training programmes for companies, consulting in organizations and conducting research on topics relevant to the organization. Many psychologists are working in governmental agencies, such as the departments of Labour Force and Transmigration, Social Service, Education and Culture, and the Municipal Government of Jakarta. Recently the department of Labour Force and Transmigration launched a project of vocational guidance, directed at graduates from secondary schools requiring psychological services.

Social Psychology

As a developing country Indonesia is still at the stage of stabilizing its economy and is faced with many social problems, requiring contributions from social psychologists often in cooperation with other social scientists. Transmigration, urbanization, family planning, rural development and the like involve problems of adaptation faced by people in situations of rapid social change and often require a total restructuring of attitudes and values before the transition can be made.

Problems faced by metropolitan cities like Jakarta where youth is exposed to influences from western cultures, such as from films, television and literature, involve parents who are themselves confused about which of the old traditions to maintain and which of the new values to reject or to accept. Juvenile delinquency, aggression, drug addiction and prostitution are but some of the problems requiring the work of psychologists. At this stage of development the demand for research on social psychological problems cannot be met by the existing departments of social psychology.

Clinical Psychology

Though perhaps not to the same extent nor at the same rate as industrial and educational psychology, clinical psychology is developing and has many applications. More and more hospitals require a psychologist for diagnosis, counselling and psychotherapy, in cooperation with medical staff and psychiatrists in particular. Clinical psychologists also have positions in mental heath centres, student guidance services, mental hospitals and in institutes for juvenile delinquents and adolescents with emotional and/or behavioural problems. One of the crucial problems faced by clinical psychology is the competition from other clinical fields in which psychology is also applied (psychiatry, public health and medical therapy). The problem is how to achieve a sound and effective working relationship beneficial to all parties.

CONCLUDING REMARKS

A word of caution should be spoken. The fact that psychology in Indonesia has become popular within a short period of time may be to its disadvantage. Lack of competition might result in work not being critically controlled and tasks might be undertaken by those not fully qualified. Confronted by a diversity of tasks and many job opportunities, it is difficult for psychologists to confine themselves to their own field; they are thus often unable to explore their subject in depth, something which is, after all, a prerequisite for the advancement of the profession.

One of the advantages of the development of psychology in Indonesia is that the Government recognizes the important role that psychology plays for the benefit of the country, and hence gives it its full support.

NOTES

1. This paper is a revised version of the paper "The Current Status of Psychological Studies in Indonesia", by S.C.U. Munadar presented at the First Asian International Conference of Psychology, Kyoto, November, 2-4, 1978, and published in Psychologia, XXII, no. 1, March, 1979.

2. Information in this section was assembled by the editors and is taken from the book All Asia Guide (12th ed.) 1982, which is compiled from information contributed by Far Eastern Economic Review correspondents in the region.

3. Pancasila, the state ideology, means belief in one God, democracy, humanitarianism, social justice and national unity.

4. According to 1982/83 figures there are just over 120,000 primary schools and 24 million primary students; over 12,000 junior secondary schools and over 4 million junior secondary students; over 3,000 senior secondary schools and 1.5 million senior students. There are 49 state universities scattered over 25 provinces, with a student population comprising 83,961 females and 272,965 males.

REFERENCES

BP3K Overarching Goals and Action Plan. Seven Year Plan of Educational Services for the Gifted and Talented, Ministry of Education and Culture 1982.

BUDIARDJO, M., ASSEGAFF, D. H. and SOENARTO, K. Indonesia. In Y. Atal (Ed.) Social sciences in Asia, Abhinav Publications, New Delhi 1974.

DITJEN PENDIDIKAN TINGII, Gambaran Keadaan Pendidikan Tinggi Indonesia. Dep. P and K, 1976.

DUBOIS, C. The people of Alor: a social psychological study of an East Indian island, University of Minnesota Press, Minneapolis. 1944.

ENGLEHARD, C. F. Het Onderzoek Naar de Geestesgestheldheid met Behulp van Platen, Toegespast big den Javaan, Eduard Ydo, Leiden. 1923.

FAKULTAS PSIKILOGI, UI, Buku Pedoman Fakultas Psikologi Universitas Indonesia. 1978-1983.

ISKANDAR N., Universitas dan Institut Negeri di Indonesia pada Dewasa ini. Lembaga Demografi Fak. Ekonomi UI, Jakarta. 1975.

KITS van HEYNINGEN, A. Wetersche Intellectproeven en Primitieve Psyche, Eduard Ydo, Leiden. 1925.

KOENTJARANINGRAT, (ed.) Social sciences in Indonesia, (in press).

KOENTJARANIGRAT, Anthropology in Indonesia: a bibliographical review, Martinus Nijhoff, 'sGravenhage. 1975.

MEAD, M. and COOKE MACGREGOR Growth and culture: a photographic study of Balinese childhood, Putnam, New York. 1951.

MEAD M.and WOLFENSTEIN, M. Childhood in contemporary cultures, University of Chicago Press, Chicago. 1955.

MINISTRY OF EDUCATION AND CULTURE, Education and Culture in Development, 1977.

MUNANDAR, A. S., Psikologi Perusahaan: Masa Kini dan Masa Yang Akan Datang. Jakarta. 1977.

MUNANDAR, S. C. U., The Current Status of Psychological Studies in Indonesia. Psychologia, 1979, XXII, no. 1.

OFFICE OF EDUCATIONAL AND CULTURAL RESEARCH AND DEVELOPMENT, MINISTRY OF EDUCATION AND CULTURE, The Education Sector. A Review of Fact and Comment Regarding the Current Status of Education in Indonesia, Jakarta. 1976.

UNIVERSITAS GADJAH MADA, Buku Pedoman Fakultas Psychologi Universitas Gadjah Mada Tahun Ajaran 1967-1968, Yogyakarta. 1976.

UNIVERSITAS GADJAH MADA, Buku Petinjuk Tahun Adademi. 1977-1978.

UNIVERSITAS GADJAH MADA, Fakultas Psikologi, 1977. Daftar skripsi mahasiswa Faultas Psikologi UGM 1963 s.d. 1977.

UNIVERSITAS INDONESIA, Laporan Rektor 1977. Dies Natalis ke XXVII Universitas Indonesia. 1977.

UNIVERSITAS INDONESIA, General Information 1978-1979. Universitas Indonesia. 1978.

UNIVERSITAS PADJADJARAN, 20 Tahun 1957-1977.1977.

UNIVERSITAS PADJADJARAN, Pedoman 1978-1979. 1978.

17

Decolonizing the Filipino Psyche: Impetus for the Development of Psychology in the Philippines

Virgilio G. Enriquez

BACKGROUND

The Republic of the Philippines comprises 7,107 islands located on the western edge of the Pacific Ocean, east of Vietnam, south of Taiwan and north of Sabah. Philippine climate is tropical with three main seasons. There are approximately fifty million multi-ethnic and multilingual Filipinos who are primarily Malayo-Polynesian. However a good number of them look more <u>Chinito</u> (or Chinese), <u>Bumbay</u> (or Indian), <u>Tisoy</u> (or Spanish), and <u>Bisoy</u>[1] (or American) in various degrees.

From the point of view of tourist promotion, the Philippines is the "third largest English speaking country in the world." English is spoken and understood by Filipinos who went through American-oriented schools with English as medium of instruction. However, one has to settle with the heavy accent in "<u>Tenkyu beri mats</u>." The new Philipino constitution of 1986 is likely to retain the English language as an official language but it is the Filipino language which is used across across the archipelago by the man-on-the-street on the other side of the Great Cultural Divide. The legally minded elite refuses to acknowledge the existence of a Philippine national language; writers and language scholars argue between <u>P</u>ilipino and <u>F</u>ilipino; and the University of California-trained Filipino teachers of English argue passionately for the colonial language but the fact remains that the language of the Philippine masses is the language of the Philippines.

The dominant home-grown religion is <u>Iglesia ni Kristo</u>. The historian Agoncillo (1974) explains:

Like the Philippine Independent Church, the Iglesia is by the masses. The masses who belong to the Catholic Church are superficial Catholics, while those belonging to the Iglesia are devoted followers and loyal adherents of their Church.... The Catholics, it is true, go to Church on Sundays and holidays, but they do so not because they understand and appreciate the mysticism and poetry of the Catholic rites, but because it is the fashion to be seen in the Church on such days. And so, while statistics show that the Catholics comprise 83% of the total population, actually the genuine Catholics do not probably comprise 0.5% of the whole population.

The Catholics form a majority in the Philippine islands of Luzon and Visayas. The Catholic faith plays an important role in Philippine economy and polity. To be sure, the friar lands have been gradually transferred since 1903 from the Catholic Church to government and private hands but the religious orders have a long way to go in making good their vow of poverty in the islands. The Spanish Dominican priests are still embroiled in a struggle with Filipino priests for financial control of the University of Santo Tomas, the oldest Catholic university in the Phillipines. The struggle surfaced anew just after Filipino consciousness was shaken by the historical assassination of Benigno Aquino at the Manila International Airport. Jaime Cardinal Sin, as leader of Filipino Catholics argued for "reconciliation with justice" as the nation recoils from the shock of a politically motivated murder which ignited a spark that led to the fall of a dictator and a change in leadership.

Islam is dominant in the Southern Philippines as it is dominant in neighbouring Malaysia and Indonesia. Regardless of what the future has in store for the Moro National Liberation Front, the Mindanao calendar includes the Hari Raya Puasa on top of the more familiar Christmas holidays in Luzon. Just the same Filipino religious pscyhology is best found in folk Islam and folk Catholicism but the traditional indigenous religion, animism and respect for nature, are deeply held in various aspects of life.

PSYCHOLOGY IN THE PHILIPPINE COLONIAL CONTEXT

Philippine colonial education fosters the belief that scientific psychology in the country is an American creation, a process which supposedly started soon after Commodore George Dewey won the mock battle of Manila Bay. To begin with, undergraduate psychology courses beyond the introductory course were taught in the College of Education, University of the Philippines, using American textbooks and the English language as medium of instruction less than a decade after the university itself was established in 1908 with Murray Bartlett, an American, as its first president. At the time, Spanish had not altogether given way to English; literary writing in the Filipino language was on the ascendancy, and the socalled Filipino essay "in English" was still a fledgling effort, a tug-of-war between the Hispanic and the indigenous in an attempt to approximate idiomatic English. As Americans gave psychology lectures in the university, the goodwill of many upper and middle-class Filipinos was being won gradually by Governor-General Francis Burton Harrison's policy of attraction.

Agustin Alonzo: early American psychology minus the laboratory animals

The early influence of American education and the colonial culture on Philippine psychology took concrete form in the person of Agustin Alonzo. Harrison's policy of Filipinization and five years of training with advanced psychology paved the way for Alonzo to assume the psychology chair in the state university. Although personnel indigenization annoyed the American community in the Philippines, it was actually a practical policy for the Americans because it cost less to hire a Filipino. Critical positions were of course reserved for the American colonial administrators but the chairmanship of the psychology department of the state university was not considered a "critical" position then or now. The end of the Harrisonian era in 1921 marked the completion of the first M.A. Psychology thesis in English written by Alonzo at the University of the Philippines. Right after completing his M.A. requirements in 1922, Alonzo proceeded to the University of Chicago where he received his Ph.D. in experimental psychology. It was no accident that while in Manila he initially worked on a people-oriented

thesis on the psychology of feeling, but shifted to the
mechanistic determinism of rat psychology in the American
midwest. Alonzo's conscious experience as an Asian in a
white midwestern city impelled him to work for fellow
foreign students towards the establishment of the
International Centre at the University of Chicago.
Filipino scholars who later passed through the University
of Chicago's International Centre, and enjoyed its
facilities little realized that Alonzo's efforts had led
to the Centre's creation. Likewise, Alonzo's pivotal role
in early American colonial psychology in the Philippines
passed unnoticed as he passed away in 1981.

Of course, neither Alonzo nor the Americans should
be credited with the introduction of western psychology
to the Philippines. Psicologia was not unheard of in the
Philippines at the time the American Senate ratified the
Treaty of Paris which legitimized the American annexation
of the islands. In fact, the Filipino term sikolohiya was
derived from the Spanish psicologia and the term itself
was already a part of the layman's vocabulary even if the
spelling was standardized much later. However, what
matters most to the "Philippine-psychology-as-an-American-creation" theorists is what they perceive as a
difference in kind between Spanish Rational psychology
and American behavioural psychology. After all, one can
credibly argue that rational psychology is a form of
philosophy, and as such, appropriately in the realm of
speculative thought. Similarly, the psychological
treatises of Plasencia and Delgado were not meant for the
indios who now call themselves Filipinos. The works of
Jacinto, del Pilar, and Pardo de Tavera are rich sources
of psychological theories and insights but they were
mainly propagandists and not psychologists. Besides, it
took more than two centuries from its founding in 1611
before the University of Santo Tomas changed its admission policy to accommodate Filipinos; it was not their
mission to teach Thomistic psychology to the indios. And
in all likelihood, the psicologos del verbo Tagalog,
referred to by Emilio Aguinaldo in his inaugural speech
as president of the First Philippine Republic, were not
Ph.D. (Psychology) degree holders anyway. Neither were
del Pilar and Jacinto. Heroes of the revolution they
were, but certified psychologists they were not.

If we must demand credentials from Emilio Aguinaldo's psicologos then let us ask the same of William
McKinley's "psychologists." Historians tell us that no
less than a President of the United States of America,

William McKinley, justified his venture to the Philippines on the basis of a dream and divine inspiration which
impelled him to send soldiers to the Philippines to
civilize and Christianize the islanders. The English
language and the American system of education proved to
be the most efficient instruments for this noble purpose.
In fact, the first American teachers of psychology in the
Philippines were not trained in psychology. To be sure,
they spoke English and administered psychological tests,
but that was not good enough to dislodge rational
psychology which held sway in the Philippine psychological scene at the time. The Pontifical University of
Santo Tomas was not named after Thomas Aquinas for
nothing. Just the same, William Howard Taft's move to
impose English as the medium of instruction in the
Philippines was the single masterful stroke which quite
conveniently transferred the burden of developing
psychology as a discipline in the Philippines from the
hands of the Spanish speaking friars to the shoulders of
native American speakers of English. But not for long.
The colonial masters reserved the position of Minister of
Education for an American national as a holdout even as
they intensified the pragmatic pursuit of the policy of
personnel indigenization at lower levels. The American
teachers of psychology in the twenties were gradually,
but soon enough, replaced by a new breed of Filipino
teachers. The new teachers were unfortunately trained in
fields other than psychology, just like their American
predecessors. As late as the sixties, we find instructors
armed with a copy of an American textbook and a background in English Literature, Education or Law, handling
undergraduate psychology courses. They all had one thing
in common: they could lecture in reasonably good English
naman.

The "Philippine-psychology-as-an-American-creation
Theory" has a sizeable number of adherents. The "theory"
has no name because it is less a theory than an un-
challenged assumption in the minds of American-trained
Filipino psychologists. The strong version of the
"theory" states that Americans brought psychology to the
Philippines together with the blessings of civilization
and democracy. If we must believe this claim then
psychology as a science and profession was a "factory
sealed" importation from the West, from theory to method
and application, including all the appurtenances that go
with psychological practice, and its establishment was
rather fast and easy. No resistance was met and problems

were minimal. Thanks to the efficiency of the American colonial administration, it did not take too long for American style western psychology to take hold in Philippine soil. To borrow a word from the historian Renato Constantino (1975), the "miseducation" of Filipino psychologists was thorough and almost complete. Not content with welcoming the Thomasites to Philippine shores, psychologists retraced the Thomasites' voyage back to North America. Indeed, Alonzo was one of the first to take such a voyage but it is to his credit that in spite of his training he did not feel compelled to bring home to Manila, as pasalubong, a colony of rats and a T-maze. He shifted his research and teaching activities from experimental to educational psychology. He cannot be faulted for not directly exploiting his training. In the late 20's and early 30's, the university and the country had a greater need for the application of psychology to educational measurement than basic research on animal learning. But looking back, one realizes that while he did not bring his white rats from Chicago with him, he brought something else, something truly precious to Philippine education as handmaiden of colonial policy. Alonzo unwittingly came back from Chicago proficient in American English, with psychology as topic of discourse. To paraphrase and modify Constantino (1975) as his ideas apply to the psychological situation:

> The use of English as the medium of instruction in psychology made possible the speedy introduction of American-oriented psychology and values. With American textbooks in psychology from Thorndike, Krech, Crutchfield, and Ballachey to Hilgard, Filipinos began learning not only a new psychology but a new culture. Education became miseducation because it began to de-Filipinize the Filipino psychologists, taught them to look up to American departments of psychology as always years ahead of Philippine counterparts, to regard American psychology as always superior to theirs and American society as the model par excellence for Philippine society.

Yet from the Filipino standpoint, Philippine culture was able to hold its own in the face of Americanization, then as now. The initial stirrings of conflict and the manifestations of the Great Cultural Divide between the have's and the have-not's could not be ignored by the first generation of American-trained Filipino psychologists of the twenties. The initial entry in the cultural struggle scoreboard was one-all as Alonzo made good his long shot for a relevant Philippine educational psychology but at the same time scoring for American English. It was for Manuel Carreon to make a follow-up attempt for the Filipino in the area of psychological measurement.

Manuel Carreon: a call for relevance in psychological measurement

The current Philippine objection to the uncritical importation of western psychological models is at least sixty years old. The credit for the first attempt at indigenous psychological test development goes to Sinforoso Padilla who took over from Alonzo the position of psychology chairman at the University of the Philippines. However, his teaching and administrative duties kept his hands full, so to speak. It was his articulate and prolific colleague, Manuel Carreon, who took up the cudgels for appropriate and relevant psychological testing. In 1926, Carreon published in New York his Ph.D.dissertation retitled Philippine Studies in Mental Measurement. His motivation for writing the book, his thesis and arguments were valid, but as a faithful colonial he committed the mistake of writing in English. To think that his psychological writing could have shared the fate of its literary counterparts in the native language! Copies of the Malaya, Ilang-Ilang, and Sinag-Tala sold briskly at 5¢ a copy. Not to mention the popular and durable Liwayway and Bulaklak, which were available then as now in the streets of Manila, weathering the American colonial administration, a World War, the Japanese Occupation, student activism, Martial Law, the closure of the "We Forum," "People's Power," and the "revolution" of 1986. For his mistake, Carreon paid dearly. Copies of his book were not shelved with other books on psychological testing, but instead landed in the Filipiniana section of the university libraries in America and the Phillipines. A librarian wields a lot of power, for by classifying a book as Filipiniana he unwittingly dooms it to limited readership. A reader of Carreon's book at the Northwestern University library rewarded Carreon's effort to communicate in English with

an unsigned remark on a page margin castigating his poor
mastery of the language of his colonial masters. If
Alonzo was blessed with a Governor-General Harrison and
the policy of "Filipinization", Carreon was less lucky
with Harrison's successor in the person of a certain
Major-General Leonard Wood who believed that the Filipinos were "not prepared for independence and that it
would require much more time and experience before they
could prove worthy of America's trust" (Agoncillo, 1974).

Perhaps Carreon was born at the wrong time, with the
right ideas. He should have written for _Liwayway_ instead.
In a manner of speaking, nobody listened to him. Educationists and guidance counsellors went ahead and merrily
administered psychological tests developed in America to
unsuspecting respondents in a language hardly mastered by
them. Some understood part of Carreon's message and
modified items in tests to fit Philippine conditions.
They became satisfied with what was later known as the
"change-apples-to-bananas" approach to improving test
validity: an approach to Philippine psychological testing
which held sway from the time Hartendorp studied the
correlation between breast size and the intelligence of
Filipinas up to the questionable rush to test Filipino
workers to certify that they are psychologically fit for
work in the deserts of Saudi Arabia.

Isidoro Panlasigui: identifying with the new culture--from Apalachicola to Boogaloo

The third generation of American trained Filipino
psychologists as typified by Panlasigui completely forgot
the horrors of Balangica, Samar[2] and proudly identified
with the "Protestant churches, schools and colleges; the
concept of democracy; the structure and practices of the
(American colonial) educational system and government;
Baguio City and the zigzag road; the American dollar; _our_
(italics mine) economic and industrial system; the
American sports--baseball, basketball, tennis, golf, etc"
(Panlasigui, n.d.).

Panlasigui's admiration for Mother America showed
clearly even as he wrote about the psychology of the
Filipino and as he argued for the colonial language. On
the basis of a quotation from H. G. Wells, Panlasigui was
quick to remind us that "the language of the conquered
may be adopted by the conqueror or _vice versa_." He
considered it a boost to Philippine national dignity to

be "culturally classified with the great natives of the Americas and Europe."

The awesome task of Americanizing the Filipino psychologist was therefore completed in the person of Isidoro Panlasigui, intellectually and emotionally. But Panlasigui was not without opponents. A good attitudinal arch-enemy for him was Manuel L. Quezon who wanted a Philippine national language perhaps even at the expense of the colonial language. The most memorable quotation from Quezon is of course his fiery "I would rather have a government run like hell by Filipinos than a government run like heaven by Americans." Quezon can have his "Filipino government" so long as Panlasigui can listen to Anita Bryant's "Paper Roses," dance the American boogaloo which replaced the Latin apalachicola, wear his Americana[3], enjoy hotdogs and ice cream, and the like (compare Colonialism in the Phillipines Panlasigui n.d., pp. 65-76).

Panlasigui's contribution to Philippine psychology can of course not be found in his Elementary Statistics, Educational Measurement and Evaluation (1951) which was really a lengthy description of how to compute the correlation coefficient but in his more authentic Ti Agtutubo (19-) and Ti Ubing (1916). His successor as chairman of the University of the Philippines Psychology Department, Alfredo V. Lagmay, was touched by the re-awakening of Filipino nationalism in the early 1950's but somehow Panlasigui was spared.

Alfredo V. Lagmay: the meeting of East and West

With a background in philosophy from a department steeped in Logical Positivism and staunchly against the sectarianism foisted by the Catholics through the then powerful University of the Philippines Student Catholic Action (UPSCA), Alfredo V. Lagymay was ostensibly sent to the United States on a fellowship precisely to weaken the U.P. Department of Philosophy led by an articulate, charismatic and controversial agnostic, philosopher, Ricardo Pascual. Lagmay's colleagues in the department were also sent abroad not in order to strengthen the Philosophy department but to neutralize it. Alfredo V. Lagmay went to study psychology at Harvard where he trained with B. F. Skinner in experimental psychology.

Lagmay came back to join the U.P. Department of Psychology which was then administratively a part of the

College of Education, thus giving psychology an applied educational perspective. Lagmay's first move was to transfer the department to the College of Liberal Arts, thus transforming the applied educational perspective into a basic scientific orientation. He chaired the department for two decades of historical developments and charted a direction for psychology in the country. He argued for experimental psychology even if his colleagues at the College of Education raised eyebrows at the mention of a science-oriented psychology. He was partially successful, for experimental psychology is now an integral part of the undergraduate psychology curriculum in Philippine schools. He did not quite succeed in promoting behaviour analysis in the Skinnerian tradition, for even to date, this course is not offered in a good number of Philippine colleges and universities. Just the same, Lagmay is better known as a "Skinnerian," and the U.P. Department of Psychology was perceived as behavioural in orientation from the 50's to the early 70's.

PSYCHOLOGY IN PHILIPPINE INSTITUTIONS OF LEARNING

The German roots of psychology in the Central Philippines

Psychology as a discipline in Philippine institutions of learning thrives or struggles in a variety of ways on matters of staffing, curricular development and instructional facilities. In a sense, psychology is struggling for survival at the University of San Carlos in Cebu City. San Carlos is the oldest centre of learning in the Philippines for it even antedates the University of Santo Tomas in Manila. The only difference is the little known fact that in 1661 Santo Tomas was established as a university ahead of San Carlos. In any case, psychology in the western tradition has been taught at the University of San Carlos since 1954. The medium of instruction is English while the theoretical perspective is basically German. Goertz taught experimental psychology in the tradition of Wundt in what has been called the "genealogy of psychology" in the Visayas: Wundt, Kulpe, Lindworsky and then Goertz. He taught and used Theoretical Psychology (after J. Lindworsky) as a textbook (1965) but he was one step away from the original German edition and he was using the English language in communicating with his predominantly Cebuano-speaking students. The perception experiments in the

German tradition were performed semester after semester up to the mid-seventies, thus tempting a Manila-based psychologist to refer to psychology at San Carlos as "brass and cymbals" psychology. The department needs trained psychologists to further develop their programmes. Unfortunately, the people they sent for advanced training in Manila or Honolulu failed to come back.

The University of San Carlos is presently run by the Society of the Divine Word, a Catholic religious order. However, the action in psychology is actually happening not in Cebu City but northeast of it, in a copra-rich island called Leyte, where the Portuguese Magellan and the American MacArthur both landed. The university of interest in Leyte, aside from the University of the Philippines at Tacloban, is Divine Word University where the journal Samar-Leyte Studies comes from and where the Pambansang Samahan sa Sikolohiyang Pilipino (National Association for Filipino Psychology) held its first regional conference. The output of the conference is probably a landmark in psychological publishing in the Philippines: a book entitled Filipino Religious Psychology not simply because of the conference theme but also because the title is more "sellable" than the staid Proceedings of the First Regional Conference of the Pambansang Samahan sa Sikolohiyang Pilipino.

The Spanish influence and philosophical psychology in Espana and Intramuros Manila

It is hard to decide if psychology is thriving or struggling at the University of Santo Tomas (UST). Regardless of conflicting opinions, important contributions to psychology in the Philippines come from there. It is true that Estefania Aldaba-Lim chided the university for "lack of activity" in a Psychological Association of the Philippines convention. It is also true that for a long time their Ph.D. programme could use professors with doctorates in psychology but just the same UST has the distinction of having initiated the offering of advanced training in psychology in the country.

One might care to note that, aside from the University of Santo Tomas, another Dominican-run institution also offers training in psychology. Colegio de San Juan de Letran in Intramuros, Manila distinguished itself in the 1970's for being the only school reportedly teaching psychology in Spanish, a culture similar to Filipino, psychologically speaking as claimed by Rosales (1965).

The Belgian Missionary Influence in the Cordilleras

As psychology develops in Manila and the south, a programme of teaching and research is also independently developing up north in the Cordilleras. St. Louis University (SLU) took the lead with Fr. Evarist Verlinden, a Belgian missionary priest, at the helm. SLU as a major institution of higher learning in the northern Philippines started to offer psychology as a field of undergraduate study in 1964. Guided by a scientific attitude, the Catholic faith and a graduate degree in psycholgy, Fr. Verlinden manages the University's Psychology Laboratory which boasts of equipment such as a tachistoscope made from old camera parts reportedly functioning even better than a first-hand apparatus. In addition to regular classroom activities, the department also provides training and research in psychology through an active programme in community service.

In spite of Verlinden's commitment to the context-ualization of psychology into the Philippine setting, he claims that "we cannot afford to hire an MA Psychology graduate from Ateneo de Manila." Instead, he has invited his fellow missionaries from Belgium with Ph.D's in Psychology as guest professors. Curiously, the Belgians outnumber the regular local faculty in SLU's M.S. psychology programme and the teaching schedule coincides with the allowable period of time a tourist can legally stay in the country.

American training at Loyola Heights, Diliman, and Manila's university belt

It would be healthier for Philippine psychology if Filipinos looked at other centres of learning outside the United States as alternative sources of psychological skills and knowledge, and as antidote to overdependence on the American brand of scholarship. Even assuming that psychological knowledge is limited to the English speaking world, one immediately notices the fact that Americans lord it over Philippine psychology. The Philippine Journal of Psychology hardly ever includes any article with references to non-American English language journals. Australia, New Zealand, Canada and England might as well disappear from the psychological map. Even Philippine references started to appear only in the middle seventies. Training Filipino scholars in other parts of the globe should not do damage to Philippine psychology. Quite apart from the University of Santo Tomas, only five other universities offer a Ph.D. training in psychology. These are Centro Escolar University, Manuel L. Quezon University, de la Salle University, Ateneo de Manila University, and the University of the Philippines.

THE FORMAL EMERGENCE OF PHILIPPINE PSYCHOLOGY

Field methods and the Bulacan Community Field Station

While the University of the Philippines offers training towards the Ph.D. degree in Psychology with an option to concentrate in learning, personality, physiological, clinical, and social psychology, it is Philippine psychology which makes psychology quite distinctive at this university. Philippine psychology as a "special topics" course was taught by Alfredo Lagmay prior to its institution as a separate graduate course by the University Council, University of the Philippines in 1978. The course has since been offered by Virgilio G. Enriquez and Zeus A. Salazar. Apart from discussing theoretical and scientific issues, graduate students debate on social and political issues; psychologies in contact; the "national," indigenous and emic; and the extent to which psychology in the Third World is international or western.

The Philippine orientation in psychological research and teaching was further strengthened by the establishment of a community field station in a rural area which serves as gateway to the uplands of Sierra Madre in Narzagaray, Bulacan. Professional and student researchers were re-orientated to the rural communities of Balagtas, Bulacan instead of drawing all their motivation for further advancements in transnational corporation-orientated Makati.

The Sikolohiyang Pilipino perspective

The new consciousness, labelled Sikolohiyang Pilipino reflecting Filipino psychological knowledge, has emerged through the use of the local language as a tool for the identification and rediscovery of indigenous concepts, and as an appropriate medium for the delineation and articulation of Philippine realities hand in hand with the development of a scientific literature which embodies the psychology of the Filipino people. A cursory examination of the Filipino language provides a basis for proposing sikolohiyang Pilipino as the study of diwa ("psyche"), which in Filipino directly refers to the wealth of ideas referred to by the philosophical concept of "essence," and an entire range of psychological concepts from awareness to motives to behaviour.[4]

Sikolohiyang Pilipino, as a perspective, demands that the Filipino psychologist confront social problems and national issues as part of his responsibility. Cipres-Ortega (1980) reported a ferment in its earliest stage of development. Issues considered in Sikolohiyang Pilipino's incipient stage include the question of which language must be used in psychological research, teaching and publication: Pilipino or Filipino. Choosing between P and F is seen as trivial, once the language issue becomes a matter of choosing between a multi-language based 31-letter alphabet and a Tagalog based 20-letter abakada. Such a choice is definitely simpler than choosing between a colonial and an indigenous language. The language issue stirred nationalist sentiments in Manila's college corridors and triggered feverish debate in the 1971 Constitutional Convention. In the meanwhile, the national lingua franca was slowly being forged by the man-in-the-street in his day-to-day transactions. For the Filipino social scientist, the choice after all was not between a P and an F but between the language of the man-in-the-street and a colonial language. Sikolohiyang Pilipino chose what The Constitutional Commission of 1986 later called the "Filipino language" with Pilipino, the national lingua franca, as a basis.

A second concern also reported by Cipres-Ortega (1980) has to do with the delineation of the "Filipino" in Filipino psychology. "Filipino" may refer to the mainstream urbanised Manileno or the "unsophisticated" provinciano. The word "Filipino" conjures the image of one who belongs to a major ethnic group but one from a minority group is just as much Filipino. Samson (1965) therefore referred to "psychologies" of Filipinos because of the cultural and ethnic diversity of the Filipino people.

While excitement regarding language and cultural heterogeneity may bring to the fore volatile socio-political problems, the concern for professionalization, social problems and universality has brought about issues which have stirred professional and academic circles and caused intellectual flurries at Loyola Heights and Diliman. A genuine concern for professional growth and commitment to psychology as a discipline has fostered unity despite attitudinal and theoretical differences.

Philippine psychology's colonial character as a captive of an American dominated, English-speaking world is one of Sikolohiyang Pilipino's major areas of protest. Psychology as a western-oriented discipline is supposed to be partial to universal findings, to "generalizability" and external validity. The scientific character of psychology is accepted by Sikolohiyang Pilipino, but its universality is questioned by the Filipino as it is being questioned elsewhere (for example, in Mexico by Rogelio Diaz-Guerrero 1977). The history of psychology as it has evolved in the western tradition can be interpreted as moving towards the goal of a truly universal psychology. Unfortunately, psychology is still far from that goal in spite of over a hundred years of scientific research. Universality must be the motive behind the series of systematically replicated experiments from pigeons to humans, from the laboratory to the field. To be sure, academic psychologists are no longer contented with sophomore students from the universities, they are now equally interested in minority and other ethnic groups. Filipino psychologists have gone beyond the convenience of captive university classes and air-conditioned Makati offices; they have themselves gone to the field. Some went to the South to Muslim Mindanao. Just like their colleagues in anthropology, the psychologist, Filipino or otherwise, will now occasionally face the discomfort of mud huts and mosquitoes. A researcher interested in Maranao psychology once intimated that in the Southern Philippines, if the mosquitoes don't get the psychologist, the dissidents will. This development has its parallel in the international scene since more and more countries say "no" to cross-cultural researchers (Brislin 1977). However, while this development may not always be welcomed socio-politically, it is probably a turning point in the growth of western-orientated psychology for the data base of western-orientated psychology is now broader. It should be stressed, however, that a broader base is far from adequate in assuring a universal psychology unless alternative perspectives from non-western psychologies are put to use. In fact, there is a need to rewrite the history of psychology with due consideration to Asian experience and perspectives.

Regardless of differing theoretical persuasions, Filipino psychologists have slowly come to recognise the importance of cultural validation. Sikolohiyang Pilipino as a subject was instituted and offered for the first time at the undergraduate level at the University of the Philippines in 1978. Jose Ma. Bartolome was painfully aware of the slow pace of theoretical reorientation, especially with a class of undergraduate juniors and seniors who enrolled in this course as an elective hoping to find a teacher ready to deliver a dissertation on the psychology, values and behaviour of the Filipino only to find that the course was meant for psychology majors who must be shown the scope and the limits of a psychology based on the Filipino culture and experience. The problem of theoretical reorientation as reported by Atal (1979) is still being sorted out by Bartolome and his colleagues at the University of the Philippines department of Political Science and St. Scholastica's College:

> While there is too much iconoclastic talk about the domination of alien models and theories and their inappropriateness, there is very little to commend as respectable replacements. Along with severe criticism of the so-called "capitalist", "status quoist", "western", "American" social science, one may come across writings that very enthusiastically prescribe "Marxism" as an alternative. Efforts are still needed to test the proclaimed universality of established theories and models in a variety of setting. It is not so much a replacement that is really needed if one wants to pursue the goal of a universal science - and not of setting up "schools of thought", like sects creating a priesthood and a blind following. Such genuine efforts that go beyond reactive rhapsodies are rare to find (Atal, 1979).

Atal recognised that some effort is being made, citing as an example the work of the Pakistani economist Mahbub Ul Haq, who reconsidered basic premises of a development paradigm learnt at Harvard and Yale thus allowing a reformulation of strategy. Unresolved theoretical issues did not deter Bartolome's students from integrating selected research studies on Filipino psychology even if this meant including Ateneo-IPC studies viewed as "American" social science by David (1977) and others.

Armed with a history of personal involvement in the development of the theoretical underpinnings of Sikolohiyang Pilipino and with the confidence of one who had concrete experience with the actual application of indigenous methods, Rogelia Pe-Pua took off where Bartolome left. Pe-Pua faced the problems of articulating the concepts and methods of Filipino psychology head-on with a book entitled Sikolohiyang Pilipino: Teorya, Metodo at Gamit (Filipino Psychology: theory, method and application (1982). For the first time, a compilation of papers on Filipino psychology is available for student use. The compilation is in English and Filipino thus reflecting the language situation in the Philippine academic setting. English is still dominant, but Filipino has emerged as the language of the educated Filipino of the seventies.

Sikolohiyang Pilipino as a theoretical perspective has finally come to print in textbook form instead of in isolated articles, thus satisfying the form-orientated "scholar" that perhaps there is a basis to the indigenous psychology movement. The form of articulation is not a measure of validity, but the mystique of the printed word, especially if in English and imported from the U.S.A., still enthralls the Filipino.

The growth of the Sikolohiyang Pilipino literature in the eighties would give one the feeling that the Filipino language is making up for lost time in the discipline of psychology. Since the publication of Pe-Pua's book, at least three psychology theses have been written by non Tagalogs in the Filipino language, thus disputing the mistaken belief that Filipino is the preserve of Tagalogs.

The philosophical position of Sikolohiyang Pilipino turns the problem of regionalism and language diversity in the Philippines into an advantage. Ethnic diversity and consciousness enriches national culture and helps define the Filipino psyche. It is perhaps a happy coincidence that the majority of the contributors to the Sikolohiyang Pilipino literature are in fact nonTagalogs. The same observation holds for psychologists who pioneered teaching psychology in Filipino. In fact, a goodnumber of non-Filipinas, primarily Americans, contributed to the anthology on new directions in indigenous psychology - Sikolohiyang Pilipino: Isyu, Pananaw at Kaalaman by Agannon and Assumpta (1986)

Psychology organisations

At present, there are eight major national organisations related to psychology in the Philippines. These are the Pambansang Samahan sa Sikolohiyang Pilipino (National Association for Filipino Pyschology); the Psychological Association of the Philippines; the Samahang Pilipino sa Sikolohiya ng Wika (Philippine Society for the Psychology of Language); the Samahang Pilipino sa Sikolohiya ng Bata (Child Psychology Association of the Philippines); the Philippine Psychiatric Association; the Philippine Guidance and Personnel Association; the Philippine Mental Health Association, and the Pambansang Samahan sa Kasaysayan Sikolohiya (National History of Psychology Association).

Established in 1962, the Psychological Association of the Philippines (PAP) aims to advance learning, teaching and research in psychology as a science, to promote human welfare and to advance the practice of psychology as an independent, scientifically-oriented and ethically-conscious profession.

The Samahang Pilipino sa Sikolohiya ng Wika was founded in 1971 and has been active with seminars held twice a year since then. The one-day seminar in February and in September of each year is a constitutional mandate which the association regularly holds to generate ideas and report empirical researches on the psychology of language. The association is now envisaged as one likely to play an important role in the Philippine struggle against a colonial language.

The Samahang Pilipino sa Sikolohiya ng Bata (Child Psychology Association of the Philippines) was established in 1982 with Esther A. Reyes as Founding President and Leticia Lagmay as President-elect. The child holds a special place in the psyche of the Filipino. Even among Christian Filipinos the child Jesus (Santo Nino) wins more attention and veneration than the adult Jesus. The Association is primarily open to psychologists but also to other professionals in the area of child study and welfare.

The Pambansang Samahan sa Sikolohiyang Pilipino (National Association for Filipino Psychology) is of interest to Filipinologists and psychologists. In fact, the association explicitly states in its constitution the avowed purpose of developing active and scientific cooperation with similar organizations in the Philippines and abroad with particular emphasis on Asia. Its other purposes include the delineation and use of psychology and related disciplines in applied settings such as education, medicine, agriculture and industry. Finally, it aims to develop all aspects of the Filipino consciousness towards an active scientific and universal psychology. Established in 1975, the PSSP is the most active national organization of psychology in the Philippines. It publishes its annual convention proceedings, a journal and a quarterly newsletter. Most of its publications are in Filipino. The association maintains a national secretariat and a research and training centre, the Philippine Psychology Research and Training House. Its training programmes are mainly focused on the training of teachers to teach psychology in Filipino and with a Filipino and Asian orientation. The programme on the teaching of psychology in Filipino was developed and tested with a group of psychology teachers and researchers in 1977 under the direction of Ma. Angeles Guanzon of the University of the Philippines at Clark Air Base. The Philippine Psychology Research and Training House facilitates the exchange of ideas from other countries and the Philippines through lectures by visiting psychologists from other parts of the Philippines and abroad.

Prospects for the nineties

The writ of habeas corpus was suspended in the early seventies, and martial law was declared shortly after. Filipinos from all walks of life, academics, student leaders, labourers, were affected in varying degrees by the New Order. Physicists, historians, political scientists, writers and journalists alike were detained for political reasons but it was business as usual for psychologists - as though they were the most apolitical among the academics and the professionals. Psychology conventions were not bereft of heated discussions on social issues but somehow psychologists were noncommittal on the martial law regime. Only a handful among the psychologists went underground or were openly against the

Marcos government.

The death of Aquino at the airport tarmac changed all that. Concerned psychologists joined the Makati businessmen in rallies of protest. Once more the anti-colonial stance received an added boost as artists demanded freedom of expression and the national language movement reiterated its position against English as a colonial language. The painful awareness of the unwanted presence of American military bases on Philippine soil was felt with greater intensity.

Prior to that painful day in August 1983, the Philippines as a country and psychology as a profession and academic discipline were both gearing for the nineties with optimism. Buoyed by the optimism brought by the February "revolution of 1986" and the new leadership, five concrete moves which may still find full realization are in the offing in the psychology scene. First, the Pederasyon ng mga Mag-aaral sa Sikolohiya or PsychFed, a federation of psychology student organisations, was finally in operation after three years of unsuccessful attempts at getting established. Co-operative exchange among undergraduate psychology students from various institutions augurs well for the growth and development of Philipine psychology.

Secondly, the Psychology Act of 1982 was introduced by Assemblyman Ronaldo Zamora to the Batasang Pambansa to regulate the practice of psychology as an autonomous and responsible profession in the Philippines. The act aims to govern the certification of psychometricians and the licensing of psychologists.

Third, the National Institute of Psychology as a national centre for advanced training and research in psychology was proposed. It was envisaged as having three departments: 1) the Department of Psychology to take care of graduate instruction in seven divisions within the department - Psychobiology, Experimental Psychology, Personality and Developmental Psychology, Social and Industrial Psychology, Clinical Psychology, Educational Psychology and Philippine Psychology; 2) an Office of Research and Publications and 3) an office of Extension Services.

Fourth, the Akademya ng Sikolohiyang Pilipino was established to further develop and strengthen the Philippine Psychology Research and Training House. The Akademya aims to promote a competent and relevant Philippine social science. The major thrust of the Akademya is still primarily to conduct studies on

Filipino behaviour and psychology, Filipino personality, Philippine language, culture and history by using appropriate and culturally relevant theory and methodology. The Akademya is not exclusively manned by psychologists. It includes historians, artists and scientists in its staff based on the avowed belief that the Filipino psyche is too important to leave in the hands of psychologists alone.

Finally, but not the least significant, an intriguing redefinition of psychology in the Philippine setting is foreboded by an increasing interest among Filipino psychologists in the arts. Nothing definitive has surfaced as yet and it is early to assess the significance of this development in the early eighties. Perhaps the therapeutic and liberating characteristics of the creative process shall be delineated or perhaps the Asian soul will be rediscovered. Sining Sikolohiyang Pilipino is an organizational venue for psychologists in the arts and was launched in 1983 as an upshot of the Marawi Conference on the Filipino personality and the Indigenous Arts. Drama, music, dance and the visual arts lend a new excitement to psychologists as the artists exchange views with them.

More importantly, the new surge of interest changes the image of the psychologists themselves and perhaps even their identity. After all it can be argued that we can take a step towards art not in order to avoid psychology but precisely in order to approach its very core.

NOTES

1. From Bisayang Tisoy, a popular T.V. character.
2. My Lai, Vietnam, in more recent memory.
3. Philippine label for the coat and tie.
4. In a paper for the University of the Philippines Psychological Society on the occasion of Psychology Week in 1974, the author explained Sikolohiyang Pilipino through a metaphor -- a characteristic way of clarifying concepts in the Asian manner. Attention was called to the difference between a "person in the house" (tao sa bahay) and a "house person" (taong-bahay). A "person in the house" may be someone who just passed by, a visitor who is not voluntarily or necessarily interested in staying there. But a "house person" (taong-bahay) has a role and a meaning in that house so long as she or he is there.

Sikolohiyang Pilipino is like a "house person" as it focuses on indigenous developments in the field of psychology from the Filipino perspective. It is most commonly understood to mean the psychology of the Filipinos - their character, values and paninindigan or principles. But more importantly and precisely Sikolohiyang Pilipino refers to psychological theory, knowledge, method and application developed through the Filipino culture (Enriquez, 1974).

REFERENCES

AGANNON, A. & ASSUMPTA, D. Sikolohiyang Pilipino: isyu, pananaw at kaalaman (New directions in indigenous psychology) Manila: National Book Store, 1986.

AGONCILLO, T. Filipino nationalism 1872-1970, R.P. Garcia, Quezon City. 1974.

ATAL, Y. The call for indigenisation: the indigenisation of social sciences in Asia. In J. J. Loubser, (ed.) The International Federation of Social Sciences Organizations Occasional Paper No. 1, Mutual Press, Ottawa. 1979, 1-21.

BRISLIN, R. Ethical issues influencing the acceptance and rejection of cross-cultural researchers who visit various countries. In Lenore Leob Adler (ed.) Issues in cross-cultural research, (Annals of New York Academy of Sciences). 1977, 185-202.

CARREON, M. L. Philippine studies in mental measurement, World Books, Yonkers-on-Hudson, New York. 1926.

CIPRES-ORTEGA, S. Sikolohiyang Pilipino. Mga implikasyon sa pagtuturo at pagaaral (Pilipino psychology: implications for teaching and learning). Paper read at the Annual Meeting of the Linguistic Society of the Philippines, Philippine Normal College. 1980.

CONSTANTINO, R. A history of the Philippines from the Spanish colonization to. the Second World War, Monthly Review Press, New York. 1975.

DAVID, R. Ang Pagkagapos ng Agham Panlipunang Pilipino (The colonization of Philippine social science). Ulat ng Ikalawang Pambansang Kumperensya sa Sikolohiyang Pilipino, Pambansang Samahan sa Sikolohiyang Pilipino, Diliman, Quezon City. 1977.

DIAZ-GUERRERO, R. A Mexican psychology. American Psychologist, 1977, 32, 934-944.

ENRIQUEZ, V. G. Mga batayan ng sikolohiyang Pilipino sa kultura at kasaysayan (The bases of Filipino psychology in culture and history). Sikolohiyang Pilipino: batayan sa Kasaysayan, perspektibo, mga konsepto at bibliograpiya, Departamento ng Sikolohiynag, Universidad ng Pilipinas, Quezon City. 1974, p. 1-29.

GOERTZ, J. Introduction to Theoretical psychology (After J. Lindworsky), University of San Carlos, Cebu City. 1965, p.149.

NACARIO, E. N. Psychology at the University of San Carlos Today, (1954-1980). Unpublished manuscript, 12 p. 1980.

PANLASIGUI, I. Ti Ubing, Imprenta Evangelica, La Union. 1916.

PANLASIGUI, I. Ti Agtutubo, Mission Press, Manila. 19--.

PANLASIGUI, I. Elementary statistics and educational measurement and evaluation, Community Publishers, Manila. 1951.

PANLASIGUI, I. The language problems of the Philippines, Quezon City. n.d.

PE-PUA, R. E. Filipino psychology: theory, method and application, Philippine Psychology Research House, Diliman, Quezon City. 1982.

SAMSON, J. A. Is there a Filipino psychology? Unitas, 1965, 38, 447-487.

18

Psychology in
Papua New Guinea:
A Brief Overview

Barry Richardson

HISTORICAL BACKGROUND

"A capsule history[1]"

The island of New Guinea is only a hundred miles off
the north coast of Australia, across the Torres Strait.
In 1828 the Dutch annexed the western half of New Guinea,
which is now under Indonesian control and known as Irian
Jaya. In 1884 the British yielded to pressure from
Australia and annexed the southeastern coast, which
became known as British New Guinea; a few days later, the
Germans annexed the northern part, which became known as
German New Guinea. When the Commonwealth of Australia was
formed in 1901, British New Guinea was transferred to its
charge and renamed Papua. During World War I Australian
forces occupied German New Guinea. In 1920 Australia was
granted a mandate by the League of Nations to administer
that area as well, and until World War II treated the two
parts as separate entities. During the war the Japanese
occupied New Guinea but not Papua. Afterwards, Australian
civil administration was re-established on a unified
basis, and the country became known as the Territory of
Papua and New Guinea. In 1975 Papua New Guinea became
independent.

Missionary influence

In a non-formal sense, the psychological study of
Papua New Guineans could be said to have begun when
traders first set foot in East New Guinea between five
and nine thousand years ago. More formally, it can be

seen from the writings of missionaries that the "psychology" of Papua New Guineans was a subject of considerable interest which may have begun when fourteen children from Mailu were captured in 1606 by Torres and Prado, taken to Manila and there baptised (Loeliger, 1982).

The gradual increase in mission activity in the Pacific Islands continued for two hundred years but the Mainland of East New Guinea was not the object of earnest missionary effort until the late nineteenth century. To the extent that missionaries were the first ambassadors of Western social sciences, psychology had a poor beginning in Papua New Guinea. Many educational, medical, and social benefits were, and still are, attributable to the unselfish efforts of missionaries - but the progress of social sciences in PNG has been affected by those who only dabbled in those sciences. Paramount among the dabblers were missionaries because it was they who prescribed, predicted, controlled, and explained behaviours of a significant proportion of the Papua New Guinean population before psychology emerged as a discipline. Psychology has not yet outlived its shaky beginnings in Papua New Guinea.

Education in Papua New Guinea

Mission schools were first set up about one hundred years ago, but rapid growth in educational opportunity did not begin until after World War II. By 1979, 56 per cent of school-aged children were attending community schools. Primary education for all is anticipated by 1990.[2] There are now eighty-five post-secondary training institutions serving more than 10,000 students. Most of these institutions are for the training of public servants but there are ten teachers' colleges and two universities (University of Technology in Lae, and the University of Papua New Guinea in Port Moresby).

The University of Papua New Guinea (UPNG) was opened in 1965, and teaching commenced in 1966. The first students were Preliminary Year entrants (1966), and in 1967 the first eighty-three students enrolled for degree courses in Arts, Law, and Science. The Faculty of Education was established in 1968, that of Medicine in 1971, and of Agriculture in 1973. The first Papua New Guinean academic was appointed in 1972, and the next, Mr. R. Lohia, who was later to become Vice-Chancellor of UPNG, in 1973.

Professional psychologists in Papua New Guinea

In 1957, a government report on mental health in the then Territories of Papua and New Guinea recommended the setting up of a Psychological Services Branch of the Public Service. The Branch came into being in 1961 and was originally staffed by expatriates whose primary function was within the clinical area. As independence approached, psychologists with testing and selection skills were hired, and a strong "professional" or "applied" emphasis became evident and was not challenged until 1970 when psychology was introduced at the University of Papua New Guinea.

A year earlier (March 1969) the Papua New Guinea Branch of the Australian Psychological Society held its inaugural meeting and, from the very beginning, was concerned with training Papua New Guinean psychologists. The nature of that training was a subject of some controversy, as is indicated by an exchange between G. Ord (elected Chairman of the PNG branch of the Australian Psychological Society) and J. Price (Chairman of the Psychology Section at the University), which was published in Psychology in Papua New Guinea: 1972, a documentation of the first conference of the PNG Branch of the A.P.S.

Dr. Price had delivered a paper in which he had outlined the course offered in psychology at UPNG, these being Introduction to Psychology, Introduction to Experimental Psychology, Social and Personality, Individual Differences, General Experimental Psychology, Cross-cultural Psychology, Psychological Theory, and Guidance and Measurement. Mr. Ord enquired as to what group had planned these courses, and, upon learning that it was strictly a faculty operation, strongly expressed the view that "if you want to relate this course to the requirements of the country ... practicing psychologists who have had quite a start on the academic psychologists" should also have been involved.

Mr. Ord was arguing from a position of some strength, because in 1972 there were roughly forty "practising" psychologists in Papua New Guinea and only two "academic" psychologists. Campbell (1972) pointed out that the foothold gained by "professional" psychologists in Papua New Guinea led to a PNG Psychological Society membership which was in sharp contrast to that of the Australian Psychological Society whose "founding fathers" were drawn mostly from universities.

Two months later (July 1972) the Chief Minister, in his opening statement at the Constitution talks, diverted interest from arguments between psychologists within the newly formed PNG Branch of the A.P.S., when he made it clear that the dissolution of this Society was inevitable. By 1975, the year of independence, the PNG Branch of the A.P.S. had given way to the Papua New Guinea Psychological Association; its first Papua New Guinean president, a graduate of UPNG, was elected in 1976. In the ensuing years, expatriate psychologist positions in the Public Service were gradually withdrawn but national psychologists were not available to replace them – at least not in sufficient numbers. This decline was accompanied by a severe drop in membership of the PNG Psychological Association and of the members remaining, too many were stationed in regional centres such as Rabaul, the Solomon Islands and Lae, and were unable to attend meetings in Port Moresby. The last meeting of the PNG Psychological Association was held in 1980.

Perhaps even more serious was the loss of the New Guinea Psychologist, which began in 1969 and published its final issue in December 1974, by which time both editors had left Papua New Guinea. Plans to revive the journal after independence never came to fruition, but an analysis of the contents of the seventy-one articles published during its five years of existence revealed that thirty-three were to do with work done in the PSB and fifteen of those were in the area of test development (St. George, 1974). This testing bias may have proved unpopular with the PNG government although no reason other than budget constraints was given for the total closing-down of the Psychological Services Branch of the Public Service in 1982. It is ironic that the "useful" psychologists were dispensed with and that "academic" psychology has gained strength over the last few years.

The increase in the number of students majoring in psychology has caused a renewed interest in a journal which UPNG plans to launch in 1984, to be called the South Pacific Journal of Psychology. Contributions will be invited from all countries within the South Pacific region, but the emphasis will be on psychology in the island nations. Although the PNG Psychological Association has not been reborn, in 1983 a UPNG Psychology Association was formed; this has a student executive and at present numbers more than twenty-five members including four academic staff.

THE UNIVERSITY OF PAPUA NEW GUINEA

Students

Selection of students. Ninety percent of the PNG population live in rural areas in village communities. Students are selected mostly on the basis of their achievement at school although 40 per cent do not receive schooling at all. Education is not compulsory and some villages are too small to justify a school or are too widely separated for a single site to be chosen to which village children could walk. Many villages are accessible only by river and walking tracks. The normal requirement for admission to UPNG is grade 12. Frequently, students are streamed according to their school performance, vacancies within the various university faculties, and perceived need for, say, teachers, economists, doctors, dentists, or lawyers. Switching streams (for example from Education to Arts) is not always possible as students may have received National Scholar-ships restricting them to a particular programme of study.

Language problems. There are roughly seven hundred indigenous languages in Papua New Guinea and the result is that nearly all students have, as their first language, a "Ples Tok" or village language which is often quite distinct (not merely dialectically different) from that of the neighbouring village. In the southern coastal regions Hiri Motu emerged (in the late 19th century) as an important lingua franca, and has since spread to some highland regions.

European influence has introduced "Tok Pisin" (a kind of Pidgin English), which is now pervasive and spoken by more than sixty per cent of the PNG population. English is the university language but, in spite of vigorous teaching programmes throughout the country, very few Papua New Guineans are sufficiently fluent for it to compete with Tok Pisin or Hiri Motu as a lingua franca. Thus students at UPNG are at least bi-lingual and more typically they are polyglots. In this sense PNG is a psycholinguists' paradise, but many students suffer from inadequacies in English, particularly when they are required to grapple with the subtleties inherent in academic English. Possible reasons for English deficiencies are the subject of ongoing research in the Psychology/Philosophy Department at UPNG.

Student performance. It is difficult to assess student achievement on an international scale, but recently it has become clear that many honours graduates who go overseas for higher degree work experience some difficulties which cannot be attributed to culture shock alone. This realization has resulted in a recent tightening of standards. The question of the general ability of UPNG students is complex, and sensitive to the extent that research aimed at revealing specific weaknesses and attempting a remedy is sometimes a catalyst for hostile exchanges and critisms and, at other times, a valuable source of cohesion among national and expatriate staff committed to the development of Papua New Guinea.

Effects of social and cultural norms on independent and critical thought. To generalize about cultural influences in a country with sufficient diversity to boast seven hundred languages is obviously dangerous. However, it is our observation that UPNG students are more inclined to seek authoritative answers to questions than they are inclined to question or debate. Sorcery is still prevalent in PNG, but belief in its powers does not obviously conflict with the subject matter of most psychology courses which, from the PNG students' point of view, embodies different and to-be-learned principles rather than different and to-be-challenged principles. Students who take Abnormal Psychology do occasionally capitalize on the weaknesses of Western attempts to explain abnormal behaviour, and offer traditional explanations which usually involve possession by a spirit originating from dead relations.

It is noteworthy that traditional village societies are usually structured such that "bigmen" provide an authoritarian setting in which children receive little or no encouragement to express their individualities. In addition, there is marked sexual discrimination such that females receive less encouragement still. This may account for the less than 15 per cent female student population at UPNG.

All students go through "Foundation Year" (either after Preliminary Year or, in the case of grade 12 graduates, directly upon entering UPNG), and most disciplines offer Foundation Year courses which can be compared with introductory courses in overseas universities. As is the case for Preliminary Year, there is a necessary emphasis on fundamentals in Foundation Year such that the basic mathematics course affectionately entitled "Say it with Figures"[3] is compulsory, as is "Advanced Comprehension and Composition," and most recently a one-year long course in World History.

Introduction to Psychology is a non-compulsory, one-semester course. In spite of the stress on basics in Preliminary Year and Foundation Year there is still an evident weakness in reading, expression, and numeracy, and lecturers in the more advanced courses cannot assume that their students have adequate preparation.

Thus cultural factors and the emphasis placed on basic skills are likely contributors to the observed lack of independent and critical thought. However, the Philosophy Section of the Department of Psychology and Philosophy is now offering a Foundation Year course called "Philosophical Enquiry" which is designed to provide exposure to methods of critical analysis and argument, previously offered only in post-Foundation Years.

Psychology students at UPNG. Most students who take Introduction to Psychology do so as part of a broad general education. However, enrollment in Introduction to Psychology has risen from 20 in 1980, to 136 in Second Semester 1983. Interestingly, the latter number is equal to enrollment figures for the compulsory courses referred to earlier! No other non-compulsory course can claim such popularity. Although the larger proportion of intro-ductory students will not major in psychology, we have seen a steady increase in the number of students taking advanced courses and registering as majors. Since 1975, two Ph.D. students (expatriates) have graduated in psychology, and there have been four honours BA graduates and twelve BA pass graduates (nationals). We now have two expatriate Ph.D. students, and one national honours BA student. This non-impressive record is likely to show an improvement in the near future because the overall enrollment in psychology courses has risen so markedly. We anticipate at least ten pass BA graduates in 1984.

As an academic discipline, psychology has grown more than any other in the history of UPNG. Since 1980 the staff establishment has almost doubled, and it is the only discipline which has been forced to restrict enrollment in first, second, and third years. The popularity of psychology courses is likely to continue in spite of the fact that we awarded fewer 'A' grades and more 'fail' grades than any other discipline in the university in Second Semester 1983. The foothold estab-lished by expatriate psychologists during the years of Australian administration and lost shortly thereafter appears likely to be regained and more firmly established by a second generation of psychologists, this time from

Papua New Guinea.

One national has recently returned from the U.K. with an M. Ed. and is now a lecturer in psychology. Another is due to return in 1984 after completing a Master's in clinical psychology at the Australian National University. Both have been supported by grants and, upon returning, are expected to teach for at least two years before proceeding to Ph.D. studies. Shortage of funds has forced a policy in which UPNG is unlikely to give financial support for overseas doctoral study, and nationals are therefore encouraged to seek aid from elsewhere. In general, the university has had difficulty in attracting and keeping graduates with higher degrees because salaries outside are too alluring. In addition, some postgraduates quite reasonably perceive their potential contribution to the non-academic community to be greater than that likely at UPNG.

The demand for psychologists comes mainly from organizations (public and private) which require graduates in the area of testing and selection. Since the Psychological Services Branch of the Public Service closed down in 1982, an increased need for organizational, educational and clinical specialists has become apparent and three courses recently introduced (Organizational Psycholoy, Guidance and Counselling, and Applied Psychology) are showing upward enrollment trends. But at present we are unable to satisfy the needs of either the public or private sector. The Post-Office and Telephone Commission asked for six graduates in 1983, but none were available, as the few BA graduates we had, had been sponsored by other agencies such as OK Tedi Mining for a year or more, and were therefore obliged to work for the sponsor upon graduation.

Academics

Composition and qualifications of academic staff. Less than 10 per cent of the two hundred academic staff are female, and less than 20 per cent are Papua New Guinean. In psychology, there is one expatriate female senior tutor with an M.Sc. and one national female lecturer with an M.Ed. The turnover rate is high. Contracts for expatriates are normally three years in duration and renewable, but these may be cut short if a national returns to UPNG with at least a master's degree. Until recently, a lecturer's position was more or less guaranteed for such a national, but now moves are afoot to make such appointments less automatic such that nationals may have to compete with overseas applicants. This seems even more likely if equality of basic pay is introduced in 1984.

In the past, a master's degree was often sufficient for a lecturing position at UPNG, but now an overseas applicant generally has to have a Ph.D. It is not uncommon for an expatriate staff member with a Ph.D. (and some years experience) to be hired at tutor or senior tutor level, which has a pay scale roughly equivalent to that of lecturer. This is because UPNG has duty statements for tutors and lecturers which differ in that lecturers are required to do research while tutors are not. However, the contributions of each are considered to be about equal since teaching is seen to be at least as important as research.

If a national student completes an honours BA or B.Sc. at UPNG, he or she may then become a teaching fellow. Typically, teaching fellows receive financial support from the Staff Development Office and go overseas for higher degree studies. Master's and doctoral degrees are offered here but it is generally felt that overseas training is desirable in the interest of improving or maintaining standards. Somewhat paradoxically, most post-graduate students at UPNG are expatriates or their spouses, wishing to up-grade their qualifications.[4]

In general, national and expatriate staff are likely to admit that the academic standard at UPNG leaves much to be desired. The fault is sometimes seen as being that of expatriates who, some maintain, come and go with little or no commitment during their stay. On the other hand, some expatriate staff complain that they are confronted with the impossible task of teaching students who are not prepared for university. One of UPNG's four national Ph.Ds recently led a team of academics whose task was to evaluate the honours BA programme, and one of the important conclusions of the resulting report was that the quality of students (and therefore national staff as a whole) was not likely to improve until the schools throughout PNG improved. Many critics are quick to point out that the schools are suffering because underqualified nationals have been prematurely appointed as teachers and that standards have dropped as a consequence. The rejoinder of some nationals is that maintaining an overpaid and self-interested expatriate teacher population will never see to the long-term localization goals of PNG.

PNG's localization aspirations might best be served by the presence of expatriates who do not fall into the locally well known categories of "missionaries, mercenaries, or misfits," but instead, expatriates who genuinely do not mind sacrificing superannuation, homecountry career paths, better facilities, and the like, and who receive satisfaction from working in a developing country. Such expatriates would be well qualified, dedicated to the task at hand, willing to go when the job is done, and non-resentful about the difficulties of re-entering the work force in the home country. Nationals would need to be appreciative of the expatriates' efforts, committed to academic study, and non-resentful about salary differences. These are tall orders!

Teaching Loads. Most staff are expected to accept twelve hours per week of class contact. If this contact involves repetition of material, the hours may increase such that fifteen per week is not unusual. Less than eight hours per week is very unusual. The year is divided into two semesters, each fourteen weeks in duration; first semester classes begin in February. Between mid-November and the end of January we run "Lahara" (the local name for the gusty winds of this time), classes which are the rough equivalent of summer school classes in the Northern Hemisphere. It is a contractual obligation to teach in Lahara sessions which are, for students from the islands and remote mainland regions, the only opportunity for intramural studies. Extension Studies courses are offered by correspondence throughout the year.

Psychological Research at UPNG. Approximately 150,000 kina ($180,000 Australian) is made available to the university for research. Much of this figure is unspent by October of each year, a consequence of a heavy teaching and administrative load which leaves little time for research. In spite of the increase in the number of students now enrolled in psychology, the current staff have managed to maintain active research programmes. These include testing multilingual students to determine the extent to which second and third-learned languages tend to be lateralized in the right or left hemisphere as a function of age of acquisition, an investigation of the effects of chewing betel nut (a ubiquitous habit in this part of the world), and, more recently, a systematic study of cognitive styles and information processing skills in which UPNG students show some marked differences when compared with their Western counterparts.

INTERACTIONS

Between UPNG psychologists and the medical profession

The absence of a clinical programme at UPNG has not encouraged interaction between psychologists and medical practioners. In any case, there are only two psychiatrists in PNG and one, Dr. Burton-Bradley, is now retired. Dr. Bradley, who recently became Patron of the UPNG Psychological Association, has regularly accompanied students on visits to the psychiatric wards of Port Moresby General Hospital and Laloki Psychiatric Institute, situated a few miles outside Port Moresby. These visits are part of the Abnormal Psychology course at UPNG. Medical doctors occasionally request intelligence or aptitude testing and we sometimes get patient referrals, though none of the academics at UPNG has formal training in clinical psychology.

Between UPNG psychologists and other academics

These interactions are generally good with the exception of occasions upon which we clash with sociologists who sometimes see our research as poaching on their territory, or as insensitive to the special reasons for UPNG students' weakness in reading and writing. As a Department, we have had joint research projects with the Departments of Law (crime research), Chemistry (the effects of betel-nut chewing), Electrical Engineering at the University of Technology in Lae (tactile device for the profoundly deaf), and we have acted as consultants for various PNG Government bodies including the Electricity Commission, Department of Finance, Post Office and Telephones Commission, and the Law Reform Commission.

Between UPNG psychologists and overseas academics

Overseas psychologists visit UPNG at an average rate not exceeding one per year, most being researchers who have obtained affiliate status at UPNG. This relatively sparse contact with the outside world is partly a consequence of the fact that PNG is not geographically convenient for a break in a journey between major cities, and partly because internal air fares are expensive. In addition, the approving bodies with which an intending researcher must negotiate are daunting in number (the appropriate university department, the UPNG Research Committee, the PNG Institute of Studies, and the appropriate Provincial Government), and strict in application of rules. This often criticised impediment is a consequence of a well entrenched scepticism dating back to the works of Malinowski (such as The sexual life of savages) and Mead (such as Growing up in Papua New Guinea), and many subsequent publications, the accuracy of which has been vigorously challenged in recent years. In some areas, the attitude towards social science researchers is downright hostile and the Trobriand Islands are completely off limits.[5] Such prohibitive measures have been introduced to guard against the gross generalizations and distortions of which some researchers have been accused. All visiting researchers must submit a copy of their research reports to the PNG Institute of Studies and UPNG before publication.

However, UPNG pays up to K1100 ($AUS 1400) in air fares for an expatriate to attend a conference provided that the applicant has had a paper accepted, that it has some relevance to PNG, and the applicant does not exceed one conference trip per year. National academics are not required to have a paper accepted for presentation, and their air fares may exceed the K1100 maximum applicable to expatriates. The air fare limit effectively restricts expatriate conference participation to Australia, New Zealand and Singapore unless such staff are willing to pay the extra expense of travelling further afield. Another alternative is to divert from a leave journey (leave to the country of origin being paid for by UPNG).

ATTITUDES TOWARDS PSYCHOLOGY IN PNG

Testing and consultancy

The majority of people in Papua New Guinea live in rural areas where psychology has little or no meaning. However, most government employees have been exposed to psychological tests of one kind or another, and there is a vague understanding that one may be promoted or demoted following tests administered by psychologists. In this context, the prevailing attitude is not positive. In recent years, consultants from overseas (notably Australia) have been hired to advise government bodies on matters of management and staff development, but although fees have been high benefits have been minimal. It is made public by the media that psychological tests are used by these overpaid consultants, and as a consequence, the image of psychology is not enhanced. As national psychology graduates enter the work force in PNG, a more thrifty use of our limited resources and an expansion of the file of tests normed and validated for PNG are to be expected.

Psychologists in the field

When the Psychological Services Branch had regional offices in outlying areas there were usually good relations between the regional pychologist and the people in the district. It would take many pages to document the excellent work of the regional psychologists in this country. Many of the "sacked" government psychologists have found jobs in other departments or in private companies and are therefore still available as sources of valuable and unique information. The contribution regional psychologists made was much valued by those who received their services, varied and unconventional though they sometimes were, and it is a great pity that these services were so inconspicuous that the PNG government saw fit to withdraw them.

SUMMARY AND CONCLUSIONS

It was the missionaries who gave the first accounts of Papua New Guineans' behaviour. Like the anthropological reports which followed, the authenticity of such data has been questioned in later years, but neither the missionaries nor the anthropologists were guilty of deliberate misrepresentation. Nevertheless, research in the social sciences is closely monitored. After World War II, the question of relevance and contribution of psychology to Papua New Guinea was much debated, but mainly by the colonials. Papua New Guineans were more interested in the concept of independence, and the emotion behind this movement was stronger than concern for such things as psychology. Expatriate psychologists within the PNG Government found themselves facing a bleak future. They believed that they served a purpose and wanted to remain in the country, but they received less and less support from the post-independence government. In anticipation of retrenchment, many left of their own accord, although when the government closed down the Psychological Services Branch of the Public Service at least half a dozen psychologists found work elsewhere within the country.

While support for professional psychologists has dwindled, academic psychology has begun to flourish at the University of Papua New Guinea. But this is probably because the University affords the protection of autonomy and prestige not enjoyed by the practitioners. Although the psychologists at UPNG feel the same pressures towards localization as are experienced by their colleagues in government, academics have been more successful in maintaining standards - but not without a price. The most serious threat to psychology (or any other discipline) in UPNG remains that of the polarity between those who hold the "must maintain standards" viewpoint, who, in extreme cases, are really saying "must maintain standards I learned were important where I come from," and those who say "psychologists must be nationals" who in extreme cases are saying "psychologists must be nationals no matter how poorly qualified those nationals may be".

When Sir Julius Chan, previous Prime Minister of Papua New Guinea, said "There's no 'Melanesian way' to pilot a plane", he was surely right, but it is also incumbent on expatriate professionals to adapt if they are to serve any real purpose in P.N.G.

NOTES

1. This "capsule history" was taken from Fodor's _Australia, New Zealand and the South Pacific_, Fodor's Modern Guides, inc., New York, 1981 (Eds.).

2. This goal may not be reached. Schools were once seen as places where children could learn skills which would enable them to get well paid jobs. Many parents paid school fees as an investment, in the expectation that money sent home would be the return. Lack of parents' confidence in this kind of investment (especially where girls are concerned) in evidenced by recent enrollment statistics (Lancy, 1983).

3. The standard of mathematics involved in "Say it with Figures" is so elementary that it has become known even more affectionately as "Say it with Fingers".

4. It is extraordinarily difficult to enroll as a student at UPNG if you have not been resident in PNG for at least six months. Since you are not allowed to reside in PNG unless you have a job or student status, it is virtually impossible for a single overseas student to attend UPNG. 5. Two members of the UPNG Psychology Department were given permission to conduct research into attitudes towards crime in the Trobriand Islands in 1983. Attitudes were found to be very different from those in other regions, and crime (in the Western sense) to be almost non-existent. Also interesting was the warm welcome we received, with the frequent assurance that researchers were not unwelcome from the islanders' point of view.

REFERENCES

CAMPBELL, E. F. A Papua New Guinea Psychology Society? in M.A. Hutton, R.E. Hicks, & C.I.S. Brammall (eds.) Psychology in Papua New Guinea. Port Moresby, Australian Psychological Society (PNG Branch), 1973.

LANCY, D. F. Cross-cultural studies in cognition and mathematics. New York, Academic Press, 1983.

LOELIGER, C. Christian missions in P.N.G., in D. King & S. Ranck (eds.) Papua New Guinea Atlas, Hong Kong, Robert Brown, 1982.

MALINOWSKI, B. The sexual life of savages in Northern Western Melanesia. London, Routledge and Kegan Paul, 1932.

MEAD, M. Growing up in New Guinea. Harmondsworth, Middlesex, Penguin, 1930.

PRICE, J. (in press) A look at psychology in Papua New Guinea since independence, South Pacific Journal of Psychology, 1984.

ROBINS, R. The presence, influence and effects of Christian missions on the people of the Southern Highlands, Papua New Guinea. Ph.D. dissertation, University of Papua New Guinea, 1980.

ST. GEORGE, R. The New Guinea Psychologist: the first five years. An analysis of content with comments, New Guinea Psychologist, 1974, 6, 118-121.

19

Psychology in the Australian Context

Alison M. Turtle

INTRODUCTION

In 1988 Australia will celebrate the bicentennial anniversary of the arrival of the first fleet from Britain, which landed on the east coast of the vast and very lightly populated continent in 1788 to establish the first of several penal settlements. The system of convict transportation continued until well into the nineteenth century, though before it ceased the population had been extensively rounded out by free settlers; soldiers who decided to remain in the country, prospective farmers, women in search of employment and/or matrimony, and gold-seekers comprised the main groups. Until 1901 there were six separate colonies or administrative units, gradually building up both responsible government and manhood suffrage in their local parliaments. In 1901 these units formed themselves into a federation, with a constitution broadly modelled on the British one, but with an elected rather than hereditary upper house. The country remains a member of the British Commonwealth, and recognizes the British monarch as its own, although direct political intervention from Britain has occurred extremely rarely in recent decades.

The indigenous people of Australia (known as Aborigines) were highly nomadic in habit, and had no written language. Both culture and health of the Aboriginal peoples suffered badly from the arrival of the new settlers, and subsequent political, social and educational institutions reflect little if any of the images or influence of the original inhabitants. Almost all the permanent settlers of the nineteenth century were British, with coolie labourers from the neighbouring

Pacific regions being imported but fairly promptly exported again; only the Chinese, who came in for a variety of reasons including gold-seeking, managed to remain, and to retain a distinctive identity despite their relatively very small numbers. The so-called "White Australia" policy introduced soon after Federation both brought the country the disapprobation of its neighbours, and perpetuated the British composition of the population until after World War II. Thereafter Australia accepted large numbers of European refugees, and followed up this opening of hitherto unwelcoming doors by actively encouraging and sponsoring migrants from selected regions. Southern Europeans in particular flocked in, to be followed by Middle Easterners. In the early 'seventies the White Australia policy was abandoned, and large numbers of Asians from a variety of countries have been migrating for the past decade. The current population numbers nearly seventeen million, spread over a continent as large in area as the United States.

As well as belonging to the British Commonwealth, Australia has formal alliances with the United States, New Zealand, and a number of its Asian neighbours. The official and by far the most common language is English, and the most common religion is Christianity, though adherence to the church is often purely nominal. Because of their geographical isolation, Australians until recently have had direct contact with overseas countries only on a rather haphazard basis, with Britain usually being the main goal for travellers.

In educational, scientific and professional spheres, as in many other social structures, the influence of British forebears may readily be discerned. Only as recently as 1965 was the Australian Psychological Society, the single independent professional organization open to psychologists of all persuasions in Australia, established. Prior to that had existed, since 1922, the Australasian Association of Psychology and Philosophy and, since 1945, the Australian Branch of the British Psychological Society. Since 1983 however, a section for Mental Science and Education had existed in the Australasian Association for the Advancement of Science. This brief chronology indicates some of the most significant facts about the history of Australian psychology - its early appearance on the Australian scene, its initial close ties in terms of cognitive content with philosophy and education and in terms of cultural contact with British, the push towards a separate professional identity given to it by the second World War, and the subsequent severance of the umbilical cord firstly with the parent discipline of philosophy and then with the parent country.

By and large Australia has produced neither individual psychologists of outstanding distinction nor a distinctive psychological tradition; one serious contender for the first category, Stanley Porteus, was not trained as a psychologist and in any case spent the larger part of his academic career after designing the noteworthy Porteus-Maze test, in the USA. What is of interest in its history is the particular way in which this new discipline was transported to an adolescent colonial society and has subsequently matured there. This was a society where, as it happened, the beginnings of the universities coincided with the beginnings in world terms of modern psychology, closely followed by a major revision of the local system of primary and secondary education and of teacher training.

As treated in this paper, the history spans some nine decades, and may be seen as falling into three periods. The first period is one of differentiation of psychology into a discipline in its own right, distinguished from both philosophy and education. The second is a time of propagation of a first generation of Australian psychologists, bred for the most part in local departments of philosophy and sometimes matured in psychology departments in Britain and the United States and occasionally Germany, and of application of their new skills in practical fields, educational, vocational and industrial. The third is the period of independence of the young academic progeny from both parent discipline and country, and of professionalization and tremendous expansion since World War II.

CONCEPTION

There are nineteen universities in the country. The University of Sydney was the first to be incorporated in 1850, followed by the Universities of Melbourne (1853), Adelaide (1874), Tasmania (1890), Queensland (1909) and Western Australia (1911). The first universities were staffed almost exclusively by British scholars and their formal organizational structures still adhere closely to the British model. As in Britain, the main doorway through which psychology made its formal entry onto the

Australian stage led via departments of philosophy.

The University of Sydney was the pacesetter here. In 1888 Francis Anderson, Master of Arts from Glasgow University, was appointed to the first lecturing position there in Philosophy, which was upgraded in 1890 to a chair of Logic and Mental Philosophy. Fired with enthusiasm by developments in the social sciences, throughout his career Anderson actively advocated the inclusion of education, psychology, anthropology, economics and sociology in the university curriculum; at various times he gave lectures on all of these except anthropology, and from the beginning made psychology an integral part of his philosophy course. The texts for psychology were taken from the modern school emerging overseas; in 1891 for instance they were Baldwin's Elementary Psychology and Education and his Handbook of Psychology, Clark Murray's Handbook of Psychology and Sully's Outline of Psychology (University of Sydney Calendar 1891, p.175).

In 1910 Anderson appointed as part-time Reader in Psychology in his department Henry Tasman Lovell, one of his own graduates who had just returned from Jena with a doctorate on the educational theories of Herbert Spencer. Whilst in Germany, Lovell had also furthered his knowledge of the new experimental techniques being developed there in psychology; by then he had as well been introduced to Binet's work on mental testing and to Freudian theory (O'Neil 1977, p.5). Promptly he organized the purchase by the University of a set of psychological laboratory equipment from Zimmerman of Leipzig (Turtle 1979, p.264), and when in 1913 his post became a fulltime one, he included demonstrations of experimental work in the expanded first year course. Texts at this stage were James's Textbook of Psychology, Myers' Introduction to Psychology, Stout's Manual of Psychology, and McDougall's Physiological Psychology and Social Psychology (University of Sydney Calendar 1913, p.173); the British influence was still clearly paramount. Gradually courses expanded, and in 1920 Lovell became Associate Professor in Psychology, which was then recognised as a separate department though still linked through its first and third year courses to Philosophy. In 1929 student numbers in Psychology had increased to such an extent that Lovell's position was elevated to a full chair, the first in Australia, and the only one until 1946.

But although the formal partnership was with philosophy, there was a continuing liaison with education, a discipline like psychology struggling for recognition. Anderson in Sydney was one of the main spokesmen for the proper training and recognition of the teaching profession, and his efforts are generally considered to have been in large part responsible for the establishment of Sydney Teachers' College in 1906, and for the Chair of Education at the University in 1910. Alexander Mackie was the first Principal of the former, and foundation professor of the latter. Prior to that, most teachers simply picked up their trade by first-hand experience. From 1889 to 1894 a teacher-training scheme, organized by the Minister for Public Instruction, flourished, whereby selected trainee primary teachers attended lectures in the Faculty of Arts, sometimes taking out degrees and sometimes studying Philosophy; the gradual decline of this system provided ammunition for Anderson's volleys against the inadequacy of the state's training of its future teachers (see for example Anderson 1901). Constantly Anderson argued that psychology should be a major component in teacher education (Anderson 1903), and was prepared actively to collaborate with Mackie to that end. In 1916 for instance, the departments of Philosophy and Education combined to offer two half courses in Experimental Psychology and Experimental Education (University of Sydney Calendar 1916). By 1923, courses on Educational Psychology and Experimental Psychology in the two departments bore a remarkable resemblance to each other, in respect both of content and textbooks (University of Sydney Calendar 1923).

This early liaison with education, closer in Australia than was it counterpart in Britain, manifested itself also in the first scholarly organization in which psychologists in Australia became involved. In 1888 the Australasian Association for the Advancement of Science[1] was established, and as early as 1893 its sections included one on Mental Science and Education. In Britain on the other hand the entry of Psychology to the British Association was delayed until 1920. The founding presidential address for the new section was delivered by Henry Laurie, Professor of Mental and Moral Philosophy at Melbourne University, his theme being the emergence of psychology as a natural science, independent from philosophy (Laurie 1893, p. 198). In point of fact the papers offered at this meeting comprised eleven on educational topics, and one on psycho-physical experiments (AAAS Report of the Fifth Meeting, 1893).

The sixth meeting in 1895 saw another professor of philosophy, Francis Anderson, as president. To this meeting was submitted a "Report of Committee on the best means of encouraging psychophysical and psychometrical investigation in Australia." Laurie was chairman of this Committee, which had communicated with both Titchener and Galton regarding practices in these areas in their countries. Regretfully it concluded that Australian universities could not yet afford the facilities of chairs and laboratories for experimental psychology, but urged "professors of mental science" to work through contacts in physics and physiology, and with students. It aimed "to devise a scheme of statistical inquiries of theoretical and practical value, in connection with the State school systems of the Australasian colonies" (AAAS Report of the Sixth Meeting, 1895). This emphasis on the potential of applied psychology in a young society continued to appear in papers presented to the Association for many years. In addition to having the usual incentives to the development of practical tools that prevailed in Britain and the States, Australians sought reassurance that their country was following the correct paths of development in educational, moral, intellectual and even physical directions. As late as 1932 in the report of a committee to the Association on the "Range of Physiological Variables in the Inhabitants of Australia and New Zealand," we find the following statement: "Is our race improving or deteriorating in these new lands is a question of first importance, and frequently asked about tropical Australia" (ANZAAS Report of the Twenty-first Meeting, 1932, p.477). (Though made to the Sections of Medical Science and National Health, and Physiology and Experimental Biology, this Report included measures of intelligence based on formal psychological tests.)

GESTATION

Within a few years patterns similar to the Sydney one were manifesting themselves elsewhere (Bucklow 1977, O'Neil 1977, Taft 1982), although only two other universities had established separate departments of psychology prior to World War II (Western Australia and New England University College). In Melbourne Henry Laurie, another philosopher from Scotland who was appointed as lecturer in Logic at the university in 1881 and to a chair of Mental and Moral Philosophy in 1886, played a role similar to that of Anderson in Sydney, in that he both pleaded for educational reform and taught psychology in his courses. His successor, W. R. Boyce-Gibson, did likewise, though a chair of psychology was not established in Melbourne until 1946. Melbourne Teachers' College was however established in 1903, and its first Principal, John Smyth, a graduate of Edinburgh and Jena, became in 1917 professor of Education at the University. Smyth set up the first experimental psychological laboratory in Australia at the Teachers' College in 1903 (Taft 1982, p.33). In 1913 the University of Western Australia appointed a Melbourne philosophy graduate, P. R. Le Couteur, who had studied psychology as well at Oxford and Bonn, as Lecturer in Moral and Mental Philosophy. The war caused a lapse in this position, but in 1928 H. L. Fowler, who had taken a doctorate with Spearman at University College, London, was appointed part-time lecturer in psychology, and an independent department was established in 1930. The University of Queensland in 1911 appointed Elton Mayo, an Adelaide graduate who had also studied at Edinburgh and London, to a lectureship in Psychology and Ethics, and in 1919 to a chair of Philosophy. Until 1923, when he went to Harvard and made his name in industrial sociology, Mayo's courses emphasized psychology. A classicist from Oxford, R. L. Dunbabin, took up a lectureship at the University of Tasmania in 1902 in "Mental and Moral Sciences", and the tie with philosophy continued there until psychology became a separate department in the 'fifties.

The main source of intellectual sustenance for this early Australian psychology was thus the newly emerging British psychology, a combination largely of British empiricism and evolutionary biology, supplemented by an input from German physiological psychology. Contact however was early established with the discipline as it was shaping up in the United States, as the use even before 1900 of American texts indicates. Rapidly after the first World War this input was to be enlarged by direct contact with pioneers, both British and American, of the mental testing movement, as students sought out teachers such as Spearman, Thorndike, Woodworth and Terman. The first World War came too soon in terms of the state of growth of Australian psychology to cause an explosion of mental testing activities there as it did in the United States, but Australia certainly felt the reverberations. Smyth for instance in 1922 began applying intelligence tests to entrants to Melbourne Teachers' College (AAAS Report of the Eighteenth Meeting, 1926, pp.709-710), and Phillips, by then Principal of Sydney

Teachers' College, in 1925 published a Sydney revision of the Binet tests (Martin 1925, p.42).

A definite impact was made in the area of psychopathology, where psychoanalytic concepts were, as in Britain, given a considerable boost by the observation of shellshock phenomena. J. W. Springthorpe, a Melbourne medical practitioner, became a most vocal advocate of the inclusion of psychology in medical couses in Australia; topics he addressed in his extensive publications on psychotherapy included the treatment of war neurosis, the use of hypnosis, and the theories of Freud (Springthorpe 1919, 1920, 1932). Chairs of psychiatry began to make their appearance in the 'twenties, and this may have delayed the development of clinical courses by the psychologists. The theory and concepts of psychoanalysis were however carefully and extensively presented and discussed by both psychologists and philosophers, Lovell being a major performer here.

By the early 'thirties then the Universities of Sydney and Western Australia were producing graduates with three years in psychology, and others were producing graduates in philosophy and education with some courses in psychology. Trained manpower was therefore available for a variety of psychological enterprises. Even before this, proponents of the subject had come to feel the need for some sort of specialist scholarly organization. In 1922 Francis Anderson was succeeded to the Sydney chair of Logic and Mental Philosophy by a former pupil, Bernard Muscio. Almost the first action of Muscio on taking up the chair was to found the Australasian Association of Psychology and Philosophy, which held its first annual general meeting in May 1923 and produced the first issue of a new journal, the Australasian Journal of Psychology and Philosophy, in the same year.

Muscio's own most clearly defined area of interest within psychology was industrial psychology. From 1914 to 1916 he had been Demonstrator in Experimental Psychology at Cambridge with C. S. Myers; during three years spent in the Sydney Philosophy Department before returning for another stint at Cambridge he presented four lectures on industrial psychology to the newly formed Workers' Educational Association (Muscio 1917). This was the first time such material had been presented in Australia; furthermore, according to Myers, Muscio was "responsible for the development of the subject throughout the British Empire" (quoted in Anderson 1926, p.159). Subsequent to Muscio's lectures Myers set up the National Institute of

Industrial Psychology in London. Muscio himself died of illness in 1926. The following year A. H. Martin, Lecturer in the University of Sydney's new Department of Psychology[2], established at Sydney the Australian Institute of Industrial Psychology, affiliated to the British Institute.

This body, which survived until the 'seventies, achieved special success in the area of vocational guidance; it paid less attention to the study of practical industrial problems. It worked from time to time in collaboration with the Vocational Guidance Bureau established in 1926 by the New South Wales Department of Education to provide a free counselling and guidance service to school children (Bucklow 1977, pp. 25-26). In fact all states but one had developed vocational guidance services by 1932, but only in New South Wales were psychological tests used rather than simply advice by teachers (Giles 1932). Thus by the time of the second World War, Australian psychology was demonstrating its potential in applied fields other than educational; the war was to accentuate this trend to a marked degree.

In Melbourne in 1930, with assistance from the Carnegie Corporation, the Australian Council for Educational Research (ACER) was established as an independent body, with K. S. Cunningham, a Columbia Teachers' College graduate, as its first Director. It adapted overseas tests for Australian use, and constructed new ones. During the war, ACER was asked by the Commonwealth Training Scheme to devise tests to discern suitability of men for different branches of technical training; the munitions industry also discovered the usefulness of aptitude tests in the selection of prospective employees for rapid training (Mellor 1958, pp.183-185). Following British precedents from World War I, Australian psychologists in the second war came to be used in the investigation of conditions affecting industrial efficiency; in 1942 a Controller of Factory Welfare was appointed by the Department of Labour and National Service, and an Australian Institute of Industrial Management was set up (Mellor 1958, pp.188-190).

The Armed Services were also persuaded of the value of psychologists' skills in the areas of selection, placement and training of personnel. In 1940 the Royal Australian Air Force set up a psychological organization for the selection of pilots; in 1942 the Army followed suit, and the Royal Australian Navy in 1944 established a vocational guidance service for members being discharged

(Mellor 1958, pp.186-188). The war thus consider-ably enhanced the prestige of the profession. In fact in 1943 psychologists were included among the scientific groups of whom the Director-General of Manpower demanded compulsory registration, so that advisory committees could direct them to where they were most needed (Mellor 1958, p.195). Psychologists of the period were actively involved in and aware of this process of promotion of their discipline, as a contemporary paper on the very topic by the director of ACER evidenced (Cunningham 1943).

SEPARATION AND MATURATION

As well as making Australian psychologists more conscious of their distinctive practical role in the community, the war served the purpose of bringing together members of the profession from different states who had hitherto hardly met each other (O'Neil 1977, p. 14). The need for a professional organization to regulate standards of conduct and to represent the interests of psychologists was also emerging. So 1945 saw the forma-tion of the first professional organization in Australia exclusive to psychologists, the Australian Branch of the British Psychological Society; simultaneously psychology withdrew from the strictly academic Australasian Associa-tion of Psychology and Philosophy. The ties with the parent discipline were thus formally severed. The first volume of the first journal of the new society, the Australian Journal of Psychology, appeared in 1949, edited by D. W. McElwain from the University of Mel-bourne.

A period of tremendous expansion then began. Until 1956 the only chair of Psychology had been at the University of Sydney; in that year Melbourne established a second, six more were established in the 'fifties, and another five in the 'sixties (Nixon and Taft 1977, pp.18-19. At present there are seventeen departments of psychology or behavioural science in the country. In the 'forties undergraduate courses for Honours students in Arts and Science were first extended to four years, with more time being devoted to the development of research skills. In the 'fifties the universities began to introduce their own doctoral training programmes in psychology, and by the 'sixties the Federal Government's post-war policy of funding scientific research was starting to affect the behavioural sciences. Funds flowed in particular via the Australian Universities Commission (established 1959) and the Australian Research Grants Committee (established in 1965), followed later by the (now defunct) Australian Advisory Committee on Research and Development in Education and the Advisory Committee for Child Care Research. The research output in psychology boomed in consequence. Whilst the tertiary education and research sectors expanded generally as a result of the increased flow of public funds during the 'sixties and early 'seventies, psychology's enormous popularity with the students led to its being a particular beneficiary.

Broad cultural and ideological factors of course played their part in this fashion, as they did in the United States. But enhanced opportunities for employment as psychologists undoubtedly influenced the students as well, as the field of applied psychology, having tested its wings during the war, really took off. After the war, all three of the Armed Services established permanent psychological organizations. The Commonwealth Department of Labour and National Service became a permanent department, and set up the Commonwealth Employment Service to expand the counselling and vocational guidance services undertaken during the war. By 1947 this was established in all states but New South Wales, where an independent arrangement was already functioning. The Commonwealth Employment Service came to advise adults as well as young clients, its emphasis gradually changing from narrow vocational guidance to general counselling. The Industrial Welfare section of the Department continued on post-war, its psychological functions being taken over by the Personnel Practice Section in 1953 (Bucklow 1977, pp. 28-29). Until 1970, the field of applied psychology was dominated by counselling services in educational institutions, clinical and personnel psychology and vocational guidance, in that order (Kidd 1971). These areas often depended heavily on testing, a situation which contributed to the already growing reputation and activities of ACER.

Post-war ACER was no longer a small, independently financed establishment, but a flourishing organization dependent on government finance and actively liaising with other government bodies, especially the new Commonwealth Office of Education. A test division was established in 1947, separate from the broader research activities of the body; developments in both are outlined

in a recently published history of the organization
(Connell 1980). In 1970, approximately two-thirds of the
country's two thousand odd persons employed as psychologists were practitioners in the applied field (Kidd
1971, p.67).

By 1965 the body of Australian psychologists was so
large that the professional society cut its ties with the
British organization, and set up the Australian Psychological Society. One of this group's first gestures of
independence was the publication, beginning in 1966, of
the Australian Psychologist, to deal with matters of
applied as opposed to academic psychology, of local
relevance. Since 1979 a news bulletin has been produced
as well. By 1982 the Society had 2962 members and
fellows, and a total membership of 4104 (Australian
Psychological Society 1982, p.20). Despite the break with
the British body, the Society frequently takes its parent
as a model for its own practices, though the American
Psychological Association is often copied as well. One of
the main achievements of the Society has been in the area
of official recognition of the profession. Beginning in
Victoria in 1965, Psychological Practices Acts have now
been passed in all states except New South Wales; these
regulate conduct in areas such as hyponosis and psychotherapy, and provide for registration by a government--
appointed council for the purposes of professional
practice.

The Society is still in the process of attempting to
resolve a dilemma which has confronted the discipline for
some time, that of how to represent and reconcile the
interests of its academic and other professional members.
Despite the fact that the membership overall has doubled
over the last few years, the proportion of academic
membership dropped steadily throughout the 'seventies
(from 76.4% in 1970 to 59.2% in 1980) (Over 1981a,
p.227). As the result of a referendum in 1980, there has
now been established a two-Division structure, one for
each of the areas of Scientific and Professional Affairs.
Such passage may be more a recognition than a resolution
of dilemma. Academics continue to be critical of the
standards and theoretical frameworks of the practitioners, in areas where they themselves usually have no
first-hand experience, whilst the practitioners question
the understanding of the academics. Until recently, the
only regular conventions for psychologists were the
annual one organized by the Society, and the much smaller
yearly event sponsored by the Psychology Division of

ANZAAS. Now specialist conferences, some regular and some occasional, some for academics and some for professionals, are becoming a more prominent feature of the Australian scene, and this divisive trend will probably continue. Perhaps it reflects the dual origins of the subject, in academic philosophy and educational applications.

The lingering relationship of Australian psychology with philosophy, much longer-lasting than that of its British counterpart, does require explanation, particularly in view of this flourishing other affair with education. Here it is relevant to recollect that the philosophers also were newcomers to the Australian scene, and themselves in need of colleagues. Only a handful of universities, sparsely staffed, existed in the country until quite recently, and these were separated by vast distances. And with funding for university research quite modest until the 'fifties theoretical issues, conceptually closely related to the traditional concerns of philosophers, continued to occupy much of the energy of academic psychologists. Since the mid-'fifties, the proportion of theoretical papers produced by academic psychologists has declined markedly (Day 1977, p. 62), an indication that independence from philosophy has become more than formal.

But here, as in other aspects of its current research and applications, Australian psychology is by no means atypical. A review of research in universities and colleges conducted between 1945 and 1973 produced the conclusion that "research effort is concentrated largely in accepted and traditional areas of research interest," with a dearth of work in clinical psychology and somewhat slight attention being paid to applied psychology (Day 1977, p.68). A study in 1980 which covered 80 per cent of Australian academics identified their five main areas of research interest as being, in order, Experimental, Personality/Social, Development, Evaluation/Measurement, and Comparative/Physiological (Over 1981, pp. 225-226). There is no characteristically Australian school of research methods of problems, and there has been but a slight attempt to shape up the study to fit the local environment. With a few important exceptions, little work has been done on the psychology of the Australian Aboriginal or of Australian native fauna. Occasionally local social issues such as the effects of immigration or unemployment are addressed, but neither official nor private bodies are much inclined to subsidize such undertakings. As yet, no theoretical contributions of major stature or of unique status have been produced in any field.

The geographical distances separating Australian psychologists from each other and from colleagues overseas mean less frequent conferring and personal exchange of ideas than in most western countries. However, generous programmes for overseas study and conference leave have been maintained by all the universities, with the result that Australian psychologists are quite well connected to the North American and British networks. A study of citation statistics for local psychologists in the 'seventies produced a comprehensible picture: they are somewhat less 'visible' than their North American counterparts, but not less productive (Over and Moore 1979). From its inception, the Australian Psychological Society has been active in the International Union of Psychological Science. Mainly through the work of cross-cultural psychologists there are contacts with Australia's immediate neighbours in South-East Asia, but these are not numerous; at a different level such contact is sustained by the continuing influx of students therefrom.

A SOMEWHAT UNSTEADY PRESENT STATE

During the 'sixties and early 'seventies employment prospects proliferated for Australian psychologists, both within and without the universities. This was in part due to the generous funding policies adopted towards the universities during that period, and to the election in 1972 of the first Labour government in a quarter of a century. As part of its broad policies on social welfare, this body hastened to increase clinical and counselling posts in the public sector. The general recession however reversed both these trends; cuts were made in the budgets for tertiary education and research as well in social welfare by the Liberal government returned in 1975, and the re-election of Labour in 1983 has not as yet resulted in any conspicuous recovery in these respects. The result is that the traditional employers of psychologists are seeking fewer recruits.

In 1981 the Graduate Careers Council of Australia reported that 30 per cent of psychologists work in broadly academic areas (Kampf and Smith 1981). The transition from rapid growth to no growth within the

particular academic arena of the universities has led
already to a situation where, as Over (1981a) points out,
the psychology departments in Australian universities
face the "impending crises" of no new blood and ageing
staff. Meanwhile, individual doctoral graduates face an
only one in ten prospect of academic employment. The
situation of the latter is exacerbated in the Australian
context by the increased recruitment from overseas that
has occurred over the last decade, provoked obviously by
similar problems in the funding of tertiary institutions
elsewhere. Between 1976 and 1982 only 57 per cent of
lectureships and 42 per cent of more senior appointments
were gained by applicants who held at least one qualification from an Australian university. As at this time the
annual growth rate of two per cent for position in
psychology departments was only one fifth of its value in
the 'sixties (Over 1983), such trends will be slow to
have any effect on the overall complexion of university
staffing. Whether they are better interpreted as an
exemplification of cultural dependence or as a profitable
extension of international connection it is as yet too
early to decide.

Since the disappearance of the early generation of
imported philosophers, this overall complexion has been
very largely an indigenous one. Of the forty-five
different individuals who have occupied Australian chairs
of psychology to date, only twelve have no Australian
degree.[3] Furthermore, the influence of the pioneer
department at the University of Sydney remains paramount,
at least in terms of this professorial criterion:
thirteen out of the thirty-four professors of psychology
in Australia in 1979 were Sydney graduates, and eight
others had at some time held an appointment at that
university (Over 1981a, p. 224). There is considerable
inbreeding within the Australian departments. For
example, out of those thirty people holding appointment
at the University of Sydney at the level of lecturer and
above in 1983, only seven did not take their first degree
there (University of Sydney Calendar 1983). Mobility
rates after first appointment are not high - between 1976
and 1982 there were on average only two moves per year
between universities in Australia (Over 1983, p. 131).
This state of affairs results in part from the broad
cultural norm, whereby in a vast and lightly populated
country Australians of all persuasions tend towards
stability in their city of residence. Also, academic
salaries across the country are regulated by a Federal

tribunal, and are hardly subject to negotiation; there is
thus little financial inducement to keep moving. Other
Australian practices in academic appointment and conditions of employment exacerbate the situation: tenurable
positions are usually advertised only at the top and
bottom levels (professor and lecturer), and superannuation schemes are not readily portable.[4]

The decision as to whether or not to undertake a
higher degree is a difficult one for today's psychology
student. Surveys by the Graduate Careers Council between
1975 and 1979 show an increasing proportion of psychology
first degree pass graduates going into non-psychology-
based employment (Kampf and Smith 1981), presumably
because they are unable to find specialized work. The
number of students graduating during the 'seventies with
psychology as their major subject is still increasing,
due to the expansion in psychology programmes available
throughout the country. That supply now exceeds demand is
indicated by the numbers of psychology graduates registered as unemployed with the Commonwealth Employment
Service (145 in 1977, 331 in 1979) (Over 1981b, p.335).
Over the last few years the number of students entering a
fourth year of training, at either the Honours undergraduate or Master's by course work level, has increased
sharply (Over 1981b, p.341). This is probably due in part
to the students' perception of employers' requirements,
and partly to the fact that the academic prerequisite for
full membership of the Australian Psychological Society
is now four years of formal study.

The balance between the areas of professional
employment for psychologists has changed somewhat during
the 'seventies, as revealed by a comparison of Kidd's
(1971) survey with a summary of graduate destination
figures put out by the Graduate Careers Council in 1981
(Kampf and Smith 1981). The main variant is an increased
number of clinical positions within the public sector.
According to this summary, the areas of non-academic
employment of psychology graduates by the government are,
in order of numbers absorbed, educational, clinical,
vocational, and occupational and counselling. There has
been little growth in employment by the private sector -
only about five per cent of new psychology graduates
begin their working careers here, though some do move
there later. A small body of private practitioners exists
in the fields of clinical, industrial, counselling and
educational psychology, but its growth in hampered by
lack of public awareness. This is exemplified by the fact

that no medical fund as yet provides benefits for
psychological services.

In respect of public recognition, Australian
psychology still lags behind that of the countries from
which it derived. Few research grants have been forthcoming from industry. Whilst many psychologists are in
the employ of a variety of government bodies, this is on
an individual basis; professional groups are rarely
consulted, and private consultative organizations are
few, existing for the purpose of advising private
enterprise or persons. No popular psychological journals
or magazines such as Psychology Today or New Behaviour
are published in Australia. The subject is unknown at the
secondary examinable level in most of the states. It has
however been popular with adults throughout most of the
century in courses offered for general interest rather
than for formal qualification by cooperative, government
and university bodies (such as the Workers' Educational
Association, the New South Wales Department of Adult
Education, and the University of Sydney's Board of
Tutorial Classes). Only very recently has there been much
indication of private enterprise capitalising on the
popular image of the discipline, with the advent of such
phenomena as Erhardt's Seminar Therapy groups and the
Australasian College of Psychology.

IN CONCLUSION

The scene emerging from these sketchy outlines is
one of a surprisingly early appearance of psychology on
the Australian stage, as early as that of philosophy
itself, followed by a slow and at no time spectacular
movement towards independence in both national and
disciplinary terms. Such early appearance was due both to
the reliance on British models of philosophy, and to a
perceived need for concepts and techniques in the rapidly
evolving field of practical education. Interest in the
practical applications of psychology manifested itself
from the beginning, in the pronouncements of the early
professors of philosophy such as Anderson, Laurie, Mayo
and Muscio. Students were increasingly directed towards
the prolific psychological productions of the United
States, where the broad functionalist approach provided a
rationale for the development of applied psychology. It
was not difficult for Australian psychologists, themselves persuaded that their discipline was fundamental to

322

the practice of a variety of forms of social endeavour, to persuade a developing society to allow them to display their expertise. The temporal juxtaposition of the importation from overseas of the new psychology with the total, and much needed, transformation of teacher training schemes in Sydney and Melbourne was fortuitous for both disciplines, education as well as psychology. Psychology had the opportunity to prove its value, and it acquired additional pupils. World War II provided these former pupils with a much expanded range of opportunities to show their own usefulness.

Since the war, academic and applied psychology have grown in conjunction, though the relationship has not been unproblematic. The post-war scenario has been less distinctive than was the pre-war progress. Academics have coped well with their peculiar geographical handicaps in terms of international connection and general achievement, whilst applied psychologists are well established in the sphere of public employment. Developments however have been belated in terms of comparison with those in Britain and the United States, both as regards past expansion and present contraction. Because of this, it is as yet uncertain whether psychology, along with the other social sciences, will be as much a particular victim of the recession in Australian as it has been in those countries.

NOTES

1. From 1930 known as the Australian and New Zealand Association for the Advancement of science (ANZAAS).

2. Martin's appointment in 1921 was the first in Australia of a holder of a degree in psychology, this being a doctorate from Columbia University where he studied with Woodworth.

3. Derived from data in O'Neil (1983).

4. 1982 saw the introduction of a new national scheme designed to overcome this problem, but many of the universities have not yet joined it.

REFERENCES

ANDERSON, F. The Public School System of N.S.W., Angus & Robertson, Sydney, 1901.

ANDERSON, F. Letter to <u>Daily Telegraph</u>, Sydney, 4th December, 1903.

ANDERSON, F. In Memoriam Bernard Muscio, <u>Australasian Journal of Psychology and Philosophy</u>, 1926, 4, 157-159.

AUSTRALASIAN ASSOCIATON FOR THE ADVANCEMENT OF SCIENCE (AAAC, later ANZAAS), <u>Reports of Meetings</u> for 1893, 1895, 1926, 1932.

AUSTRALIAN PSYCHOLOGICAL SOCIETY, Annual Report, <u>Bulletin of the Australian Psychological Society</u>, 1982, 4, 17-20.

BUCKLOW, M. Applied psychology in Australia - the history, in Nixon, M. and Taft, R. (eds.) <u>Psychology in Australian: achievements and prospects</u>, Pergamon Press, Australia, 1977.

CONNELL, W. F. <u>The Australian Council for Educational Research 1930-80</u>, ACER, Melbourne, 1980.

CUNNINGHAM, K. S. The use of psychological methods in war-time Australia, <u>Occupational Psychology</u>, 1943, 17, 111.

DAY, R. H. Psychological research in universities and colleges, in Nixon, M. and Taft, R. (eds.) <u>op.cit.</u>, 1977.

GILES, G. R. Vocational guidance in Australia in 1932, <u>International Labour Review</u>, 1932, 26, 530-543.

KAMPF, D. and Smith, S. <u>Careers for Psychology Graduates</u>, Careers Information leaflet published by Graduate Careers Council of Australia, Melbourne, 1981.

LAURIE, H. Recent progress and present position of mental science, in AAAS <u>Report of the Fifth Meeting</u>, 1893, 196-206.

MARTIN, A. H. The present status of psychology, <u>Australasian Journal of Psychology and Philosophy</u>, 1925, 3, 40-51.

MELLOR, D. P. The Role of Socience and Industry, Part 5 from Series 4 (Civil) of <u>Australia in the War of 1939-1945</u>, Griffin Press, Australia, 1958.

MUSCIO, B. <u>Lectures on Industrial Psychology</u>, Angus and Robertson, Sydney, 1917.

NIXON, M. and TAFT, R. (eds.) <u>Psychology in Australia: achievements and prospects</u>, Pergamon Press, Australia, 1977.

O'NEIL, W. M. Teaching and practice of psychology in Australia in the first phases, in Nixon, M. and Taft, R. (eds.) <u>op. cit.</u>, 1977.

O'NEIL, W. M. Psychology and its history in Australia, Bulletin of the Australian Psychological Society, 1983, 5, 8-20, 36.

OVER, R. and MOORE, D. Citation statistics for psychologists in Australian universities: 1975-1977, Australian Psychologist, 1979, 14, 319-327.

OVER, R. Impending crises for psychology departments in Australian universities, Australian Psychologist, 1981a, 16, 221-233.

OVER, R. Employment prospects for psychology graduates in Australia, Australian Psychologist, 1981b, 16, 335-345.

OVER, R. Career prospects in Australian psychology departments, Australian Psychologist, 1983, 18, 130-132.

SPRINGTHORPE, J. W. War neuroses and civil practice, Medical Journal of Australia, 1991, 2, 279-284.

SPRINGTHORPE, J. W. Psychology and medicine, Lancet, 1920, 199, 940-941.

SPRINGTHORPE, J. W. Education - medical and otherwise, Letter in Medical Journal of Australia, 1932, 1, 67.

TAFT, R. Psychology and its history in Australia, Australian Psychologist, 1982, 17, 31-39.

TURTLE, A. M. Anniversary year for psychology - 1979, Australian Psychologist, 1979, 14, 261-272.

UNIVERSITY OF SYDNEY Calendars for 1981, 1913, 1916, 1923, 1983. Sydney.

ACKNOWLEDGMENTS

An earlier version of this paper was published under the same title in the International Journal of Psychology, 1985, 20, 111-128.

The encouragement of Emeritus Professor R. Taft in my research in this area is very much appreciated. Comments made by him and by Emeritus Professor W. M. O'Neil on matters of detail in the paper are gratefully acknowledged.

20

Psychology in New Zealand:
A History and Commentary

Ross St. George

Napoleon is reputed to have said that history is but lies agreed upon. While this is not quite the stance adopted in attempting briefly to review the development of psychology in New Zealand, for some matters of fact will be discussed and some lies will not be agreed upon, it is the case that some imagination will be exercised with respect to the whys and wherefores of psychology in New Zealand.

Further, this report on psychology in New Zealand is not a study of the psychology of Maori and European New Zealanders in a national character, behavioural or ethos sense. Nor is it strictly about the distinct or unique contributions New Zealand has made to the discipline of psychology, indeed they may be hard to find. However the use of a little imagination on these matters might not be altogether out of place either. The focus is primarily upon the development of academic psychology and the psychological profession in the social, economic, political and intellectual context of New Zealand.

SETTLER PSYCHOLOGY AND THE UNIVERSITY COLLEGES

The European settlement of New Zealand and colonial status within the British Empire brought amongst others, medical practitioners and missionaries. Both bore world views and perspectives on human behaviour that accorded with the intellectual traditions of Western Europe and particularly those of Britain during the major settlement phase (1840-1880s). It is perhaps not surprising then, that the Protestant union of the scalpel and the cloth, with its emphasis on education, should have flourished in collaboration with settler men of letters and commerce to establish Otago University in the largely Scottish settlement of Dunedin. The University was founded in July 1871 with a staff of three professors, including an appointment in Philosophy consisting of Mental and Moral Science. By the Calendar of 1880 psychology as an entity had gained a mention in the course prescriptions. At this time psychological thought and practice were largely the province of the medical profession and the church. Meanwhile, provincial and colonial legislatures made provision for the mentally insane, and by 1885 New Zealand's largest public building was the Seacliff Asylum north of Dunedin (Belshaw, 1980).

Today, some of the remnants of this period[1] can be found in the books in settler museums, complete with phrenological charts, along with instruments for trephination. Freud and the psychoanalytic movement were not unknown in this corner of the Empire if the existence of early copies of Freud's works is any measure. Wundt's experimental psychology was not far behind but travelled to New Zealand via the United States. Although in its infancy, New Zealand psychology was distinctly British. Meanwhile the teaching of psychology under the title Mental Science incorporated topics as diverse as "the physiology of the nervous system, instinct, the sense and the intellect, abstraction, perception", while the Ethics component of the same paper considered the "psychology of the will, the ethical standard, the moral faculty, hedonist, intuitionalists and utilitarian methods" (Hunter, 1952, p. 101).

In 1874 the University of New Zealand was established as an examining authority with eventually four colleges, Otago, Canterbury (Christchurch - founded 1873), Auckland (founded 1882) and Victoria (Wellington - founded 1889). Initially only Otago College had a chair in philosophy. Appointments in philosophy began at the other colleges in the early twentieth century, culminating in chairs at Victoria in 1908, Canterbury in 1914 and Auckland in 1920. Such psychology as was taught within the Bachelor of Arts degree remained under the tutelage of philosophy departments and as Thomas Hunter (later Sir Thomas Hunter, Vice-Chancellor of the University of New Zealand and acknowledged founder of modern psychology in New Zealand) makes clear, change was slow and difficult (see Hunter, 1952). The constituent colleges had all to agree on course and prescription changes, teachers of philosophy were resistant to increasing the psychological component in courses on mental science and some were strong in their opposition to separate courses in psychology. Furthermore, at this time the University of New Zealand examinations were set and marked by external examiners half the world away, usually in Britain. Examiners in philosophy were more inclined towards the traditional aspects of their discipline and matters were not remedied for psychology until a recognised psychologist was appointed to act with the examiner in philosophy in setting and marking the psychological papers. Amongst those who performed this task for New Zealand students of the emerging discipline were Professors James Drever, T. H. Pear, C. S. Myers and Dr R. H. Thouless.

THE 1920's: A DECADE OF DEVELOPMENT

The early political battles over the place of psychology within the structure of the University of New Zealand as the controlling authority and on the college campuses are evident in the accounts of Hunter (1952), Winterbourn (1953) and in the Hunter-Titchener letters (Brown and Fuchs, 1969, 1971). For those wishing to promote psychology, and especially an experimental psychology, the attitudes of some philosophers had to be overcome along with the antagonism in British philosophical and psychological circles to an experimental perspective. In addition, the University of New Zealand structure made change more difficult than is usually the case in essentially conservative institutions. Getting agreement across the four colleges clearly impeded developments. However there was to be progress, but for those involved it must have been exceedingly painful and slow. And, while philosophy did not always provide fertile ground for the growth of psychology, the university-based study of education was more receptive.

The 1926 Royal Commission on the University of New Zealand enabled some progress to be made. As a consequence, staffing was improved, research and support services (libraries) were granted greater recognition and some flexibility in courses and examinations between colleges was sanctioned. It was a first step.

During the 1920's departments of education were established at the colleges which encouraged the teaching of psychological approaches to educational issues. Assistance was sought from courses and instructors of mental science, and where this was not possible education departments began their own teaching in areas of psychology deemed relevant to students of education.

The position of psychology had been further enhanced by the establishment of both 'Psychological Laboratories' and 'Child Clinics'. Hunter established the first psychological laboratory at Victoria College in 1908 on his return from leave with Titchener at Cornell University and visits to Harvard, Yale, Johns Hopkins and Pennyslvania. Professor John Beaglehole in his history of Victoria University College was to write that Hunter returned from the U.S. "all Cornell and Titchener" (Beaglehole, 1949, p.97) and convinced the college council to grant him fifty pounds for a laboratory. According to Brown and Fuchs (1971), Hunter's laboratory was the first in Australasia and was established in the same year as the laboratory at Cambridge with a grant of similar size.

However, the development of laboratories and clinics was more a phenomenon of the 1920's. In 1925, Canterbury College introduced experimental work in psychology in courses on education with the appointment of Clarence Beeby, a New Zealander who later became Director of Education from 1940 to 1960. He set up a laboratory servicing primarily the psychological components of courses in education (see Beeby, 1979). Similarly, laboratory work had began at Otago, and has been reviewed by Ferguson (1979) who came from Scotland as Otago's first appointment directly in psychology in December of 1930. Developments at Auckland appear to have been less dramatic in the psychological field under the professorship of the philosopher W. Anderson, although, in keeping with the university prescriptions, instruction in psychology was part of the course in 'Moral and Mental Philosophy' (see Auckland University College Calendar, 1922, pp.77-78).

The orientation of psychological teaching in the colleges of the University of New Zealand during the 1920's was essentially British. It is evident in Beeby's (1979) account of the early years at Canterbury and Ferguson's (1979) account of Otago during a similar period. The personal contacts, the overseas examiners and the prescribed texts were often British. It followed quite naturally in the wake of the pattern of recruiting the early academic psychologists from Britain. Continental European psychology, especially the German experimental school was known and respected, as were Freud and the psychoanalytic paradigm, but it was English language presentations of these perspectives that were often relied upon. Of course, Hunter at Victoria was considerably influenced by North American experimental psychology with its German Laboratory origins, and Watson's behaviourism was known and debated. The general experimental or at least empiricist orientation of psychology at this time was also to play a part in its striving for recognition as a science and in 1924 passes in psychology were recognised in the Bachelor of Science degree.

Another important impact on both the acceptance and content of psychology in New Zealand in the twenties, whether pursued in the colleges under the heading of psychology or education, was the advent of individual and group intelligence tests. Following their reported success in the United States and adoption in Britain in military and educational settings, testing became very popular in the practice of psychology in New Zealand. Although a social history of the introduction and use of such tests has yet to be written, it is tempting to suggest that advocates of various social and educational reforms could take ideological comfort from the use of and data produced by such tests. In relation to a range of social and educational issues, both 'white empire supremacist' groups advocating eugenic solutions at one end of the spectrum and liberal egalitarians supporting environmental change through the reform or revolutionizing of social and educational programmes at the other, could argue their case from the test data (see Fleming, 1981, McKenzie, 1924).

All the accounts of the founding of the psychological laboratories and child clinics make reference to the demonstration and use of psychological tests. The state Department of Education also took an early lead in 1925 with the national standardization and norming of the Terman Tests (Marsden, 1925). As the accounts of Watson (1979) and Reid (1980) also show, in New Zealand from the mid-1920's there was a fair measure of interest in test use, adaptation and development, and their importing and marketing were quite well established. This must have conferred a degree of respect and respectability upon the new discipline for it apparently had an applied contribution to make.

A recurrent theme in the accounts referred to above covering the 1920's was the isolation between teachers of psychology in the colleges, the lack of library resources and lack of funds. But, necessity fostered invention and ingenuity. Beeby (1979), Ferguson (1979) and Hunter (see

Brown and Fuchs, 1969) were all able to build or supplement apparatus with either technical assistance or a
little trading. Some of the barriers to contact with
peers and developments in psychology in a regional sense
were weakened with the founding in 1923 of the Australasian Association of Psychology and Philosophy which
established the Australasian Journal of Psychology and
Philosophy in the same year. Martin (1926) reviewed
progress in the development of the discipline in Australia and New Zealand in this journal.

THE 1930's AND 1940's: THE DEVELOPMENT OF EDUCATIONAL,
INDUSTRIAL AND OCCUPATIONAL PSYCHOLOGY

During the 1930's the teaching of psychology
continued as part of departments of philosophy. Experimental psychological laboratories were established and
accepted with their positivist-empiricist orientation.
The child clinics with their applied developmental and
educational orientation provided assistance of a psychological nature to the community. Victoria had its
psychological clinic for children founded by Hunter
(1928) along the lines of Witmer's clinic in Philadelphia. Beeby at Canterbury, with the support of Shelley as
Professor of Education, had established a clinic with an
educational and guidance flavour. At Otago a child
guidance clinic was formally inaugurated in 1939 but had
been operating informally as early as 1934 (see Connor,
1959; Mitchell, 1954).

The growth of applied psychology under the aegis of
education in the 1930's also came with the development of
vocational guidance services. Winterbourn's (1974)
detailed history traces the early beginnings of the
vocational guidance movement in New Zealand from the
efforts of the Young Men's and Young Women's Christian
Associations which initiated the dissemination of
vocational information to school leavers, through the
formation of the regional Dunedin Vocational Guidance
Association which fostered the guidance concept, to the
establishment of the dual state department (Education and
Labour) Youth Centres in 1938. Five years later, control
was passed to the Department of Education with the title
'Vocational Guidance Centres'.[2] As analyses by Winterbourn (1974) and Small (1976) show, the vocational
guidance centres, movement was influential in the
dissemination of psychological ideas, practices and

products.[3]

Concurrent with the development of Vocational Guidance Centres, the movement to improve the educational provisions for children with special needs gained momentum. The early development of the university-sponsored child clinics has been mentioned. In addition, the state educational system had made early provision for 'special classes' with the appointment of a national supervisor in 1923. With no doubt agonising slowness, partly dictated by depression-induced retrenchment, moves were then made to develop a psychological service for schools. Sutch (1972) and Winterbourn (1974) have detailed the twists and turns of policy in the attempts to provide special services of a psychological nature to schools during the 1930's. They record the attempt to appoint the first 'Psychological Officer' in 1936, a move which failed because the then Minister of Education held "...some reservations about importing a specialist in psychology" (Sutch, 1972, p.205).[4] The second attempt to establish such a service followed in 1940 with an offer being made to F. J. Schonell, but the offer was not accepted. It was not until 1946, with the secondment of Winterbourn from Canterbury University College to the Christchurch Vocational Guidance Centre, that a 'Psychological Division Centre' was established. Offices were established in other cities in the 1950's, with notable expansion during the 1960's (see Sutch, 1972). Without going into detail, since these are covered in the reviews of Sutch and Winterbourn, the reader's attention is drawn again to the role that education has played in the fostering of psychology in New Zealand. Much as support for the teaching of psychology within the university colleges came from educationalists, it also appears to be the case that applied psychology gained support from the needs of teachers. Between these two disciplines this relationship has also led to a measure of conflict which will be touched on later.

The 1930's also saw the beginning of central government involvement with the social sciences in other ways. In 1937 the Social Science Research Bureau was established within the Department of Scientific and Industry Research. Professor Don McElwain (now at the University of Queensland) cut his statistical teeth with the Bureau as a young graduate of Victoria College. The Bureau primarily analyzed and reported on social and economic data for government and, although disbanded four years later for reasons regarded by some at the time as political (see Robb, 1980, however, for an account on this point), it helped to further establish a place for social scientific input in government activities. World War II was shortly to take an even more direct hand in the promotion of psychology.[5]

In 1942 the Department of Industrial and Scientific Research (D.S.I.R.) established an Industrial Psychology Division to "...service industry, particularly war industries, in matters of industrial psychology, and, in addition, to be a centre of information on all matters of this nature and on any vocational use or testing which may be required from time to time" (Winterbourn, 1974, p.50). Leslie Hearnshaw, who was teaching at Victoria, was appointed as director in Wellington and offices with psychologist appointments were established in Auckland and Christchurch.

The Division operated until 1947 when it was disestablished and staff moved to the Personnel Advisory Division of the Department of Labour and Employment. Hearnshaw (1948) reports this move as stemming from the high involvement in advisory activities. Nonetheless, during its life the Division was active in industrial and occupational research on topics as diverse as industrial absenteeism, the design of factory seating, factory ventilation and heating and the reduction of fatigue and monotony. Further details can be found in the papers by Hearnshaw (1948, 1965) and Jennings (1951). Involvement of the D.S.I.R. with psychology continued for a further three years through the Occupational Psychology Research section until this was closed as a result of reductions in government expenditure.

New Zealand's entry in 1939 into the Second World War also saw the application of psychological principles and methods in the military context. The initial emphasis was on RNZAF aircrew selection and training. Psychological methods, especially in selection, were also extended to the Navy and Army during hostilities. Following World War II the organisation of psychological services in the defence forces experienced a number of changes until the establishment of the joint services Defence Psychology Unit in 1976 which has led to the more stable development of psychological services in the New Zealand military context (see Toulson and Williams, 1979). A little recognised contribution to psychology in New Zealand was made through the Ministry of Defence in the early 1950's by way of the Defence Science Corps. During a five year term with the Corps, two years were committed to doctoral studies. Psychologists to benefit from the scheme included Laurence Brown, Tuan Emery and Hugh Priest. Brown was to subsequently found the Department of Psychology at Massey, Emery to direct the Educational Research Advisory Unit at the University of Canterbury and Priest became senior member of the Department of Psychology at the same campus.

THE FIFTIES TO THE PRESENT DAY

Departments and Chairs

The establishment of autonomous departments of psychology and the appointment of professors of psychology has been a phenomenon of the 1950's and early 1960's. For New Zealand it is the period when psychology gained an autonomy hitherto denied the academy and the period that laid the foundations for the post-graduate study of psychology in New Zealand by New Zealanders.

At Victoria University College, where psychology had been nurtured by Hunter since his appointment in 1904, a chair in Psychology and Philosophy was established in 1949 with the appointment of Ernest Beaglehole. Two years later the disciplines and departments separated with Beaglehole as professor of psychology. He fostered both the experimental psychology tradition brought from Titchener by way of Hunter and an ethnopsychological or cross-cultural perspective in keeping with his anthropological background. Ritchie's (1979) memoir conveys in very personal terms the scope of Beaglehole's contribution.

By 1949 Canterbury College had also established a department of philosophy and psychology. In 1953 psychology separated from philosophy under the headship of Alan Crowther. From 1963 to 1979 it operated as a joint department of psychology and sociology, returning then to single discipline department status. Psychology at Canterbury during the 1950's and early 1960's appears to have drawn a lot of its strength from the applied occupational and clinical fields.

The same pattern of psychology moving towards full departmental status from an association with philosophy also took place at Auckland. The department was established in 1957 with Harry Scott, a graduate of McGill, as head. Tragically a mountaineering accident took his life three years later. Barnie Sampson, also of McGill, picked up the reins with the department making its mark in such fields as experimental psychology, perception and optometry, social psychology and more recently behaviour analysis.

In 1961 the University of New Zealand was devolved and each of the four colleges became autonomous under separate Acts. Three years later an independent department of psychology was established at the University of Otago with Stephen Griew appointed to the chair. In 1964 both Waikato and Massey universities were established, with the appointment of James Ritchie to the chair at Waikato and Laurence Brown to the chair at Massey.

The department at Otago has established a tradition in experimental psychology in the cognitive, perceptual, social and neuropsychological fields, along with forays into parapsychology. Meanwhile at Waikato a strong interest has always been evident in social and cross-cultural psychology, clinical psychology, and behaviour analysis. The department has also had an important role in the promotion of women's studies. Psychology at Massey has shown considerable interest in the applied occupational and vocational fields, coupled with clinical and rehabilitation studies.

Of course, all departments teach a wide range of undergraduate courses leading to a sound education in general psychology. The specialities tend to become more evident through postgraduate course offerings and staff research and activity areas but, as noted by St. George (1979), it would be instructive to systematically collate such data and go beyond what must remain essentially impressions.

Psychological societies, registration and professional issues

Since the appointment of teaching staff in psychology to the university colleges was principally from the United Kingdom, it is no surprise that the appointees were often members of the British Psychological Society (B.P.S.), and that, in time, a New Zealand Branch of the B.P.S. would be established. The Branch was established in 1947. As Mitchell's (1961) account of the formation and activities of the Branch shows, it provided a focus at the four university college centres for academic meetings on topics of interest in psychology and promoted national conferences of the Branch. In 1954 the Branch

produced the New Zealand Bulletin of Psychology but this
could not be sustained as a journal and was transformed
into the News Bulletin of the New Zealand Branch of the
British Psychological Society which was issued at
irregular intervals.

The growth in the teaching of psychology in the
universities, the development of public and private
sector employment opportunities and no doubt a feeling
that it was time to sever the colonial connection led in
1968 to the formation of the independent New Zealand
Psychological Society (N.Z.Ps.S.). The N.Z.Ps.S. has
acted as both an academic and professional focus for
psychologists. Following the pattern established through
the B.P.S. association, the N.Z.Ps.S. has an organisational structure made up of regional branches, sub-
discipline and interest area divisions and a national
council responsible for the administration of the Society
and its relationships with other agencies, professions
and the community. A national conference is held annually
which provides a focus for academic and professional
activities within both the Society and the field of
psychology in general.

The Society continued the publication of the
Bulletin of the New Zealand Psychological Society which
focusses primarily on reporting the business of the
Society, information on topical events of interest to
members, notices, advertisements and the like. In 1972
the Society commenced the publication of the New Zealand
Psychologist (from Volume 12, New Zealand Journal of
Psychology) as a forum for both theoretical and empirical
research based papers in psychology.

In recent years the Society has become increasingly
involved in matters related to the professional practice
of psychology in New Zealand. Leland and Trainor (1976)
surveyed the membership in terms of employment histories
and commented on the implications for graduates. Interest
in career development and public education about the
contributions of psychology has continued. The Society
has also been active in the making of submissions on
proposed legislation and to committees of inquiry where
the discipline has a clear contribution, for example,
penal reform, health services, education, welfare. In
recent years for example, it has also commented on
matters of public concern, especially in the social
arena.

Professionally one of the most significant developments supported by the Society has been the enactment of

the formal registration of psychologists under the Psychologists Act, 1981. The Psychologists Registration Board, under its first chairman Professor Ken Strongman, administers the Act with support services provided by the Department of Health.

The functions of the Psychologists Registration Board include maintaining a register of psychologists qualified in terms of the Act, advising the Minister of Health on matters relating to the education and registration of psychologists, advising the universities on matters relating to the education of psychologists, and promoting high standards of professional education and conduct. Registration is voluntary, although an employer may require registration. The Act is a nominal act in that it says in effect that no person not on the Register may be called 'Registered Psychologist'. It is not a functional act, in that it does not describe what psychologists may or may not do. The Board is empowered to receive complaints against a Registered Psychologist and to investigate. The Board has the power to strike off the Register, to suspend, fine or censure.

For staff of the Psychological Service of the Department of Education, the Psychological Services Association, which was formed in the mid 1970's, has acted to both represent employees on terms and conditions of service and to provide a professional focus for psychologists within the Service. It publishes the Journal of the New Zealand Psychological Service Association.

Similarly, psychologists employed in clinical, rehabilitative and therapeutic roles within hospitals formed, in the mid 1970's, the New Zealand Association of Hospital Psychologists. Here too the focus of the Assocation has been upon both employment matters and more general professional concerns.

Total membership of the N.Z.Ps.S. stood at 801 covering all membership levels as of July 1984, having grown from a membership of probably less than 100 at its inception.[6] While some New Zealand branch members of the B.P.S. have maintained their B.P.S. membership, most also belong to the N.Z.Ps.S. Certainly the involvement of most psychologists in New Zealand, especially the New Zealand graduates, in both professional and academic matters in psychology, is now seen largely within the N.Z.Ps.S. This does not mean however that psychologists in New Zealand are separated from professional and academic involvement in other fields. There is joint membership of kindred organisations such as the New Zealand Association of Research in Education or the New Zealand Counselling and Guidance Association. However, some bones of contention are beginning to emerge between disciplines and areas of professional activity.

It is clear that in the university context, departments of education in particular have contributed to the growth of psychology. All of these departments teach papers with a psychological content and employ staff who are psychologists, often members of the N.Z.Ps.S., and who are either registered psychologists or eligible to register. The relationships between the disciplines have largely been supportive and sympathetic. But, it is now the view of some educational sociologists in particular that psychology and psychologists have had too much influence upon the New Zealand education system (see Nash, 1983; Freeman-Moir, 1984).[7] Be that as it may, relationships between psychology and other disciplines are also beginning to show some unease on other fronts as well. It is evident, for example, in relation to N.Z.Ps.S. membership criteria giving different treatment to psychological studies undertaken within departments of psychology and education. Similarly, criteria for registration under the Psychologists Act, 1981, also reflect aspects of the same dilemma and are likely to be questioned as interpretations become known. Furthermore, the public nature of what constitutes psychology is now making this sort of question wider than any differences just between psychology and education.

For the N.Z.Ps.S., the growth in psychological content in other professional and academic fields in New Zealand such as business studies and management, nursing education and guidance and counselling is presenting new challenges. The N.Z.Ps.S. has now to grapple with the dual role of being both the major professional and academic focus for psychologists who in turn are becoming increasingly diverse in their orientations, interests, employment and in their views on the appropriate involvement of psychologists with New Zealand society. What might have been once an academic club is now an organisation caught up in a wide range of professional activities in a territory with more fluid boundaries and allegiances than in the past.

338

Some uncharted territories

In the early years of psychology in New Zealand there were no graduate study opportunities, meagre research support in any form and few employment opportunities. Not surprisingly, New Zealand exported much of its psychological talent. As early as 1920 Hunter was to send C.C. Braddock in his footsteps to the psychological laboratories of the United States.[8] In time Mary Dry left to pursue her studies in Jungian psychology (Dry, 1961), Don McElwain went to London to take his doctorate when Burt was at his best, and Reo Fortune moved between psychology and anthropology sharing life in New Guinea with Gregory Bateson and Margaret Mead.

The changes in policy and direction in the Industrial Psychology Division of the D.S.I.R. during the upheavals of the Depression of the 1930's, partial recovery and World War II brought many changes. Leslie Hearnshaw, for example, returned to the United Kingdom and T. A. Churton moved into what was probably the first private practice in the industrial and occupational psychology field in New Zealand. The organisational changes in the Ministry of Defence and the burdens of war fell partly upon Jack Jennings and Ralph Waite. They were to see the changes through into the post-war years, while E. M. Wrigley carried forward his psychometric skills developed in the defence context to an advanced level first in London and then in the United States.

Similarly, in the clinical domain there are, as Taylor's (1979) review suggests, events and personalities whose influence is worthy of closer attention. Certainly the interface between clinical psychology, psychiatry and the medical profession in New Zealand awaits exploration. Equally the often associated field of forensic psychology was and still is very much in its infancy with Tony Taylor for many years being a lone spokesperson in the New Zealand context (see Taylor, 1977). But the law will not leave psychology alone, and new reputations are about to be forged as professional, community and family questions are placed before the law through legislation and litigation in which psychologists in New Zealand increasingly claim an interest.

From time to time, professors, along with some of their staff, are able to foregather at meetings sponsored by the Vice-Chancellors of the universities. One presumes (but without evidence) that matters of pedagogics are at times discussed at conferences but, to date, only Jules

Older (1979) appears to have gone to the trouble of really talking about the teaching of antipodean psychology.

CONCLUSIONS AND PROSPECTS

The pattern of development of psychology in New Zealand has not, it seems, been unique or special. This is particularly so in relation to developments in Australia, which, in the context of this volume, is an obvious country of comparison given the sharing of some historical experiences. The points of similarity, but also some of the differences are commented upon in the papers by Ord (1977) and St. George (1979).

In New Zealand, psychology was taught within and as part of philosophy from the founding of each of the university colleges and was largely pursued within the frameworks propounded by the British educated academics who came to this corner of the Empire. Hunter's interest in the experimental psychology of continental Europe as mediated via America was a little different. If nothing else, the seemingly more functionalist approach, as evidenced through the founding of 'laboratories' and 'child clinics', might have helped mollify some critics of the discipline in its struggle for identity and autonomy. And in retrospect, it does appear that the promises of applied psychology, whether or not fulfilled, have contributed as much to the growth and establishment of the discipline in the universities as any arguments about the intellectual necessity of studying psychology for its own sake. The child clinics were in response to particular social and individual needs and, along with the vocational guidance centres, were the forerunners to the educational psychological services. The early and continued interest in psychological testing, notably ability testing, also reflected a belief in the contribution of an applied psychology through the structuring of elements of the educational system. Psychology, at first in association with the universities, sought to assist industry directly at the 'shop-floor', and more recently through a wider range of occupational career development and managerial servicing operations. Similarly, clinical psychology and therapeutic extensions outside of the classical psychiatric settings have gained increasing acceptance. A case in point would be the role of the Mental Health foundation with its broader community focused orientation (see Turkington, 1983). Perhaps it should not come as any great surprise that in a country that prides itself on its "do it yourself, give it a go" tradition, the applied emphasis should come to the fore in the development of New Zealand psychology. It does accord with the appeals for utilitarian outputs from the universities that are voiced here from time to time.

It might also be speculated that the kind of psychology developed in New Zealand has been, until recent years, a cheap 'paper-and-pencil' psychology. Nothwithstanding the establishment of the laboratories in the early days of Mental Science, continuously well maintained laboratories, staffing, and technical support capable of advancing experimental, physiological and neuropsychological studies, have been the exception rather than the rule.

Psychology in New Zealand can also be seen in terms of the dependent status of the country as a whole. It has historically been an importer of refined psychological products, be they staff, texts, tests, equipment or ideas. At the same time it has been an exporter of only partially processed psychological talent. Probably this is inevitable given the career/employment opportunities in a small society where psychology is an international discipline with its centres of intellectual life and research still some distance from these shores.

At this time it is difficult to detect a New Zealand psychology as such, or clear evidence of one emerging. Bound in as we are with the course of psychological thinking and practice of other western societies, with a pattern of development laid down by both British and North American traditions and now reinforced by the power of their publications, any change short of a revolution will be slow. Perhaps it is not necessary to search for a distinctive New Zealand psychology, but in terms of the social and multicultural experimentation New Zealand has engaged in, psychology here might yet have something interesting to say about cultures, communities and human behaviour. Whether any indigenous conceptualizations, methodologies or restructuring of the discipline will emerge or whether we continue to largely emulate the thinking and behaviour of our more influential psychological peers in Europe and North America, remains to be seen.

NOTES

1. The period in mind covers the foundation of the universities (1870's) up until the clearer emergence of psychology. By the 1920's psychology was openly talked about.

2. In 1978 administration and control of the centres was passed back to the Department of Labour.

3. More recently school guidance-counsellor positions have been established in conjunction with specialist university based training. The courses include relevant psychological content.

4. Sutch does not make clear the nature of the 'reservations' but does refer to the Department of Education files for 1936.

5. Robb's analysis suggests that the demise of the Bureau cannot be solely traced to the assumed political embarrassment over the report on the standard of living of dairy farmers. He notes that in its life and death the Bureau was a "...complex set of forces, personal, political, ideological, scientific and administrative..." He argues that the disposition of these forces gave rise to the Bureau and to its demise (see Robb, p.10).

6. The Minutes of the first A.G.M. of the N.Z.Ps.S., 11 August, 1968, do not record actual membership numbers. Forty-four members were present, thirty proxies held and five apologies recorded.

7. Their thesis, based it seems on the contention that various Directors-General of Education and departmental officers have studied more psychology than sociology, is that thought and action in education have been dominated by psychological perspectives.

8. Ms. Braddock died of influenza at Cornell in 1922 with her Ph.D. research incomplete.

REFERENCES

AUCKLAND UNIVERSITY COLLEGE, Calendar Auckland University College. University of New Zealand, Auckland. 1922.

BEAGLEHOLE, J. C. Victoria University college. New Zealand University Press, Wellington. 1949.

BEEBY, C. E. Psychology in New Zealand fifty years ago. In R. St. George, (ed.) The beginnings of psychology in New Zealand. Department of Education, Massey University, Palmerston North. Delta Research monograph, 1979, No. 2, 1-6.

342

BELSHAW, B. Seacliff. A house of horrors? New Zealand
Listener, 1980, February 234, p. 21.

BROWN, L. B. and FUCHS, A. H. The Letters between Sir
Thomas Hunter and E. B. Tichener. Publications in
Psychology, University of Wellington, Wellington.
1969.

BROWN, L. B. and FUCHS, A. H. Early experimental psychology in New Zealand: The Hunter-Titchener letters.
Journal of the History of the Behavioural Sciences,
1971, 7, 10-22.

CONNOR, D. V. A child guidance clinic in a university
setting. Australian Journal of Psychology, 1959, 11,
202-208.

DRY, A. M. The psychology of Jung. A critical interpretation. Methuen, London. 1961.

FERGUSON, H. H. Psychology at the University of Otago and
beyond with special reference to the period
1931-1938. In R. St. George, (ed.) The beginnings of
psychology in New Zealand. Department of Education,
Massey University, Palmerston North. Delta Research
Monograph, 1979, No. 2, 7-21.

FLEMING, P. J. Eugenics in New Zealand, 1900-1940.
Unpublished M.A. thesis, Massey University. 1981.

FREEMAN-MOIR, J. Review-Strike K.A. Educational Policy
and the just society. New Zealand Journal of
Educational Studies, 1984, 19, 83-86.

HEARNSHAW, L. S. Industrial psychology in New Zealand.
Occupational Psychology, 1965, 22, 1-6.

HEARNSHAW, L. S. Psychology in New Zealand. A report.
Bulletin of the British Psychological Society, 1965,
18, 17-24.

HUNTER, T. A. Psychological clinic for children, Victoria
University College, Wellington. Australasian Journal
of Psychology and Philosophy, 1928, 6, 300-303.

HUNTER T. A. The development of psychology in New
Zealand. Quarterly Bulletin of the British Psychological Society, 1952, 3, 101-111.

JENNINGS, J. R. Psychology applied to industry and
commerce in New Zealand. Occupational Psychology,
1951, 25, 254-258.

LELAND, L. S. and TRAINOR, M. E. A profile of the New
Zealand Psychological Society: Education, sex and
first employment. New Zealand Psychologist, 1976, 5,
62-67.

McKENZIE, N. R. Group test of mental ability. Education
Gazette, April, 1924, 52-53.

MARSDEN, E. Terman Intelligence Tests in New Zealand schools. In New Zealand Official Yearbook. Government Printer, Wellington, 1925, 832-834.

MARTIN, A. H. The present status of psychology. Australasian Journal of Psychology, and Philosophy, 1926, 3, 40-51.

MITCHELL, F. W. A note on the University of Otago child guidance clinic. Austalian Journal of Psychology, 1954, 6, 94-96.

MITCHELL, F. W. The Branch Society in New Zealand 1947-1961. In H. Steinberg, (ed.) The British Psychological Society 1901-1961. British Psychological Society, London. 1961.

NASH, R. The Director-General and his crisis. P.P.T.A. Journal, Term 1, 1983, 25-30.

OLDER, J. Improving the introductory psychology course. Teaching of Psychology, 1979, 6, 75-77.

ORD, I. G. Australian psychology and Australia's neighbours. In M. Nixon and R. Taft, (eds.) Psychology in Australia: Achievements and Prospects. Pergamon, Sydney. 1977.

REID, N. A. Research on educational measurement and testing in New Zealand. In Research in Education in New Zealand: The state of the art. Department of Education, Massey University, Palmerston North. Delta Research Monograph, 1980, No. 3, 209-235.

RITCHIE, J. E. Ernest Beaglehole at Victoria: A personal memoir. In R. St. George, (ed.) The beginnings of psychology in New Zealand. Department of Education, Massey University, Palmerston North. Delta Research Monograph, 1979, No. 2, 61-67.

ROBB, J. H. The life and death of official social research in New Zealand. Paper to the Sociological Association of Australia and New Zealand Conference, University of Tasmania, Hobart. August, 1980.

ST. GEORGE, R. Psychology in an Australian neighbour: improving upon some impressions about New Zealand. Australian Psychologist, 1979, 14, 375-380.

SMALL, J. J. Guidance: Retrospect and prospect. In J. A. Codd, and G. L. Hermansson, (eds.) Directions in New Zealand secondary education. Hodder and Stoughton, Auckland. 1976, 231-243.

SUTCH, M. S. Psychological and guidance services. In S. J. Havill, and D. R. Mitchell, (eds.) Issues in New Zealand special education. Hodder and Stoughton, Auckland. 1972.

344

TAYLOR, A. J. W. Forensic psychology: Principles, practice and training. New Zealand Psychologist, 1977, 6, 97-108.

TAYLOR, A. J. W. Clinical psychology in New Zealand: An historical note. In R. St. George, (ed.) The beginnings of psychology in New Zealand. Department of Education, Massey University, Palmerston North. Delta Research Monograph, 1979, No. 2, 70-76.

TOULSON, P. K. and WILLIAMS, W. C. J. History of personnel research and psychological services in the New Zealand armed forces. In R. St. George, (ed.) The beginnings of psychology in New Zealand. Department of Education, Massey University, Palmerston North. Delta Research Monograph, 1979, No. 2, 77-84.

TURKINGTON, C. Private foundation rallies New Zealand behind mental health. APA Monitor, 1983, 14, 7.

WATSON, J. E. Fifty years of test supply. The New Zealand experience. Paper to New Zealand Psychological Society Conference, Massey University, Palmerston North. August, 1979.

WINTERBOURN, R. A review of psychology in New Zealand. Australian Journal of Psychology, 1953, 5, 17-27.

WINTERBOURN, R. Guidance services in New Zealand education. N. Z. C. E. R, Wellington. 1974.

21

Psychology in Fiji: The Pioneering Stages

Subhas Chandra

INTRODUCTION

Fiji is an archipelago of more than three hundred islands, about a third of which are inhabited. The present population is approximately six hundred and fifty thousand, and consists in about equal proportions of Melanesians mixed with Polynesians, and Indians. The forebears of the latter group came in as contracted labourers between 1879 and 1916 to assist with the production of sugar, which remains the main source of income. The population is therefore not highly urbanized, and current government policy is to encourage people to stay on the land. Indians form the majority in the towns, and are dominant in commercial and professional life.

The Fiji Islands lie 1100 miles south of the equator, Sydney and Auckland being the closest international airports to them. The islands were first sighted by Europeans in 1643, and contact with European traders and missionaries increased steadily throughout the nineteenth century. In 1874 the islands were voluntarily ceded to Britain, and in 1970 resumed an independent status, instituting a form of parliamentary democracy.[1]

The establishment of psychology as an independent discipline with the responsibility for the training of psychologists both academic and professional is essential in a developing Fiji with constant and varied demands for psychological services. Government institutions and private industry have so far successfully excluded the psychologist from their occupational classifications, and have essentially relied upon both locally available and imported professionals to assist predominantly in educational assessment, personnel selection and the

training in personnel management on a consultancy basis.
The teaching of psychology in the tertiary institutions,
especially the University of the South Pacific, has
increased significantly over the last decade or so, and
the need for new programmes in psychology is being
identified, whereby trained personnel would be available
to fulfil the academic and professional responsibilities
of this discipline. A review of the contributions of
psychologists in teaching, research and consultancy is
presented.

THE TEACHING OF PSYCHOLOGY

The University of the South Pacific was established
in 1968 as a regional institution to serve the needs of
ten South Pacific governments (the Cook Islands, Fiji,
Kiribati, Nauru, New Hebrides, Niue, Solomon Islands,
Tokelau, Tonga, Tuvalu and Western Samoa). English is the
language used in teaching, and all textbooks are written
in this language. Students follow a Foundation programme
which forms the basis for further study at both the
degree and diploma levels; a pass in the New Zealand
University Entrance examination establishes eligibility
to undertake studies at this level. In areas where
teaching for this external examination is not available,
the University has established Preliminary programmes to
prepare them for entry into the Foundation level courses.
A comprehensive review of the University was undertaken
on the occasion of its tenth anniversary. The Review
Committee summarized the past performance and future
prospects of the University as follows:

> Any University is a complicated and difficult
> enterprise. New ones are more difficult than
> established ones. Being in the position, as USP
> is, of having to seek finance from dozens of
> sources throughout the world makes it vastly
> more difficult. And having to assess and
> effectively serve the needs of eleven member
> countries speaking over two hundred languages
> and with great ethnic diversity creates a task
> of enormous complexity... (USP Calendar, 1982,
> p.58).

The first calendar of the University was published
in 1968 in the form of a Student's Handbook, and listed

twelve academic staff members, mainly in the physical sciences. Towards the end of the same year M. J. Bennett, an occupational psychologist from the United Kingdom who had developed the Wire Bending Test in Zambia, was appointed as Lecturer in Education in the School of Education. This School offered the following two teacher training programmes, a three year non-graduate diploma course, and a four year undergraduate course leading to a B.A. and B.Sc. with education.

In 1970, T. Gilbert, another Englishman, joined the School as Lecturer in Educational Psychology. Bennett and Gilbert shared the teaching of two diploma level education courses described as "the study of the development of children in a variety of social and cultural settings ... and the factors which affect children's learning" and "more detailed study of child development and learning theory, and psychological bases of classroom practice" (USP Calendar, 1970, p.45). At the degree level in the concurrent programme, Education Psychology and Child Development were listed as compulsory first year education courses. In 1970 Ian Stewart from New Zealand took up an appointment as Reader in Education and assumed responsibility for teaching the Child Development course, while Bennett offered a course in Educational Evaluation to final year diploma students. At the degree level the Educational Psychology course was modified to include Principles of Measurement. The English section offered a course entitled Psycholinguistics, which covered a selection of topics in the area in which language and psychology overlap. The same year Dr. D. W. McElwain, Professor of Psychology at the University of Queensland, came to the School of Education on sabbatical leave.

In addition to on-campus teaching, the School of Education began to offer Classroom Learning and Child Development as diploma level courses through extension studies in 1972. The latter course was modified in 1980 as part of an independent learning package in Human Development, and this has been taken by more than 1800 degree and diploma students both on and off campus.

The next four years continued to yield staff changes, firstly in 1973 through the appointment of S. Chandra, a local psychologist educated in Sydney who had worked at the University on secondment from the Fiji Government since 1971, and the departure of Bennett in 1972 followed by that of Gilbert in 1973, and of Stewart in 1976. During this time a three year Bachelor of Education programme was introduced by the School of

Education in which the existing psychology courses were incorporated. Staff replacements were made so that Drs. J. Crawford and W. B. Elley, educational psychologists from the United States and New Zealand respectively, commenced teaching in 1977. A third year level course in Educational Measurement was introduced so that the existing Educational Psychology course concentrated essentially on the teaching-learning process. After Dr. Elley's transfer to the Institute of Education a year later, Dr. R. A. C. Stewart of New Zealand,who had previously held senior academic positions in Psychology and Educational Psychology in Canada and New Zealand, was designated Reader in Educational Psychology. The same year the Waikato team of Professor J. and Dr. Jane Ritchie and Professor D. Thomas came to the School and offered a special course in cross-cultural personality development.

Two other appointments were made when Crawford terminated his services to the University in 1979, of M. Brooks (who left within a year) and Dr. Jeanette Mass, a clinical psychologist, both from the United States. This resulted in an establishment of three staff in psychology within the Education discipline at the end of 1980. The most recent staff appointment is that of Nand Kishor, another local with a Master's degree in educational psychology from this University in 1981. Dr. G. Davidson from the University of New England arrived in 1981 as visiting Senior Lecturer and offered a course in cross-cultural cognitive development.

In addition to the existing courses already identified, special degree courses have been offered during the past three years, such as the Study of Exceptional Individuals and Introduction to the Counselling Process. At the post-graduate level, two students have completed a course in Cross-Cultural Psychology as part of the MA degree. In 1984 a new three semester programme leading to the award of the Diploma in Guidance and Counselling and a four year BA plus GCEd with a major in guidance and counselling are being offered by the School of Education. Approval was obtained about five years ago to provide courses at the Master's level such as Advanced Human Development, Research on Learning and Achievement in Developing Countries and Advanced Educational Measurement and Evaluation.

As well as being taught as an ancillary subject in the teacher education programmes, psychology has made an increasing contribution to the training of medical personnel. In 1971 a Behavioural Science course was offered for second year medical and dental students at the Fiji School of Medicine, and a year later an Introduction to Psychology course was made compulsory for all Foundation level medical students. These offerings have been retained, except for the inclusion ofthe former course in the third year diploma programme in medicine and surgery in 1975. When the diploma was replaced by a new five-year MB BS programme two years ago, a course in Human Development was also included in the curriculum. In 1983 all three courses were offered on a university-wide basis, and this practice is to be maintained and developed in the future.

UNIVERSITY COUNSELLING SERVICE

This service to both staff and students was made available through the appointment in 1973 of Brian Hazell, a Sydney graduate working at the University of Newcastle in Australia. Mary Montu, a local with an American BA, joined as Assistant Counsellor the following year, and was promoted to Counsellor status in 1975 when Hazell departed. During 1976-8 she was given the opportunity to undertake an M.Ed. in counselling at the University of Hawaii.

The main service to over fifteen hundred full-time students involves academic counselling for those who encounter difficulties in coping with academic work either through academic deficiency, lack of interest, conflict with a lecturer or illness. Students applying for overseas study programmes are always seeking assistance with application forms and career information. The Counselling Service deals with referrals of discipline cases, the most common being consumption of alcohol on campus, and personal squabbles. Attention to pregnancy cases is often a complex and tiresome process.

PSYCHOLOGICAL ASSESSMENT

C. W. Mann, Professor of Education at Sydney Teacher's College, was the first investigator of the government-controlled system of education in Fiji. During the thirties he and his wife came at the invitation of the Methodist Missionary Society of Australasia to investigate certain aspects of mission education. They were assisted by a grant from the recently formed Australian Council of Educational Research, and the outcome of their work was the publication in 1936 of Education in Fiji. While here, Mann (1934, 1939) developed the Fiji Test of General Ability which was applied to some four thousand school children. This non-verbal test consisted of both power and speed subtests and yielded high correlations with teacher assessments, the Otis Self Administering Test and the Goodenough Draw-aman test, but does not seem to have been put to any use. Between 1962 and 1964 the Campbell Picture Test and the Jenkins Intermediate Non-verbal Test were used in order to gain "a clearer assessment of the intellectual potential of pupils who were handicapped by a lack of facility in English" (Stevens 1967, p.4). There is little evidence of any other psychological work having been done before the University was set up.

In conjunction with the Government of Fiji, the University in 1970 established a Psychological Assessment Unit in the School of Education, the terms of reference of which were "to carry out research, and give advice on, matters relating to educational and vocational guidance to both the public and the private sectors" (Bennett 1971, p.2). Bennett was appointed Head of this unit and was joined by Chandra in 1971. McElwain's participation in the development of this unit during this year was most timely and significant. In a review of psychological assessment at the XVIIth International Congress of Applied Psychology, Ord concluded that "Fiji now has a small, but solidly based unit with excellent prospects of expansion and viability" (Ord 1972, p.151).

I. G. Ord of the Psychological Service Division in Papua New Guinea had visited Fiji for three weeks in 1968 and tried out a number of tests he had developed for public service selection in that country. The Pacific Reasoning Test (Ord 1968) was selected as the basis on which to develop a test of general ability to supplement secondary school allocation. In 1970, Bennett {1971 (a), 1971 (b), 1971 (c)} developed two parallel versions of a non-verbal General Ability Test for this purpose.

In 1971 the Psychological Assessment Unit developed a battery of six psychological tests (Bennett, 1974; Chandra, 1974), which was administered together with the Pacific Vocational Interest Analysis (Hicks 1970) to all students in Forms 5 and 6. In subsequent years, those in Form 6 were given a Fiji Scholastic Aptitude Test developed from the Commonwealth Secondary Schools

Scholarship tests from the Australian Council for Educational Research, the results of which were used in selection to the University of the South Pacific Foundation programmes.

After the departure of Bennett in 1972, the Unit continued with its programmes, with the services of one local psychologist who was also responsible for teaching at the University, and four administrative support staff. However, a major review of the University in 1976 resulted in the closure of the Psychological Assessment Unit and the establishment of an Institute of Education to strengthen the University's developmental role in education, which included among its priorities educational evaluation and assessment.

Another significant development occurred in 1975 when a Selection and Aptitude Section of the Fiji National Training Council was set up by a British Aid Officer, C. C. Potts, to continue the use of aptitude tests for occupational and trades selection purposes. The major types of services offered to employers by this section are advisory services in job analysis, recruitment selection procedures, placement, promotions and training, training courses on various aspects of occupational assessment, and aptitude measurement and interpretation for prospective employers. Two of the five staff are classified as professional selection and aptitude officers, even though they do not possess any formal qualifications in psychology.

The Careers Service in the Ministry of Education was established in late 1973 to be responsible for the employment aspects of the work of the Ministry of Labour. It was to provide accurate and up-to-date information about employment and careers, to offer vocational guidance to young people in their later years at school and subsequently, to help them find suitable employment and employers to find suitable workers, and to follow up the progress of young people in employment and give them any further advice and help that they may need with problems of adjustment. Its initial development occurred under the leadership of a consultant provided under British Aid who was given a local counterpart. To date there are seven staff designated as Careers Officers, the most senior of whom has obtained a Diploma in Counselling from a British university while the others are qualified school teachers. The guidance function relies almost exclusively on school and external examination results, and there is a total absence of psychological testing.

RESEARCH

Despite the fact that the teaching load of the four psychology staff exceeds the weekly norm of twelve contact hours for each staff, efforts have been sustained to conduct and publish research findings. The University has established a Research Committee which provides limited funds for investigations, preferably of the cross-cultural type within the South Pacific region, and government approval is generally not difficult to obtain for such research. Some funds from international agencies have been forthcoming for studies in collaboration with psychologists from abroad.

The University has provision for study leave, whereby most staff are able to visit overseas institutions and colleagues for periods of up to six months after three years of service. As yet there does not appear to be any specific trend in their itineraries. Visits from overseas psycho logists occur from time to time, and Australian psychologists have sought to spend extended periods of up to a year at this University. Conference leave is granted every three years so that research findings can be presented to interested scholars in Australia and Hawaii. With the assistance of external financial aid, a few staff have travelled as far as Canada and Hong Kong to attend conferences. As no professional society or journal exists in Fiji, most staff have submitted their research for publication in international journals with considerable success. All research and teaching activities are evaluated by an external examiner who visits the University every two years.

In 1982 the University hosted an international conference on thinking (for Proceedings, see Maxwell 1982). Although this was an interdisciplinary conference, most of the international participants, who included Margaret Boden and Edward de Bono from the United Kingdom and David Perkins from Harvard, were distinguished psychologists. While only two local research papers were presented, one on Fijian indigenous games and memory development by Kishor and Davidson, and the other on philosophies on human nature by Stewart, the conference did create an awareness among academics and the general public of the importance of psychological knowledge, service and research.

A general perspective of research in psychology at the University may best be obtained by a review of the

published research of the staff. Bennett wrote several
articles on psychological testing and educational
selection, as well as a doctoral dissertation about the
prediction and determination of educational performance
in Fiji. Chandra has investigated factors in urban
delinquency, the effects of group pressure, perceptual
acuity, and patterns of response on the Queensland Test.
His more recent studies have been in the area of population psychology, covering specifically social and
psychological variables and cross-cultural model testing
in contraceptive decision-making. Stewart has completed
studies about beliefs and human nature in adolescents in
the South Pacific and has edited Pacific Profiles,
consisting of short narratives written by individuals,
largely students, reflecting upon their developmental
experiences. He is also the editor of Social Behaviour
and Personality and Psychology and Human Development,
both of which are international journals. Kishor has
concentrated on the effects of self-esteem and locus of
control in academic achievement and career-decision-
making, and has also published on truancy in schools.
Finally, Maas has investigated the beliefs relating to
temporal dimensions among the main ethnic groups in Fiji,
and is also concerned with the relationship between
personal attitudes and background variables and thinking
strategies.

Scholars from overseas insititutions have also
conducted research in Fiji. Susan Basow of Lafayette
College, Pennsylvania, studied achievement motivation,
self-esteem and attitudes toward women, using samples of
Fijian and Indian secondary school students. D. Thomas
from Waikato University and N. Singh of the University of
Canterbury in New Zealand have published cross-cultural
studies on social distance in Fiji.

THE FUTURE OF PSYCHOLOGY

There is abundant evidence to confirm the impact of
psychology in the education of teachers, not only in Fiji
but in all the smaller countries of the University region
as well. It is well established as a service course for
other areas of teaching, especially medicine and to a
lesser extent administration, both public and private. In
all these instances, continued efforts are being made to
ensure that the course contents are of cultural relevance
and appropriate difficulty, in order to promote the

contribution of psychology to the development of multi-racial Fiji.

In 1978 Ritchie suggested that a case existed for the recognition of psychology as an essential component of general education in the University and made the following observation regarding the nature of courses that could be designed and offered. He wrote:

> There seems to be no applied social psychology taught as such, no personality, no consistent principles and practice of behaviour modification, no advanced development, no research technique or design and neither the strong natural science link (to biology, ecology, human geography and environmental science) nor the humanistic link (to literature, history, the history of ideas, philosophy and metaphysics) has been explored or developed (Ritchie 1978, p.2).

In partial response, the University included a major in guidance and counselling within the four year concurrent degree programme, the basic aim being to provide an opportunity for students to obtain a thorough grounding in the area of guidance and counselling. This Diploma in Guidance and Counselling is designed to enable the acquisition of basic knowledge and skills which should strengthen the services of the Careers Section of the Ministry of Education. It will also provide teachers in secondary schools with some competence to address the needs of students in vocational guidance and educational counselling and to identify exceptional students for special education. Further courses in this area, particularly in research methodology, are still required.

Provision for special education in Fiji has increased significantly over the past twenty years. Since the foundation of the Fiji Crippled Children's Society in 1961 and the registration of a school two years later, there are now seven schools with over 470 children and 52 teachers. Separate schools exist in various parts of Fiji that are at present responsible for the teaching of 215 physically handicapped and deaf children, 230 children who are mentally retarded and 32 children and young adults with visual deficiencies. All this is ample evidence of a rapid change in attitude toward the disabled. The success in the development of special education services must to a large extent be attributed to the dedication and tireless efforts of Frank Hilton, who was sent to Fiji in 1967 under the Commonwealth Cooperation in Education Scheme as Head Teacher of the Crippled Children's School. There are still many children however who cannot benefit from such schools because they live in rural areas.

Hilton (1980) identified the lack of guidance for parents during the vital early years of a handicapped child as being the greatest weakness of the present provisions of special education. The existing link between home and school must be strengthened if full use is to be made of the resources presently available. He also pointed out that the ordinary class teacher is not prepared by his or her training to identify those children with less severe handicaps and learning disabilities. While some teachers in special education have formal qualifications from overseas institutions, most only receive on-the-job training.

In a recent review of mental health programmes in Fiji, Iyer concluded that, in line with trends observed in other developing countries, the incidence of mental illness is increasing here. While the rate of first admission of 1.8 per 10,000 is considerably lower than those for other developing and Western countries, he maintains that this is not a true indication of the overall incidence of mental illness in Fiji, explaining that "The family or social structure in the Islands is such that it tends to tolerate and accommodate individuals exhibiting extremes of abnormal behaviour" (Iyer 1983, p.2). This practice makes a case for the exploration of a combination of modern and traditional methods for the prevention of mental illness, and the care of those afflicted with a mental disorder.

Some research does exist on specific mental disorders in Fiji. Studies include one by Price and Karim (1978) on hypomania; a comparison of the Indian and Fijian rates of suicide by Karim and Price (1973), which found the former to be ten times that of the latter; and an investigation by the Royal Commission on crime in Fiji into the socially disruptive effects of alcohol-abuse, especially its positive relationship with the increase in serious crime (Grant 1975).

Price and Eastwell (1980) investigated some of the psychological problems relating to the educated elite in the South Pacific. Their statement of the essential conflict of the educated salary earner is an follows: "To refuse to give money to less affluent members of the

356

extended family offends them - they have little experience of Western attitudes and such a rejection is not
readily understood, lying outside their mores. But the
salary earner who gives freely will have to forego his
ambition to live in the Western style" (p.200).

At present mental health services are provided by
one government mental hospital - St. Giles, with two
hundred in-patient beds. The staff consists of a consultant psychiatrist, four medical officers, a psychiatric
nurse and eighty ward staff. Murphy (1978, p.67) described this as "a place for custodial care rather than
for active therapy," although the inclusion of clinical
psychologists as mental health personnel was recommended
as early as 1966 by Burton-Bradley (Burton-Bradley 1966),
and has been an issue for at least the last five years.
Witchdoctors remain common in both Fijian and Indian
cultures. It is safe to assume that almost every individual who seeks psychiatric help from the hospital has
been "diagnosed and treated" through witchcraft and found
little or no relief. Witchdoctors are occasionally
brought to court when their treatment appears to have
been detrimental to patients.

In spite of the limited influence of psychology in
various areas in Fiji, a start has been made such that
existing offerings can be further refined and new
programmes devised to meet increasing manpower needs. The
establishment of psychology as a discipline in the
university would serve as a necessary base for a sustained and effective contribution in the future.

NOTE

1. The background information in the first two
paragraphs was taken from Fodor's Australia, New Zealand
and the South Pacific, Fodor's Modern Guides, Inc., N.Y.,
1981 (Eds.).

REFERENCES

BENNETT, M. J. Some problems of ability testing in Fiji,
     Maori Research Publication No. 1, 1971, University
     of Waikato, New Zealand (a).
BENNETT, M. J. First Annual Report of a Psychological
     Assessment Unit. Suva, Government Printer, 1971 (b).

BENNETT, M. J. Predictors and determinants of educational performance. Proceedings of XVIIth International Congress of Applied Psychology, Liege, 1971,(c).

BENNETT, M. J. Some predictors and determinants of educational performance in Fiji. Unpublished Ph.D. thesis, The University of the South Pacific, 1974.

BURTON-BRADLEY, B. G. Preventive psychiatry in the South Pacific: Some suggestions. In Mental health in the South Pacific. Report to the South Pacific Commission, Noumea, 1966.

CHANDRA, S. The Psychological Assessment Unit - Organizations and Functions. Fiji, Indian Printing Ltd., 1974.

GRANT, C. H. Report of Royal Commission into Crime. Suva, Government Printer, 1975.

HICKS, R. E. Manual for the PV1A. Psychological Services Branch, Public Service Board, Papua New Guinea, 1970.

HILTON, F. Special education in Fiji: Current issues and the role of the teacher, Education Gazette, Fiji, Second Term, 1980, Vol.LV, No. 2.

IYER, B. K. Mental health programme in Fiji. Paper presented at the World Health Organization Conference in Manila, 25-31 October, 1983.

KARIM, I., & PRICE, J. Suicide in Fiji, Fiji Medical Journal, 1973, 1, 49-54.

MACGREGOR, D. F. Mental health in the South Pacific. South Pacific Commission Technical Paper No. 154. Noumea, New Caledonia. 1966.

MANN, C. W. Fiji Test of General Ability. Suva, Government Printer, 1934.

MANN, C. W. A test of general ability in Fiji, Journal of Genetic Psychology, 1939, 54, 435-454.

MAXWELL, W. (ed.). Thinking - the expanding frontier. Philadelphia, Franklin Institute Press, 1982.

MURPHY, H. B. M. Mental health trends in the Pacific Islands. Report to South Pacific Commission, Noumea, 1978.

ORD, I. G. Manual for the Pacific Reasoning Series Test. Melbourne, Australian Council for Educational Research, 1968.

ORD, I. G. Education and occupational selection in developing countries - a review. Proceedings of XV11th International Congress-of Applied Psychology, Liege, Belgium, 1972.

PRICE, J. & EASTWELL, H.D. Psychological problems relating to the educated elite in some Pacific peoples, Australian and New Zealand Journal of Psychiatry, 1980, 14, 199-202.

PRICE, J. & KARIM, I. Matiruku, a Fijian madness: An initial assessment, British Journal of Psychiatry, 1978, 133, 288-230.

RITCHIE, J. E. Psychology at USP - Possibilities. Unpublished report. School of Education, The University of the South Pacific, 1978.

STEVENS, J. L. Selective tests in Fiji Primary and Secondary Schools. Paper presented at South Pacific Commission technical meeting on the selection and assessment of pupils for promotion or vocational guidance. Goroka, Papua New Guinea, 1967.

UNIVERSITY OF THE SOUTH PACIFIC Calendars for 1970 and 1982.

ACKNOWLEDGMENT

The historical review of psychological testing in Fiji was greatly facilitated by Bennett's (1974) doctoral dissertation.

Notes on Contributors

HAMIDA AKHTAR BEGUM, M.A. (Dhaka), M.A., Ph.D. (Manitoba) is an Associate Professor in the Department of Psychology at the University of Dhaka. Her major interest is in the area of social psychology, particularly research methodology, attitudes and values.

DUANGDUEN BHANTHUMNAVIN, A.B. (Berkeley), M.A. (Illinois), Ph.D. (Maryland) is an Associate Professor and Deputy Director of the Behavioural Science Research Institute of Sri Nakharinwirot University, Bangkok. She is best known for her work on moral socialisation and her empirical approach to the psychological development of the Thai people. She is consultant to the Civil Service Institute and has been a member of the National Research Council of Thailand since 1974.

GEOFFREY H. BLOWERS, B.Sc. (Sheffield), M. Phil. (Sussex), Ph.D. (Hong Kong), is a Senior Lecturer in the Department of Psychology at the University of Hong Kong. His main research interests are in psychophysiology and perception and he has written previously on the history of psychology in Hong Kong. He is a Fellow and former President (1980/81) of the Hong Kong Psychological Society.

JAE-HO CHA, M.A. (Seoul National University), M.A. (Arizona), Ph.D. (UCLA) is an Associate Professor at Seoul National University, and was Chairman of the Department of Psychology there from 1980-1983. Since 1983 he has been General Secretary of the Korean Social Science Research Council.

SUBHAS CHANDRA, B.A. (NSW), M.A. (Sydney), Ph.D. (USP) is a Senior Lecturer in Education at the University of the South Pacific. Previously he was head of the Psychological Assessment Unit in Fiji.

VIRGILIO G. ENRIQUEZ, A.B. (University of the Philippines), M.A. (Northwestern), M.A. (University of the Philippines), Ph.D. (Northwestern), is Professor and former Chairman of the Department of Psychology, College of Arts and Sciences, University of the Philippines. He has research interests in the history of psychology, cross-cultural and indigenous psychologies.

PHAM MINH HAC, B.Sc., Ph.D., D.Sc. (Moscow National University) is Director-General of the National Institute of Educational Science, Hanoi. His main research interests are in the field of personality. He was recently appointed Vice-Minister of Education for the Socialist Republic of Vietnam.

AKIRA HOSHINO, B.A. (Tokyo), is Professor and Head of the Department of Psychology, Education division, in the College of Liberal Arts and Graduate School of International Christian University in Tokyo. His main research interests are in the fields of personality, clinical, and cross-cultural psychology and among his publications he has translated many of the works of G. W. Allport into Japanese.

JOSEPH SHIH-ZEH HSU, B.S., D.V.M. (National Taiwan University), M.A., Ph.D., D.Med.Sc. (National Tokyo University) is Professor of Medical Psychology at National Yang-ming Medical College, Taiwan. His current research interests are in the area of the psychology of politics, specifically socialist and capitalist mentalities.

H. WING LEE, M.Ed., M.A., Ph.D. (Ottawa) is a Lecturer in the Department of Psychology at the University of Hong Kong, and Coordinator of the Department's M.Soc.Sc. Programme in Educational Psychology. His current research interests are in divergent thinking across the life span, and second language learning.

FOO YEE LONG, B.A. (NSW), M.A., Dip. Psych. (Sydney) is at present the Senior Psychologist of the Ministry of Health, Republic of Singapore, and a clinical teacher in the Department of Psychological medicine, National University of Singapore. He was President of the Singapore Psychological Society in 1979, 1980 and 1983.

S. M. MOGHNI, M.A., Ll.B. (Aligarh), Ph.D. (London), is Professor and Head of the Department of Psychology at Peshawar University and the founder President of the Pakistan Psychological Association. He has wide ranging research interests in motivation, learning, group behaviour and programmed instruction.

A. S. MUNANDAR was Dean of the Faculty of Psychology, University of Indonesia from 1981-84 and Professor of Industrial and Organisational Psychology.

S. C. UTAMI MUNANDAR is Professor in Educational Psychology in the Faculty of Psychology at the University of Indonesia.

MATTHIAS PETZOLD, Dr.-Phil., Dipl.-Psych., is Lecturer in the Institute for Developmental and Social Psychology, University of Dusseldorf, W. Germany. His research interests are in Developmental Psychology (cognition), History of Psychology and Psychology in Asia.

M. P. REGMI, Ph.D. (Saugar) is Chairperson of the postgraduate Department of Psychology in Tribhuvan University. His main areas of research are perception, cognition and personality.

BARRY RICHARDSON, B.A., Ph.D. (Queen's), M.Sc. (Sussex) is Associate Professor in Psychology at the University of Papua New Guinea, and Head of the Department of Psychology and Philosophy.

DURGANAND SINHA, B.A. (Patna), Ph.D. (Cambridge) is Director of A.N.S. Institute of Social Studies, Patna. From 1961 to 1982 he was Professor of Psychology and head of department at Allahabad University. Offices he has held include presidency of the Indian Academy of Applied Psychology (1975 and 1976), of the Indian Psychological Association (1978), and of IACCP (1980-82); he is currently an Executive Committee member of IUPS and of the International Association of Applied Psychology.

ROSS ST. GEORGE, B.Phil (Hons), D. Phil. (Waikato), is a Senior Lecturer in the Department of Education, Massey

University, Palmerston North, New Zealand. He specialises in measurement and evaluation and has written previously on the history of psychology in New Zealand. He has been a member of the New Zealand Psychological Society Council since 1981 and President for the 1982-83 year.

ALISON M. TURTLE, M.A. (Sydney) is a Senior Lecturer in the Department of Psychology at the University of Sydney. Her main areas of research are in the history of psychology, and applied social psychology. At present she is working on a large-scale historical study of the development of psychology in Australia.

TAKEO UMEMOTO, B.A., Ph.D. (Kyoto), is Professor of Psychology in the Department of Educational Psychology in Kyoto University. His main research interests are in cognitive and educational psychology and the psychology of music. He is the Editor of Psychologia and a member of the editorial boards of the Japanese Journal of Psychology and the Japanese Psychological Review.

COLLEEN WARD, B.S. (Spring Hill, Alabama), Ph.D. (Durham), is a Lecturer in the Department of Psychology at the University of Canterbury, New Zealand. She has held lecturing posts in the Department of Social Work at the University of Singapore and in the School of Social Science, the Science University of Malaysia. She has research interests in cross-cultural psychology, in particular, in perceptions of gender, traditional healing practices, and the psychology of women.